American Industry
in the War

American Industry in the War

A REPORT OF THE
WAR INDUSTRIES BOARD
(MARCH 1921)

by

BERNARD M. BARUCH, CHAIRMAN

Including, besides a reprint of the report of the War Industries Board of World War I, Mr. Baruch's own program for total mobilization of the nation as presented to the War Policies Commission in 1931, and current material on priorities and price fixing.

WITH A FOREWORD BY
BERNARD M. BARUCH

AND AN INTRODUCTION BY
HUGH S. JOHNSON

EDITED BY
RICHARD H. HIPPELHEUSER

New York: PRENTICE-HALL, INC., *1941*

Copyright, 1941, by

PRENTICE-HALL, INC.

70 Fifth Avenue, New York

Printed in the United States of America

Foreword

BY BERNARD M. BARUCH

TOTAL DEFENSE must plan to fight, to win, and above all to survive war. This means some plan along lines similar to the experience tested by the United States War Industries Board of 1917 and 1918. It must mobilize men, money, materials, morale—all resources—to give to the war-making agencies and those allied with them, such as shipping and blockade, what they want when they want it, without unnecessary deprivation or exploitation of civilians.

This volume contains documents which will show what should be done and what should be avoided. The War Industries Board plan contemplated getting ahead and keeping ahead—avoiding bottlenecks rather than breaking them. It was arrived at by trial and error— which are proving in 1940 and 1941 what they proved in 1917 and 1918. It is regrettable that we have to re-travel any of that road. England and France did not act in time to get ahead of their necessities. France fell. England is not yet organized. German military experts have said, "Except for a few minor changes, the German economic mobilization system was conscientiously built in imitation of the similar American system."

A study of the War Industries Board plan will show, among other things:

> Protection of civilian needs by the retention of the highest possible standard of living at the lowest cost.
>
> Organization of demand and supply. This means not alone a mobilization of things but all trades, callings, and professions to which application can be made for the needs that must be met.
>
> Priority.
>
> Price control—with an increased tax program to pay as much as possible as we go.
>
> Conservation—to make both ends meet where there are shortages.
>
> Conversion of facilities.

Finding of substitutes and new sources of supply.

Control of imports and exports with a world-wide economic strategy to insure supplies to our friends and to withhold them from our enemies.

Wise location of plants and new facilities having special reference to housing, transportation, and labor, spreading to all communities the opportunity to take part in defense work. Not too many eggs in one basket or too much work in one place.

Regional organization with special emphasis upon subcontracting, using small business for making parts to be assembled in larger units.

Avoidance of even any appearance of acting in a dual capacity for the government, themselves, or the businesses in which they have an interest.

Methods proved for all this and more are outlined in this volume.

At times the reader will have to raise his eyes from these pages to wonder whether he is reading what took place a quarter of a century ago or what is unfolding before us daily.

All must be done without losing sight of our condition after the war—not merely to fight and win the war, but also to survive it economically, with a low price structure and an industrial system dislocated to a minimum degree, well prepared for post-war conditions in the international markets.

Whatever organization or plan may be adopted for industrial mobilization, I know all Americans will join in endeavoring to make it a success. There must be no holding back or sulking because we do not approve of this or that particular plan or the personalities involved.

After a full discussion, under our American system, the final decision rests with the Commander-in-Chief. It is for us then to fall in line.

Let all men and women, and that includes boys and girls, remain at their daily tasks until called upon to act in another assigned capacity. America has the resources and the brains; and, with the *will* to do so, it will be able to say again: "It can't be done—but here it is."

B. M. B.

Contents

BOOK ONE

American Industry in the War

BOOK TWO

Taking the Profit Out of War

Introduction

BY HUGH S. JOHNSON

THIS IS a timely and valuable compilation of the writings of B. M. Baruch on industrial mobilization for war, a subject to the study of which he has devoted most of his spare time for many years—and almost all of his time in recent years. As the director and genius of our trail-blazing organization along these lines in World War I, he had a more intense experience with these principles than any other living man —and it was successful. This pioneer work created a pattern of organization and method for war-regulation of industry which both the Germans and the British have acknowledged and adopted as far as it is adaptable to their systems.

At the close of the First World War, this work was applauded by nearly all the great war leaders—Woodrow Wilson, Lloyd George, Winston Churchill, Clemenceau, Hindenburg, Ludendorff, and Pershing, to name only a few. Year after year since then, Mr. Baruch has collaborated, lectured, or advised with the War College, the Industrial College, and the General Staff of the Army, with Committees of Congress, in the press, and at civilian colleges, to try to help keep the economics of the Industrial Mobilization plan of the Army alive and adaptable to the changing circumstances of a world in almost constant turmoil.

In 1935, partly inspired perhaps by his close contacts with European statesmen and especially with Mr. Winston Churchill, Mr. Baruch became very much alarmed at the rapid rise of Nazi military and air power, at the apparent indifference to this growing danger in France, in England, and in the even more directly theatened small states of Europe. He was especially disturbed by the almost complete nonchalance of our government and the comparative helplessness of our own Army in numbers, equipment, organization, and training to compete with the kind of armament that he knew was proceeding so rapidly in Europe.

Continuously afterward, and with increasing insistence as the tragic world situation developed in the awful direction of the 1940 holocaust

of nations, Mr. Baruch, in newspaper interviews and in conferences
with the highest officials of our government, sounded warning after
warning, documented and buttressed with reliable reports from abroad.
He did it so frequently and with such increasing emphasis that he
began to feel himself a sort of twentieth century Laocoon who might
expect a visit from Minerva's strangling serpents almost any day.

Nothing effective was done about it in all those years while disaster
was overtaking the world.

It is mere coincidence but none the less interesting that, in some
of the oldest records of our religion, it is written that a Baruch helped
Nehemiah rebuild the defenses of Jerusalem. Generations later another Baruch, who was a sort of Chief of Staff to another major
prophet, warned the king over and over again of just such a developing danger to his country as the present one has been to ours. That
king didn't want any advice either, but Baruch kept on giving it.
When the king had his scroll of warning publicly burned in scorn,
Baruch rewrote it from memory and so disposed it that it could not
be suppressed. He did not cease to repeat his warnings up to the end
of bitter disaster.

The Baruch of the present generation has not confined himself to
prophecy. He offered plans and asked that surveys be made of our
equipment and organization for war on land and sea and in the air,
of our ability to turn quickly to war-production of modern equipment
and other preparation against possible enemies.

Once he was told to return to Europe, recheck his observations, and
then come back and himself make the domestic survey he suggested.
When he returned, official opinion had apparently changed again.
Later another board, the so-called Stettinius War Resources Board,
was appointed to make the domestic survey, but was soon disbanded,
and whatever report it made was suppressed.

In the early months of World War I a Council of National Defense
was created by statute and an "Advisory Commission" of industrialists
and labor leaders with no authority whatever was named to consult
with it.

That invertebrate setup, with no experience, yet under the stress
of war, fumbled around for some months, lost much time, and wasted
a good deal of effort and money; yet, by methods of cut-and-try, trial
and error, there was evolved the plan that later worked so well after
March 4, 1918—the War Industries Board.

In the post-war years, all these experiences were intensely studied
in the War Department in consultation with all the experienced actors
of the World War economic drama—largely guided by the veteran

impresario, B. M. Baruch. What had proved right and successful was recommended; what had faltered or failed was discarded. New aspects of that plan, to adapt it to new situations in the organization of government and to the problems of the country, were worked out. This was the War Department industrial plan.

It was Mr. Baruch's belief that this Plan would at least avoid the fumbling and blundering of 1917 and take up where we left off in 1918 in experience, progress, and knowledge. In reorganizing Selective Service, exactly that principle was adopted in the mobilization of man power. The 1918 experience has been faithfully followed, and it has worked as nearly to perfection as such things can work. But a strange reversal of that policy has been applied to industrial mobilization.

We went straight back to 1917, re-created the old Council of National Defense with its inept and amoebic Advisory Commission, and fumbled along for just as many months. The War Department mobilization plan was hardly even considered. Every fumble and blunder of the World War mobilization was repeated. As this became more and more apparent and the storm of criticism rose, there was a partial centralization of authority in the Knudsen-Hillman "one man with two heads," but it didn't remotely resemble the War Industries Board precedent in intelligent foresight, organization, planning, and action, and it doesn't resemble it yet.

Why the record has been thus is beyond my power of conjecture. There is just one comforting crumb. Apparently reluctantly, but none the less certainly, step by fumbling step, the new planless pattern is gradually being brought back and draped on the proved pegs of the old. It is being brought back by the clutch of circumstance and the pressure of necessity. It will eventually be adopted piece by piece because it is right and is the only method ever developed anywhere that worked so well.

The astonishing thing is that all this precious time should have been lost. The encouraging thing is that there may yet be time and that all this experience will not be wasted forever.

Because people are interested—and every American ought to be interested—many will want to read this book—especially the simple, concise, but adequately stated principles of American mobilization on pages 377 to 408. It should be read to get some glimpse of what has been done well in the past, what is being so miserably done now, and what must be done if we are to snatch success from failure in the future.

A great value of this book is that it is not an advocate's argument in this present debate. It is a collection of utterances made over many years without the change of a word or syllable to adapt them to the present discussion. They are as good today as when they were first spoken, and their wisdom is proved by every recent blunder into which departures from their counsels have taken us.

H. S. J.

BOOK ONE

American Industry in the War

A REPORT

OF THE

WAR INDUSTRIES BOARD
(MARCH 1921)

By BERNARD M. BARUCH
CHAIRMAN

LETTER OF TRANSMITTAL

MARCH 3, 1921

The PRESIDENT,

    Washington, D. C.

SIR: I have the honor to submit to you the more detailed exposition of the work of the War Industries Board which was promised in my report of December 24, 1919.

In closing this undertaking, new as it was in many of its aspects to our institutions of government, I want to thank you in behalf of myself and the members of my staff for the opportunity which you vouchsafed to us thus to serve our country.

Respectfully submitted,

BERNARD M. BARUCH

"The highest and best form of efficiency is the spontaneous cooperation of a free people."—Woodrow Wilson.

Preface to Book One

THIS REPORT is an analysis and narrative of the activities of the War Industries Board, whose function it was so to supervise the industries of America that the energies of each should, as far as practicable, supplement those of all others, and that all should contribute to the limit of their combined ability to one common purpose—the winning of the war.

The volume has been written in pursuance of a promise contained in the following brief report to the President:

WASHINGTON, D. C.,
December 24, 1919.

MY DEAR MR. PRESIDENT: I have the honor to submit herewith a report of the activities of the United States War Industries Board.

The statement covers the period from its inception in the Council of National Defense, July 28, 1917, through its reorganization, by your letter of March 4, 1918, until the dissolution of the Board, after the war had been won, on November 30, 1918, when you accepted the chairman's resignation because the abnormal needs caused by extraordinary military effort had passed.

An estimate of the spirit of service and the success that characterized the work of the Board's members, with whom I had the honor of being associated, is generously expressed in your own words when you said, with reference to them, that they had "turned aside from every private interest of their own and devoted the whole of their trained capacity to the tasks that supplied the sinews of the whole great undertaking. The patriotism, the unselfishness, the thoroughgoing devotion, and distinguished capacity that marked their toilsome labors, day after day, month after month, have made them fit mates and comrades of the men in the trenches and on the seas." Not only to those men is due a great measure of appreciation, but the obligation extends to a far wider field, and in recognition of this fact, which I know has your hearty acceptance, it is proper for me to repeat here that sense of gratitude which was expressed in the dedication of the handbook of the War Industries Board thus "To American Industry; to Employer and Employee, to Capital and Labor, to each of whom is due a large share of such success as the War Industries Board has achieved; to their spirit of service, of patriotism, and of cooperation, I make acknowledgment and dedicate this booklet, which is largely a record of their own activities and of achievements their support made possible."

In measuring our victory the importance of the battle line at home must ever be a great factor. The mobilization of America's industrial forces and

3

their conversion from peace and construction to war and destruction was a
gigantic task and responded to in gigantic manner. Its value in the final outcome rates second only to the mobilization of the nation's man power and in
that enterprise the War Industries Board, which commanded, under you, the
forces of industry, was likewise of aid by indicating those trades from which
the workers could be more readily spared than from others, the continuation
of which were essential to the war's development.

The problem confronting the War Industries Board was vast and complex
and the difficulties were added to in that it was not possible to set a program
of fixed limitations which could be worked up to, and, having been achieved,
the task completed. The needs of the Army and Navy and the other war
agencies of our country and our associates changed and expanded over night.
It was no part of our work to make the program; our duty was to help execute it by supplying the materials that made success attainable. To be able
to do this; to know what we had to do and then to plan to do it; to coordinate and synchronize the multiplicity of national and international efforts and
make them effective in supplying the war demands so that our armies and
navies could discharge their duty of fighting and winning, the War Industries
Board evolved a general formula,[1] which is herewith appended because it contains its theory, organization, and policy of procedure—because it shows what
the Board was and what it tried to do. It read:

Wars are fought and won—or lost—on the land, on the water, in
the air, and on those battle lines behind the front where the civilian
forces stand.

It is not enough to mobilize the Nation's military strength. There
must be a mobilization of her full economic resources—industrial,
agricultural and financial. These must be organized, coordinated,
and directed with the same strategy that governs the operations of
the purely military arms of service.

The prodigious strain upon the world's productive capacity must
be met and balanced to provide the means of warfare and to maintain the civilian population as well as to preserve the economic fabric.

America to-day is the chief source of strength to the forces engaged
in the conflict against German world domination. That strength is
expressed in terms of man power and material—the one military,
and the second industrial.

To control and regulate industry in all its direct and indirect relations to the war and to the Nation, the President has created the
War Industries Board and placed the responsibility for its operation in the hands of the chairman. * * * [2]

The War Industries Board is charged with the duty of procuring

---

[1] The formula referred to was embodied in the foreword of a War Industries
Board pamphlet, *An Outline of the Board's Origin, Functions and Organization,*
compiled as of November 10, 1918 (Government Printing Office).

[2] The sentence deleted here referred to the fact that Woodrow Wilson's letter

an adequate flow of materials for the two great war-making agencies of the Government—the War and Navy Departments—and for the two agencies in immediate affiliation with these military arms—the Emergency Fleet Corporation and the Railroad Administration.

Also, the Board provides supplies necessary to the military needs of our associations in the war, and those commodities required by neutrals in exchange for materials essential to us.

Finally, and of paramount importance, the Board, in alliance with the Food, Fuel, and Labor Administrations, provides for the country's civilian needs, the protection of which is a particular duty of the organization.

It is not only the duty of the War Industries Board to stimulate and expand production in those industries making war essentials, it is equally the Board's duty to protect, as far as may be, those industries not immediately essential to the war program.

It is the policy of the Board, where retrenchment and curtailment are necessary, to keep alive, even though it be necessary to skeletonize, the enterprises in this group, and not to destroy them.

Whenever possible, conversion of industries from a nonwar production to an essential output is effected.

The War Industries Board is a method of control devised by the President to equalize the strain placed upon the American industrial structure by the war.

It stimulates and expands the production of those materials essential to the war program and at the same time it depresses and curtails the production of those things not of a necessitous nature. This is done by regulation, in consonance with other executive branches, of the basic economic elements: (*a*) Facilities, (*b*) materials, (*c*) fuel, (*d*) transportation, (*e*) labor, and (*f*) capital.

The method of control is through a preference list, on which are placed those industries whose output is essential to the war's progress. The priority indicated by the preference list is the master key to the six elements named.

Further, the Board regulates all and controls certain other industries of first-rate war importance, it fixes prices through the price-fixing committee, it creates new and converts old facilities, it clears the national business requirements, and it leads to conservation, which is needed to bridge the gap between the extraordinary demand and the available supply—a gap which exists in almost all the great commercial staples.

The War Industries Board embraces all and each of the Nation. Food and fuel are separately administered, but with every other

of March 4, 1918, to Bernard M. Baruch and the proclamation of May 28, 1918, delegating Mr. Baruch's powers as chairman, were to be found in the first pages of the above-mentioned pamphlet.

article of military need and of ordinary life the Board has a direct connection, and it has a basic relationship with food and fuel, too, for both require in production and distribution the materials that the War Industries Board provides. Its strength lies in the full and patriotic cooperation that American business, including both the employers and the employees, gives in working out the problems common to us all.

The abnormal conditions of the war demand sacrifices. It is the price of victory.

Only actual needs, not fancied wants, should and can be satisfied.

To save heavy and long privation, temporary deprivation must be the rule.

America's willingness to accept these conditions marks her ability to quicken the end of the conflict.

It is not within the province of the writer to render judgment upon the success achieved by the organization of which he was the head, but it is not amiss for him to say not one default was recorded on any demand made by the military establishments. They were given all they asked in measure so full and so quick as to be noteworthy, especially when it is remembered that most of the years of our existence had been given over to life and thought of peace with small inclination or opportunity to familiarize ourselves with the arts and needs of war. If the love of country shows itself in the readiness of men to fight it is equally proven in the willingness of capital and labor—of the men and women workers—to serve. * * * [3]

There will be submitted later a detailed exposition and study of the Board's origin, function, and organization. Further, there also will follow the reports of the members of the Board and the divisional chiefs in whose hands fell the authority you delegated to me, decentralized according to an attached chart.[4] Finally, in addition to general comments, I am submitting certain conclusions as to the lessons taught us by the war, expressed in the form of recommendations which, if translated into practice, will bring us a greater readiness for the worst that the future may hold and which can be enacted without violence to our traditional predisposition to peace and the pursuits thereof.

Between the time of the signing of the armistice and the discontinuance of the War Industries Board, the problem was faced of reversing the Board's machinery in order to demobilize industry from war service and assist it back to its normal channels. The German collapse had been spectacular in its suddenness. When fighting ceased, war production in the United States was reaching its peak. Every unit of the vast machinery was keyed up to high speed. There is no doubt but that knowledge of this fact contributed ma-

---

[3] In paying tribute to the loyalty and patriotism of his aides and associates in the War Industries Board, and to the "spirit of service" shown by industry generally, Mr. Baruch said he was appending a complete roster of the War Industries Board. That roster has been omitted in this reprint.

[4] The chart appears between pp. 14 and 15.

terially to Germany's sudden realization of the hopelessness of her position. The Board did all that was possible to prevent any injury to industry as it was put back on a peace basis. The price-fixing committee of the Board determined as a general policy that price agreements should continue for the period originally fixed. The President directed the various departments of the Government not to market, in competition with private producers, materials in which there was no shortage and which were not of a perishable nature. The Board, through recommendations and advice, aided in cancellation of contracts so as to stabilize as far as possible the flow of materials, labor, and plant facilities back to peace channels. It was arranged with all of the war-making agencies of the Government that the Board should be advised of revisions and adjustments of all Government contracts in excess of $100,000. The Board's facilities section, for a brief time, remained as the clearing house for all information relating to contract adjustment. Contact also was maintained with the Labor Department so that as labor was released from war work, it was distributed to peace-time industries needing it. If the proper authority had been at hand, it would have been possible for the War Industries Board to have continued its functions during the period of readjustment. Much good could have been accomplished. But with the signing of the armistice, the purchases by the Allies and our own great departments coming to an end, the power of the Board, without further additional legislative authority, ceased and it was possible to do only what was done—to wind up its work as quickly as possible.

It would be impossible in any statement of the activities of the War Industries Board, or any story of the mobilization of the industries of the country, not to conclude with definite recommendations based upon the lessons learned. A similar emergency may arise in the future and it can more easily be coped with if the experiences of the last two years are profited by. The writer believes:

First. There should be created a peace-time skeleton organization based on the experience of the war-making agencies. It should be headed by a chairman, who, when the emergency arises, should be granted the powers necessary to coordinate and synchronize the economic resources of the country. With him should be associated the representatives of the Army and the Navy or any other department vitally interested, as the Shipping Board, who should have centralized under them the various purchasing branches of their departments. There also should be in the skeletonized organization a vice chairman, a secretary, a counsel, and members in charge of raw materials, finished products, facilities, prices, labor, planning and statistics(during peace under the Department of Commerce), priority and conservation. Under these there should be also the various section or commodity heads. The peace-time organization would meet at least once a year to discuss and outline plans and to keep in touch with the general world situation and with one another. Each sectional head would name committees in each industry in order that, in the event of an impending crisis, it would be possible within a few days to create an organization which immediately would mobilize all of the industries of the nation and quickly make available for the Government all of its resources. These men, with the exception of the Secretary, who would keep the records, would serve without compensation and the actual expense of maintaining such an organization would be small. I would recommend that all priorities, including those of shipping, should be centralized in the chairman.

Second. Through a system of stimulation by a protective tariff, a bonus, an exemption from taxation for a limited period, licensing, or any other effective means, every possible effort should be made to develop production of manganese, chrome, tungsten, dyestuff, by-products of coal, and all such raw materials usually imported but which can be produced in quantity in this country. Above all, immediate and persistent effort must be made to develop production of nitrogen and its substitutes, not alone for war but for agricultural purposes.

Third. Under the supervision of the proper departments of the Government some industries must be given encouragement to maintain a skeleton organization through which can be developed the rapid manufacture of guns, munitions, airplanes, etc. Some facilities already developed might be kept alive through outright purchase or by small orders for munitions and airplanes while at all times there must be kept on hand the necessary dies, jigs, fixtures, etc., needed for the manufacture of munitions. The expert personnel of the War and Navy Departments in addition to keeping abreast of the times in new war-making agencies should keep the industries of the Nation attuned in a skeleton form to meet immediately that enlarged demand which would come through war.

Very sincerely yours,

(Signed)   BERNARD M. BARUCH.

Hon. WOODROW WILSON,
> *President of the United States,*
> *The White House, Washington, D. C.*

In the report which follows, attention is directed to the things accomplished rather than to the individuals who did them. The world will desire to judge the quality of these men by an untinseled record of their work rather than by their biographies, and such a record is here set down. It is known to all that every loyal American citizen contributed whole-heartedly to the common end, and it was this unfaltering spirit of patriotism that finally crowned the war effort with success. There is no calculus by which the value of each man's activities, even within such a group as the War Industries Board and its staff, can be rated, and no such attempt has here been made.

This record has been made by no one man. Each member of the Board prepared an account of his work. Each director of a division and each chief of a section reported the conditions and problems which he found in his industry and the manner in which such problems were handled. All of these reports have been worked over and condensed, duplications and repetitions eliminated, and an endeavor has been made to weave the story into a consecutive whole.

The compilation is the work of Edwin B. Parker and Frank Fritts. It is with regret that I found that there could not be placed in this volume a fuller and more detailed report of the work of each division and section head—their difficulties and their successful accomplishments.

It is believed that a condensed yet comprehensive record of the activities of the Board, with explanations of the principles and policies by which it functioned, together with a discussion of the place in the great World War occupied by the leading industries of America, is worth preserving for the information, and it may be for the guidance, of this and future generations.

BERNARD M. BARUCH,
Chairman, War Industries Board.

Contents of Book One

PART I

THE WAR INDUSTRIES BOARD

PART II

COMMODITY SECTIONS

APPENDICES

THE WAR INDUSTRIES BOARD

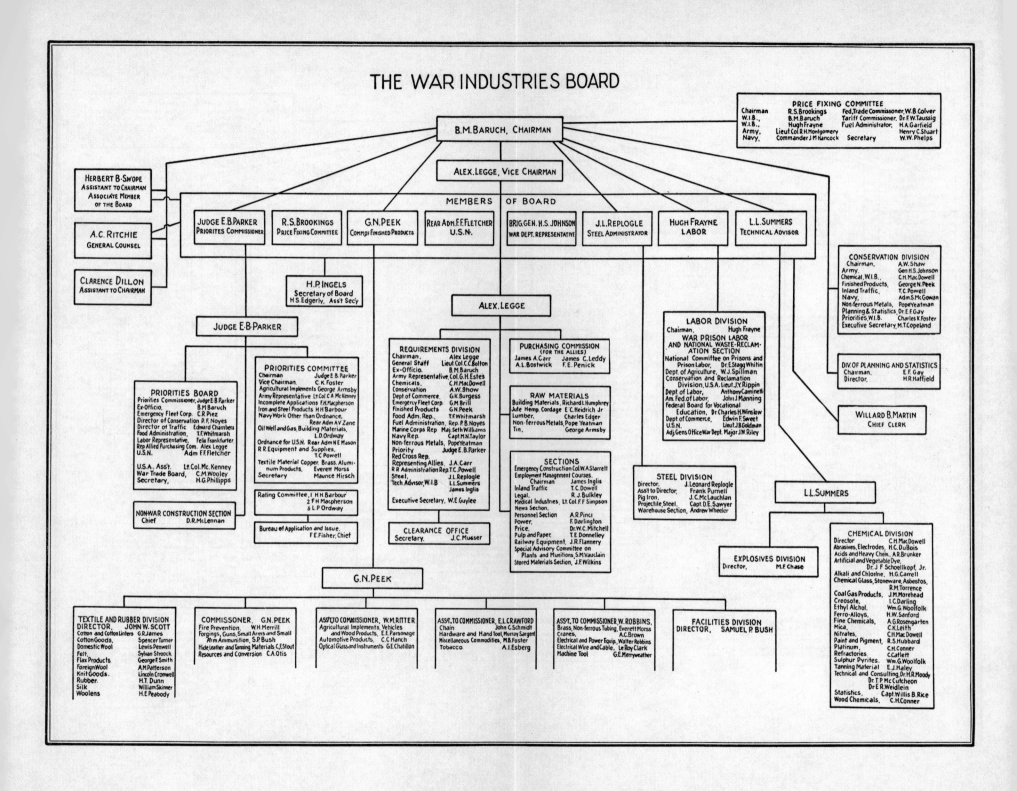

THE WAR INDUSTRIES BOARD

CHAPTER 1

Origin and Purpose

FOR YEARS to come the activities of the United States in meeting the many problems involved in its participation in the war will furnish a wealth of material for the economist, the political scientist, and all others interested in public affairs. During the period before this country became a party to the conflict, much of the attention of those who fostered preparation for the inevitable day was devoted to plans for producing a trained personnel. And that early work was of an importance which is easily underestimated. The speed with which our Army grew from 200,000 to 4,000,000 men and the success with which it was being moved to Europe at the rate of 225,000 troops per month during the summer of 1918 were phenomena new to history and phenomena which amazed not only our enemies but our allies.

The prime characteristic of this war, however, was the extent to which it involved the material resources of the participating nations. As attention was turned to immediate preparations, it was soon felt that the problem of supplies was going to involve difficulties of the most far-reaching and important character. Private industry in this country was already making important contributions to the supply of the Allies, but without proper coordination in the supply of our own requirements and those of the Allies it could well have happened that our entering the war might have had the effect of impeding rather than stimulating the flow of supplies to Europe and thus actually hindering the progress toward victory. The strain on industrial resources which the war was causing in Europe was well known here, but it was exceedingly difficult to estimate the extent to which our vast resources would have to be brought to bear on the undertaking.

In casting organizations to meet the problem, we had the experience of the Allies which was placed freely at our disposal. But the temper and habits of our people, the extent of our territory, and the magnitude of our industrial wealth gave many new aspects to the situation. There is a general theory deeply ingrained in our political habits to the effect that Government should not interfere with the

15

processes of business any further than is necessary to preserve the principle of fair competition and to insure the observance of ordinary legal obligations. For development and progress, individual initiative is relied upon. The public welfare is to be served by the spontaneous common purpose of a free people. The sentiment of our people was at one in regard to the purposes of the war. Men in all parts of the country, the owners and workers in every trade and industry, were more than ready each to do his part.

The common purpose was already in existence on April 6, 1917. The problem was to bring about a coordination of effort. Our citizens had been reading for three years of the sacrifices and privations, of the regulations and restrictions, which the allied peoples had been undergoing for the war. There would be no hesitation anywhere in acquiescing in restrictions affecting fortunes or freedom. The only question was what restrictions were going to be necessary and how they ought to be applied. The people of the country were in a mood to make any system work well, and after all that is perhaps the only condition under which the most cautiously built system of control would work at all. Methods and organizations developed as problems came forward. Before the end it was found necessary to establish a very comprehensive scheme of control over the entire industrial life of the Nation, and indeed toward the end control was extending beyond our borders to every part of the world from which war supplies were drawn. This came gradually and it was founded always as the result of common council with those directly involved. It depended always in largest measure on the good will and sound purpose of the people; and it was operated with far less machinery of organization than that used in any other country engaged in the war.

The harmony with which the greatest military program in our history was moving forward in the summer and fall of 1918 is proof enough that the plan which was developed would work, at least in such circumstances as then prevailed. Whether a card system of distribution, a priority and price-fixing system, or any other system would work unless supported by the complete confidence of the people is questionable. We can only know that in applying the procedure which was developed we found our people convinced that control was necessary and we found them always willing to acquiesce whether they considered certain particular rules wise and necessary or not. It is the purpose of this book to tell how and why the principal features of direction and control were inaugurated in respect to the great body of our industries. The story will make every American proud of the magnitude of the natural wealth of his country and the skill of his fellow citizens in making that wealth minister to human needs. It will make him prouder still of the unselfish patriotism which prompted every individual to do or refrain from doing, according to his lot, for the accomplishment of the common purpose.

Early thoughts on the question of supplies pointed to the fact that there would be shortages in a number of fields. It would perhaps have been impossible to have anticipated these shortages and provided against them beforehand because of the extreme difficulty of defining military needs. The war was constantly developing new needs so that a comprehensive undertaking in war manufacture, inaugurated five years before we entered the war, might have been largely wasted. The program of supplies had to be developed in closest harmony with the military program proper. At any rate, whether for better or for worse, few important steps in preparation of the supply service were taken before the war was actually upon us.

Three official movements began in 1916. The Naval Consulting Board appointed a committee which made a comprehensive survey of some 18,000 industrial plants throughout the country. This so-called industrial inventory was an ambitious attempt to list, describe, and classify all of the industrial establishments of importance in the country. It was made, however, at a time when the nature of the problem and the character of the data needed were not clearly determined, and does not appear to have been as useful in practice as might have been expected.

Another survey of importance was made by the Kernan Board, appointed by the Secretary of War to investigate the country's munitions resources with a view to determining the advisability and practicability of the Government's manufacturing its arms, munitions, and other war equipment.

The action of greatest importance, however, was the provision in the Army appropriation act, approved August 29, 1916, for the establishment of the Council of National Defense.[1] The council was given advisory powers only, but it was charged, among other things, with the "coordination of industries and resources for the national security and welfare," and with the "creation of relations which will render possible in time of need the immediate concentration and utilization of the resources of the Nation." The council was composed of the six Secretaries—of War, the Navy, the Interior, Agriculture, Commerce, and Labor.

---

[1] See Appendix I for sec. 2 of the Army appropriation act, approved Aug. 29, 1916.

As a corollary to the council proper, the act provided for the "advisory commission" of the council, to consist of seven persons appointed by the President upon the recommendation of that body, each of whom should be specially qualified for some particular line of endeavor which would make his services of peculiar value. The commissioners were to serve without compensation.

Provision was made for a director and a secretary, and both the council and the advisory commission were permitted to enlist the services of such experts, advisors, and committees as they saw fit. Individual experts might be employed, but subordinate bodies were to serve without compensation.

The two bodies were formally organized October 11, 1916. The Secretary of War was designated as chairman of the council, Walter S. Gifford was appointed director, and Grosvenor B. Clarkson (later director) secretary of both bodies. The advisory commission was composed of the following members: Daniel Willard, Hollis Godfrey, Howard E. Coffin, Dr. Franklin H. Martin, Bernard M. Baruch, Julius Rosenwald, and Samuel Gompers. Each of these commissioners took charge of a special field. One was assigned to transportation, one to engineering and education, one to munitions and manufacturing, one to medicine and surgery, one to raw materials, one to supplies, and one to labor.[2] For some months there occurred little more than conferences and discussions. A plan of organization and definition of purpose were evolved through conversations not only among the members, but with leaders of industry, and those who were in contact with procedure in Europe. A system of contacts through "committees of the industries" was worked out by the commissioner in charge of raw materials, and it was on March 3, 1917, that the idea of a large organization was made effective.

There was then attached a number of divisions, sections, and committees, the memberships of which were largely composed of trained executives who placed their services at the disposal of the council without compensation. As time went on, these various subordinate bodies underwent constant change both in character and personnel.

---

[2] Daniel Willard, of the Baltimore & Ohio, was given the transportation post; Dr. Hollis Godfrey (deceased), then president of the Drexel Institute and the originator of the Council of National Defense plan, took over engineering and education; Howard Coffin (deceased), a leading automotive engineer, handled manufacturing and munitions; Dr. Martin (deceased), then Secretary-General of the American College of Surgeons, was assigned to medicine and surgery; Bernard Baruch assumed control over raw materials; Julius Rosenwald (deceased), of Sears Roebuck & Co., handled supplies; and Samuel Gompers (deceased), president of the A. F. of L., supervised labor relations.

The broad idea of the council was to serve as a center of contact between the Government and the industrial life of the Nation. The purpose was to make available to the United States the best thought and effort of American industrial and professional life for the successful prosecution of the war. The council had no administrative power. It was only advisory. Its organization was large and loose, many of its ablest men serving only part of their time. It consciously or unconsciously served as a great laboratory devoted to discovering and making articulate the new administrative problems which the war was to involve.

Within the council, committees emerged in response to needs as they arose, and these committees developed for the most part both the personnel and the plan of organization of nearly all the special administrative organs which the exigencies of war made necessary. Thus in the course of development the committee on transportation became by act of Congress the Railroad Administration; the committee on coal was the forerunner of the Fuel Administration; the Food Administration emerged from another committee; from others came the Shipping Board and War Trade Board; and through a series of developments, which we will outline more fully, emerged the War Industries Board, which played such an important rôle in directing the whole ramification of the country's industrial life to the purposes of the war.

As early as February 28, 1917, the council created a body known as the Munitions Standards Board. Frank A. Scott was made chairman,[3] and the board was composed of technically competent persons serving without compensation to cooperate with the War and Navy Departments in establishing standards for the manufacture of munitions of war. A month later the General Munitions Board was established, with the duty of coordinating the buying of munitions by the War and Navy Departments and to assist those departments in acquiring raw materials and manufacturing plants to meet their requirements. This new and larger board had the same chairman, and included the civilian personnel of the Munitions Standards Board; but it had in addition in its membership representatives of the several supply bureaus of the War and Navy Departments. It was the purpose of this board to exercise sufficient supervision over the distribution of Government orders to prevent competition in buying

---

[3] Frank Scott, then president of the Warner-Swasey Co., Cleveland machine tool manufacturers, was one of the earliest advocates of industrial preparedness in the United States.

between the two departments and among the several purchasing
agencies of the War Department.

Almost as soon as war buying commenced, shortages began to appear or to be threatened in a number of trades. In fact, allied purchasing had already produced shortages in some industries. Prices
of particular commodities, whose use in unusual quantities was anticipated, began to rise rapidly and to fluctuate with great uncertainty.
The advisory commission called rapidly into being a large number
of committees of producers and manufacturers dealing with commodities which would enter into war needs. The thought was that
these committees could serve in an advisory capacity, acting as centers
of contact from which the Government purchasing agencies could get
full and authoritative information concerning both immediate and
prospective supply capacities and the industries could get information
showing immediate and projected Government needs. The question
of fair prices and suitable methods for making equitable distribution
of Government orders could be discussed by the advisory commission
with these committee members, who were for the most part the most
influential and best informed men in their respective lines of business.
Evidences of unparalleled good will in every quarter made this plan
seem more feasible than experience proved. The unprecedented rapidity with which expansion occurred on every hand was soon accompanied by confusion and overlapping of duties and jurisdiction. Dissatisfaction began to come to light on the part of firms not directly
represented on the committees. The possible misconception of the
position of the committees in appearing to represent, even in a vague
sense, both the buying and selling interests was very soon felt.

The council took prompt action to cure these difficulties. On July
28, 1917, it created, "with the approval of the President," a new body,
to which it gave the name War Industries Board. This board took
over the duties of the Munitions Standards Board and the General
Munitions Board, which bodies were abolished; and it was further
charged with the duty of reorganizing the several committees advising on particular industries and materials so as to make those
committees in the first place subordinate to the Board, and in the
second place composed of direct representatives of the Government
who should have no financial interest, direct or indirect, in the industries concerning which they advised. Frank A. Scott was designated as chairman of the Board; Bernard M. Baruch, commissioner
of raw materials; Robert S. Brookings, commissioner of finished products; Robert S. Lovett, priorities commissioner; Hugh A. Frayne,
labor commissioner; Col. (later Brig. Gen.) Palmer E. Pierce, Army

representative; and Rear Admiral F. F. Fletcher, Navy representative, being the other members.[4] The resolution of the council, by which the War Industries Board was created, defined its duties in general terms as follows:

The Board will act as a clearing house for the war industry needs of the Government, determine the most effective ways of meeting them and the best means and methods of increasing production, including the creation or extension of industries demanded by the emergency, the sequence and relative urgency of the needs of the different Government services, and consider price factors, and in the first instance the industrial and labor aspects of the problems involved and the general questions affecting the purchase of commodities.

The development from this step forward was along the line of the organization which was functioning when the armistice was signed. It should be noted, however, that there was a marked change in the responsibility and powers of the Board upon its reorganization, March 4, 1918.

By the end of July, 1917, the elements of the problem had become sufficiently defined to indicate the main features of the machinery which would be required to meet them. Of first importance, there was and would be an insurmountable current shortage in certain commodities. To cause those commodities to flow in channels most conducive to the purposes of the war, the Government had either to outbid all others in the market, or to take measures to control purchases and prices. The most significant, and for us the most novel, functions of the Board were the solutions which it developed for these problems in the form of the priority system and the price-fixing plan. Government price-fixing for all purchasers has been practiced from time to time as far back as the oldest known code of law.[5] But the priority system, applying to Government and private purchasers alike, represents, so far as we know, a new method of control over the products of industry.

The other functions of the Board came to appear broadly as follows: (1) To analyze the needs of our Government, of the Allies, and of the civil population; (2) to study the extent to which the resources could meet these needs; (3) to provide means and encouragement for increasing production; and (4) to promulgate rules and suggestions for preventing waste and unnecessary use. Various subdivisions were

---

[4] Robert Brookings (deceased), founder of the Brookings Institution in Washington, was president of Washington University in St. Louis; Judge Robert Lovett (deceased) went to the War Industries Board from the chairmanship of the Union Pacific Railroad; and Hugh Frayne (deceased) was general organizer of the A. F. of L.

[5] See code of Hammurabi, Babylonia, about 2250 B. C.

shaped to forward these purposes, the duties of each supplementing those of the others. Legal and technical engineering problems of a general nature, arising in connection with various features of the work, required separate divisions in those fields. The cordial support of labor was essential to increased war production, and to assure this a Division of Labor was established.

The several committees reorganized to handle the interests of the Board in respect to particular commodities grew in importance. They were composed of men thoroughly trained and experienced in individual industries. As time went on, it became more and more evident that the divisions exercising general functions would have to depend upon these commodity units first for the information on which they would base their policies and second for the direct administration of the policies themselves. There was a gradual growth in the number and strength of the commodity sections as the field of the Board's supervision widened. It was soon seen, however, that these commodity sections in turn were experiencing great difficulty in dealing directly with the very numerous individual competitive units of which most industries were composed. The situation required a series of groups who could represent before the commodity sections and the functional divisions of the Board the interests of all members of the respective trades to be affected by a war regulation. Such groups had begun to take shape from the early days of the council, particularly in the industries producing raw materials. Some trades already had national organizations of a sort; but none of these were authorized representatives of all units of a given industry.

Beginning in the early fall of 1917, the Chamber of Commerce of the United States supplemented the work already under way by lending its powerful support to the task of organizing the remaining principal industries of the country in such a way that each should be represented by a war service committee to serve on behalf of the trade as a point of contact with the Government. Where a national organization already existed, the chamber had it appoint a war service committee with authority to represent it, and where a trade was not organized, the chamber took steps to secure its organization and the appointment of such a committee. Special care was taken to see that the committees represented entire trades, small firms as well as large. The advantages of this scheme of organization are set forth to greatest possible effect in a pamphlet published by the war service executive committee of the chamber February 28, 1918.[6]

---

[6] See Appendix II for a quotation from this pamphlet.

The significance of these organizations for the future was pointed out by Harry A. Wheeler, president of the chamber, in the following terms: [7]

Organization for war service is giving business the foundation for the kind of cooperative effort that alone can make the United States economically efficient enough to take its place with the nations in world trade * * *. Creation of war service committees promises to furnish the basis for a truly national organization of industry whose proportions and opportunities are unlimited * * *. The integration of business, the expressed aim of the national chamber, is in sight.

During the summer and fall of 1917, the Food, Fuel, and Railroad Administrations, the Shipping Board, and the War Trade Board were established by acts of Congress. The War Industries Board remained a subordinate body to a council having advisory powers only. As necessities for its action arose, however, it developed and acted, relying on the one hand upon the support of the President, the Secretaries of War and the Navy, and other legally established agencies, and on the other hand upon the voluntary support of the business men of the country. For the most part there was cooperation and cordial good will, but sometimes legally responsible services of the Government would be doubtful about their obligation or their right to defer to the determinations of a body possessing only advisory powers. Priority rules were promulgated, prices were fixed, and projects for vast increases in production were inaugurated on voluntary agreements with the industries. Success depended upon the cooperation of other branches of the Government. Technically the Board had no administrative powers whatever at this time. It had no legal responsibility. The agencies of the Government, however, on whom legal responsibility for making purchases rested, found themselves dependent upon it for many important determinations.

As the spring of 1918 approached, it was felt that the scope and effectiveness of the Board's work would have to be materially increased with the increasing demands of the war in prospect. There was a widespread demand for the creation of a ministry of munitions with full administrative powers to take over and combine the work of the Board and the purchasing function of the War and Navy Departments. It was decided to leave with the War and Navy Departments the work of determining what military and naval supplies were required and the actual placing of the purchase orders. But to cure the defective powers of the War Industries Board for exercising a more

---

[7] In an article contributed to *The Nation's Business* for August, 1918.

comprehensive control over the entire industrial fabric, the President, under his general powers as Chief Executive and commander in chief of the armed forces, reconstituted the War Industries Board, removing it from the jurisdiction of the Council of National Defense and making it, with enlarged powers, an administrative agency directly responsible to himself. This reorganization was effected (1) by the President's letter, dated March 4, 1918, to Bernard M. Baruch, appointing him Chairman and setting forth specifically the powers and duties of the Board; and (2) by a formal Executive order dated May 28, 1918, after the passage of the Overman Act.[8]

The President's letter constituting the charter of the Board read as follows:

THE WHITE HOUSE,
Washington, March 4, 1918.

MY DEAR MR. BARUCH: I am writing to ask if you will not accept appointment as Chairman of the War Industries Board, and I am going to take the liberty at the same time of outlining the functions, the constitution and action of the Board as I think they should now be established.

The functions of the Board should be:

(1) The creation of new facilities and the disclosing, if necessary, the opening up of new or additional sources of supply;

(2) The conversion of existing facilities, where necessary, to new uses;

(3) The studious conservation of resources and facilities by scientific, commercial, and industrial economies;

(4) Advice to the several purchasing agencies of the Government with regard to the prices to be paid;

(5) The determination, wherever necessary, of priorities of production and of delivery and of the proportions of any given article to be made immediately accessible to the several purchasing agencies when the supply of that article is insufficient, either temporarily or permanently;

(6) The making of purchases for the Allies.

The Board should be constituted as at present and should retain, so far as necessary and so far as consistent with the character and purposes of the reorganization, its present advisory agencies; but the ultimate decision of all questions, except the determination of prices, should rest always with the Chairman, the other members acting in a cooperative and advisory capacity. The further organization of advice I will indicate below.

In the determination of priorities of production, when it is not possible to have the full supply of any article that is needed produced at once, the Chairman should be assisted, and so far as practicable, guided by the present priorities organization or its equivalent.

In the determination of priorities of delivery, when they must be deter-

---

[8] See Appendix III for copy of the Overman Act, approved May 20, 1918, giving the President power to redistribute functions among the executive agencies.

mined, he should be assisted when necessary, in addition to the present advisory priorities organization, by the advice and cooperation of a committee constituted for the purpose and consisting of official representatives of the Food Administration, the Fuel Administration, the Railway Administration, the Shipping Board, and the War Trade Board, in order that when a priority of delivery has been determined there may be common, consistent, and concerted action to carry it into effect.

In the determination of prices the Chairman should be governed by the advice of a committee consisting, besides himself, of the members of the Board immediately charged with the study of raw materials and of manufactured products, of the labor member of the Board, of the Chairman of the Federal Trade Commission, the Chairman of the Tariff Commission, and the Fuel Administrator.

The Chairman should be constantly and systematically informed of all contracts, purchases, and deliveries, in order that he may have always before him a schematized analysis of the progress of business in the several supply divisions of the Government in all departments.

The duties of the Chairman are:

(1) To act for the joint and several benefit of all the supply departments of the Government.

(2) To let alone what is being successfully done and interfere as little as possible with the present normal processes of purchase and delivery in the several departments.

(3) To guide and assist wherever the need for guidance or assistance may be revealed; for example, in the allocation of contracts, in obtaining access to materials in any way preempted, or in the disclosure of sources of supply.

(4) To determine what is to be done when there is any competitive or other conflict of interest between departments in the matter of supplies; for example, when there is not a sufficient immediate supply for all and there must be a decision as to priority of need or delivery, or when there is competition for the same source of manufacture or supply, or when contracts have not been placed in such a way as to get advantage of the full productive capacity of the country.

(5) To see that contracts and deliveries are followed up where such assistance as is indicated under (3) and (4) above has proved to be necessary.

(6) To anticipate the prospective needs of the several supply departments of the Government and their feasible adjustment to the industry of the country as far in advance as possible, in order that as definite an outlook and opportunity for planning as possible may be afforded the business men of the country.

In brief, he should act as the general eye of all supply departments in the field of industry.

Cordially and sincerely yours,   WOODROW WILSON.

MR. BERNARD M. BARUCH,
    Washington, D. C.

The Executive order, like several other orders under the Overman Act, simply ratified an existing status. It read in part as follows:

I hereby establish the War Industries Board as a separate administrative agency to act for me and under my direction * * *. The functions, duties, and powers of the War Industries Board, as outlined in my letter of March 4, 1918, to Bernard M. Baruch, Esq., its Chairman, shall be and hereby are continued in full force and effect.

The new chairman reappointed the personnel of the Board as it had been during the greater part of the winter just passed. The Board was composed of the following members: Bernard M. Baruch, Chairman; Alex Legge, Vice Chairman; Rear Admiral F. F. Fletcher, Navy representative; Maj. Gen. George W. Goethals, Army representative; Robert S. Brookings, chairman price-fixing committee; Edwin B. Parker, priorities commissioner; George N. Peek, commissioner of finished products; Hugh Frayne, labor representative; J. Leonard Replogle, steel administrator; L. L. Summers, technical advisor; Albert C. Ritchie, general counsel; and H. P. Ingels, secretary. Herbert B. Swope was an associate member of the Board, and, together with Harrison Williams and Clarence Dillon, was assistant to its Chairman.[9]

---

[9] Alex Legge (deceased) was vice-president and general manager of International Harvester, advancing after the War to the presidency of that company. When Mr. Baruch asked Legge to suggest someone for the post of Commissioner of Finished Products, Legge named George Peek, of Deere & Company in Moline, Illinois, saying to Mr. Baruch: "He's my biggest competitor. Get him down here. I want to watch him." Edwin Parker (deceased) was a leading member of the bar in Houston, Texas. J. Leonard Replogle gave up the presidency of the American Vanadium Company to become Baruch's director of steel supply. Leland L. Summers (deceased) was a New York consulting engineer who had previously acted as advisor on Allied purchases in this country. Albert Ritchie (deceased) was the Attorney General of Maryland, later governor of that state. Howard P. Ingels was vice-president and consulting engineer of the Milton Manufacturing Co., and had had considerable experience in turning out explosives for England. He is secretary of the War Industries Board Association, an informal organization of several hundred of those associated with Mr. Baruch in the war days. (The Association has held frequent reunions, the last being on Armistice Day, 1938, when, after a prophetic view of the world situation by Mr. Baruch, a resolution was passed urging President Roosevelt to give fullest consideration at once to U. S. industrial preparedness.) Herbert Bayard Swope then was city editor of the New York *World,* later to become its managing editor. Harrison Williams and Clarence Dillon went to Washington from Wall Street, the former being a utility financier, the latter an investment banker. Major General Goethals served for only a short time on the War Industries Board before being assigned to other duties in the War Department. His place was filled by Brig. Gen. Palmer Pierce, who, in May, 1918, was succeeded by Brig. Gen. Hugh S. Johnson.

By direct act of the President, authority for all principal controls except price fixing had thus at last been centralized in the new Chairman. He in turn took immediate steps to decentralize the execution of his powers, making each of his colleagues fully responsible for a particular field. Thus it was that there was created an organization which was able to mobilize the industrial resources of the country in order that the fighting forces could draw upon them with as little dislocation as possible in the industrial fabric and so as to avoid at the same time conflicts of demand. This was done, however, without taking away from any of the permanently established departments either the making of contracts or the power to determine the types and quantities of materials needed.

Upon the reorganization, the Board entered with renewed energy and confidence into the work of exercising an enlarged control over the industries of the country as they affected, both directly and indirectly, the plans for prosecuting the war. Further commodity sections were rapidly organized and the existing ones enlarged and strengthened. Representatives of Government purchasing bureaus interested in the commodity were placed in each, and the importance of these sections, as substantial administrative centers of the work of the Board, developed rapidly.

No legislation was ever passed making specific provision for the establishment of the War Industries Board. Its power still depended in large measure upon its ability to demonstrate its effectiveness in accomplishing the common purpose and the willingness of other agencies to be assisted by it, together with the voluntary support of the business interests of the country. Several times during the summer of 1918, bills giving the Board larger legal powers were prepared and discussed by committees of Congress, but the general conclusion was that the Board was accomplishing its purpose well enough without further legislative powers. The legal foundation of the priority power and the price-fixing power is discussed more fully in the chapters devoted to those subjects.

An extraordinary feature of the organization from a legal point of view was its detached nature through which it was able to maintain an expansive view of the whole undertaking and to act in a quasi-judicial capacity in respect to the many conflicting elements. The Board has been criticized as an institution with tremendous powers and no responsibilities; that democracy created in it a tyrant with power to shatter the ordinary rules of business practice even to the extent of undoing contract obligations. A fuller study of what was actually done will modify this conception. That the powers of the Board were of a quality easily susceptible to abuse and of a kind which should be intrusted only to men of extraordinary integrity and talent cannot be denied.

The Chairman of the Board from his earliest connection with this work conceived it as his highest duty to surround himself with men peculiarly qualified in temperament, knowledge, and experience for the particular tasks as they developed. It was not his theory to make a large paper organization before the facts. Out of the very large number of men from all sources who were brought to Washington for advice and discussion and for service during the earlier and more confused months of the council's work a large part of the Board's personnel was chosen. There had been a study of men as well as a study of the nature of the problems which were to emerge. With the right men, almost any organization will work. In general the men selected for the important work of the Board were of the type who in private life had been managers rather than owners of large industrial undertakings. Upon appointment to the staff they ceased to engage in their private business affairs.

The aim was to have men who possessed special knowledge each in his own field, but men with catholic and broad-gauged vision who could correlate the problems of their neighbors with their own. Constant conflicts were to be involved. Much of the work would have to be done by forcing or reaching agreements. These features required on the part of 100 or more of the men in key positions not only the qualities usually termed "executive ability," they also required tact in a high degree, patience, endurance, and buoyancy; enthusiasm which could inspire, and inspiration which could accomplish.

Some of the men who came were of independent means; for some the coming at a dollar a year or a very small salary meant a real sacrifice. Some were Democrats and some Republicans. Men worked side by side for many months without learning each other's politics, for politics was adjourned in the War Industries Board. It was the purpose of the Chairman to support the members of his staff in every way consistent with duty, to make each man really responsible for the work before him. The enthusiastic and cordial support, which he in turn received from them, is the foundation and measure of such success as the Board enjoyed. A task of this character would have failed completely if the men engaged in it had not been willing entirely to sacrifice personal interests, time, money, and sometimes even health for their work. The men were willing at all times to work long hours without holidays and without pay, forgetting personal anxieties and personal fortunes in the patriotic effort of each to do his part to win the war. This was an extraordinary example of the natural organizing power of the American people.

It is difficult to give a summary conception of the organization and its work. The Board was inspired by a picture of our industry so mobilized, and with all conflicting efforts so synchronized, that the fighting forces of the world could tap it at will for such supplies as they needed. This ideal was perhaps never quite attained, but it was the guide. The Board set out to prevent competition among those buying for the war, and to regulate the use by the civil population of men, money, and materials in such a way that civilian *needs*, not merely civilian *wants*, should be satisfied; and to do all of this with the least possible dislocation and destruction of the essential features of our ordinary industrial life.

Through application of the principle of priorities, the processes of manufacture and trade were made to move in response to a national purpose rather than in response to the wills of those who had money to buy. Through price-fixing, men were discouraged in any unwholesome ambitions to make inordinate profits out of the war. Through the conservation work of the Board, many wasteful trade practices were reformed and millions of hours of human labor were made more fruitful. Before the war ended, the American method of industrial control was coming to be applied, through the medium of international executives, to the several war materials whose sources were in distant parts of the earth.

The plan of the vast organization was simple enough in form. The President's authority was centralized in the chairman of the Board. The chairman delegated, so far as practicable, the power of final decision to the several members of the Board, each in his respective field. The machinery of the 60 commodity sections was used in carrying forward the part of the general purpose for which each was responsible. Each of the commodity sections contained members from the Government purchasing agencies and each section came into contact with the industries for which it was responsible through the medium of the war service committees of the several trades. Guidance for all hands in the general plans of the war came through the activities of the chairman, who sat in the war council and gave to his men, through the channels described above and through regular meetings for conference, such information as was necessary to keep the whole organization functioning harmoniously toward a common purpose.

CHAPTER 2

The Program of Requirements

THE STATEMENT is frequently heard that a bill of requirements and specifications covering the military needs of the Government should have been prepared during the early spring of 1917 before war was declared. Had this been possible, it would unquestionably have saved millions of dollars and a vast amount of confusion. The impossibility of such a performance, however, is only too evident to one who will stop to consider the ramifications involved in the production of a war element so simple and direct as a shell. Even direct military needs change from month to month with the changing fortunes of war, and always these changes are accompanied by adjustments reaching deep into the industrial life.

A shell is made principally of steel, brass, and copper. It is filled with an explosive and is fired by either a fixed or separate charge of propellent powder. The production of such a shell involves first the preparation of a plant or plants to forge, machine, and measure it, equip it with a firing mechanism and with a band to take the rifling of the gun. It requires another plant for loading, packing, and shipping. Each of these processes involves, directly or indirectly, a vast group of industries turned to a new field. But the steel and copper used in the shell involve another set of forces as they are developed from the ore through the processes of extraction and refinement to the forges. The blast furnaces have to be supplied with coke, with lime, and with manganese. They have to be lined with refractory brick. Coke involves mining bituminous coal and passing it through coke ovens. They all involve a large amount of railroad transportation, for the most favored spot on earth does not contain all the elements for a piece of steel.

Turning to the explosive and propellant for loading and firing the shell, the nitric acid is made from nitrate of soda, which has to be mined and refined in a desert part of Chile,[1] carried to the coast on

---

[1] The improved condition of nitrate supply in the present emergency is discussed in Part II of Book One, in the Commodity Section on Chemicals.

railroads whose rails, rolling stock, ties, and fuel have to be taken there from distant parts, and then it is carried 5,000 miles in vessels to our shores; the sulphuric acid required in great quantities is made from pyrites ore coming from Spain or brimstone from Texas, platinum from Russia being needed for the equipment of the acid-producing plants. From some cotton field of the South has to be collected a little of the fine lint sticking to the seed as it comes from the gin to form the basis of the propellent powder. And after all this preparation, a shell on the front is fired in a few moments. One day its use is necessary, another day it is not, but its preparation has to go on and on until the conflict is over.

Shells are but one small feature of the equipment of an army. There must be guns and rifles, hand grenades and gas equipment, airplanes and motor cars, food supplies and uniforms, medicines and surgical dressings, sound ranging apparatus, telephone supplies, and optical instruments. Ships were required to carry the troops and supplies. When one realizes the extent to which an individual direct requirement of the Army involves the whole ramification of industry, it is not difficult to see how a large number of direct requirements projected on a vast scale will bring in their train an overlapping and confusion in indirect requirements. The program of supply had to grow with the growth of the military program on the one hand and the growing knowledge of the materials obtainable on the other.

For the purposes of supply our Army was organized to make purchases according to the use to which the commodity would be put. The Ordnance Department bought guns and ammunition; the Quartermaster, clothing, blankets, food, and trucks; the Signal Corps, telephone apparatus, field glasses, etc.; the Engineers, building materials, railroad supplies, and implements; and so on. Each service had subunits charged with responsibility for particular groups of supplies. More than one service frequently bought quantities of the same commodity. It will be seen that the Army method of classifying supplies did not correspond to any extent with the classifications of ordinary business. Particularly did requirements by services, when translated into terms once removed from direct requirements, fit awkwardly into the classifications of business usage. From the beginning the Board felt that it was advisable to develop its organization according to the classification of commodities used in business. Before the war was over, the Army found it necessary to reorganize its purchasing system, gradually drawing it together under one control and revising its classifications. Outside of the War Department, the Navy, and later the Emergency Fleet and the Railroad Administration, were making Government purchases.   In addition to all, the principal Allies had purchasing missions in this country.

All of these factors contributed to the difficulty of laying down a program of requirements.   The separate units of the Army supply bureaus could not compute their requirements until they knew the size of the particular part of the Army for which it was their legal duty to provide.   The size of the Army to be here and abroad at any given time could not easily be computed without a definite knowledge of the amount of shipping that would be available both for men and for supplies.   Frequently the kind of equipment could not be determined until it was known what materials could be found available.   Sometimes types, designs, and specifications were delayed in an effort to develop a more perfect product.   It soon became clear that the comprehensive supply organization would have to be mobile enough to respond promptly to an ever-changing demand.

When the General Munitions Board was formed, the activities of all Government purchasing agencies consisted in energetically placing orders without any certainty of their being filled.   The board received statements of immediate requirements only as they were brought before it, when it joined in the effort to supply them in the shortest possible time.   When a request for assistance came, the board would consider whether the proposed order involved a conflict with other necessary orders and whether it required emergency action to provide material or determine prices, and then it attempted to assist in discovering the best available source of supply.   At first there was no system forcing all orders to be brought before the board even in lines where there was a known shortage.

Action on such orders as were brought was advisory only, and there was no report back showing whether the advice had been followed. Many Government bureaus placed the bulk of their orders without reference to the board.   Each sought those plants whose manufacturing facilities promised the best results as judged from experience in normal times.   This procedure had a tendency to localize orders in the northeastern manufacturing district of the country, and congestion soon began to appear, with inevitable slowing up of deliveries.

By the fall of 1917 many plants had orders far beyond their available capacity.   Fuel and raw materials could not be transported in sufficient quantities to supply the plants. Each Government purchaser wanted his order filled first and each manufacturer wanted his coal and railroad service given preference on the ground that he was filling a Government order.   There was competition in buying even between different Government agencies, and the competition between

Government contractors was increasing in intensity. Prices rose not only because of actual shortages, but because of options and inquiries made to cover bids on Government orders. * * *[2]

The first effort directed specifically to bringing system into the confusion of Government orders was the formation of the "clearance committee" as an administrative unit of the General Munitions Board, which became later the War Industries Board. The clearance committee was composed of a chairman, a secretary, and a representative from the Army General Staff, the Navy, several bureaus of the Army, the Marine Corps, the more important sections of the Board, and later the Allied Purchasing Commission. This committee prepared what is called a "Clearance List" setting forth those materials in which a shortage was believed to exist. Government agencies were requested not to place orders for any materials on this list without first having those orders cleared by the committee. The committee considered requests for the clearance of orders with a view to preventing their being placed where there was congestion and where they would interfere with the fulfillment of other orders of equal importance, with a view to adjusting the relative importance of deliveries and to preventing abnormal rises in price. The method was by discussion and agreement between the respective interests, each being represented. Each buying department read its proposed orders before the committee, and, if no objection developed, the orders were cleared. If objection was made by another department because of conflict with its program or by an agency of the Board because curtailment, substitution, or other plan of conservation was being hindered, the order was re-formed or clearance delayed until the matter could be adjusted.

It was not many weeks before the clearance committee began to be overwhelmed with duties. Shortages showed themselves in one commodity after another and the clearance list increased week by week. The function of deciding on the relative merits of two or more conflicting agencies who wanted delivery of the same thing and of ruling on which should be preferred in cases where all could not be served, in other words, the priority function, presented increasing difficulties and appeared as increasingly important. In the summer of

---

[2] The deleted material described an additional factor in the confusion of procurement: that caused by the placing of Allied orders in this country. To handle these orders, to co-ordinate Allied buying with that of the U. S. Government, there was set up an Allied Purchasing Commission (whose members were the Messrs. Baruch, Brookings, and Lovett), which assisted the Allied missions in this country in obtaining the best prices, terms of delivery, priority preference, etc., that were practicable.

1917 a new agency, the priorities committee, was formed to take over this function, which later, as we shall see, became such an important feature of the work of the Board. It was found, also, that the clearance process had little effect in the control of prices. This function also was early isolated and placed in the province of a price-fixing committee created to handle it. But the clearance function proper had not been developed in vain. It was evident by the spring of 1918 that one committee could not handle the volume of work which the administration of this function implied. Furthermore, its performance by a single body was not necessary.

By July, 1918, the commodity sections, following the reorganization put into effect by the new Chairman, had developed such strength, containing as they then did representatives from each of the supply bureaus interested in their respective commodities, that these sections could take over the clearance function, and they did, the clearance committee being reorganized into a Clearance Office whose function it was merely to receive requests for clearance, record them, and transmit them to the proper commodity sections, the sections in turn reporting back through the Clearance Office. The first chairman of the clearance committee was Frank A. Scott. He was succeeded by Lieut. Col. C. C. Bolton, who in May, 1918, was succeeded by Rear Admiral F. F. Fletcher.

During the winter of 1917 and 1918 the clearance schedule not only increased by reason of the addition of many new groups of commodities, but the ruling was issued that all orders to be placed in the so-called congested district (outlined in the ruling) would have to be cleared, and that all orders involving the creation of new or additional facilities should be cleared. The clearance function, as developed through the commodity sections, was the means by which the record was maintained, commodity by commodity, of standing orders, and it was the means used for so distributing the Government orders that their benefit or their burden might be equitably shared by all the interests of the respective trades. Clearance, however, was never effective as a means for developing a program of requirements. Requests for clearance were statements of immediate requirements only.

When, in the spring of 1918, it had become evident that an enlarged control of industry would be necessary, the need for a systematic statement of requirements, projected far enough into the future to allow time to provide for their production, was keenly felt. In order "to anticipate the prospective needs of the several supply departments of the Government and their feasible adjustment to the industries of the country," a Requirements Division was organized in June, with Alex Legge as chairman, and embracing in its membership authorized representatives of each of the Government purchasing agencies (Army and Navy), the priorities commissioner, the commissioner of finished products, chiefs of divisions, section chiefs, manager of Allied Purchasing Commission, representatives of the Food, Fuel, and Railroad Administrations, the Capital Issues Committee, the Department of Commerce, the Red Cross, the Shipping Board, and other departments and bureaus.[3]

Each of the several Government departments was requested to submit a statement of its requirements projected as far in advance as practicable. These statements were received by the Requirements Division, where they were discussed from the point of view of their general relations to other requirements, and then handed on to the appropriate commodity sections, where detailed studies were made and reports sent back to the source of the statements concerning the possibility and means for meeting such requirements. * * *

The scope involved made this procedure very difficult of application, but the principle was sound. For the first time during the war, and perhaps for the first time in Government operations generally, this organization provided systematic machinery by which the various department buyers had the opportunity of learning one another's needs, and of knowing at what points their respective efforts conflicted or overlapped. It gave Government bureaus and section chiefs alike a more comprehensive vision of the whole course of the undertaking.

The procedure of the Board, as it developed with respect to these two functions, was about as follows: The various Government purchasing units and the Allied Purchasing Commission were sending to the Requirements Division their best estimates of future requirements projected for six months or a year in advance. The commodity sections of the Board used these statements in their studies of curtailment and conservation programs, increased production programs, and other plans necessary in looking forward to meeting the needs. They also used them for the instruction of the trade through the war-service committees, and in the consideration of problems arising in connection with priorities and price-fixing. These statements were in the nature of estimates and did not necessarily imply that orders would actually be placed. They meant at least that orders were contemplated. The changing nature of military plans will make obvious the fact that full and accurate statements of all require-

---

[3] See Appendix IV for a copy of the circular creating the Requirements Division.

ments for a year or even a half year in advance are quite impossible, however desirable they might be from the point of view of the officials responsible for mobilizing industry. * * *

The commodity sections, on whom the burden of clearing rested, would act on requests in one of six ways. (1) Clear without comment, in which case the purchaser was permitted to go into the market and order as he saw fit; (2) clear with restriction as to the area in which the order might be placed; (3) clear with restriction as to the electric power system on which the order would draw; (4) clear subject to restrictions as to certain named plants or with restrictions inhibiting the creation of new facilities for the execution of the order; (5) clear with an actual allocation of the order to a particular named source of supply; (6) clear with advice as to suitable source of supply. The application of this system varied with the peculiar problems incident to different lines of trade. There was no attempt to make it rigid. A licensing system for civilian as well as Government purchases was used in several industries, as will be observed in connection with the work of the commodity sections discussed in Part II of this book.

That much of the confusion experienced in collecting the supplies for this war could have been avoided by a more painstaking, thorough, and comprehensive effort on the part of the Government supply bureaus to work out a program of requirements, even a program tentative in many of its details, there is little doubt. That such a program would have been exceedingly difficult to frame is quite certain.

The experience of the Board in this respect suggests the thought that there should be established a large unit of specially qualified officers of the War Department devoted in time of peace to studies of supply programs for supposititious military undertakings. As these programs would always have to be based upon the obtainability of the supplies outlined, the bureau should be required to go deeply into a study of the industrial resources and possibilities of the country as they relate to war needs. These studies are a military function, but they might have also, as a by-product, a healthy effect upon business.

Editor's Note: Hugh S. Johnson, as the Army representative on the War Industries Board, was concerned specifically with the problem of supply; and in *The Blue Eagle from Egg to Earth* (1935), he said:

It is not serving the public interest to withhold the observation that the American Army Supply System just didn't work. It didn't work because there was no proper co-ordination and organization of purchase bureaus. I can say this because part of that co-ordination was my own responsibility. I have often reflected that in the organization of the whole nation for the draft, starting with nothing, we turned in an almost perfect job, but that in the reorientation of an existing "going system," we never really rang the bell.

The cause is not far to seek—the tremendous tenacity of life of a Government bureau. The draft system was a temporary emergency improvization, and we did it mostly with kids. There was no hierarchy or vested rights in federal functions. The supply system was just a cluster of jealous and ancient bureaus. They fought the exterior control of the War Industries Board at every step, even after we had contrived a plan of integration that put their men in control of practically every economic unit. We did, by major assault, concentrate purchase activities in single units, but as soon as the war was over the old chambered nautilus was back just where it was before Sarajevo; and there methinks it will remain in spite of hell and high water.

Although the supply bureaus were split up after the Armistice, and are still apart, considerable procurement planning has been done in the last twenty years. In the National Defense Act of 1920 (which, in large measure, was the result of agitation by those civilian leaders who had contributed so greatly to the war effort), Congress gave the Assistant Secretary of War broad authority over procurement planning and plans for industrial mobilization, resulting in the establishment of the Planning Branch and the Army Industrial College. Furthermore, a prominent place in the curriculum of the Industrial College has been given to lectures on procurement and other phases of industrial mobilization by such acknowledged experts as Mr. Baruch, General Johnson, George Peek, Frank Scott, and others who gave their time so that the lessons of World War I would not have to be learned over again.

The General Staff, however, remains firm in its belief that decentralization of Army procurement is necessary because of the specialization of the various supply branches. Yet the last war gave convincing proof that some kind of centralization is absolutely necessary. The result has all the appearances of a compromise. The Assistant Secretary of War—instead of the civilian leaders in charge of mobilizing *all* the economic forces of the country —is given the job of checking on procurement schedules and maintaining a co-ordination between the supply branches.

CHAPTER 3

The Study of Resources

WHILE ORGANIZATIONS were being developed with a view to evolving a program of requirements, several institutions were created whose function it was to aid in discovering or obtaining resources to fill the requirements. No statistical data existing at the beginning of the war was of any great value in this direction. The needs were immediate. Hence the efforts to discover resources and to develop and convert resources went forward hand in hand.

The purchases of the Allies had given a war atmosphere to our industries before April, 1917. Many extensive developments had taken place. The DuPont Co. had increased its facilities for the production of military powder from 500,000 pounds per month to nearly 30,000,000 pounds per month. Our great steel plants and many others were engaged on very large war contracts. But it was important that the Allies should not be hindered by our entrance into the war. These facilities and more were going to be needed for the allied supply programs. Our problem then was to provide for our own needs without interference with the allied program and with the least dislocation of industry. This would have to be done in many instances by the creation of new facilities, but in most instances by the conversion of existing facilities to new work. Factories making fine watch springs could manufacture time fuses; plants making steel rails could forge shells; carpet looms could make Army duck; automobile factories could make airplanes. A thousand and one industries could be converted to making direct war necessities, some with great difficulty, some with little difficulty.

Many of the supplies required by the war were required in the same form in which they are used in civilian life. In some fields the work involved no more than an increase of production. Most of the raw materials entering into the implements of war were the same as the materials of peace. A few of peculiar importance had to be produced in quantity for war purposes for the first time, but in respect to most basic materials a great increase in quantity of production was required, because civilian needs and war needs overlapped.

The first steps taken to discover the facilities of the country available for war use have already been referred to. Both the industrial inventory and the report of the Kernan Board were made during the winter of 1916–17. These data were in the hands of the Council at the beginning of the war, and an Industrial Inventory Section was early formed to take them over and continue the line of investigation. As the work of the Board developed, this field was expanded to include the following divisions and sections: (1) The Resources and Conversion Section, for discovering plants suitable for conversion and suggesting and supervising the operation; (2) the Facilities Division, for supervising the construction of new plants; (3) the Advisory Committee on Plants and Munitions, with general duties in coordinating the work of various agencies in the field; and (4) the Division of Planning and Statistics.

The commodity sections, of course, did very important and far-reaching work in connection with the discovery and conversion, as well as creation, of facilities. For the determination of raw material resources we had had some peace-time reports. The demand for facts by highly organized industries, like the iron, steel, copper, lead, coal, oil, and other industries, had resulted in compilations of periodical statistics by private enterprises, by the Census Bureau, and by the Bureau of Mines. The statistical work in these fields was carried forward almost entirely by the commodity sections.

By May, 1918, the Industrial Inventory Section had not only extended the inventory to include 28,000 separate plants but had reclassified the plants according to a system better suited to the uses of the Government. The original inventories had been made up accordcording to a form used in the 1914 census of manufactures. This showed the factories in terms of their capacity to produce definite finished articles. For the purpose of making a decision on the placing of most of the war contracts it was necessary to know the "processes" for which a given factory was equipped rather than the product which it normally turned out. With this reclassified inventory, the section was to become a valuable source of information for the commodity sections and the Government purchasing agencies.

The work of re-forming and extending the industrial inventory was greatly assisted by a number of business organizations, among them the Associated Fire Underwriters, which furnished to the section duplicates of its active files. The United States Chamber of Commerce also assisted by furnishing the section with a current record of all war service committee organizations. The commodity sections assisted also by the use of questionnaires. Several Government departments maintained organizations for the study of plant facilities. These also sent out many questionnaires seeking particular items of information.

By the spring and early summer of 1918, the number of questionnaires being sent out by various Government organizations was becoming so great that complaints were received from manufacturers to the effect that they were a positive hindrance to progress. To remedy this, the newly organized War Industries Board established a Questionnaire Section in the newly formed Division of Planning and Statistics, and an effort was made to have all Government questionnaires harmonized through this section. Duplications could be avoided and forms could be suggested which would more adequately supply the information desired.

As has already been pointed out, the spring of 1918 saw the great manufacturing center of the country north of the Potomac and east of the Alleghenies completely congested. At the same time the war program was expanding. Several other parts of the country were not engaged in war work to any important extent and in many instances the peace-time business was declining. The clearance system has already been mentioned as one step taken to relieve this situation. Through clearance it was the purpose to spread the development of war industries into other parts of the country as much as practicable. This would naturally throw a greatly added burden on the Industrial Inventory Section. A more powerful and extensive organization was required.

Resources and Conversion Section.—On May 27, 1918, the Board established the Resources and Conversion Section, which took over the records and the work of the Industrial Inventory Section and began to organize on an enlarged scale under Charles A. Otis as chief.[1] An organization decentralized geographically and subjectively was determined upon. The work was too large to be effectively handled from one office. The country was divided into 21 geographical areas, called "industrial regions," for each of which a regional advisor was appointed with an office in the principal center. Each regional advisor organized a regional committee, with a member representing each of the principal war industries operative in the area, and having in addition special members to handle the priorities function, industrial stimulation, and statistics on plants, on power, and on raw materials. Each member of this regional committee be-

---

[1] Charles Otis, an investment banker, was president of the Cleveland Chamber of Commerce prior to going to Washington in 1918; in that capacity he had already made, on his own initiative, an inventory of the Cleveland area.

came in turn chairman of a subcommittee of the region devoted to the particular subject matter which he represented. The regional advisors were local business men of highest standing, chosen by the business organization or organizations of the respective regions. They served without pay and usually without expense money. Headquarters were established in Boston, Bridgeport, New York, Philadelphia, Pittsburgh, Rochester, Cleveland, Detroit, Chicago, Cincinnati, Baltimore, Atlanta, Birmingham, Kansas City, St. Louis, St. Paul, Milwaukee, Dallas, San Francisco, Seattle, and Denver.

The Resources and Conversion Section had in its membership representatives of the Army, Navy, Marine Corps, Emergency Fleet, and the Department of Commerce. Two lines of work, each supplementing and assisting the other, were undertaken in the several districts. The general work of perfecting the industrial inventory was carried forward by having each region attempt to collect and send to Washington the following list of information:

(1) Existing facilities for producing direct and indirect war needs, both raw materials and finished products; (2) the extent to which these facilities were occupied with unfilled orders and the extent to which they could take on additional orders; (3) if a plant were overloaded, the feasibility and extent of expansion necessary for relief; or, in the alternative, a suggestion for transferring a part of the load to other plants; (4) existing facilities not employed on war work but capable of undertaking it; (5) facilities whose production was about to be curtailed because of war conditions and the extent to which they were susceptible of conversion for the production of war needs; and (6) the existence of available labor, of new sources of supply of raw materials, of unused power facilities, of available transportation facilities, etc.

The armistice came before this body of information was anything like complete, but particular items collected in this way had already begun to serve the purpose contemplated, particularly in the less congested areas of the country. * * *

It would be difficult to isolate and list the work of the section, giving specific credit for particular accomplishments. It would require many pages to enumerate all cases of plant conversions, a large percentage of which were carried out at the suggestion or under the supervision of the section. A few examples will illustrate the scope of the work and at the same time show how many plants, which might otherwise have found little work during the war, were kept in full activity.

Plants for making gas holders were converted into munitions plants;

carpet plants began to make blankets and duck; automobile factories made airplanes; refrigerator plants were converted into plants
for making Navy filing cases and field hospital tables; furniture
plants manufactured ammunition boxes; horseshoe plants made trench
picks; toy plants turned to making packing boxes; factories for
ladies' waists became plants for making signal flags; electric vacuum
plants made parts for Liberty motors; factories for making fishing
rods turned out staffs for the Signal Corps; shirt factories sewed
mosquito nets; factories for rubber goods produced gas masks; peaceful stove plants turned to making hand grenades and trench bombs;
corset factories labored on Medical Corps belts and fencing masks;
gear plants learned the art of making gun sights; plants for pipe
organs made mosquito nets, and so on.

Facilities Division.—By the fall of 1918 so many problems were
arising in connection with the location and construction of new plants
for war work that a Facilities Division was formed for the purpose
of harmonizing the activities. S. P. Bush was made director of the
division.[2] It had been organized only a short time when the armistice
was signed.

The functions of the division were outlined in the plans for its
establishment as follows: (1) The division will make a comprehensive
study of all aspects of new construction projects, advising in respect
to proposed locations on the availability of transportation, power,
fuel, labor, building materials, raw materials, etc.; (2) it will advise
on the selection and specifications of materials of construction so as
to avoid long hauls especially through the congested districts and
so as to avoid conflicts with orders already placed; (3) it will look
to the adoption of forms of contract such as will insure uniformity
and consistency in all Government building activities; (4) it will
compile and from time to time revise lists of responsible contractors
and architects throughout the United States equipped to undertake
construction work of various kinds, furnishing such lists to Government
agencies upon request, and it will keep a record of existing Government contracts with a view to preventing interference between new
and old orders; (5) it will prevent the creation of new facilities in
localities where the condition of existing facilities is such that new
ones would be inadvisable; (6) it will endeavor to coordinate the
activities of all departments and agencies of the Government in construction work of every kind, except shipbuilding; and (7) it will

---

[2] Samuel P. Bush, who was president of the Buckeye Steel Castings Co., of
Columbus, Ohio, went to Washington in the early days of the Council of National Defense.

study prospective departmental needs and make plans for the new facilities necessary to meet them.

The procedure contemplated was that, after future requirements should have been received by the Requirement Division and passed upon by the appropriate commodity sections, they should be passed on to the Facilities Division, whose business it should be to determine what steps would be necessary to provide facilities for such requirements. When later on the schedule of orders should be received, the Facilities Division would clear the orders subject to such restrictions as it might impose and return them to the departments from which they came with a schedule of available facilities attached.

Advisory Committee on Plants and Munitions.—This committee was formed May 28, 1918, to take over the work of the committee on production of the council. S. M. Vauclain,[3] who had been chairman first of the Munitions Standards Board, then of the committee on production, became chairman of the advisory committee and took with him the records and most of the personnel of the earlier organization. The committee worked in a general way to stimulate production, to advise on plant extensions, etc. Particular attention was given to the production of freight cars and locomotives for the Army. Work on standardization of types of cars and locomotives was carried on. The committee was given a special assignment to assist the Czecho-Slovak Government in securing supplies in this country. The plan at the end was to have the work of this committee absorbed by the Facilities Division on the one hand and the Railway Supply Section on the other. The chairman had arranged to go to France as manager of the Chateauroux tank plant.

Division of Planning and Statistics.—In the early days of the council a Statistical Division was organized under Dr. Leonard Ayres.[4] This division devoted its principal energy to assembling statistics which would be of particular value to the General Staff of the Army in laying down a program of requirements. In April, 1918, Dr. Ayres and most of his staff were commissioned and he was asked to transfer his work to the War Department and to take the title of chief of the Statistical Division of the General Staff. This gave the Army a central statistical organization for the first time and it left the War Industries Board without such an organization.

Although most of the commodity sections were doing very im-

---

[3] Samuel Vauclain, then first vice-president of the Baldwin Locomotive Works, was chairman of the board of that company upon his death last year.

[4] Dr. Ayres, the economist and statistician of the Cleveland Trust Co., was lent to Washington by that institution.

portant statistical work, the need for a central bureau was definitely felt. Dean Edwin F. Gay,[5] who was Director of the Division of Planning and Statistics of the Shipping Board and Chief of the Bureau of Research and Tabulation of Statistics of the War Trade Board, was asked to organize such a bureau. He became Director of the Division of Planning and Statistics of the War Industries Board, which was conducted under the immediate charge of Dr. Henry R. Hatfield.[6] The division operated through six sections.

The *Section on Price Statistics* was put in charge of Prof. W. C. Mitchell.[7] This section worked in close co-operation with the price-fixing committee, for which it prepared many special reports. It early began a study of war-time price movements, showing actual and relative prices of several hundred commodities and groups of commodities most affected by the war. Monthly price quotations for the period 1913 to 1918 were collected as a basis for the study. Immediately after the armistice the section was expanded, by transferring personnel as it could be released from other sections, and this work was pressed speedily forward. The studies were published early in 1919 in a series of War Industries Board Bulletins, Nos. 1 to 57. The general title of the series is "History of Prices During the War," and each bulletin covers a particular group of commodities. The reasons for price fluctuations are discussed and graphs picturing relative prices as well as tables of monthly prices for each of the principal war products are printed.[8]

The *War Contracts Section* of the division, established under the early régime (Aug. 17, 1917), continued to collect information on war contracts and deliveries. This work never proceeded as satisfactorily as those engaged in it desired. Although the Secretary of War issued orders directing the five purchasing bureaus of the Army to furnish information to the section, regular and complete reports never came in from these sources. The section then tried a system of circular letters sent to manufacturers asking for regular monthly reports on contracts and deliveries. But even with most vigorous work on the part of the office staff, the returns on the vast number of contracts were insufficient to afford really satisfactory bases for statistical judgments. In February, 1918, however, the section began

---

[5] Dean Gay was head of the Graduate School of Business Administration at Harvard from 1908 until 1919. He returned to the Harvard faculty as professor of economic history in 1924 and retired in 1936.

[6] Dr. Hatfield retired as dean of faculties of the University of California in 1923.

[7] Wesley C. Mitchell went to the War Industries Board from Columbia University, where he has been a professor of economics since 1914.

[8] See Appendix V for a list of the War Industries Board Price Bulletins, Nos. 1 to 57.

to issue bulletins based on partial returns, and even these proved of value. * * *

A *Questionnaire Section* was organized during the summer. The division had taken up this work from the beginning, giving advice on the framing and handling of questionnaires with a view to lessening duplications and to securing forms suited to the various purposes. With the multiplication of questionnaires by every Government agency and the increasing complaint from manufacturers over the growing burden of answering them, more rigid action seemed necessary. An order was issued on August 12, 1918, that all questionnaires sent out by any branch of the Board should first be submitted to the section. The section advised as to desirable forms and methods of tabulation and on request would undertake the entire work of preparation, issue, and tabulation. A complete indexed file of questionnaires sent out by the Board is preserved in the records of the section.

It was the duty of the *Editorial Section* to make available to war agencies information on the status of the supply program and on changes in the industrial conditions affecting it. This was done by a series of bulletins.

The relation of the division to the commodity sections in respect to their statistical work was of particular importance. Some of these sections had well-organized statistical subunits. All of them based their work on statistical information.

It was the function of the *Commodity Statistics Section* of this division to assist the commodity sections either (1) by tabulating, charting, and preparing data secured from a section, or (2) by detailing statistical clerks to work in the office of a section, or (3) by organizing and installing a complete statistical service in a section, or (4) by co-operating in the establishment of joint statistical offices representing commodity sections of the Board and other war agencies.

As part of the work of this division, Dr. Gay undertook a special mission which is perhaps of unusual interest. In the spring of 1918 the President asked the chairman of the Board to prepare for the President's personal use a *conspectus of progress* in the accomplishment of the supply program, to be brought up to date as promptly as possible and supplemented weekly. The purpose was to afford a more businesslike, comprehensive view of the entire undertaking, in order that, when necessary, adjustments might be made or steps taken to synchronize to the highest possible extent all elements involved. This purpose made necessary the collection of secret information from many sources, unrelated except through the President as chief of all. * * *

The activities of this division, as they took shape immediately after the armistice, were unusually important. The work on a "History of Prices During the War" has already been referred to. Another work of importance was the rapid preparation of a report for the peace conference. This was undertaken as a joint enterprise by the statistical offices of the Food Administration, the Fuel Administration, the Shipping Board, the War Trade Board, and the War Industries Board. The effort was to set forth an extended body of data on the economic situation of the world, particularly of the United States, in respect to 60 principal groups of commodities. * * *

The experience of the Board in respect to the part of its work discussed in this chapter would point to the desirability, in case of a future analogous situation, of forming immediately a decentralized organization with one unit of the Board, like the Resources and Conversion Section or the Division of Planning and Statistics, in the form of a staff organization at Washington, whose function it would be to supervise the field organizations and harmonize the statistical work of the commodity sections.

There could perhaps be no more valuable measure of "preparedness" than the establishment in peace time of a bureau of planning and statistics (a fact-finding body), organized into about 60 commodity sections, whose function it would be to maintain current data on the productive capacity of the country. This organization could probably be established successfully as a bureau of the Department of Commerce.

Editor's Note: Considerable development along the line suggested above has taken place in the last eight years, assuming final form in the statistical work of the Bureau of the Budget and the National Resources Planning Board.

Profiting from the experience of the War Industries Board, Hugh S. Johnson saw to it that the National Industrial Recovery Act of June, 1933, contained a provision for a separate agency known as the Central Statistical Board, which lived on after NRA. In the government reorganization of 1939, the Central Statistical Board was abolished and its functions were transferred to the new Bureau of the Budget in the Executive Office of the President.

The National Resources Planning Board, likewise created in the reorganization of 1939, stems directly from the National Resources Committee and the Federal Employment Stabilization Office in the Department of Commerce. The old National Resources Committee, in turn, had evolved from the National Planning Board of the Federal Emergency Administration of Public Works.

Furthermore, in addition to the work of the National Resources Planning Board and the centralization of statistical studies in the Bureau of the Budget, the 1939 reorganization also provided a means for centralizing circulars and questionnaires in the Office of Government Reports, another branch of the new Executive Office of the President.

CHAPTER 4

Priorities

NEITHER THE function of drawing up programs of requirements, synthesizing them, and throwing them into comparison with catalogues of resources, nor the effort to provide for action to a common purpose in the supply process through clearance lists and the method of clearing orders, ever got at the root of the confusion. A new method of control was to be invented here, a method by which one body of officials would sit in judgment to determine the sequence in which materials should be manufactured and orders filled. What came to be known as the priority system was destined to become the most characteristic feature of the whole scheme of wartime supervision over the industrial forces.

When it once became clear that the Government had machinery which could turn out definite rulings on the order in which demands might be supplied, when he who came with the largest purse could not necessarily obtain his materials first, the importance of abnormal demands in affecting prices immediately began to diminish. The priority system was, perhaps, as important as any other single factor in stabilizing prices. It was also of profound importance as a corollary to price-fixing. When prices are fixed under circumstances in which demand far exceeds supply, the right to buy cannot safely be left to the forces of chance and personal favoritism. The flow of materials had to be directed, to every extent possible, from one central authority whose eye was everywhere. With priority control established, conservation programs could be enforced, rationing programs and curtailment programs could be made effective, necessary new undertakings could be materially encouraged; the regulations of the Board became enforceable, and that small minority, whose tendency to disobey rules which an overwhelming majority were ready to follow, could be brought into line without unreasonable delays. Yet this priority control was strictly American in its nature. The central authority was only the organism necessary to make articulate and definitive the desire of each man to do his part. The long list of rules and regulations was developed out of conferences and hearings trade by trade, Government and governed taking each other into fullest confidence.

It required some months to discover the gravamen of the system and to realize its effectiveness, and even after this discovery there was always a feeling for the importance of caution in the exercise of such power.

The first uncertain steps in the exercise of priority control † extended back to the formation of a priority subcommittee of the General Munitions Board on May 3, 1917. The director of the council at that time briefly defined the priority function by stating that the committee—

shall exercise full power in the determination of priority of delivery of materials and finished products whenever there is a conflict in delivery in accordance with the general policy of the Government. It is further understood that at present the priority committee of the General Munitions Board has no power in regard to the determination of priority in regard to civilian needs in which the Army and Navy requirements are not involved. It is further understood that as between the needs of our allies and our civilian population, the priority committee of the General Munitions Board for the present has no authority to act. In this connection, however, the priority committee should keep full information as to such cases or instances as come to its attention, in order that plans may further be developed for properly handling the matter.

This function was thrust upon the General Munitions Board by the fact that a multitude of manufacturers and contractors engaged in Government work were asking which orders they should fill first. Before midsummer the committee was receiving 50 to 75 inquiries or requests per day for preference policies; but this committee was only giving advice without binding effect, designed to assist individual concerns who had accepted more orders than they could hope to fill in laying down their production plans. The real work of control by priorities did not begin until early in the fall of 1917, after the formation of the War Industries Board, with Robert S. Lovett as priorities commissioner. Edwin B. Parker was by Judge Lovett designated as chairman of the new priorities committee, and as such placed in active charge of it on August 23, 1917. When Judge Lovett retired to join the Railroad Administration as director of capital expenditures, Mr. Parker was appointed by the Chairman to succeed him as priorities commissioner and head of the rapidly developing

† *Editor's Note:* Your attention is called to Mr. Baruch's discussion of priorities, and related problems, in the article on page 465.

Priorities Division, upon the reorganization of the Board, March 4, 1918. * * *[1]

Action began by the issuance of Priorities Circular No. 1 on September 21, 1917, the day on which the price of copper was fixed and a few days before steel prices were announced. The first formal priority certificate issued bore date of September 25, 1917. But the great possibilities of this system and its necessity as a cure for the confusion of the day were not, perhaps, fully and generally appreciated, nor its full application believed to be authorized, until the reorganization of the Board on March 4, 1918, from which time forward priority control became a characteristic feature of the work. Priority rulings were given finality by the President's direct authority and they became most effective, because the Nation to a man was then in a mood to follow the leadership of its designated commander in chief.

The legal foundation of the right to issue priority rulings rests on a variety of statutes and principles. The committee, however, soon found itself in a position where it did not have to depend upon direct legal sanction for the enforcement of its regulations; the spirit of service exhibited by the people made such sanction perhaps unnecessary. But the President, the Secretary of War, the Secretary of the Navy, the Chairman of the Shipping Board, the President of the Emergency Fleet Corporation, the Fuel Administrator, and the Director General of Railroads determined to centralize in the chairman of the Board, and through him the priorities commissioner, the exercise of such powers of priority as lay within their legal right, and unity of machinery brought effective results.

The national defense act of June 3, 1916, gave broad powers to the President to place orders for the manufacture of any supplies needed by the Government for war purposes, with any concern engaged in the manufacture of such supplies or whose plant was capable of being transformed so as to manufacture them, which orders should be mandatory and be given preference over all other orders. If satisfactory arrangements could not be made with the owner of such a plant, the Secretary of War was authorized to take over and operate it, paying just compensation. Section 120 of this act provided, in part, as follows:

such possession to be taken where the owner or operator refuses to give preference to Government orders or to manufacture or to furnish arms,

---

[1] The vice-chairman of the Priorities Division was Charles K. Foster, of Chicago, who for many years has been a vice-president of American Radiator & Standard Sanitary.

ammunition or parts of ammunition or other supplies or equipment at a reasonable price, as determined by the Secretary of War.

    *   *   *   *   *   *   *

The President is hereby authorized, in his discretion, to appoint a Board on Mobilization of Industries Essential for Military Preparedness, nonpartisan in character, and to take all necessary steps to provide for such clerical assistance as he may deem necessary to organize and coordinate the work hereinbefore described.

The act of August 29, 1916, providing for the creation of the council, directed "the creation of relations which will render possible in time of need the immediate concentration and utilization of the resources of the Nation." The resolution of April 6, 1917, declaring a state of war, read in part as follows:

* * * and that the President be, and he is hereby, authorized and directed to employ the entire naval and military forces of the United States; and to bring the conflict to a successful termination all the resources of the country are hereby pledged by the Congress of the United States.

Under the naval appropriation act of March 4, 1917, the Secretary of the Navy was given the same extraordinary powers in directing purchases as those possessed by the Secretary of War. The urgent deficiency act of June 15, 1917, conferred analogous powers upon the President in respect to the placing of orders for ships and shipbuilding materials. The food and fuel control act of August 10, 1917, authorized the President to commandeer foods and fuel, and gave him very exhaustive control over the distribution of coal and coke.

Under the act of May 29, 1917, amending the interstate commerce act, power was given to the Interstate Commerce Commission to regulate and control the car service of interstate carriers, including the right, either upon complaint or upon its own initiative, to suspend the operation of any or all rules, regulations or practices established with respect to car service and to make such directions for the use of cars as in its judgment would best promote the public interest. But the act which finally placed the executive branch of the Government in a position to exercise priority power was the preferential shipments act of August 10, 1917, which read, in part, as follows:

During the continuance of the war in which the United States is now engaged the President is authorized, if he finds it necessary for the national defense and security, to direct that such traffic or such shipments of commodities as, in his judgment, may be essential to the national defense and security, shall have preference or priority in transportation by any common carrier by railroad, water, or otherwise. He may give these directions at and for such times as he may determine, and may modify, change, suspend, or annul them, and for any such purpose he is hereby authorized to issue orders direct, or through such person or persons as he may designate for the purpose. * * *

Thus it will be seen that, although Congress gave authority in so many words to issue priority orders having mandatory force only in the case of transportation, the priorities committee, by drawing into one body through representation on it of each of the Government agencies interested in priorities and through direct authorization from the heads of these agencies, was able to muster adequate power to enforce compliance, if enforcement should be necessary, with any order or request that it might issue. The power to control the use of freight cars and the supply of fuel, and in the last resort to secure the commandeering of plants, was enough and more than enough. Legally, priority orders outside the sphere of transportation were, possibly, no more than requests; in fact, they usually were stated in the form of requests and their issuance was ordinarily in conformance with understandings reached through negotiations with the trade involved; but actually they had all the force and vigor of orders, since every concern affected knew that if it did not comply its supply of fuel might be cut off, its materials and supplies might not be received for transportation, or its establishment might be seized by the Government. Throughout its history the Board found few occasions in which it was necessary to secure compliance with its "requests" by actual use of any particular enforcing powers.

The manner in which priority control brought a degree of system into the chaos of the conflicting and ambitious industrial forces of the day can be read from the record of the commodity sections in Part II of this volume. Its first important application, viz., to the vast problem of iron and steel, is fully described in chapter 2. The commandeering powers of the Army, the Navy, and the Emergency Fleet Corporation came into sharp conflict with each other in respect to the steel supply and the supply of numerous other commodities. Each department was given full power, and confusion was the result. The priority system brought concerted action by a scheme which made actual commandeering unnecessary. The Priorities Division was given control of the situation through a letter from the President to each department, ruling that no commandeering order could be issued without the approval of the chairman of the War Industries Board.

The essential features of the mechanism of the system are readily understood. It was a system which would apply only under circumstances in which extreme shortages were the order of the day. Its distinctive characteristic and the foundation of its effectiveness lay in the fact that the Priorities Division placed itself in a position where its acts took the form of assistance to the industries and to individual concerns. The division could bargain for pledges and expect conformity to its regulations in return for assistance, which it had power to grant or withhold. As soon as the railroads began to follow priority rulings, and the distribution of fuel began to be based on them, the supply of the necessities of industry began to fall away from those not receiving the advantages of these rulings. The iron and steel industry, which is the foundation of such a considerable share of all manufacture, was first placed under the committee's rulings,[2] and in the circular of instructions issued to this trade were outlined the general directions as to priority and the method of applying for priority assistance.

These and subsequent circulars attempted to classify and rate orders in accordance with their relative importance for war and national purposes. Producers of iron and steel and their products were required to rate all their orders. In order to get the system satisfactorily started, all orders which had been placed prior to September 21, 1917, by or on behalf of the War Department, the Navy Department, or the Emergency Fleet Corporation, were automatically rated as class A-1 unless otherwise directed, and likewise all orders for military supplies and equipment placed by or for the Allies as class A-2.

The classes of producers required to observe priority ratings in the fulfillment of their contract orders were extended gradually from that beginning until, on July 1, 1918, Priorities Circular No. 4[3] was issued, providing that—

during the war in which the United States is now engaged, all individuals, firms, associations, and corporations engaged in the production of raw materials and manufactured products (save foods, feeds and fuels) are requested to observe regulations respecting priority.

From this time forward priority control was rapidly extended. The President's letter of March 4 had definitely centralized the pri-

---

[2] See Appendix VI for Priorities Circular No. 1, dated September 21, 1917.
[3] See Appendix VII for Priorities Circular No. 4, dated July 1, 1918.

orities function in the chairman of the War Industries Board in the following language:

The functions of the Board should be * * * (5) the determination, whenever necessary, of priorities of production and of delivery and of the proportions of any given article to be made immediately accessible to the several purchasing agencies, when the supply of that article is insufficient either temporarily or permanently.

Sixty priorities circulars in all were issued between September 21, 1917, and December 20, 1918, when No. 60 revoked, as of January 1, 1919, all rules, regulations, and directions of every nature issued by the Priorities Division.

Two concurrent and mutually supplementary methods of procedure were employed by the division in accomplishing its purposes. These will be studied separately. On the one hand, all orders were rated, either by the issuance of priority certificates to the persons placing the orders, or by a system of automatic ratings; and on the other hand, in order better to guide the forces of production into channels leading to the possible fulfillment of all rated orders, there was issued a "Classification of Purposes Demanding Preferential Treatment," which was followed by a series of "Preference Lists."

First must be understood the scheme of classifying orders by priority certificates.

All orders and work were divided into five general classes: Class AA, class A, class B, class C, and class D, with subdivisions of class AA, class A, and class B indicated by suffix numbers, as, for example, classes AA–1, AA–2, etc., A–1, A–2, A–3, etc., B–1, B–2, etc. Orders and work in class AA took full precedence of orders and work of all other classes; those in class A took precedence of those in classes B, C, and D; those in class B took precedence of those in classes C and D; and those in class C took precedence of those in class D; all irrespective of the dates the orders were placed or the certificates issued. But the classification of an order meant that it should be given such precedence over orders of a lower classification as was necessary—and only such as was necessary—to insure delivery on the date of delivery specified in the order. It did not mean that work should cease on orders of a lower classification, or that the order should be completed and delivery made in advance of all orders taking a lower classification, unless such procedure should be necessary in order to effect delivery within the time specified. * * * [4]

---

[4] See Appendix VII for a detailed explanation of the classification system.

The procedure for obtaining priority certificates on the part of any person having work to be done which fell within one of these classifications was simple enough. He would make application to the priorities committee, following a form established by the committee, blanks for which had been freely distributed. The application was for an order running against a manufacturer or distributor and calling for delivery by a certain date. The priorities committee, after consideration and frequently after reference to the appropriate commodity section, if it were determined that the application should be granted, would assign one or another of the above ratings to the order and issue a certificate. This certificate was issued directly to the applicant; that is, the person desiring to make a purchase or enter into a contract to have materials manufactured for him, unless otherwise requested, and not to the person against whom it ran. The applicant then presented his certificate to the person against whom it ran and the latter arranged his production program so as to give delivery to that priority order in its relative turn with respect to other priority orders.

The volume of work undertaken by the division in connection with the issuance of priority certificates can be appreciated from the following figures: Between September 25, 1917, and November 11, 1918, 211,430 applications were received; 191,966 priority certificates were issued, of which 8,448 were reissued certificates; and 27,912 applications were denied or withdrawn. The highest number of applications received and catalogued in one day was 1,901, on July 8, 1918. The highest number of certificates issued in one day was 2,121, on September 30, 1918.

There was printed on the cover of practically every circular of instructions concerning rules of priority, the following significant statement:

The test.—In requesting priority the petitioner should join with the committee in applying the test: To what extent, if at all, will the granting of this application contribute, directly or indirectly, toward winning the war; and if at all, how urgent is the need?

As the system of granting priority certificates showed more and more success and one new industry after another was taken under this method of control, the administrative difficulties increased to the point where a large addition to the work involved danger of a breakdown, unless a compensating practice could be devised. By July 1, 1918, as already noted, the committee had decided to make all industries subject to the regulation. A way out of the administrative difficulty appeared in the fact that certain classes of orders so obviously deserved preference that priority ratings could be assigned to them automatically.

A scheme of automatic classifications was set up accordingly on July 1, 1918,[5] the day on which control was extended to all industries.

This plan made unnecessary any application for written priority certificates to cover certain classes of orders, no reference to the priorities committee being necessary for such cases. A person whose order fell within the automatic classification would simply attach to it an affidavit in prescribed form setting forth the facts essential to automatic rating and naming the war uses for which the materials were needed. The new procedure gave no automatic rating higher than A–4, thus leaving the ratings AA, AA–1, AA–2, etc., A–1, A–2, and A–3 to be given only by specific action of the priorities committee. Orders of the War and Navy Departments and the Emergency Fleet Corporation falling within class A were automatically rated A–5 upon proper signature to the following statement:

Unless rerated by express order in writing by the priorities committee of the War Industries Board, this order is by authority of said priorities committee rated as class A–5, and its execution shall take precedence over all your orders and work of a lower classification to the extent necessary to insure delivery according to the date specified herein, as prescribed by Circular No. 4, issued by the priorities division of the War Industries Board, of date July 1, 1918, and all amendments thereto.

Priorities Circular No. 4 contained a list of purposes with their corresponding automatic ratings below A–4, by reference to which a person desiring to obtain a rating for one of his orders could prepare his affidavit, stating that the materials were to be used for such purpose, name his own rating, and proceed as if by a priority certificate.

The priorities committee handled the certificates and the rules for the automatic rating of orders, and was the sole priorities agency of the Board until March 27, 1918. The President, in his letter of March 4, suggested the creation of a further agency to work with the one already in existence in bringing about more concerted action respecting priority of delivery and in synchronizing priorities within the Government and industry.

In pursuance of this suggestion, the Priorities Board was created March 27, 1918; Edwin B. Parker, priorities commissioner, became

---

[5] See secs. 7, 8, and 9 of Priorities Circular No. 4, Appendix VII, for rules of automatic priority ratings.

chairman of the board, its other members being Bernard M. Baruch, chairman of the War Industries Board, ex officio member; Brig. Gen. Hugh S. Johnson, Army representative; Rear Admiral F. F. Fletcher, Navy representative; Clarence M. Woolley,[6] representing the War Trade Board; Edward Chambers, representing the Railroad Administration; Charles R. Piez, representing the United States Shipping Board and Emergency Fleet Corporation; P. B. Noyes, representing the Fuel Administration; T. F. Whitmarsh, representing the Food Administration; Alex Legge, Vice Chairman of the War Industries Board, also representing the Allied Purchasing Commission; and Felix Frankfurter, chairman of the War Labor Policies Board. From this time forward the Priorities Division functioned through these two main units, authority for final decision on priority resting always with the priorities commissioner to whom it was delegated by the chairman.

The first act of the Priorities Board was to issue, on the day of its establishment, a General Classification of Purposes Demanding Preferential Treatment,[7] a document designed to guide all governmental and other agencies in the production, supply, and distribution of raw materials, finished products, electrical energy, fuel, and transportation. That list gave preference to the raw materials going into or supplies necessary to the manufacture of ships, aircraft, munitions, military and naval supplies, fuel, food, and collateral industries, clothing, railroads, and public utilities. This classification, created as it was by the united action of all the purchasing agencies of the Government and the Allies, went a long way toward bringing about concerted action.

By way of refinement and explanation of this idea, a list of 45 industries, known as "Preference List No. 1,"[8] was issued by the Priorities Board on April 6, 1918. These industries were announced as those whose operations were considered of exceptional importance during the war. The list was issued for the guidance and instruction of all Government agencies in the supply and distribution of coal and coke, and in the use of transportation. The list was from time to time extended by the issuance of supplements until it finally covered 73 industries and was reissued with broadened scope as "Preference List No. 2," on September 3, 1918.[9]

---

[6] C. M. Woolley was also, by special appointment, coordinating member of both the War Industries Board and the War Trade Board.

[7] See Appendix VIII for copy of General Classification of Purposes Demanding Preferential Treatment, issued March 27, 1918.

[8] See Appendix VIII (2).

[9] See Appendix IX for copy of Preference List No. 2, dated September 3, 1918, excluding the list of 7,000 individual plants.

This new list contained a classification for 73 industries and, in addition, a rating for about 7,000 separate plants, plants whose importance, for some special reason, was considered above or below the class to which their product was assigned on the principal list. A supplement to this list was issued on October 1, 1918.

The purpose of this classification of industry was stated to be for the regulation of all Government agencies and others in the production and supply of fuel and electric energy and in the supply of transportation and of labor. All industries and individual plants on the list were divided, according to their relative importance, into four classes, viz. Class I, Class II, Class III, and Class IV. The issuance of this list was not intended to act as an embargo on all plants and industries not included on it, but the requirements of such plants were to be deferred until the needs of those on the preference lists could be satisfied. It was intended that the preference lists should be interpreted in the same spirit as the priority rating of orders. Industries and plants in Class I were construed as of exceptional importance in the prosecution of the war and their requirements in respect to fuel, power, transportation, and labor were to be fully satisfied in preference to those of the three remaining classes. As between Classes II, III, and IV there was no complete or absolute preference, the ratings being designed only as a general guide to the relative importance in the composite picture. The supply of fuel, power, transportation, and labor to industries and plants not on the preference lists was considered, so far as it should not be affected by special rulings of the priorities committee, as of minor importance for the purposes of the war.

Whenever a plant not on the list took a war order, it was promptly placed thereon if its needs required this action. This situation obviously gave a renewed incentive to owners to convert their plants to war work. The general scheme of automatically directing the flow of certain fundamental industrial necessities into channels designed to forward the work of those producing for the war, to the detriment, if need be, of those engaged in efforts not materially necessary to the emergency, was of extraordinary importance in supplementing and completing the control obtained by priority certificates and automatic priority ratings for individual orders.

Toward the end of the war period further additions were made to the organization of the Priorities Division. The problem of diverting labor, capital, and materials from building operations of a character not essential to the purposes of the war became an especially serious one. High prices and shortages did not seem, even in the summer of 1918, to be automatically curtailing nonwar construction as rapidly as was believed to be necessary to the emergency; for, through Government control, prices were declining and their levels were largely compensated by widespread prosperity. A Non-War Construction Section was formed in the division, with D. R. McLennan [10] as chief. This section worked largely through the State councils of defense and the system of regional advisors described elsewhere in this book. Under the provisions of Priorities Circular No. 21, issued October 15, 1918, there was inaugurated a scheme for controlling large building operations not essential to the war by a permit system. Applications under oath were made first to local representatives of the Board, with appeal, in cases of refusal, to the Non-War Construction Section, and finally to the Priorities Commissioner. No building operation involving a considerable expenditure of capital or labor could be undertaken without the issuance of a permit from the section. Enforcement was had through use of the priority power in controlling the supply of materials and transportation.

Several delicate cases arose in this connection. There was a strongly supported movement in Chicago for the construction of a large temporary memorial to the soldiers. A permit was refused and, after consideration of the explanation given, the application was withdrawn. Permits were refused for the building of Billy Sunday tabernacles and, in the light of the explanation furnished, Mr. Sunday and his followers expressed their satisfaction in the ruling. A large public-school building project, involving $8,000,000, was likewise suspended in the city of New York.

The important relation between priority control and the regulation of railroad transportation brought about the early formation of an Inland Traffic Section of the Board. T. C. Powell,[11] an experienced railroad executive, took charge of the section, whose work, although it was so successfully merged with that of the Priorities Division and the Railroad Administration that it cannot easily be described separately, was nevertheless of far-reaching significance.

The division also established a Labor Priorities Section, with A. W. Clapp as chief.[12] The purpose of this section was to bring about a control over the ever diminishing supply of labor, by a system of

---

[10] Chicago insurance executive.
[11] Thomas Powell was director of capital expenditures of the wartime Railroad Administration before joining the War Industries Board. He retired as chairman of the board of the C. & E. I. in 1931.
[12] St. Paul attorney.

priorities. Reference to this work is made in chapter 7, below. The end came before it had gone very far.

An obvious indirect effect of the processes of priorities was to curtail the production of nonwar industries and release labor, materials, capital, and transportation for use in war industries. These processes were necessarily slow and uncertain, and as the war progressed and greater and greater demands were made on war industries, while at the same time the substantial increases in our Army were making greater inroads in the labor supply, the necessity for direct action curtailing the production of less essential industries became more and more imperative. There was much discussion in Congress, in the several executive departments of the Government, in the press, and elsewhere, of "non-essential industries" and the expediency of suppressing them during the war. The problem had the careful consideration of the President, who appointed a committee composed of Vance C. McCormick, chairman of the War Trade Board; Bernard M. Baruch, Chairman of the War Industries Board; Herbert C. Hoover, Food Administrator; and Harry A. Garfield, Fuel Administrator, to investigate and report what industries were non-essential to the point that they should in the public interest retire from business during the war. This committee in turn formed a subcommittee, composed of Clarence M. Woolley, of the War Trade Board, as chairman; Edwin B. Parker, priorities commissioner; T. F. Whitmarsh, of the Food Administration; Edward Chambers, of the Railroad Administration; Edwin F. Gay, of the Shipping Board; and P. B. Noyes, of the Fuel Administration, to which were later added Felix Frankfurter, chairman of the War Labor Policies Board, and George May, of the Treasury Department.

This committee, after careful and painstaking investigation and consideration, made its report under date of June 22, 1918,[13] in substance recommending:

1. That no industry should be absolutely prohibited and destroyed.
2. That a plan of general curtailment could and should be devised, broad enough to remove the conflict between the necessities of war and nonwar industries in the matter of raw materials, fuel, transportation and labor. * * *

Following this report, the industrial adjustment committee of the

---

[13] A copy of this report, together with a copy of Mr. Hoover's letter of July 3, 1918, transmitting same to the President, with the President's O. K. thereon, forming as it does the charter of the industrial adjustments committee, is embraced in Appendix X.

Priorities Board was formed, with the approval of the President, with a membership composed of the subcommittee above mentioned. * * * Ample notice of proposed curtailments of nonwar industries was given and their representatives appeared before and agreed with the committee on bases of curtailment. This enabled them so to reorganize their businesses as to engage in the production of war necessities or reduce the volume of their output, or both. No industry was branded as nonessential, but every effort was made to preserve the organization of every unit in each industry through the use of its facilities for war production or otherwise, to the end that it would be prepared to go promptly forward with its normal activities following the conclusion of peace, but at the same time men, materials, and capital were released and transportation was relieved for the more efficient prosecution of the war.

As illustrating the methods pursued and the results accomplished by the industrial adjustments committee, reference is made to the latter part of chapter 2, Part II of this volume, dealing with the rationing of iron and steel.

The results of the work of the Priorities Division cannot be fully described nor well illustrated in the confines of a single chapter. This division functioned through, and with the systematic assistance of, not only the other agencies of the War Industries Board, but other departments and bureaus of the Government. Priority became a procedure, not alone an organization. The purposes and results of priority control will necessarily be illustrated in every chapter which follows.

Editor's Note: At the present time, the legal basis for priorities *on Government orders* in a war emergency rests in section 120 of the National Defense Act of June 3, 1916, which provides that, in time of war or when war is imminent, the President may place orders for "such products or materials as may be required" and that "compliance with all such orders for products or materials shall be obligatory . . . and shall take precedence over all other orders and contracts theretofore placed. . . ." In peacetime, priorities on government orders can be enforced on the basis of the act of June 28, 1940, which states that all the Army and Navy orders shall, in the discretion of the President, take precedence over all deliveries for private account or for export.

Neither of these statutes specifically legalizes priorities to govern *civilian purchases.* Such an extension of the system, unless an enabling statute is passed, would have to be based on voluntary agreements, backed by public opinion, or by the threat of commandeering plants or goods of uncooperative producers under the Selective Service Act of 1940, or finally by the power to cut off by priorities regulations their supplies of steel, fuel, transportation, or anything else that might become scarce. The power to apply priorities in transportation is granted in the act of February 4, 1887, which enables the President to demand preference for shipment of troops and materials in time of war, and the act of February 28, 1940, which authorizes the ICC to direct priorities in transportation. Further authority is granted indirectly in the act of August 29, 1916, which authorizes the President through the Secretary of War to take possession and assume control of transportation if necessary in time of war.

CHAPTER 5

Conservation

THE WORK of the Priorities Division was intimately related to that of another very important and very energetic division of the Board—the Conservation Division. The President's letter of March 4, 1918, charged the War Industries Board with the duty of promoting "the conservation of resources and facilities by means of scientific, industrial, and commercial economies." But the work was at that time already well under way, and the establishment of the Conservation Division under the Board on May 8, 1918, represented only a transfer from the council, and a reorganization of the Commercial Economy Board, which had been created as early as March 24, 1917. Arch W. Shaw † was chairman of both organizations in succession and took active charge of conservation work throughout the war period.

The attention of the earlier organization was devoted initially to conservation in distribution rather than in production. It was felt that economies could be effected so as to release men and equipment in the distributive trades with the least destruction to the essential processes of industry, because on the whole they perhaps were more inclined to practices not wholly necessary. The aim was to bring

† *Editor's Note:* Grosvenor B. Clarkson, in his authoritative work *Industrial America in the World War*, made this enlightening comment on the relationship between Mr. Baruch and Arch W. Shaw, a Chicago publisher of business books and magazines, which goes far toward explaining the co-operation between Mr. Baruch and his associates:

The amazing thing about the harmony that pervaded the organization was that the executives were all strong, forceful, and outspoken men. Mr. Shaw, for example, was disappointed by the selection of Mr. Baruch for chairman of the Board, and bluntly told him so. Although they had been in the Government service for a year, under the central authority of the Council of National Defense, they were barely acquaintances and each knew little of the other or his work. Shaw spoke as an impartial critic and not as a partisan. And Baruch in no way resented Shaw's position. On the contrary, he asked Shaw to remain at the head of the Conservation Division and assured him that he would have in his work all the authority that he (Baruch) and the Board had. Then the two men sat down and amicably discussed Shaw's objections to Baruch as chairman. The outcome was that Baruch "sold" himself to Shaw "in principle," as the diplomats say, and subsequent experience applied the principle.

about reductions in the use of men, capital, and materials in ways that would least disturb essential economic purposes.

The section on foreign experience carried on studies of conservation measures practiced in England, France, Italy, Germany, and Austria. Although our methods differed radically from those of Europe, because our circumstances differed radically, information concerning their raw-material shortages, manufacturing capacities, methods of substitution, of curtailment, etc., afforded many suggestions for the solution of our own problems. This information came to the division largely through the activities of the Department of Commerce and of the War Trade Board.

Besides general publicity through motion pictures, newspaper and magazine articles, advertisements, signs in stores, special pamphlets to women's organizations, proclamations by governors, and other means, setting forth information, suggestions, and arguments concerning desirable and workable economies, which, by the way, received a cordial and spontaneous response, the Board canvassed trade practice after trade practice with a view to finding defined methods for eliminating large blocks of waste. A few examples of the earlier work will tell the story.

It was an established trade custom among bakers to allow the retailers to return unsold bread, and this bread was disposed of largely as waste. Calculations showed that the elimination of this practice would save bread enough to feed 200,000 people and would save about 4 per cent of the total man and equipment power devoted to handling bread between bakers, retailers, and consumers. The wealth and energy thus released would naturally turn to war effort. Agents were sent to many wholesale bakers, conferences were held in Washington with others, and a schedule of inquiries was circulated widely in the trade. Everybody seemed willing to discontinue the practice. A circular was issued on June 6, 1917, to all wholesale bakers, setting forth the general understanding and stating that it was the will of the Government that the return-of-unsold-bread privilege should be stopped on and after July 10, 1917.

While this was going on, a study was being made of the use of the return-of-goods privilege by customers of retail stores. Data and opinions were gathered from about 500 retail grocery stores and more than 1,000 retail dry goods and department stores in all parts of the country. An investigation was made of cooperative delivery systems in over 35 cities and towns by the National Wholesale Grocers' Association. Based on this canvas of sentiments, all retail merchants of the United States were requested to restrict delivery service to not more than one trip per day over each route, to eliminate special deliveries, to restrict the return-of-goods privilege to three days, and where possible to establish cooperative delivery systems. For enforcement of these rules reliance was had principally upon the patriotic desire of everybody to assist the purposes of the Government. The State councils of defense, State officials, and many other war-service organizations were of greatest value in securing the adoption of these rules in various cities of the country.

Reports show that the merchants of more than 315 of our larger cities adopted the one-delivery-a-day rule, and that cooperative delivery systems were inaugurated in 189 cities. Spread of the sentiment that a package under the arm was a mark of patriotism was effective also in releasing man power. As a typical example, the report shows that 33 dry goods and department stores in one city, by restricting delivery service to one trip per day, operated with 545 delivery employees where 848 had previously been employed. The number of automobiles needed was reduced from 324 to 195, and 17 horse-drawn vehicles were discontinued. In another city four department stores were able to save the services of 21 drivers, 14 wagon boys, 29 horses, 2 stablemen, and 21 motors or delivery wagons, by a cooperative delivery system. In general, department stores reduced man power by about 25 per cent and retail grocery stores by 50 per cent through fewer deliveries; and cooperative delivery systems saved from 50 to 75 per cent in labor employed.

Activities had been going on also in the direction of economies through reduction in the number of styles and types of articles, prior to the organization of the work under the Board in May, 1918. With the new and more positive powers of the War Industries Board under its reestablishment, this division set about to accomplish more specific results and to extend its activities more intensively in the field of production. As the priority power began to show its effectiveness, there appeared a method of enforcing rules of conservation, and the possibility of genuine enforcement would make these rules fair alike to that vast majority which wished to do everything in its power for the cause and to those few who preferred their private gain.

In addition, two new sets of organizations were now in the field to make definite and expeditious action possible. The commodity sections of the Board could study, bargain, and administer in behalf of the Government, and the war service committees of the national associations of the several trades could bargain and administer in behalf of their respective trades. The purpose of the Conservation Division was to release man power, materials, manufacturing facilities, and capital by reducing the number of different types, patterns, and styles of articles manufactured, and by requiring the substitution of more plentiful for less plentiful materials. The method was by agreement with the respective industries organized so as to act as units. The aim of every measure was to forward the war program, and its contribution to that end was the test by which it was judged. But the method sought was always that one which would cause the least disturbance to the essential features of the normal course of industry. The procedure of the division is succinctly described in a notice given to the public on July 24, 1918, about the conservation of tin.

The Board calls meetings of representatives of each important trade using tin, states the necessity for economy, asks for patriotic cooperation and seeks advice as to how to get the results desired. Each industry is asked to organize, to consider the problem and submit specific recommendations. These recommendations are digested and sent to everyone in each trade concerned. Conferences are held with those who may not agree with the recommendations so as to get as complete unanimity as possible. A set of recommendations or regulations is then drawn up for each industry and these are enforced by the War Industries Board.

The plan of conservation laid down by the division for the guidance of the commodity sections and of its own agents was to undertake studies of industries, particularly those in which there were shortages of materials, facilities, or labor, with a view to formulating sets of regulations to accomplish one or more of the following purposes:

1. To secure all feasible reductions in the number of styles, varieties, sizes, colors, finishes, etc., of the several products of the industry in question. This would accomplish economies in manufacture by reducing the number of operations, and the amount of reserve stock, raw and finished, which had to be carried; it would speed up the turnover, reduce the labor and expense of selling, and decrease the loss due to depreciation.

2. To eliminate styles and varieties of articles which violated the principle of economy in the use of constituent materials; for example, garments requiring unusual yardage could be eliminated.

3. To eliminate features of adornment which added nothing to the usefulness of articles.

4. To reduce the production and sale of such articles as were of lesser importance for the comfort and satisfaction of the population.

5. To foster the substitution of articles and materials which were plentiful for those which were scarce and difficult to produce.

6. To discourage the use for unimportant purposes of articles which were needed for more important purposes.

7. To standardize sizes, lengths, widths, thicknesses, weights, gauges, etc., in such a way as to preserve sufficient strength and durability, but to effect economies in materials and labor.

8. To reduce the waste of materials in manufacturing processes generally.

9. To secure economies in the use of samples for selling purposes.

10. To secure economy in containers by eliminating the smaller and odd sizes.

11. To secure economy in packing by increasing the number of units per package.

12. To secure economy in shipping space and packing materials by baling instead of boxing wherever this was practicable.

The process of drawing up tentative schedules of regulations, based on the recommendations of the trade organizations themselves, and sending them out to all parties directly interested for criticism and comment, that they might be revised before being issued as binding regulations, was designed to safeguard so far as possible against unfairness and injustice to any industry or firm. By canvassing conditions in their industries, by furnishing technical information and advice, by their loyal readiness to cooperate with the Government in carrying out the plans, often for drastic changes in trade practices, the business men in industry made these conservation projects possible. When the need was explained, they were always found ready to take the necessary steps, often at heavy sacrifices. The thoughts of the men at the helms of their own industrial enterprises were linked with the thoughts of the men at the seat of government in the common purpose of winning the war.

But there was an additional sanction for these regulations which gave confidence to each business man that all his fellows in trade would observe like practices with himself, and this last means of enforcement would have been of increasing importance had the war lasted over a long period. Whenever a schedule of conservation was issued, each manufacturer and dealer was required to give a pledge that he would observe it and do all in his power to see it observed on the part of those with whom he dealt. Most American business men will observe a pledge when once given and they need not be vigilated.

But there was a further power to encourage the good will of those who were tempted to waver. By the summer of 1918, the priorities commissioner was in a position to exercise control not only over the distribution of iron and steel, copper, and numerous other elemental constituents of manufacture, but, through the cooperation of the Fuel and Railroad Administrations, he could also withhold, for the purpose of bringing recalcitrants into line, supplies of coal, coke, and oil, or the use of freight cars for transportation. With this sanction at the foundation of its efforts, the Conservation Division developed in rapid succession during the summer and fall of 1918 a series of "agreements," issued in the form of schedules of regulations to more than two hundred different groups of producers—regulations which were already showing their effect in reducing the industrial activities of the country to a more efficient basis—when the end of the war made such undertaking no longer necessary.

Curtailment plans were carried out not by agreement among the concerns of an industry but by agreement between the industry as a group, on the one hand, and the Government, on the other. Many new trade practices were inaugurated in the same way. In many instances curtailment was the negative result of positive action in some other direction. This problem has already been considered at some length in the chapter on priorities. The plans and results of the Board's activities in carrying forward the conservation program are explained at some length in Part II of this book, in connection with the work of the various commodity sections dealing with the particular industries affected. Reference, by way of illustration, to some of these will be of general interest.

The conservation schedules for makers of men's and youths' clothing limited the length of sack coats and the length and sweep of overcoats, reduced the size of samples, and restricted each manufacturer to not more than 10 models of suits per season, resulting in a saving of 12 to 15 per cent in yardage. The number of trunks carried by traveling salesmen of dry goods houses underwent an average reduction of 44 per cent. The schedule for the women's garment industry was calculated as capable of saving 20 to 25 per cent in yardage.

The standardization of colors together with certain restrictions in styles of sweaters and analogous knitted articles released 33 per cent of the wool ordinarily used in that industry. A schedule providing that hosiery, underwear, and other knit goods, with certain small exceptions, should be packed for shipment in paper covered bales instead of pasteboard boxes resulted in a large saving in shipping space, while at the same time it released pasteboard to be used as a substitute for tin plate in the manufacture of containers for articles for which tin plate had been forbidden. It was estimated that this schedule would have effected an annual saving of 17,312 carloads of freight space, 141,000,000 cartons, and nearly a half million wooden packing cases.

On the face of it, spools for thread would seem to be an industry not worth the time spent in restricting it. Yet investigation showed that thread manufacurers had reduced the yardage on spools from 200 yards to 150 yards and were considering a further reduction to 100 yards in order to avoid disturbing the unit retail selling price. The quantity was fixed by the division at 200 yards per spool, bringing about an economy of 25 per cent in lumber, labor, shipping space, wooden cases, cardboard boxes, and other shipping supplies, releasing, it was estimated, 600 freight cars per year.

These conservation schedules were issued to the several trades, their separate features to become effective at future dates fixed by agreement between the Board and the respective trades. In some industries, where the period of production is an extended one, the date for becoming effective had to be placed some months in the future.

This was true of the shoe manufacturing industry. A very exhaustive investigation was made here, far-reaching plans inaugurated, and schedules issued. The schedule provided that shoe manufacturers should be restricted to three colors—black, white, and one shade of tan. New lasts were forbidden; heights of shoes were limited; and certain other features requiring an unnecessary amount of leather were eliminated. Activity in this direction was first stimulated by the fact that in the midst of the war there developed a fashion requiring that women have shoes colored to match each gown, very high shoes for women being also a vogue; and this in face of the fact that there was a peculiarly difficult shortage in glazed kid leather, of which the majority of women's shoes are manufactured. This schedule effected savings in leather not only in stock carried by retail stores but in shoes standing in the homes. It saved capital, packing boxes, labor, and transportation in amounts very large. The savings back through the processes of manufacture, preparation, and tanning of hides, dyeing of leathers, etc., were large. One tanner reduced his line from 81 colors to 3 colors. Most manufacturers reduced their styles by about two-thirds, and retail stores by greater amounts.

The manufacturers of automobile tires agreed to a reduction from 287 styles and sizes of tires to 32, with a further reduction to 9 within two years. This had a tendency to release a large amount of rubber and capital tied up in stocks everywhere. A schedule was issued also to the rubber clothing and the rubber footwear industries, the former eliminating 272 styles and types and agreeing to bale their product instead of shipping it in cartons. Even bathing caps were restricted to one style and one color for each manufacturer.

Savings in the agricultural implement industry are among the most important effected. Implement manufacturers were able to simplify manufacturing operations and reduce their stocks of raw materials; manufacturers, dealers, and jobbers found it possible to do business with smaller stocks of finished products; the steel mills saved, because every variation in size or shape had required a different set of rolls, and so on. Schedules were issued to manufacturers of portable grain elevators, plows and tillage implements, grain drills and seeders, harvesters, mowers, hay rakes, ensilage machinery, spring-tooth harrows, farm wagons and trucks, land rollers and pulverizers, and cream separators. The number of sizes and types of steel plows was reduced from 312 to 76; planters and drills from 784 to 29; disk harrows from 589 to 38; buggy wheels from 232 to 4; spring-wagon wheels from 32 to 4; buggy axles from over 100 to 1; buggy springs from over 120 to 1; spring wagons from over 25 to 2; buggy shafts from 36 to 1; buggy bodies from over 20 to 1 style, two widths; spring-wagon bodies from 6 to 2.

By making his line of farm wagons conform to this schedule, one manufacturer reduced his variety of front and rear gears from 1,736 to 16. Yet the farmers were as well taken care of in the growing, harvesting, and marketing of their crops with this smaller variety of agricultural implements to draw upon as they had been with the wide variety previously manufactured. The habits and prejudices of localities and individual farmers had made it necessary for manufacturers to make many more sizes and types of equipment than were essential, for all of which parts had to be carried, and the number of finished implements in the hands of manufacturers, jobbers, and retailers were unnecessarily large because of this multiplicity.

Several schedules were issued to different branches of the electrical industry, particularly to manufacturers of heating appliances, fan motors, industrial lighting fixtures, panel boards, and switchboards. The preparation of many more schedules in this field was under way when the work was stopped.

Work was likewise going forward with many branches of the hardware trade. To show the scope of this undertaking, one hardware wholesaler estimated that over 90,000 items would have been removed from his catalogue if the schedule had gone into effect as planned.

The use of tin to give weight to silk dresses was eliminated. Tin-using industries were taken up one after another and conservation schedules issued. It was found possible to reduce the tin content of babbitt metal for many types of bearings without reducing appreciably the quality of the bearings. The tin content of several solders was changed. The users of tinfoil, collapsible tubes, and silver-plated ware came in for their share of abstinence in order to relieve the growing shortage of tin, which had to be imported from distant sources. The Bureau of Standards worked out a valuable method of substituting cadmium for tin in solder. To save tin in the tin-plate industry, which is ordinarily the largest consumer of this metal, the division, in cooperation with the Food Administration, worked out plans for many substitutions in the industries using tin-plate containers, measures which would have effected an annual saving of 260,000 tons of tin plate. Tin plate is 98 per cent steel, but 4,680 tons of pig tin is a saving of great importance, and the saving in steel was not unimportant.

These examples should be sufficient to show that the work of the Conservation Division was effective. It would be wearisome to catalogue at length all the schedules which were issued and all the savings effected—the mere list of industries producing different varieties of hardware would fill a page of small type. Efforts at conservation were made and either put into operation or were about to be at the time of the armistice in such diverse and unrelated industries as road-making machinery, chains, bicycles, motorcycles, children's vehicles, clocks, pens, pencils, talking machines, motion-picture projectors, burial goods, furniture, beds, vacuum cleaners, washing machines, household wringers, refrigerators, stoves and ranges, furnaces, enamel goods, galvanized ware, cameras, hand stamp and marking devices, adding machines, autographic registers, sales books, typewriters, cash registers, tabulating machines, time recorders, fire-prevention and fire-fighting apparatus, corsets, pocket cutlery, hosiery and underwear, hats, shoes, gloves, harness, trunks, overalls, bedding, nails, bolts, rivets, bottles, crockery, davenports, paint, and varnish.

Many of these conservation schedules applied to Government as well as civilian purchases. The division continued the work which was begun early in the war to bring about greater uniformity in the specifications of the Army, Navy, and other Government agencies.

An interesting illustration of the way in which several lines of conservation effort would converge on one object is afforded by the automobile industry. Rubber is imported over a long route, and the shortage of shipping dictated restriction in its use. Automobile tires, consuming 70 per cent of it, furnished the most fruitful point of attack. From another angle the shortage in petroleum forced the Fuel Administration to ask for a general reduction in the use of gasoline. From a third angle, the shortage in steel for direct and indirect war work required curtailment in every practicable way. These three forces converged toward reducing to a minimum the manufacture of pleasure cars during the latter part of the war. The plans under which the automobile plants were to be kept alive in reduced condition are explained more fully in Part II.

Although there was power to enforce conservation, the results of this division were achieved almost entirely by the voluntary cooperation of the industries to whom the needs of the Government were presented and who worked out in cooperation with the Board the various mechanisms of execution. The industries themselves had caught the spirit of the hour and most remarkable exhibitions of unselfishness were seen on every side.

The experience of the Conservation Division has clearly demonstrated that there are many practices in American industry which cost the ultimate consumers in the aggregate enormous sums without enriching the producers. These are often due to competitive demands, real or assumed. Many salesmen, in order to please the whims of particular customers, will insist upon the manufacture of new styles or new shapes of articles, requiring increased expense to the manufacturers and increased expense to both wholesalers and retailers in carrying more lines of stock, these in turn causing increased expense in maintaining salesmen and providing them with samples as well as in advertising. The consumer, the general public, is no better served by the satisfaction of these unreasonable demands, but the public ultimately pays the bill. We may well draw from this war experience a lesson to be applied to peace, by providing some simple machinery for eliminating wasteful trade practices which increase prices without in the remotest degree contributing to the well-being of the people. There is enough natural wealth in this country, and there is enough labor and technical skill for converting that wealth into objects of human satisfaction to provide abundantly for the elemental comforts of every person in the land. The problem before our Nation today is to bring about such adjustments of the industrial processes as lead toward that long-sought condition of life.

Editor's Note: The following letter is appended in the belief that it presents a concise, valuable *aide memoire* for the conduct of conservation activities in the present emergency:

"It has always seemed to me that if I accomplished anything of significance in Washington, it was early in April, 1917, when I prevailed upon the Council of National Defense not to follow a plan that had been submitted to them to eliminate non-essential businesses, *but to cut out non-essential uses of labor, materials, capital and equipment from all business.*

"I made the point that the so-called non-essential businesses made up but a very small part of the whole business structure and the greatest opportunities for saving would come from cutting out non-essential uses of these four elements from the large volume of essential businesses. The procedure suggested was a minor operation; the method that I had in mind involved a major operation.

"I remember that a list of non-essential industries was furnished to the Council of National Defense at its request by an organization of railroad operators. This list apparently had been compiled from a rate book, for I recall that three of the items were poker chips, poker chips crated and poker chips boxed!

"But what was even a more important consideration was that sooner or later the war would be ended. The fat could be taken off all business for war purposes, but the skeleton and vital organs must be left, for business would be called upon to re-absorb the fighting forces into the industrial army as rapidly as possible after the war was over.

"In the book published by the Yale University Press, *How America Went to War,* there is this concluding statement: 'And it was work done well: undoubtedly it maimed industry but it did not kill it—the indispensable amount of surgery was accomplished with such clean, swift strokes that the wounds healed after the war and left no scars.'

"Perhaps it is an overstatement, but at least the author sensed what we were trying to do."—From a letter to Mr. Baruch from Mr. Shaw, October 14, 1937.

CHAPTER 6

Price Fixing †

THE STABILIZING EFFECT of the priority system on market prices has already been the subject of comment. That the activities of the Conservation Division tended also in a large way, though indirectly, to head off runaway markets, is a conclusion not difficult to understand. But the 14 months from August, 1917, to November, 1918, will always be a period of peculiar interest to students of political economy, because it marked the first experiment in this country of direct Government control of prices of commodities for all consumers. The reason for inaugurating this pioneer effort, the authority under which it was undertaken, the method employed, and the principles applied warrant our special attention.

An understanding of the market conditions which precipitated the action can be obtained by reading Part II of this book. The prime factors were the high level to which prices had climbed by the late summer of 1917, and the fear of a further rise. Prices were soaring out of all relation to the cost of production and were fluctuating with great uncertainty. This condition was having a more menacing effect than the mere extravagance of paying high prices on the part of the Government. The present generation of business men had been accustomed, for three decades preceding 1915, to conduct their affairs under steady and sober market conditions, with extreme price fluctuations in staples only at rare and extraordinary intervals. The rapidity of the rise from 1915 to the early spring of 1917 had already thrown great confusion and irregularity in the processes of trade. Commodities had begun to flow through unusual and ineffective channels, causing unbalanced and often retarded production. The final upward swing of prices during the spring and summer of 1917 enhanced these unhealthy tendencies. Capital was turning in great quantities toward speculation and manufacturers were uncertain in their purchases of raw materials. "Cost-plus-profits" contracts brought adventurers into

---

† *Editor's Note:* The full development of Mr. Baruch's position on price fixing will be found in Parts I, II, and III of Book Two.

the field of production, who flooded the country with options and inquiries to cover their bids, and prices were being forced further and further out of joint while actual work and production were halted by the confusion.

American business could not make progress in the unaccustomed atmosphere and there was no relief in sight. Demand for goods was to increase rather than decline, and it would increase with ever more telling persistence. A war demand differs in its essential nature from the normal demands of peace. In ordinary times a rising price carries with it its own defeat. Purchasers will buy so long as they can make a profit or reap a satisfaction by doing so. This at least is true of everything except the most extraordinary luxuries. They will stop buying when the price reaches a point outside the range where the commodity can be turned over at a profit. The inflated price drops as a result. But war is economically the greatest and most scandalous of spendthrifts. No economic profit comes from the expenditure of an instrument of war and no economic profit is considered in connection with its purchase. The demand is absolute; the price is no deterrent.

The monthly wholesale price quotations of 1,366 separate commodities were studied by the Price Section of the Board to cover the period 1913–1918. "Weighted index numbers" were calculated to show average percentages of rise and fall in prices. A "weighted average" is obtained by taking the sum of a series of prices multiplied by quantities of goods sold at those prices, and dividing the result by the sum of the quantities. Using this method of computation, if the average weighted prices of the 1,366 commodities for June, 1913, be taken as 100 or normal, they had increased to only 104 by October, 1915, but to 144 by December, 1916. By March, 1917, the threat of war had brought this number up to 156. In one month from April 6, 1917, it jumped 14 points. The prices of individual groups of commodities more directly related to the war rose high above these averages. By March, 1917, the average price of metals was 247 per cent of the average for 1913, and by July of the same year it had reached its peak at 333 per cent. Basic pig iron climbed from $32.25 per ton in March to $52.50 in July; steel plates from $4.33 per hundredweight to $9. Foods went from 142 per cent to 167 per cent during this period, wheat rising from $1.98 per bushel in March to $2.58 in July. Clothing went from 157 per cent to 187 per cent, and chemicals from 159 per cent to 180 per cent.

In the face of these facts every condition pointed to further rises for the future unless a radical cure could be found. During the year ending June 30, 1914, Europe took raw materials, manufactures, and foods from this country valued at $1,471,266,488; during the year ending June 30, 1917, Europe bought goods here valued at $4,307,-310,138. Our total exports of iron, steel and their products, which were $251,488,677 in value for the year before Europe went to war, had jumped to $1,133,746,188 by 1917. The corresponding figures for copper were $146,222,556 for 1914, and $322,535,344 for 1917. These data explain why metal prices in this country got out of hand until their record rise in July, 1917, compelled Government regulation.

These are only a few specimens of the alarming facts which faced the Government in the summer of 1917. It was conceivable that the Government might pay these prices and take back much of the undue profits by excess profit taxes; but the question of costs, while perhaps the most serious, was not the only difficulty. The instability of prices was in itself hampering production and driving business into confusion.

Various committees of the Council of National Defense were struggling with the price question; suggestions and arguments were being exchanged everywhere. A few important special arrangements were made for Government purchases, but prices continued to rise. Finally, on July 12, 1917, the President announced that the Government was determined to make its purchases at reasonable costs and that prices would be fixed if it should be found necessary to do so. He added further that if it should be necessary to fix prices for Government purchases, the same prices ought to be made to apply also to civilian and allied purchases, because wherever there was a shortage, fixed prices for the Government would only make other prices higher than ever. Following this announcement prices began to decline, but the instability remained. The country had a very strong prejudice against Government price fixing. This was relieved somewhat by the knowledge that this method of control was being used successfully in England and France. Another factor which encouraged the step was the growing discontent on the part of the public as they saw prices mount while men joined the ranks and family budgets were reduced.

Price control was taken up piecemeal, commodity by commodity, as expediency dictated. Congress did not grant to the President, nor to any other agency, blanket authority to work out a scheme of price regulations. The bases in law for different regulations were varied, and in some cases doubtful. For this reason the method, if not the extent, of price fixing was circumscribed. Nearly all of it was done by negotiation and agreement between the Government and the trades.

The food and fuel control act, passed August 10, 1917, gave the President very broad powers of control, and when this had been added to the national defense act of June 3, 1916, the President, in response to the widely and keenly felt need, made himself virtually a minister of price controls. The President assumed to himself the final responsibility, in a literal sense undertaking to approve and sign a majority of all the regulations issued.

A legal foundation for the inauguration of such regulations as were established can perhaps be spelled out. Certain it is that there were ample means at hand for enforcing such rules as it was believed wise to impose. The law clearly gave the President or the Secretary of War power to "requisition," and in granting this power it gave to the same officials power to determine and pay "just compensation" or "reasonable prices." The food and fuel control act provided in section 10:

That the President is authorized, from time to time, to requisition foods, feeds, fuels, and *other supplies necessary* to the support of the Army or the maintenance of the Navy, or any other public use connected with the common defense, and to requisition, or otherwise provide, storage facilities for such supplies; *and he shall ascertain and pay a just compensation therefor.*[1]

This act was undoubtedly intended by its authors to apply only to foods, fuels, and commodities directly related to them. But the national defense act, passed June 3, 1916, authorized the Secretary of War to place orders with any concern for such product or material as might be required and which was of the nature and kind usually produced or capable of being produced by such concern. It further gave him power to "determine reasonable prices" for such products; and upon failure of compliance, gave the President power to take over any plant. Thus the Government could, by the payment of just compensation, require or commandeer the whole output of a plant and itself determine the price to be paid for everything taken under the compulsory order. The possibility of compulsory order gave a very formidable legal weapon for compelling the acceptance of price determinations on the part of the Government.

The naval appropriations act of 1916 authorized the President to place an order with any person for ships or war material, if such ships or material were of the nature, kind, and quantity usually produced or capable of being produced by such person. Upon refusal, the plant could be requisitioned. Under this act "war material" was made to include arms, armament, ammunition, stores, supplies,

---

[1] The italics are those of the War Industries Board.

equipment for ships and airplanes, and everything required in connection with their production. Another paragraph provided for the modification or cancellation of any existing contract for the building, production, or purchase of ships or war material. The so-called emergency shipping fund act of 1917 allowed the placing of an order with any person for such ships or material as the necessities of the Government, to be determined by the President, might require during the period of the war, and which were of a nature, kind, and quantity usually produced or capable of being produced by such person; and power was given to the President to determine "just compensation" to be paid for such product. In case of refusal, there was power of requisition.

There was ample legislation to give the President commandeering power over any type of commodity. Moreover, in that resolution of April 6, 1917, Congress had said to the President, "* * * and to bring the conflict to a successful termination all the resources of the country are hereby pledged by the Congress of the United States."

Over and above all this, the President, as Commander in Chief of the Army and Navy, undoubtedly had vast control without legislation. He had a right to take private property for public use upon payment of just compensation, even if such taking was not authorized specifically by Congress. But whether this right, or the rights granted by the legislation mentioned above, were sufficient or not is perhaps of minor importance. The legal authority for establishing controlled prices for sales to private purchasers and to foreign Governments has never been, and perhaps never will be, adjudicated by the courts. As a matter of fact, public opinion acceded to the President, in this emergency, power commensurate with the peril and left to his discretion the determination of the degree of peril and the power necessary to meet it.

Practically all schedules of fixed prices were reached by a process of negotiation and agreement between the Government and the industry involved. Purchases based on such schedules were all made after their announcement and, in a collective sense, prices were voluntary. The power to enforce adherence to the schedules was abundant, though never direct. The requisitioning power placed the Government in a position to address producers virtually as follows: "These are the prices to which the Government will agree; if you are willing to enter into a voluntary arrangement with us, you will be paid these prices for your goods, but if you refuse to do so, we will be compelled to ask the properly constituted authorities to commandeer your output or your plant and give you just compensation therefor, as provided by statute, and these very prices are the 'just compensation' for which the statute provides." The commandeering acts, it will be noted, provided that the Government should determine "just compensation."

In addition to the use of the requisitioning power, the Government had further weapons equally effective in the premises. Those who might be inclined to disobey a price regulation could be deprived of the assistance of the Priorities Division in obtaining supplies, use of railroads, coal, and other things essential for the operation of their businesses, and, as war operations developed, this assistance could become more and more the sine qua non of continuing in business.

The earlier efforts at negotiated price fixing, which was later to become the rule of the day, were halting and uncertain. An abortive effort was made in June, 1917, to fix the price of bituminous coal in this way. Some early work of the council in negotiating metal prices for Government purchases was a success. The food and fuel control act set a minimum price for wheat. The President fixed the price of all bituminous coal on August 21, 1917. He fixed the price of copper on September 21, and of iron and steel on September 24 following. From this period forward the War Industries Board, the Food Administration, and the Fuel Administration, each in its own field, went forward with the work of preparing price regulations for the approval and ratification of the President, covering commodity after commodity, as the needs of the time seemed to require.

The chief aim of the control by the Food and Fuel Administrations was to assist the civilian population to obtain necessary articles of supply at reasonable rates, while, in the beginning, it was the primary purpose of the War Industries Board to assist the Government in getting supplies at fair prices. The Board soon found, however, that its assistance to the civilian population was of an importance at least equal to its work for the Government purchasing agencies, and its procedure was early adapted to that need. The distinguishing feature of price control in the food group was the scheme of fixing "margins of profit" only. Very few basic prices were determined by the Food Administration. The War Industries Board, on the other hand, and later the price-fixing committee, in the field in which they operated, found, for the most part, that the most satisfactory control could be accomplished by the fixing of the prices of basic materials.

A question of principle which received cautious consideration when price fixing was being undertaken on the part of the Board was that of the meaning and proper construction to be given the term "just compensation," which lay at the foundation of the commandeering right and which the fifth amendment of the Constitution guarantees to every citizen from whom private property is taken by the Government for public use. A long line of decisions has used "market value" as a measure of "just compensation." Another set of cases shows that the fact that a given piece of property is to be "condemned" should not be used to add to its condemnation value.

In the war, market value was largely created by the Government's emergency, and hence it was not a fair test of just compensation. If an examination be made into the reasoning behind the proposition that market value is a sound measure of just compensation, it will be found that the principle is based on the economic doctrine prevailing when the rule was first pronounced. This doctrine taught that under the automatic working of the law of supply and demand, "market value" always tends to become equal to the "cost of production," and for this reason market value is a measure of "just compensation."

Adam Smith taught that the iron law of nature would always bring about its balance—things will sell for what they are worth, and they are worth what they will sell for—which, he said, was always in the long run what it cost[2] to produce them; and he illustrated by a series of examples taken from spheres of life where economic relations were very simple. Whether this principle be generally true or not, it was certainly not true under war conditions. When a demand in the nature of a war demand—absolute and unabated by considerations of a return in value—enters the field, there is no force tending naturally to adjust the market value to cost of production. Hence, it was found necessary to go back to the more elemental principle and measure just compensation by its primary cause, viz. cost of production, including a reasonable profit. This was the principle adopted by the War Industries Board.

The responsibility for negotiating fixed price schedules for such commodities as fell outside of the field of the Fuel and Food Administrations was assumed from the start until March 4, 1918, by the War Industries Board as an instrument of the Council of National Defense. On March 14, 1918, the price-fixing committee was appointed by the President and continued the work, extending it to an ever-increasing number of trades. Practically all price schedules

---

[2] Including a reasonable profit.

were ratified and promulgated by the President himself. A few special arrangements touching commodities of which the Government bought nearly the entire output were reached without reference to this procedure, but they actually amounted to little more than Government purchasing agreements.

The variety of purposes to be accomplished in respect to the separate industries, the variety of methods pursued, and the measure of success had in the exercise of price control, can be understood only by a reading of the record, commodity by commodity, as set forth in Part II of this book. A full description of the general method as it was worked out by the War Industries Board at the beginning, and which represents in outline the method prevailing throughout the period, is given in chapter 2 of Part II, in connection with its application to the iron and steel industry.

The Federal Trade Commission was found to be equipped with a very large and competent staff of cost accountants, statistical experts, and economists. As the exigencies of the day pointed to industry after industry as necessary fields for the exercise of price control, the Federal Trade Commission was invited to assign to each a corps of these experts to investigate and report on the costs of production. The studies usually extended to all producing plants, or where this was impracticable to a large number of typical plants, from the lowest to the highest cost producers, and their prosecution required usually from one to three or more months.

In the meantime it usually happened that the Board, or an appropriate section of the Board, was carrying on a series of hearings with the war service committee and other representatives of the particular trade concerned, and the trade itself was preparing its case in anticipation of a final hearing in which figures and facts should be presented on both sides; should be compared, discussed, and adjusted, to result in a schedule of fixed maximum prices. The first schedule usually covered basic materials only and was followed a few weeks later with a system of differentials, making price control complete. Most of these final meetings were prolonged affairs; often they extended over several days, and an "agreement" would emerge only after most earnest and searching debate.

The Board, and later the price-fixing committee, acted in a quasi-judicial capacity, the appropriate commodity section, representatives of the Federal Trade Commission, and other interested officials appearing on the part of the Government, and the war service committee, with other representatives, appearing in behalf of the industry. When an "agreement" upon a price schedule was finally reached, the decision of the Board (or later of the committee) would be transmitted forthwith to the President, and, in the event that it met with his approval, he would promulgate it to the country. The schedules always named the dates on which they were to become effective, which usually followed closely upon their adoption, varying according to the exigencies of particular trades. Most schedules were made effective for a period of three months only, and were subject to renewal, or modification upon presentation of facts showing that they were unjust, either as being too low or too high. Contracts made before the announcement of a schedule were not affected by the price regulations unless they in terms so provided; but contracts made after a price announcement, for delivery during the life of a schedule, were subject to the schedule, and contracts made after an announcement, for delivery after the expiration of the life of a schedule, were made subject to such prices as might be set in a new or modified schedule to cover that future period.

The promulgation of a schedule of prices was usually accompanied by statements of certain corollary agreements reached in the price negotiations; such, for example, as that wages for labor should not be reduced in the plants of the industry affected, that production should not be diminished, and the like.

All prices fixed were maximum prices, sales and purchases being freely allowed below such figures; but as these regulations were in nearly every instance inaugurated for the purpose of preventing runaway markets in commodities in which there was a marked shortage, and as they usually represented the minimum figures at which all concerns of a given trade could produce, they came, with one or two exceptions, to be regarded by most dealers as standard prices, and the Government purchasers paid them without further negotiation.

The price-fixing committee was not formed until March 14, 1918, following the separation of the War Industries Board from the jurisdiction of the council. The President made mention, in his letter of March 4 to Mr. Baruch, of his intention to appoint a price-fixing committee on which the chairman of the Board should sit as a member. It was the purpose of the President in choosing the committee to name on it no one having a personal, financial interest in any result of the committee's recommendations. The following members were appointed: Robert S. Brookings, chairman; Bernard M. Baruch, chairman of the War Industries Board ex officio; F. W. Taussig, chairman United States Tariff Commission; W. B. Colver, chairman Federal Trade Commission; H. A. Garfield, United States Fuel

Administrator; Hugh Frayne, labor representative of the War Industries Board; Comdr. John M. Hancock, representing the Navy Department; Lieut. Col. Robert H. Montgomery, representing the War Department; Henry C. Stuart, representing the interests of agriculture, and W. W. Phelps, secretary.[3]

The range of Government agencies represented on the committee makes this a noteworthy example of the characteristic practice of bringing about unified action through the device of an "interlocking directorate." Responsibility was placed in the committee as a body, the chairman being only presiding officer.

Because the price-fixing function was, by this reorganization, detached from the Board proper, and placed in the hands of a committee which reported directly to the President (only three of the nine members were on the War Industries Board), the Board itself was enabled to retain and obtain more highly specialized talent from the business world for its own work without placing such men in a position where their integrity could be challenged. The new committee found practically no occasions for reducing the prices which had been fixed by the earlier machinery. On the contrary, mounting costs and lessening man power were in most instances shown to make slightly upward revisions necessary.

The price-fixing committee took the attitude of a quasi-judicial body. It did not initiate steps looking to regulations, but upon the motion of the appropriate commodity section or other division of the War Industries Board, it heard case after case presented by the Board and other officials on behalf of the Government and by representatives of the industry on the part of the trade involved. After a full hearing and deliberation it presented its findings directly to the President, who took final action. The various agencies of the Board, with the assistance and support of other Government organizations, undertook to administer and enforce all price regulations. This was done in a multitude of ways, depending upon the characteristic nature of the particular trade in question. The committee always issued its statements under the heading, "Price-fixing committee of the War Industries Board," and its work was always carried forward in closest harmony with the activities of the Board.†

---

[3] Henry Stuart (deceased) was formerly Governor of Virginia. Phelps is president of W. W. Phelps Estate, N. Y. City.

---

† *Editor's Note:* The Price-Fixing committee, however, was an independent agency in that it did not have a responsibility to, or report to, the Chairman of the War Industries Board, but was responsible directly to the President,

While the different purchasing departments of the Government were expected to fix prices for themselves on their current purchases where there were no special problems involving a lack of supply, the price-fixing committee stood ready, on application, to solve any special price-fixing problems the nature of which seemed to require its jurisdiction, and which were in scale with the time involved.

In the light of the favorable effects of the earlier price controls; with the growing tendency on the part of business men to view the practice with little alarm, in fact, in many instances to favor it to the extent of asking for it; and with the increasing number of trades being drawn into the war interests, with accompanying price fluctuations; the committee, through the summer and early autumn of 1918, found cases on its calendar for six days in the week and it turned out schedule after schedule until the armistice made the work no longer necessary.

The tendency, particularly at the beginning, was to fix prices at the source and trust largely to the other instrumentalities of the War Industries Board so as to control the avenues of trade that reasonable prices for finished articles at retail would result. This practice, however, as time went on, and a more comprehensive understanding of the vast ramifications became possible, was gradually being supplemented toward the end of the period by action definitely establishing price control from the raw stocks, right through the processes of manufacture and trade, to the retail consumers. An example of this is found in the action taken with reference to the shoe industry, more fully described in Part II of this book.

It is impossible to make even a reasonable guess concerning the amount of money which was saved in the Government purchases and purchases by individuals as a result of the price-fixing policy. By the machinery used, prices of numerous commodities might have been held to even lower levels and successful resistance could not have been maintained by the business men of the country, but cheap prices could not in wisdom have been the single or even primary aim of Government control. The outstanding purpose was to bring as nearly as possible to reality that ideal condition in which the country as one man would be bending its energies to the satisfaction of the

---

who finally passed upon and announced all the prices fixed by the committee. Mr. Baruch and others of his associates on the War Industries Board believe the same separation of authority should be continued in the present defense set-up for the reason that only in that way can businessmen, acting for their government, be freed of the easily aroused suspicion that they are fixing prices for their own interests.

all-impelling war needs. Production in many industries had to be stimulated by every conceivable device; and the business man of America is so imbued with the habit of reaping where he sows, that even admitting for him the highest and most unselfish quality of patriotism, no device is more stimulating to his latent energy than a vision of fair reward. The aim of the committee was to establish the figures where no honest man should have sound grounds for complaint that he did not receive "just compensation," measured in terms of cost production for the commodity which he furnished; and yet so that, as far as was humanly possible, men should not use their country's distress for their own inordinate aggrandizement. The aim was to set for any given commodity the lowest price at which the producers could bring forward enough to meet the need.

In respect to very few commodities did the Government contract to take the entire output. Wool, linters, and wheat were brought in this way. But all of the great industries were required to hold their goods for the option of the Government without a guaranty that any specific quantity would be purchased. It was difficult to meet the argument of the producers who held their goods thus at the option of the Government that they should have a relatively higher price than those who, like the growers of wheat, were assured of a market both during and for a reasonable time after the war.

Critics have asked why price fixing was not extended to more fields. The relatively short period during which the committee functioned is one explanation. Everything could not be done at once. Extensive studies in costs of production were going on simultaneously in many fields. Several programs were about to go into effect when the armistice made them unnecessary. An important rule for determining the order in which industries should be taken up for price fixing was that the committee ought not to act in a given case unless Government purchases were causing a severe shortage. The price of cotton under this rule was not fixed.

Price fixing, like other controls of the Board, could not have worked had it not been for the spirit of service manifested by all of the people and the contributing effect of the other features of the Board's regulations. When demand exceeds supply in normal times, rising prices cause production to be increased on the one hand and consumption to be curtailed on the other, and in the long run prices return automatically. In war time the Government was able to make an effective appeal to the people both to increase production and curtail consumption, in order to assist the Government in accomplishing the purposes of the war. In addition to this spontaneous response, the Board, through the exercise of priorities in labor, transportation, fuel, power, capital, etc., was able to bring about both curtailments in demand and increases in production.

A by-product of price control which was not absent from the minds of those who were responsible for the inauguration of the policy, was its effect in preserving the business structure for the ordinary processes of peace. A glance at the economic history of the period following our Civil War would bring this thought home to the reader.

The task facing those who endeavored to fix prices for our Government, the Allies and the civilian population was very difficult. First, there was no direct legislative authority like that under the Food and Fuel Act; second, as has been seen, before our entrance into the war, prices had mounted to extreme levels and those who held, even if unsoundly, that "just compensation" was to be measured in terms of "market value," had strong arguments for very high prices; and, third, there was the difficulty that the Government did not contract far ahead for quantities of these materials, as it did with wheat, but prices were fixed under conditions allowing the Government to take what it needed and providing for distribution of the rest under Government control. One is led to the thought that, in a similar emergency, there ought to be not alone a mobilization of man power, but of things and of dollars.

Editor's Note: At present, there is no specific legal authority for overall price fixing. Unless an enabling statute is passed, such a system would have to be based on voluntary agreements, backed up by public opinion, or by the power to commandeer plants and commodities of unco-operative manufacturers, or by cutting off their supplies of transportation, fuel, or raw materials through the priorities system.

Indirectly the price of some farm products can be manipulated by the AAA and the Surplus Marketing Administration; interest rates can be held in line by the RFC, the Treasury Department, and the Federal Reserve Board; transportation charges can be controlled by the ICC; while prices of certain raw materials can be held in line to some extent by the Rubber Reserve Co., the Metals Reserve Co., and the Defense Supplies Co. of the RFC.

CHAPTER 7

Labor Problems

IT WILL NOT be the purpose of this chapter to give a complete picture
of the war administration of labor. That function happened in the
large to fall outside of the War Industries Board. The Board, however, did very important and energetic work in the field and such
reference must be made as will throw the relationship into relief.
That each of the various activities directed to the mobilization and
control of industries—price fixing, priority, conservation, and the
others—had its counterpart in the sphere of labor is too evident
to warrant comment. The diversity of Government agencies created
to deal with labor problems was perhaps necessary because of the
diversified character of the problems.

In general terms, the labor problem was to discover means for
guiding the flow of labor from less essential to more essential industries and to prevent the very wasteful rapid turnover which
war conditions engendered. The labor turnover was unfortunately
high throughout most of the period. It was not until nearly autumn
of 1918 that devices were perfected which were bringing more settled
conditions.

Laborers naturally turned with favor toward war work, both
because it was the patriotic thing to do and they liked the prestige
and satisfaction of it, and because it paid unusually high wages.
But the actual shortage in man power was in effect the most significant economic shortage in the war. There are perhaps 20,000,000
men of working age in the United States. About one-fifth of these
were removed from productive employment, while industry was asked
at the same time to make important readjustments calling for skilled
and unskilled workmen by the tens of thousands to enter new trades.
The flow of one-half million immigrants per year, from which new
industries had been in the habit of recruiting, was also suddenly
stopped. The new shipbuilding, ordnance, airplane, and other industries needed skilled workmen far in excess of our supply. All
of these factors united to produce a condition out of which success
could come only through the good will of the overwhelming majority.

As was natural, the first war labor agency to be created was a labor committee of the Council of National Defense. The importance attached to it is witnessed by the appointment of Samuel Gompers as one of the six original members of the advisory commission of the Council. There is significance in the steps by which he inaugurated the undertaking which grew like other pioneer work of the Council into a number of separate organizations. He began by calling a series of conferences of organized labor for the purpose of securing a general agreement as to the attitude it would take toward the war and the problems of labor involved in it. The first meeting, called as early as February 28, 1917, was with representatives of a large number of labor unions.

This was followed by a meeting of more than 150 executive officers of labor organizations, which culminated in a formal declaration (1) that union labor would give its unqualified support to the war, but (2) it demanded that the Government should curb profiteering, and (3) give labor adequate representation in all bodies dealing with industrial matters. Mr. Gompers next called a conference of representatives of both laborers and employers, including certain other prominent authorities on labor problems. The conference reached a general agreement that "neither employers nor employees shall endeavor to take advantage of the country's necessities to change existing standards." The Council issued a statement setting forth the agreement and explaining the principle involved, addressing it to employers and employees of all industrial establishments and transportation systems.

In work of this kind the foundation was laid and attitudes were established. As the war industries developed, particular problems took the center of the stage. The rule was to organize special machinery to handle particular difficulties as they came to view. There already existed in the Department of Labor three bureaus of peculiar importance to the war. The United States Board of Mediation and Conciliation had been designed to compose disputes arising in the transportation service; the Division of Conciliation, also called the "Mediation Service," to mediate labor disputes generally. To handle another aspect of the work, the United States Employment Service had been expanded to include an extensive field force. There were 20 zone offices and 62 subbranches in 1916, and the Post Office Department was cooperating in such a way as to make each local post office a substation for bringing employers and employees together. These three organizations were important factors, but they were not equipped to handle the greatly enlarged problems brought on by the war.

The war had scarcely begun when the I. W. W., stimulated no doubt by the enemy, appeared as a menacing factor, particularly in the mountain regions and on the Pacific coast. To cope with this, the President decided to appoint a special commission whose purpose should be not only to take up particular disputes and try to settle them, but also to study the conditions which made such activities possible. This commission, called the President's Mediation Commission, was headed by Secretary of Labor W. B. Wilson. It immediately entered with energy into its work, composed a series of disputes, and on January 9, 1918, rendered a report containing a most remarkable analysis of American labor conditions, with suggestions looking to their remedy.[1] Among other needs, unified direction of labor administration for the period of the war was recommended. The principles stated in this report, made effective through various agencies, represent in general the policy toward labor which was adopted by the administration for the war.

Among the special agencies formed to standardize labor conditions should be mentioned the arsenals and navy yards wage commission, composed of representatives of the War, Navy, and Labor Departments. Its function was to seek a method for equalizing wages and labor conditions in Government arsenals and navy yards in order to prevent the labor turnover incident to open competition in the face of a shortage. Another organization of this kind was the board of control for labor standards in Army clothing, whose duty it was to prescribe labor conditions to be observed by all contractors for the supply of uniforms. It should be noted further in this connection that the Shipping Board, the Fuel Administration, and the Railroad Administration each had its Bureau of Labor devoted to the study and laying down of labor conditions, wages, etc., the adjustment of disputes and recruitment.

By the beginning of 1918 a large number of Government agencies and war contractors competing against one another to attract laborers, advertising more and more favorable conditions and more and more favorable wages, was causing a turnover and inefficiency which, in the face of a growing shortage, was a dangerous menace to the war program.

The Council of National Defense, as a result of a series of con-

---

[1] See Appendix XI for "Extract from report of President's Mediation Commission."

ferences on this subject, recommended to the President a revised labor program calling for a unified administration with a labor administrator at the head. The purposes to be accomplished by it were suggested as follows:

1. A means of furnishing an adequate and stable supply of labor to war industries. This will include:

(a) A satisfactory system of labor exchanges.

(b) A satisfactory method and administration of training of workers.

(c) An agency for determining priorities of labor demand.

(d) Agencies for dilution of skilled labor as and when needed.

2. Machinery which will provide for the immediate and equitable adjustment of disputes in accordance with principles to be agreed upon between labor and capital and without stoppage of work. Such machinery would deal with demands concerning wages, hours, shop conditions, etc.

3. Machinery for safeguarding conditions of labor in the production of war essentials. This to include industrial hygiene, safety, women and child labor, etc.

4. Machinery for safeguarding conditions of living, including housing, transportation, etc.

5. Fact-gathering body to assemble and present data collected through various existing governmental agencies or by independent research, to furnish the information necessary for effective executive action.

6. Information and education division, which has the functions of developing sound public sentiment, securing an exchange of information between departments of labor administration, and promotion in industrial plants of local machinery helpful in carrying out the national labor program.

The President's Mediation Commission also recommended centralized control in labor administration and so did the Secretary of Labor.

Acting on these suggestions, early in January, 1918, the President appointed Secretary Wilson as labor administrator, and the Secretary, in turn, appointed Felix Frankfurter, of the President's Mediation Commission, as his chief assistant to act as assistant labor administrator. * * *

The next step was an important one. In order to get for the labor administrator the united approval and support of employers and employees alike, Secretary Wilson, on January 28, 1918, provided for the creation of the war labor conference board. Its composition was described by him as follows:

The national industrial conference board named five representatives of employers to sit in this conference: L. F. Loree, a railway official and coal operator; C. Edwin Michael, a builder of bridges; Loyall A. Osborne, a manufacturer of electrical equipment; W. H. Van Dervoort, a structural engineer; and B. L. Worden, another bridge builder. These five men are among the largest employers of labor in the United States. Only one of them has ever dealt with labor unions in his private business. The American Federation of Labor named as its five representatives: Frank J. Hayes, of the mine workers; William L. Hutcheson, of the carpenters; Thomas J. Savage, of the machinists; Victor Olander, of the seamen; and T. A. Ricket, of the garment workers. Each set of five representatives named another to represent the general public. The employers' representatives selected William Howard Taft, the former President of the United States. The labor representatives chose Frank P. Walsh, recently the chairman of the Industrial Relations Commission.

This board was the forerunner of the "Taft-Walsh Board," technically called the National War Labor Board. The conference board, after deliberation, made a statement of principles [2] and a set of recommendations which were submitted to the labor administrator late in March, 1918; and early in April the President, in accord with these recommendations, created by proclamation the new board, giving to it the same personnel and defining its functions as follows:

The powers, functions, and duties of the National War Labor Board shall be: To settle by mediation and conciliation controversies arising between employers and workers in fields of production necessary for the efficient conduct of the war, or in other fields of national activity, delays, and obstructions in which might, in the opinion of the national board, affect detrimentally such production; to provide, by direct appointment or otherwise, for committees or boards to sit in various parts of the country where controversies arise and secure settlement by local mediation and conciliation; and to summon the parties to controversies for hearing and action by the national board in event of failure to secure settlement by mediation and conciliation.

The principles to be observed and the methods to be followed by the national board in exercising such powers and functions and performing such duties shall be those specified in the said report of the War Labor Conference Board dated March 29, 1918, a complete copy of which is hereunto appended.

The national board shall refuse to take cognizance of a controversy between employers and workers in any field of industrial or other activity where there is by agreement or Federal law a means of settlement which has not been invoked.

The Taft-Walsh Board was a very active organization. W. Jett Lauck [3] was made executive secretary. The board set out to settle

[2] See Appendix XII for statement of "Principles to be observed," as contained in the report submitted March 29, 1918, to the labor administrator by the conference board.

[3] Washington economist and writer.

labor disputes through informal mediation by sections and local committees, and whenever such method failed the board itself would sit as an arbitration commission, making awards by unanimous decision. Cases in which unanimity could not be had were referred to an individual umpire, the umpire being selected from a panel of 10 appointed by the President. In this way several hundred serious labor disputes were composed.

The next agency to be established was of peculiar interest to the War Industries Board. The Taft-Walsh Board, while it announced a body of principles, was in essence an administrative organization and was devoted chiefly to mediating disputes. The need was felt for machinery aimed to bring the labor policies of the several war organizations into closer harmony and cooperation. In pursuance of this purpose, on May 17, 1918, a new body, the War Labor Policies Board, was created. Felix Frankfurter, assistant labor administrator, was made chairman. * * *

The theory of this board was that of an interlocking directorate. It was composed of the officials principally charged with labor problems in each of the major war agencies.[4] It worked out and agreed upon labor policies, and they in turn were executed through the respective agencies themselves.

The purposes of the board, as set forth in the announcement of its establishment, were:

The policies board will determine, directly for war industries and indirectly for nonwar industries, all questions involving the distribution of labor, wages, hours, and working conditions, and its decisions will be executed by the various production departments of the Government, each represented in its membership. This execution will be direct for all industries engaged in war work. The decisions will be given effect in nonwar industries through the machinery of the War Industries Board, which controls the flow of raw materials for all industries.

*   *   *   *   *   *   *

In the matter of wages it will not attempt to set a flat rate for any one craft or trade in the country as a whole. But it will fix standards to be determined for all industries in a given section of the country after investigations disclosing the conditions of life, including the cost of living and the service rendered. The facts will be ascertained justly and comprehensively from information to be sought from the workers' own organizations, private employers and their organizations, Government bureaus, and wherever else exact knowledge may be secured.

We must husband our labor supply so as to satisfy the war needs of the

---

[4] Franklin D. Roosevelt represented the Navy Department.

country to the fullest possible practical extent. It is necessary, therefore, that the sources of supply be wisely directed and employed. With respect to this phase of the industrial problem it will be the function of the War Policies Board to allocate the supply according to the productive needs of the country. Under decisions of the board on this score it will be impossible for one industry to draw the labor supply from another unless it has been regularly determined that the first industry has a higher claim upon the supply on the basis of a more pressing Government need than the industry from which it would draw the workers. This question will, of course, be determined by the War Industries Board. But by the establishment of standardized wage conditions the incentive for workers to leave one industry and go to another will have been removed anyhow.

In addition to controlling the labor supply by the methods just reviewed, the Policies Board will also regulate hours of labor in the various industries and determine the needs of industry with regard to housing, transportation facilities, etc.

It should not be assumed that the policies board worked at cross purposes with the Taft-Walsh Board. The first act of the former board was a resolution adopting the general principles announced by the latter, and the two boards functioned throughout the period in close harmony, the field of the policies board being the broader and more ambitious. It attacked with energy the labor turnover question, its aim being to cure the cause. The laborers went from one job to another because wages and conditions were actually better or believed to be better. In the Official Bulletin of July 25, 1918, Mr. Frankfurter published the following comment on this phase of his work:

For several days the War Labor Policies Board has been conferring with representatives of union labor and with representatives of industrial management concerning the national standardization of wages.

In seeking standardization the precedents of unionized industry are being followed. Wages have, of course, long been standardized by the agreements of employers and employees in many industries.

The same kind of standards which the railroad brotherhoods and the railroad managers established in the transportation systems, the same kind of standards which the organized coal miners and the coal operators set up in the well-developed coal fields, the same kind of standards which the carpenters, the blacksmiths, the plumbers, the organized tailors created by agreement with their employers, the War Labor Policies Board is also by mutual consent negotiating for the entire country.

Wage standardization merely extends the familiar method of wage fixing to cover the entire Nation. What has been done in many industries the War Labor Policies Board is planning for the whole people. But, although wage standardization admittedly follows familiar precedent, it is solely a war measure. * * *

Congress, through the taxes on excess profits, the War Industries Board, through its price fixing, the President, through the veto of $2.40 wheat, have prepared the way for standardization of wages. Additional methods of keeping down the cost of living are being investigated at this time.

All these measures, past and pending, have revealed the determination of the American people to let no one make money out of the war. What price fixing means for the manufacturer, wage standardization is to the workers of the country.

That means plainly that just as the price-fixing committee takes into account the cost of production and proper profits, so wage standardization must be built upon an accurate knowledge of the cost of living and a just estimate of what makes up the right American standard.

Upon these general grounds the War Labor Policies Board is advancing, as rapidly as the gravity of the problem permits, to the establishment of standard wages.

The war was over before a satisfactory scheme for "wage fixing" was actually put into practice, but the necessity for it had become very evident and a practical line of attack seems to have been evolved. Thus price fixing had its analogue in the sphere of labor.

In the same way we shall see how the principles of priority applied to labor. In this phase the War Industries Board played a leading rôle, the United States Employment Service being the essential instrument of administration. It was necessary to acquire such control over the labor supply that the priority principle could be applied in its distribution. To do this the labor administrator asked the President to make a public appeal, which he did on June 17, 1918, solemnly urging "all employers engaged in war work to refrain after August 1, 1918, from recruiting unskilled labor in any manner except through the United States Employment Service."

This appeal was followed immediately by two surveys on the part of the Employment Service, one of the common labor requirements of war industries, the other of the common labor reserves in each State. On July 15, 1918, and again on August 1, the service sent out instructions to all employers engaged in war work. They were told (1) that they should not recruit labor by private means, except that employers might continue to hire workers applying at the plants, without solicitation direct or indirect; (2) that all advertising for unskilled labor, whether by card, poster, newspaper, handbill, or otherwise, should cease after August 1, 1918; (3) that the Federal director of employment in each State might grant special permission to recruit labor within the State through private agents; but (4) that permission to do this in another State should be given only by the

Director General of the United States Employment Service; and (5) that no unskilled labor should be transported from one State to another except by such permission.

The most important new agency created for administering the system was a scheme of local "community labor boards," composed of one representative each from the United States Employment Service, the local employers, and the local workers.

In pro-rating labor where supply was less than demand, the whole scheme worked out by the Priorities Division of the War Industries Board was applied. The "preference list" was the guide to the degree of war importance in industries and individual plants. The classification of industries and all rules for automatic ratings which the priorities commissioner was applying were adopted as rules for guiding the flow of labor.

In the early fall of 1918, A. W. Clapp was appointed by the priorities commissioner as chief of the Labor Priorities Section. It was the function of this section to work out the special problems involved in applying the priorities principles to labor. The release of labor from less essential industries through rules resulting in curtailment of operations had been one of the aims of the Priorities Division from the start. More positive work could now be accomplished through the newly organized control over labor supply.

An idea of the manner in which the Priorities Division was beginning to deal with labor problems in the later period of the war can be obtained from Labor Priority Bulletin No. 1, issued September 17, 1918.[5]

This document explained that a series of labor priority bulletins would be issued from time to time containing suggestions and rules for the guidance of the various units of the United States Employment Service, and all industrial advisors who were engaged in assisting the district draft boards in working out and applying principles of industrial deferment. It explained that attempt had not been made to include in the preference list *all* essential industries and plants, the chief aim in that list being to provide automatic flow of coal and railroad service to essential industries. The flow of labor required in some instances separate treatment. The bulletin further contained instructions constituting the first example of such special treatment. The lumber industry had been left off the preference list to foster the use of wood as a substitute for coal and to dis-

---

[5] See Appendix XIII for copy of Labor Priority Bulletin No. 1, dated September 17, 1918.

courage distance shipments of lumber for civilian uses, shipments on Government orders being properly covered by a method not depending on the preference list. The obvious importance of many branches of the lumber industry in the war was emphasized, and attention was directed to the necessity for guarding its labor supply. As the war movement went forward it became increasingly necessary in drafting men for the lines to see to it that the recruits were taken from industries where they could best be spared and the program of war production would be least disturbed. Gen. Crowder appealed to the Board for help, and when the armistice was signed, the Priorities Division was engaged in assisting Gen. Crowder in revising and expanding his "work or fight" regulations to make them apply both to a larger class of individuals and to better defined classes of industries. A circular had been drawn up after conference not only with Gen. Crowder's staff but with the labor administrator, the United States Employment Service, and the American Federation of Labor. Under it there would have been no more private chauffeurs, no more traveling salesmen, etc.

More particular reference should be made to the work of the Labor Division of the War Industries Board. The division was created with Hugh Frayne as director, upon the formation of the Board, July 27, 1917. It continued through the reorganization of the spring of 1918 and until the end of the war. Mr. Frayne's work as a member of the War Labor Policies Board, in bringing the control practices of the War Industries Board into coordination with the efforts of the Policies Board, in working out a system of control over labor, was one of the most significant phases of the division's activities.

But it was by no means the only phase. The director was a member of the price-fixing committee and served there to point out the effect of policies proposed from time to time upon labor conditions and labor's attitude. * * *

Another significant phase of the Labor Division's work was in the organization of the War Prison Labor Section and the National Waste Reclamation Section. It assisted also in setting up the Conservation Division of the Army, which established machinery for repairing instead of discarding great quantities of worn clothing, shoes, and other equipment. Much of this work was done by registrants unfit for combatant service, through physical disability or the fact that they were enemy aliens or conscientious objectors. The National Waste Reclamation Section was composed of representatives of principal departments of the Government, its purpose being to educate the public to save and to contribute their waste materials to useful purposes. For carrying out the program, 86 local cooperating councils were organized in as many cities, and 200 more were in course of organization when the armistice came. The thought was to use both military and civil prison labor for converting into useful articles the waste materials collected by the service. By this service, for example, peach pits were collected for use in manufacturing an important ingredient for gas defense. After the close of the war, the Department of Commerce organized a new bureau called the Industrial Cooperation Service, to take over and extend the work begun by the Prison Labor and the Waste Reclamation Sections.

In a way less easily defined than all this, Mr. Frayne's presence and his work was of very great value to the Board. He had been for years an authorized and trusted representative of labor organizations. He brought with him labor's point of view and he argued in favor of that point of view. But he did more than that—he caught the spirit of the time and felt very deeply that the peril of his country called for a new quality of unselfishness. He preached this doctrine to labor in season and out of season, never missing an opportunity to drive home the truth that every laborer, as well as every employer, was an American first.

Editor's Note: Mr. Baruch's position on the role of labor in a war economy is presented in Book Two. However, it is well to state here briefly that he has been a steadfast opponent of the drafting of labor, arguing that a draft is not necessary in view of this country's large reservoir of labor and, furthermore, that such a draft would be dangerously detrimental to civilian morale.

CHAPTER 8

The Foreign Mission

IN JULY, 1918, the War Industries Board sent to Europe a mission of 12 men, headed by L. L. Summers. This action grew out of the process by which the international nitrate executive in London had been formed earlier in the year [1] and was designed to accomplish two main purposes—(1) to extend and make more effective the work of the War Industries Board as it related to those commodities whose principal sources lay outside of the United States and (2) to assist in coordinating the demands of all of the Allies in order that American priorities and price-fixing schedules might be more effectively and justly administered. If the war had continued, a system of international control of many of the principal war industries might have resulted.

In addition to the nitrate executive, an international tin executive [2] had actually been formed before the close of hostilities, and several other international executives were in process of formation. Jute, rubber, manganese, tungsten, platinum, flax, leather, wool, and several other commodities were under consideration. These were all commodities in respect to which the Allies were suffering from a world shortage, and whose principal sources of production were in outlying districts, so that concerted action on the part of at least the British and American Governments was necessary for any effective control. Prices were very high and production was insufficient. There existed British committees whose function it was to supervise the flow of these commodities, but the committees were only semi-governmental. The foreign mission of the Board insisted that the committees be made governmental, and requested that an American representative be placed on each committee. On account of the fact that America was the most abundant source of steel, the steel committee was given an American chairman. * * * †

---

[1] See p. 166 for an account of the nitrate executive.
[2] See p. 153 for an account of the tin executive.

---

† *Editor's Note:* To judge from Clarkson's account, it would be nearer the truth to say that the American Mission "took over" the chairmanship of

(In 1935, during the investigation of the so-called Nye Committee of the Senate, it was disclosed that there was no appropriation for the Foreign Mission of the War Industries Board, and that Mr. Baruch personally paid the $85,000 expenses of the Mission.)

In accordance with the practice in vogue during the war, the head of the mission made direct contact with the British cabinet, dealing with the ministers in charge of the particular matters under discussion without using the services of ordinary diplomatic channels. Mr. Winston Churchill, who was then minister of munitions, entered vigorously into the work; and Mr. Austen Chamberlain, who was then minister without portfolio, was appointed by the cabinet to supervise the activities of the committees in behalf of the British Government. The committees were reconstituted as governmental agencies, and it was contemplated that from these committees should emerge whatever international executives should be determined upon as necessary.

The problem in respect to each of the several commodities was threefold: (1) to assist the Interallied Munitions Council in determining the real needs of the respective allied and associated Govern-

---

the steel committee. Clarkson, telling of the unfriendly attitude of the British business interests toward the American Mission, says:

The coolness of the British members of the then forming committees of the Munitions Council continued. The Americans found that, although the completion of their organization had been delayed pending the arrival of the Mission, there was no disposition to confer with them regarding the chairmen. They (the Americans) were particularly sensitive regarding the omission to consult with them regarding the chairmanship of the Steel Committee which, they thought, should be assigned to them without question. However, the day of the organization meeting of this committee arrived without any suggestion that there should be an American chairman. Mr. Summers was greatly concerned and acted in a manner that was decidedly disconcerting and entirely in the "it-isn't-done" category.

He boldly took the chair himself, declared the purpose of the meeting, and announced that, inasmuch as America was furnishing its Allies with more steel than their own entire production, the permanent chairman of the committee, in all propriety, should be an American. Accordingly, as chairman of the American Mission, Mr. Summers nominated Paul Mackall for permanent chairman.

[Mackall had been in the sales department of Bethlehem Steel Co., and is currently a vice-president of that company.]

"There being no objection," proceeded the amazing Summers, "I will declare Mr. Mackall chairman." There were doubtless mental objections aplenty, but none was audible.

"Will you kindly take the chair, Mr. Mackall?" proceeded Mr. Summers—and that settled it. Whereupon he left the meeting to Mr. Mackall and proceeded about his other business. * * *

It was about this time that Bonar Law said to the remarkable head of the (American) Mission: "So—you are Mr. Summers. Well, you have been the most talked-about man in the British cabinet for the past two weeks."

ments, and thus to see that priorities were given to best advantage; (2) to obtain sufficient control of the sources of supply to insure fullest possible production; and (3) by eliminating competition in buying, to control prices at reasonable levels.

Another important controversy fell largely in the hands of the mission. On most controlled commodities, the British Government had two schedules of fixed prices, (1) the military issues prices; and (2) the civil issues prices. In America, we had one schedule of prices on each commodity for all purchasers, Government, allied, and civilian. It was found that the British were loath to give to the American Army the advantage of the military issues prices, on the theory that these prices were actually below costs. The mission insisted that unless the American Army was allowed the military issues prices, it would be necessary for us to readjust some of the conditions under which the British were purchasing to such advantage in the United States, and the British Government finally acceded to the principle.

The mission had no power to make purchases for the United States, but it had extraordinary power of control over the conditions on which purchases might be made. The activities of the mission as they related to the particular commodities are referred to under the several commodity headings in Part II of this book, but some of the work was of such special interest that it warrants mention here by way of illustration.

During the drive of midsummer, 1918, the motor transport began to be ineffective on account of the destruction of roads, and our Army had pressing need of mules and horses. Both time and the lack of bottoms stood in the way of furnishing mules from America. Spain had them, but refused to sell them for gold because of internal needs. Spain, however, had dire need of ammonium sulphate for agricultural uses, and, through the activities of the mission and the War Trade Board, consented to trade mules for ammonium sulphate. All possible ammonium sulphate was, of course, greatly needed for the explosives program, but, because the War Industries Board in Washington could definitely determine through its foreign mission that the need for mules was the more immediate and pressing, priority was given for the shipment of ammonium sulphate to Spain.

The mission had an important struggle with the British Government on the question of jute. All the jute of the world comes from India, and the British Government urged that it could not control the price, because it was an affair of the Indian Government. The mission pointed out that our Government was supplying silver to the Indian Government through the mediation of the British Treasury, and that if the British Government could not exercise control in India, our Government might find it necessary to withdraw from the arrangement for supplying silver, and, by thus causing a depreciation of Indian currency, buy the jute at reasonable prices. Before hostilities ceased, the British had begun vigorously to work with us in obtaining a control over jute prices. Jute products are manufactured principally in Calcutta, but also in Aberdeen and Manchester, and the mills, both in India and in Britain, are controlled principally by British capital.

In this connection it is but fair to say that in the series of matters taken up with the British they never failed to respond with full cooperation when the facts showing need of regulation or other joint action were brought fully to light. As showing this spirit of whole-hearted cooperation on their part it may be interesting to note that one of the particular things that the Foreign Mission of the War Industries Board set out to do was to make an examination of the use to which many of the things obtained from America at fixed prices was going. It had been suggested that perhaps some of the steel and such articles bought from America would replace steel that had been sold by some of our associates in the war for export. An explanation of the injustice of taking steel away from our commercial interests while they permitted their merchants to export steel immediately appealed to them. An international committee on steel, with Paul Mackall, an American, as chairman, undertook to visé the use of all steel.

Immediately after the signing of the armistice, the members of the mission began to make a personal survey of the devastated regions. They had two ideas in mind: (1) To make a general estimate of the types and quantities of materials for which there would be an immediate demand as soon as reconstruction should begin; and (2) to secure data on which an estimate of the extent of the damages could be calculated for use at the peace conference. Following this survey, the President authorized the formation of an organization to estimate the damages done in the devastated regions.

Editor's Note: The greater part of the above account of the Foreign Mission of the War Industries Board concerns the relationship between the U. S. and its Allies. However, the Chilean nitrate negotiations and the mule trade with Spain give some idea of the great importance that attaches to what Mr. Baruch calls the "war on the neutral front"—i.e., the relation of a nation at war with the neutral countries.

As Mr. Baruch pointed out at the meeting December 19, 1940, of the Consulting Committee on Industrial Mobilization of the National Industrial

Conference Board, the United States is much better equipped today to meet the challenge on the neutral front. The Reconstruction Finance Corporation is available for direct loans; the Export-Import Bank has vast possibilities in controlling the exports and imports of neutral countries; and, as concerns Latin America, the Office of the Co-ordinator of Commercial and Cultural Relations gives a special directional emphasis to what is for the United States the most important sector of the war on the neutral front.

Such agencies as these have made it unnecessary to create another agency corresponding to the War Trade Board in this emergency; just as the regulatory functions of other agencies, such as the Securities Exchange Commission and the Federal Reserve, would make unnecessary another Capital Issues Committee; and just as the RFC would take the place of a War Finance Corporation.

CHAPTER 9

Conclusion

THIS REPORT is a record not alone of new methods of Government control over business; it is also a record of many new practices on the part of business itself. With purpose always defined, but method to be discovered by a process of trial and error, through months of unparalleled effort and devotion, at first by applying varying degrees of the principle of "advice and encouragement," the Board finally developed a scheme of positive "control" over the major portion of the industrial fabric, which, by the summer of 1918, was showing results of an extraordinarily satisfactory character. Success bred courage for more success, and trade after trade was taken under control with an increasing willingness on the part of the interests affected.

The thoughtful reader will find here and there stories which carry with them suggestions of problems relating to the industrial practices of peace, and the same stories will also, perhaps, point toward peace-time solutions of some of these problems. Reference has already been several times made to the evident value, as a measure of preparedness, of a comprehensive Government bureau devoted to industrial research and statistical information.

Recommendations which would follow as the fruit of the experience of the Board might be classified in two groups: (1) Those relating to peace-time preparation for a possible war emergency, and (2) those relating to the business practices of normal times.

Three lines of industrial preparedness will be briefly suggested here as the most important direct war lessons to be derived from the work:

First. There should be established a peace-time skeleton organization following the lines of the War Industries Board. It should be headed by a chairman who should have associated with him the chiefs of the centralized purchasing bureaus of the Army, of the Navy, and of any other Government department which might be called upon to make large purchases in case of war. Other members of the Board should be selected to take charge of (1) raw materials, (2) finished products, (3) facilities, (4) price control, (5) labor, (6) priority, (7) conservation, and (8) planning and statistics. There should be a vice chairman, a general counsel, and a secretary. To function under the several principal divisions there should be selected about 50 chiefs of commodity sections. Each chief of a commodity section would name a committee to represent the industry under his charge. The committees of the different industries could meet separately as occasion required for the purpose of keeping acquainted with the general growth of the industry and the demands which a war would make upon it. The main organization should meet in general conference at least once a year to discuss and outline plans, to keep in touch with the general nature of war needs, and to keep acquainted with one another. The office of secretary should be permanent and salaried, and the division of planning and statistics ought to be a moderately large permanent organization—a reservoir of information for all departments of the Government and the Congress. All other members and subordinates of the Board should serve without compensation.

Second. During the war the country was constantly threatened with a shortage in available supply of nitrogen, manganese, chrome, tungsten, dyestuffs, coal-tar derivatives, and several other essential materials. These materials had always been imported into the United States and their production never developed, although sources for most of them exist here. The Government should devise some system for protecting and stimulating their internal production. Among these, nitrogen is of outstanding importance, not only because it is indispensable for war, but also because it is almost indispensable for agricultural purposes. There is only one natural source in the world, and the fixation process, having been proven to be practicable, should be developed to commercial proportions.

Third. Under the supervision of the proper departments of the Government, certain war industries should be encouraged to maintain skeleton organizations through which they could develop the rapid manufacture of guns, munitions, airplanes, and other direct military equipment. This might be done in some cases through Government purchases of factories, in others through the placing of sufficient orders to permit the owners to keep the plants in existence. It is extremely important that our recent development of machine tools, in the nature of dies, jigs, etc., for the manufacture of munitions, should not be allowed to dissipate. At an expense bearing very little relation to the cost of building anew in time of emergency, present stocks could be carried forward and supplemented as new designs replace the old in the development of war devices.

These measures are suggested as direct methods of insuring against some of the heavy losses and unfortunate delays which the country experienced in the process of converting its industries from a peace to a war basis. They involve very small current expenditures, but are capable of being instruments for saving many millions of dollars in an emergency.

The experience of the Board in exercising control over American industry leads it to make a further suggestion, which has less to do with war than with the normal practices of business.

During the past few decades, while the American business man, uniting his talents with those of the technical expert, has, through the control of great masses of capital, made such extraordinary strides in converting the natural wealth of this country into means for human comfort and satisfaction, the processes of trade have so changed their nature that the older and simpler relations of Government to business have been gradually forced to give way before certain new principles of supervision. We have been gradually compelled to drift away from the old doctrine of Anglo-American law, that the sphere of Government should be limited to preventing breach of contract, fraud, physical injury and injury to property, and that the Government should exercise protection only over noncompetent persons. The modern industrial processes have been rendering it increasingly necessary for the Government to reach out its arm to protect competent individuals against the discriminating practices of mass industrial power. We have already evolved a system of Government control of no mean significance over our railroads and over our merchant fleet, but we continue to argue, and in a measure believe, that the principles of competition can be preserved in sufficient power in respect to all other industries to protect the interests of the public and insure efficiency and wholesome growth in the development of natural wealth. With this in view, the Sherman and Clayton Acts have forbidden combinations in restraint of trade, monopolies, and many other vices attendant upon group action by individuals controlling great masses of capital. This legislation, while valuable for immediate purposes, represents little more than a moderately ambitious effort to reduce by Government interference the processes of business so as to make them conform to the simpler principles sufficient for the conditions of a bygone day.

The war has introduced a new element into this situation. The individual units of corporations which had been dissolved under the

Sherman Act have, in many cases, grown during the war into corporations many fold larger than the parent organization which before the war the law construed as a menace. The conditions of war made this sort of thing necessary and in all respects desirable. The war gave rise to a kind of demand unknown in time of peace—an absolute demand, which was halted neither by prices nor difficulty of procurement. There followed an absolute shortage in some trades, and a time shortage in most of them. Group action, industry by industry, accompanied by Government control of prices and distribution, was the natural and, so far as we know, the only solution which could be devised.

In line with the principle of united action and cooperation, hundreds of trades were organized for the first time into national associations, each responsible in a real sense for its multitude of component companies, and they were organized on the suggestion and under the supervision of the Government. Practices looking to efficiency in production, price control, conservation, control in quantity of production, etc., were inaugurated everywhere. Many business men have experienced during the war, for the first time in their careers, the tremendous advantages, both to themselves and to the general public, of combination, of cooperation and common action, with their natural competitors. To drive them back through new legislation, or through the more rigid and rapid enforcement of present legislation, to the situation which immediately preceded the war will be very difficult in many cases, though in a few it is already occurring spontaneously. To leave these combinations without further supervision and attention by the Government than can be given by the Attorney General's Department, or by the Federal Trade Commission in its present form, will subject business men to such temptations as many of them will be unable to resist—temptations to conduct their businesses for private gain with little reference to general public welfare.

These associations, as they stand, are capable of carrying out purposes of greatest public benefit. They can increase the amount of wealth available for the comfort of the people by inaugurating rules designed to eliminate wasteful practices attendant upon multiplicity of styles and types of articles in the various trades; they can assist in cultivating the public taste for rational types of commodities; by exchange of trade information, extravagant methods of production and distribution can be avoided through them, and production will tend to be localized in places best suited economically for it. By acting as centers of information, furnishing lists of sources to purchasers and lists of purchasers to producers, supply and demand can be more economically balanced. From the point of vantage which competent men have at the central bureau of an association, not only can new demands be cultivated, but new sources of unexploited wealth can be indicated. In case of a national emergency, the existence of these associations at the beginning would be of incalculable aid to the supply organizations. Many of these considerations apply to large individual companies as well as to associations.

These combinations are capable also—and very easily capable— of carrying out purposes of greatest public disadvantage. They can so subtly influence production as to keep it always just short of current demand and thus keep prices ever high and going higher. They can encourage a common understanding on prices, and, without great difficulty, can hold price levels at abnormal positions. They can influence the favoring of one type of buyer over another. Nearly every business man in the country has learned by the war that a shortage in his product, if it be not too great, is distinctly to his advantage. Trade associations with real power can, in respect to most of the staples, so influence production as to keep the margin of shortage at a point most favorable to high prices and rapid turnovers.

The question, then, is what kind of Government organization can be devised to safeguard the public interest while these associations are preserved to carry on the good work of which they are capable. The country will quite properly demand the vigorous enforcement of all proper measures for the suppression of unfair competition and unreasonable restraint of trade. But this essentially negative policy of curbing vicious practices should, in the public interest, be supplemented by a positive program, and to this end the experience of the War Industries Board points to the desirability of investing some Government agency, perhaps the Department of Commerce or the Federal Trade Commission, with constructive as well as inquisitorial powers—an agency whose duty it should be to encourage, under strict Government supervision, such cooperation and coordination in industry as should tend to increase production, eliminate waste, conserve natural resources, improve the quality of products, promote efficiency in operation, and thus reduce costs to the ultimate consumer.

Such a plan should provide a way of approaching industry, or rather of inviting industry to approach the Government, in a friendly spirit, with a view to help and not to hinder. The purpose contemplated is not that the Government should undertake any such far-reaching control over industry as was practiced during the war emergency by the War Industries Board; but that the experiences of the war should be capitalized; its heritage of dangerous practices should be fully realized that they might be avoided; and its heritage of wholesome and useful practices should be accepted and studied with a view to adapting them to the problems of peace. It is recommended that such practices of cooperation and coordination in industry as have been found to be clearly of public benefit should be stimulated and encouraged by a Government agency, which at the same time would be clothed with the power and charged with the responsibility of standing watch against and preventing abuses.

COMMODITY SECTIONS

CHAPTER 1

Introductory

THE COMMODITY SECTIONS of the War Industries Board were in an important sense the backbone of the whole structure. Through them the various so-called functional divisions—Conservation, Priorities, Price-Fixing, Requirements, Labor, and Allied Purchasing—obtained their expert information, made contact with the industries and with the purchasing agencies alike, received suggestions, requests, and complaints, and directed the enforcement of regulations and control.

Of indispensable value in facilitating contact between the various sections and the branches of industry corresponding to them, was the series of war service committees, originally under the Council of National Defense and later transferred to the supervision of the United States Chamber of Commerce, each representing one line of business. A war service committee spoke and acted as agent and representative of an industry and not as agent of the Board. The various units composing a particular industry would join in appointing one of these committees to act as spokesman in negotiating with the Government. The strongest men in the industry usually served on these committees.

Thus, structurally, there was unified control from the individual plants and companies through the war service committees, the commodity sections, and the functional divisions to the chairman of the Board, who took his powers directly from the President of the United States. And practically, the organization was as centralized as the heterogeneous nature of the undertaking would permit.

On the Government purchasing side harmonious action was provided for by representation on each commodity section of an officer from each purchasing agency using the commodity. And further, each purchasing agency had a representative on each functional division. Final authority on questions of priority or other regulation was for administrative purposes vested in the respective members of the Board. The rule was laid down that an appeal from their decisions to the chairman of the Board could be taken only by the Secretary of War, the Secretary of the Navy, the Chairman of the Shipping

Board, or other head of an independent department of the Government. This rule eliminated much of the debate and delay incident to the right of appeal. It fostered prompt decisions and brought action in place of words.

As has been pointed out, most of the various organs of the War Industries Board had their origin in the Council of National Defense in the various subdivisions of the General Munitions Board, which was reorganized under the name War Industries Board, and remained part of the council until March 4, 1918. The commodity sections for the most part grew out of the numerous subdivisions of the committee on supplies and the committee on raw materials, to which, as time went on and shortages or threatened shortages appeared in particular industries, experts were called to take oversight in the separate fields. These experts became the chiefs of the commodity sections with enlarged powers and responsibilities under the reorganized Board.

George N. Peek, as commissioner of finished products, had general oversight of the work of those sections devoted to manufactured articles; and L. L. Summers, as technical advisor, took general supervision of the sections dealing with unfabricated materials and chemicals. The work of these men was very important.

As the Board stood on November 11, 1918, there were 57 commodity sections, each with important and far-reaching responsibilities. The duties of one section often related to those of several others, and particularly to the work being carried on by the War Trade Board, the Shipping Board, and the Food and Fuel Administrations, as well as the several agencies of the Government which were consuming the products under attention. Each section chief had one or more assistants and an organization which worked continuously with him, and he had in addition the advantage of daily conferences with a group consisting of one man assigned by each Government agency which was buying materials in his field. There was also a general weekly conference of all chiefs of sections presided over by the chairman of the Board, who thus kept all hands informed about the war plans, the general purposes, and general needs.

The chiefs of sections and their assistants brought to Washington an expert knowledge of their trades. Most of them had been, in private life, managers of large companies.

Upon its formation a section would set to work to verify and complete the body of facts necessary in dealing with its problems. This was, of course, the most difficult, while it was at the same time the most vitally important part of the work. In some cases it was next to impossible to get vital facts accurately compiled and to get them in time for greatest usefulness in understanding and solving the problem. It is in this feature of the work that a peace-time bureau, functioning continuously, watching with studious care the development and condition of each industry having a war value, could be of extraordinary significance if it should ever be necessary again to direct the industrial forces of the country to the support of a great war.

In the first place, then, it was the purpose of each commodity section to serve as a clearing house for information in its line. The Nation's demands for extraordinary production made it necessary in some industries to spread broadcast "trade secrets," which in normal times are cautiously guarded. It was only that quality of sentiment of devotion to the purposes of the war, which transcended the desire for what we have always construed as legitimate gain, which could have brought these men to give up their sacred rights to their "trade secrets" to such an organization as the War Industries Board. The sections used questionnaires quite freely in the collection of information. Many of them established systems of monthly reports from the various firms engaged in their work.

The war service committees were constant sources of information regarding the sentiments of the trades, their complaints, and their suggestions. Whenever a section felt the approach of a critical situation, something involving unusual treatment, a conference of representatives of all firms to be affected would be called together; views would be exchanged; the importance of the Government's requirements would be carefully explained; and suggestions for the solution of the problem would be received and discussed at length. Working agreements were often reached at these conferences, agreements regarding priorities, agreements as to the form and handling of a licensing system of distribution, agreements as to price-fixing, and other methods of control. The results of these conferences would be taken before the appropriate functional division where the plans could be ratified and directions for putting them into effect issued to the section and to the trade.

Information relating to the needs of the War Department, the Navy, the Emergency Fleet, etc., came to the commodity sections formally through the Requirements Division and Clearance Office, and informally and continuously through the representatives of these agencies in each section. Early in the work there appeared signs of strained relations between the commodity chiefs on the one hand and delegates from the buying agencies on the other.

The Chairman of the Board, following the President's example in creating it, at first delegated his authority to chiefs of sections alone, instead of delegating it to the sections as a whole. The section chiefs represented the Board's authority over supply, while members from the Government departments represented demand. The Government departments were statutory organizations, vested with sole responsibility for filling their supply programs. So long as the chiefs had authority and the department representatives had none, the latter tended to avoid rather than seek contact with the sections. This difficulty was completely overcome by a delegation of authority to the sections as a whole with provision for carrying any dissent directly to the Chairman of the Board. When this was done, the purchasing departments immediately began to send more authoritative agents to represent them on the sections. These men brought to the sections all available information and received from them all the assistance within the power of the Board. They participated in the control of the particular commodity in question and the sections became what they had been designed to be. The most significant purpose of the sections was the establishment of authoritative centers of contact, and this was accomplished to a remarkable extent before the end came. As a principle of administration, the Chairman always gave fullest support to the decisions of the section chiefs, and he is happy to say that he has never had cause for regret in the abuse or misuse of such power.

It was never the policy of the War Industries Board to establish one set of rigid formulæ for industry in general. This would have played more havoc than the situation called for. Rather was its policy, acting largely on the initiative and suggestion of the respective sections, to deal with each industry according to the peculiar conditions affecting it. The regulation of the steel industry, which was said to be controlled by 17 men who could be gathered into one room at Washington, required a different method from that applicable to the regulation of cotton textiles.

There was no laying out of a program of control over every conceivable industry. In contrast the Board preferred, as the necessity to control an additional industry arose, to meet that industry separately and make individual agreements which seemed at the time most expedient. As section after section was formed in response to needs, the administrative activities of the various functional divisions had to be gradually decentralized and focused in the sections. The routine by which all requirements were received at a central point and distributed to the commodity chiefs is indicative of the policy behind the whole scheme.

Various Government and allied representatives, who throughout

Washington on the day previous had made new estimates of requirements, brought those estimates to the War Industries Board each morning. They were there read aloud in the Requirements Division and, as the representative chose, discussed. The discussions turned not on whether the future requirements should be allowed or disallowed, but rather upon whether there was a shortage from any cause, and, if so, how the requirements should be met. The requirements, after the meeting, were sent forthwith to the commodity chiefs. It was the business of the commodity chief, with the advice of all his section members, to find ways to meet the requirements and later on to allocate them if necessary. The department which originally submitted them was expected to keep account of it through the department representative in the commodity section to which the requirement had been referred.

Under the system as it finally developed, the commodity chiefs were asked to fill out a blank for the Requirements Division, upon receipt of each requirement, stating in detail whether and how the industry could meet it. The sections were asked to consider market conditions pertinent to the requirements, recommended plans to the several purchasing departments, and, if it seemed necessary to control an industry in whole or in part by allotments, to determine, with the advice of the priorities committee, the allocation of materials, commodities, and facilities to the several Government departments, to the Allies, and to civilians. In respect to those industries in which the Board adopted the policy of "allocating" each order to specific plants or regions, for the purpose of more suitably distributing the burden or fruit of Government patronage, the particular allocations were worked out in the sections.[1]

In the same way it will appear how the work of the Clearance Division was almost entirely decentralized and the division gave way to a Clearance Office which merely received all requests for clearances, recorded them, and distributed them promptly to the appropriate Commodity Sections. This became necessary because the numbers of immediate requirements which needed clearance each morning grew into the hundreds and made utterly hopeless any more than a mere perfunctory reading of them at the clearance committee meetings. The increases in Government purchases gave the committee more work than it could do either with care or expedition. As each com-

---

[1] See chap. 2, Part I, for fuller explanation of the procedure referred to here, including the clearance of orders and the importance of using the clearance as a check upon potential shortages.

modity section had competent purchasing department representatives on it, the most logical solution seemed to be that of having all immediate requirements cleared directly through the commodity chiefs, and thus the work of granting clearances of prospective orders became one of the most important functions of the sections. * * *

The relation of the sections to the work of the Priorities Division was somewhat different. Priorities control in a large way had to be exercised through one organ. The interdependence of commodities required this. It was, of course, physically impossible for one organ to examine each case as it arose. A system of automatic priority ratings was worked out, and the sections undertook the responsibility of administering the rules laid down. Each section at the same time carried on a study of the effect of these rules and the need for modifying them or making new ones, and brought its recommendations and its problems before the priorities commissioner. Whenever hearings were to be held on request for special priorities, the appropriate section would prepare the case for the Government. The sections made recommendations regarding priority policies and the issuance of certificates to concerns of the industries with which they worked.

The administration of curtailment programs was also committed to the commodity sections. Curtailment was only resorted to when a serious shortage threatened. The production of certain less essential commodities was cut off or curtailed to make way for the production of war essentials. The Priorities Division was, of course, the most effective instrument of curtailment, but a special industrial adjustment committee was appointed to work also on this rather delicate problem. That committee, after permitting a hearing to the industry affected, would determine upon curtailment policies designed to effect equitable reductions without unnecessarily crippling the industry.

An important feature of the work of many of the commodity sections was along the line of conservation programs. After a study by the section with its intimate contact and knowledge of the industry involved, data would be brought before the Conservation Division, where a set of rules would be worked out. Before putting these rules into effect, however, authorized representatives from the entire industry would be brought together, technical advice would be asked from them, their voluntary consent to the rules invited, and their active cooperation in carrying them out would be cordially solicited. Once adopted, the administration of a conservation program was left to the appropriate commodity section.

The relation of the sections to negotiations leading to price-fixing agreements and to the administration of fixed price schedules was quite analogous to their work in the other fields referred to. In clearing an order or in allocating an order, a section's action did not constitute approval of the price named in it unless there existed in the rulings of the price-fixing committee a fixed price for the materials involved.

In treating the work of the 57 commodity sections, as mentioned in the chapters which follow, an effort will be made to lay emphasis only upon the unusual problems which arose in respect to the particular industries. Besides illustrating the application of these general rules, in the solution of particular problems, reference will be made to the invention of particular methods for the solution of the problems peculiar to the individual industries.

Editor's Note: Before the National Industrial Conference Board on December 19, 1940, Mr. Baruch, speaking of the Commodity Sections, said:

All resources must be mobilized so as to be tapped at will with as much speed as possible to meet changing conditions of our own offense and defense, as well as that of the enemy. This means an organization for each commodity and facility, as in the War Industries Board. On each such organization or committee should be a representative of each interested department. Here all the needs will be exposed. To this division will be given the prices and priorities. At the head of each of these committees will be the representative of the Chairman (of the agency corresponding to the W.I.B.) who has the final authority, in the committee's decision, to carry out the policies enunciated. Always we endeavored to have some one man who could finally decide. He represents the decentralized authority of the chairman, who gets it from the President.

On the other side will sit the representatives of production, i.e., industry. To them will be given the allocations or the priorities and prices. To them will be addressed questions of increasing production, of lessening demands, of what conservation can be evolved and what substitutes found.

Mr. Baruch, of course, is only envisioning the system that was tried and proved in the last war and which has been described in detail in the foregoing chapter—the system that was copied to a large extent in the organization of industries in the NRA, and which was followed in the Industrial Mobilization Plan of the Army and Navy. The abandoned I.M.P. provided for a strongly centralized War Resources Administration, akin to the War Industries Board, which had direct contact through its facilities and commodities divisions with the war service committees of industry. Such a system, furthermore, was possible even under the old Council of National Defense set-up, or under any modifications thereof—provided, of course, that its limitations under the law were recognized and remedied.

As Mr. Baruch pointed out at the National Industrial Conference Board meeting:

After the Wisconsin oil decision, there is a grave doubt as to the clearance that a committee of industry can get from the anti-trust act. When the Defense Commission was first announced, the only public statement I made regarding it was that they had to clear the committees of industry if they wanted to get the fast, quick work that is necessary. The committees have never got it yet and I think that is one of the plugs that will have to be pulled if speed is to be attained.

Some approach to the problem has been made by Edward R. Stettinius in his Industrial Materials Division of the Advisory Commission, and in his Priorities Division of the Office of Production Management. In the Industrial Materials Division, the well-organized commodity sections have approached the problem through contact with associations of industry, such as the American Iron and Steel Institute; while in the Priorities Division of O.P.M., representatives of industry were named to advisory priority committees. There is a widespread belief, however, that the problem will have to be attacked directly by giving a legal basis for the formation of war service committees representing industries.

Some authorities in Washington believe that the Attorney General can give protection for specific action by committees of industry; but other authorities believe that, as far as the courts are concerned, such authorization would be valueless. Mr. Baruch believes the problem should be solved by an amendment to the Sherman anti-trust act permitting industries, at the request of the Government, to get together for specific purposes, such as the carrying out of price and priority regulations, conservation, conversion of facilities, and the adoption of substitutes.

In World War I, it was constantly brought to the attention of Mr. Baruch that the war service committees were an infringement of the law, and frequent discussions were had with congressional leaders regarding an amendment to the anti-trust act. But congressional action was never obtained before the Armistice. During the subsequent Graham investigation, an effort was made to bring out facts that would have resulted in the prosecution of the members of some of the war service committees—but Mr. Baruch, as chairman of the W.I.B., took full responsibility for the acts of the committees and recalled that these committee members served only because they were asked to do so by the Government and were acting at its request.

It is to give these war service committees a full legal status, and to dissipate the cloud of the Wisconsin oil decision, that Mr. Baruch believes it best to obtain congressional sanction.

CHAPTER 2

Iron and Steel

THE EXTENT to which iron and steel enter into all phases of war equipment made this industry one of the first to receive the attention of the special agency of the Government appointed to advise in regard to the enlistment of production for war. The early estimates were that only about 17 per cent of our enormous steel output (35,-000,000 tons a year) would be required to supply all war needs. When this estimate is reviewed in the light of Government control during 1918 of 100 per cent of our steel, and in the light of the struggles to cover shortages which accompanied the control, one can realize the value which a peace-time bureau devoted to the collection of information might have had as a measure of preparedness.

The Allies were purchasing steel in this country in terms of millions of dollars before the United States declared war, and prices had been steadily climbing even more rapidly than production was increasing under the abnormal demand. The anticipations engendered by the events of February and March, 1917, stimulated a still more rapid rise.

Thus it was that as soon as the advisory commission of the Council of National Defense was organized and Mr. Baruch was assigned to take charge of the committee on raw materials, he began to study the question of the steel supply and the extent to which Government control was going to be necessary to meet the purposes of the war. Early in March, 1917, he brought together the leading steel men of the country, and the problem before the Nation was discussed and debated at length with them. They finally consented, as did the producers of copper, lead, aluminum, and nickel, to offer to the Government whatever steel was needed for the preparedness campaign at prices in scale with prewar buying. But, as was pointed out in an earlier chapter, as soon as the Government needs began to appear so large, low Government prices only meant higher civilian prices unless control should extend to all, and this as has been seen was the ultimate solution.

Most important and far-reaching principles of control had already

117

been conceived and were ready to be applied when, on September 15, 1917, in the course of the development of the organization, J. Leonard Replogle was appointed director of steel supply for the War Industries Board. He became chief of the Steel Division and remained in that position throughout the war. * * *[1]

It will be the purpose here to give a continuous account of the control over the iron and steel industry as it was centered first in the Council of National Defense and then in the War Industries Board. It will be understood that various studies, suggestions, and administrative functions were carried forward by the appropriate sections under the general control of the division. * * *[2]

In order to understand the problem which was faced in bringing the steel industry to the full support of the Government in the war, it is necessary to bear in mind some of the outstanding features of its development during the years immediately preceding the spring of 1917. The iron and steel markets reflected the general industrial depression of 1914. Both production and prices fell steadily through 1913 and 1914, and it was not until the autumn of 1915 that they were back to the normal of the decade preceding. The recovery, which the trade expected through an expansion of exports when the war broke out in Europe, was retarded by the lack of shipping facilities and the derangement of world finance. Instead of bringing prosperity to this industry, the war at first increased the depression. When prosperity finally came, it was due to orders from the belligerents themselves.

By the fall of 1915, contracts running to hundreds of millions of dollars were being placed for shrapnel, steel bars for shrapnel shells, machine tools for ordnance work, barbed wire for entanglements. These orders gave a stimulus to domestic demands. Steel was required for machinery and for the construction of new manufacturing plants. Steel producers themselves required steel in order to enlarge their own works. During 1915 and 1916 the production of pig iron increased 70 per cent, that of steel ingots 83 per cent, and a large share of these ingots was used directly or indirectly for the production of war materials. Conversion of plants also took place during this period. As early as 1915 rail mills had been converted to the

---

[1] Mr. Replogle had as his assistant director Frank Purnell, whom he brought to Washington from the sales department of Youngstown Sheet & Tube and who, today, is president of that company.

[2] The deleted material sketched the geography and some of the economy of steel, including: areas of production of basic steel ingredients, the different iron- and steel-making processes, the industrial integration brought about by introduction of the rolling mill, and a brief catalogue of standard mill and foundry products.

production of shrapnel bars. During this same period the steady rise in prices, without a significant setback, was phenomenal. By the end of 1916 the average "weighted" price of iron and steel products was 240 per cent of prewar normal.

The events of February and March, 1917, stimulated the most rapid rise which the history of the industry has ever experienced, until an unprecedented peak was reached in July, 1917, when the average weighted price was 370 per cent of normal. A few examples will show what a runaway market it was. The open-market price of Connellsville coke jumped from $1.67 per ton in September, 1915, to $12.25 in July, 1917, with but two setbacks. In June, 1915, basic pig iron was selling for $12.59 per ton and it climbed steadily to $52.50 per ton in July, 1917. Bessemer steel billets advanced in a straight line from $19.50 per ton in May, 1915, to $95 per ton during June and July, 1917. Structural steel shapes rose from $1.20 per hundredweight in December, 1914, to $6.20 per hundredweight in July, 1917. Steel tank plates jumped from $1.22 per hundredweight in July, 1915, to $22 per hundredweight in September, 1917.[3]

On the whole the price of iron ore rose less rapidly than that of pig iron, pig iron less rapidly than that of steel, and steel less rapidly than that of finished steel products. This was, of course, due to the immediate and pressing demand for the finished product to be used by an agency which had no measure of value for its usefulness.

In January, 1917, Secretary Baker received the report of a special board, which he had appointed "for the purpose of investigating and reporting upon the feasibility, desirability, and practicability of the Government manufacturing arms, munitions, and equipment." The conclusion of the board advised a reliance upon private industry. By June, 1917, it was becoming clear that this principle of reliance upon private industry, unguided and uncontrolled, was not going to insure steel at reasonable prices to the Government and the Allies.

There were two features which deranged the ordinary process of business. In the first place, demand exceeded supply by a margin so great that competition between producers was practically eliminated. In the second place, the demand was absolute; there was no postponing of it. Buyers of steel in times of peace expect to realize a profit on their investment. Steel that goes into buildings and bridges must be bought at prices which will make possible satisfactory

---

[3] These prices are "open-market prices" as quoted in the *Iron Age* and other papers. The long-time contract prices, of course, underwent less violent fluctuations.

returns. Whenever these buyers believe prices are likely to decline in the near future, they withdraw from the market. Their attitude serves as an effective check on buying when prices have reached what is considered an abnormal level.

The attitude of the Government toward its war-time purchases, however, differed fundamentally from this. It bought with no expectation of earning a profit. The possibility of lower prices in the future did not check its buying. The absence of the investor's attitude in Government buying effectively removed the customary upper limit to price fluctuations. Some remedy was imperative, and it was thus, by the 1st of July, 1917, that the discussions of Government control of steel supply began to be taken seriously everywhere. Price control, with its corollary control over distribution, was the most popular proposal, though the commandeering of mines, furnaces, and mills was seriously contemplated. The President made an emphatic declaration on July 12, 1917, touching war industries with particular reference to steel, warning that those "who do not respond in the spirit of those who have gone to give their lives for us on bloody fields far away may safely be left to be dealt with by opinion and the law, for the law must, of course, command these things." He added more pointedly that "the Government is about to attempt to determine the prices at which it will ask you henceforth to furnish various supplies which are necessary for the prosecution of the war, and various materials which will be needed in the industries by which the war must be sustained. We shall, of course, try to determine them justly and to the best advantage of the Nation as a whole."

The Secretary of War, the Secretary of the Navy, and the chairman of the Shipping Board, as well as the Senate Committee on Interstate Commerce, all made statements rebuking the forces which were responsible for the rapid rise in prices, and declaring themselves in favor of a control of iron and steel, which would insure reasonable prices to the Government. These announcements were having their effect on the market and on the attitude of the industry.

By the end of July prices began to show a sharp drop, and the more conservative factions of the steel industry saw only peril ahead unless the Government brought stabilization to the market. By late September virtually the whole industry was disposed to recommend that formal regulation begin. One of their principal trade journals, the *Iron Age*, began predicting regulation in late June, and was frankly advocating it in the issue of August 30. Thus, before control was actually put into effect, the Government and the industry were in a state of mind to sit around the same table and determine together what kind of control they wanted and how it should be exercised.

Discussions and investigations continued through the summer. On the War Industries Board fell the responsibility of drawing matters together, establishing and promulgating the principles of control, and of carrying out their administration. Though by midsummer both the Government and the industry were agreed that control was necessary, the Government had still to learn both the technique of control and the general policies which should underlie it, for this was one of the first commodities over which an ambitious program was undertaken. But the Government agencies had definitely in mind at the outset that, in determining upon reasonable prices, they must stimulate rather than hamper the production of steel.

Large numbers of inquiries and suggestions required the Board to consider seriously and to reach conclusions on such questions as whether any prices, fixed for Government purchases, should be made applicable to purchases by nationals; whether Government prices should be extended to the Allies; whether the fixed prices should be determined through a flat rate or a flexible cost-plus-profit scale; whether the proposed fixed price schedule would or would not abrogate outstanding contract price agreements; whether the Government, in determining upon prices, should take cognizance of the incidental labor, fuel, and transportation problems; and whether control over the producers would take proper account of the middlemen.

That controlled prices should extend to civilian purchasers and to purchases by the allied Governments was determined in the affirmative in accordance with the opinion of the President, as expressed in his announcement of July 12, 1917. The President's striking words on this point set the fashion not only for steel but for most of the other commodities whose prices the Board found it necessary to control. "We must make the prices to the public the same as prices to the Government. Prices mean the same everywhere now; they mean the efficiency of the Nation, whether it is the Government that pays them or not; they mean victory or defeat."

The Board, in announcing the policy that the Allies should be charged no more than our own Government, stated two important limitations, first, that the policy must be reciprocal; second, that the arrangement must be limited to war materials in order to protect our own industry. "We must not allow raw materials, sold by our own producers at prices patriotically conceded to our own Government and its Allies for war purposes, to be diverted to industry and trade abroad, which may come in competition with our own manufacturers and producers." The foreign mission of the Board worked later in bringing about adjustments in accord with these principles.

The flat rate versus "cost-plus-profit" argument received extended and cautious consideration at Washington. The investigations of the Federal Trade Commission showed beyond doubt that there was no uniformity in the costs of various producers. It was brought out that there were varying costs not only as between four distinct classes of producers, classes based upon the degree of integration of their plants, but also varying costs within each class. Companies who owned their own ore, transportation, blast furnaces, rolling mills, and works for the manufacture of finished products could produce more cheaply than those who bought their ore and coke, but controlled the further stages of production. Those who purchased pig iron, but carried the manufacturing process through steel to the finished article, produced more cheaply than those who bought steel ingots and billets, and rolled plates, shapes, and other products.

The principle that no measure should be taken which would reduce the maximum possible production dominated. It was, therefore, finally determined to fix the maximum prices at a flat rate, and at a point high enough to keep substantially in full operation every mill and blast furnace which contributed appreciably to the country's supply. It was left for the excess-profit tax to take care of low-cost producers and the arrangement served in place of a subsidy for high-cost producers. This was considered more satisfactory than a pooling arrangement, which had been given serious consideration, and under which the profits of low-cost producers would have been turned over to cover losses of high-cost producers, for the latter plan would inevitably have reduced production.

Another problem, which arose first in connection with steel but which had to be determined later for many more commodities, was whether prices written in active contracts should be abrogated when the fixed price schedule went into effect. The concern was not alone over the legal right of the Government to abrogate those contracts, but the arguments turned also upon the practical advantages which would accrue to buyers who had not contracted ahead and could, under the fixed price schedule, buy steel more cheaply than had their competitors a month or two earlier under contract agreements. The adjustments which took place during the period between the determination to fix prices and the actual issue of schedules tended to relieve both aspects of this problem. It was finally determined that the prices fixed by the Government should not apply to past contracts.

The fuel, transportation, and labor problems were puzzling this and other industries during this confused period. What should be the relation of the control of prices and distribution to these problems? Time answered the question. The Government's control over the distribution of fuel and transportation proved to be the most important means it had for enforcing the rules and regulations which it found necessary to impose upon the industries. The full spirit and intention of the control could not have been enforced without the good will of the leaders of trade. But it was in no small measure the necessity on the part of industry of seeking the privilege of priority in fuel and transportation which placed the War Industries Board in the position of power which made it possible for the Board to bargain with the industries as an equal. The benefits and advantages flowing from Government recognition brought the industries voluntarily to seek to place themselves on the preference list, willingly assuming its obligations in order to obtain its benefits. The industries became plaintiffs; pledges could be required in return for privileges granted.

The place of middlemen in price fixing and the extent to which the various practices of different trades in respect to them should be recognized was also the subject of studious consideration. The concentration of iron and steel production in the hands of relatively few producers made it simpler to control prices at the source than it was in some other trades. If a price is fixed for a producer and the product passes through a jobber to the ultimate consumer, the jobber's interest in the fixed price is that of purchaser and not that of seller. Abnormal demands will simply give him abnormal profits.

When Mr. Replogle came to Washington about the middle of September, 1917, numerous conferences had been held and both sides of the case were more than ready for action. Action was soon to follow. In a report on the iron and steel situation, which he rendered to the Board on September 14,[4] he urged that the steel men be called at once to Washington for a conference that immediate steps might be taken to alleviate the chaotic steel situation. He outlined in some detail the condition peculiarly demanding the maximum production of coke, pig iron, sheared plates, shell steel, billets, and rounds. And he recommended furthermore that there be fixed on these items maximum prices to take effect at the earliest possible date.

Four days later the War Industries Board called the committee representing the steel industry to a special meeting, and asked for views on the proper method to be followed in fixing the price of steel.

---

[4] See Appendix XIV for the text of the report.

The committee said that an examination of the cost figures, furnished by the Federal Trade Commission, showed that they really reflected in general the prevailing condition of a year previous, because the materials used during the first half of 1917 had been contracted for in the fall of 1916. A special committee of the Board recommended that the question of price fixing could be best approached—

by considering the individual processes or stages comprising the manufacture of the finished product. Each of these practically constitutes an independent industry. Many of the operators are engaged in only one of the processes, while a few of the larger companies cover all operations from the raw material to the finished product. As each industry must be allowed a profit to support that particular industry, the integrated companies who cover all processes from raw materials to highly finished products must necessarily receive a profit on each of the processes.

Conditions prevailing in the steel trade for a considerable period made it necessary for all lines of industry using steel products to order their supplies further in advance than would be necessary under normal conditions, and as a consequence these industries have on hand substantial stocks of steel acquired at prices very much higher than any we could recommend as being fair or equitable. To partially meet this situation and avoid demoralizing the many industries that are largely dependent upon steel products, we recommend the establishment of what might be termed an intermediate scale of prices for a period of three months with the expectation of a further reduction at the end of that period.

With that purpose in mind we submit the attached schedule of proposed prices on the raw materials and various products, also showing the approximate market prices at the present time and the amount of the reduction from such prices.

This scale of prices is recommended on the basis of offering a premium on ship's plates and shell steel with the object of stimulating production, as the present capacity is inadequate to meet the requirements.

It is evident that to be effective any price regulations must be rigidly enforced. Serious consideration should be given to the question of abrogating contracts which were entered into prior to establishing this suggested schedule of prices.

We have asked the Federal Trade Commission to advise the War Industries Board further in regard to these contracts, which must be considered an important factor in the situation, as some furnaces have entered into contracts without regard to the price established on coal.

The Board agreed on the same day that prices should be fixed separately on ore, coal, coke, pig iron, and on transportation, for the purpose of building up a fair price for steel. It was likewise agreed that should the steel interests not be willing to give their full cooperation to the price-fixing program, the Board would take steps necessary to assume control over the steel plants.

The iron and steel industry of the country, as represented by 65 executives, met the War Industries Board at Washington at 10 o'clock on the morning of September 21. The steel men were told that the President had requested the Board to call them together and ask their opinions on proper prices to be fixed. A prolonged discussion followed. Each side had its case fully prepared, and there was vigorous conflict with regard to the facts as well as the principles to be applied. The Board finally stated to the industry the theory which it believed was a sound one for computing the price schedule and the representatives of the industry disagreed and retired. At the request of E. H. Gary, the meeting reconvened, and he, speaking for the steel industry, explained to the Board that the trade, in its desire to meet the Board's views as far as possible, had appointed committees covering ore, coke, and pig iron, and that these committees would make and explain separate recommendations. The schedules were prepared, and after long debate and many revisions by the Board they were finally agreed to by the steel interests subject to the approval of the President.

Thus, on September 24, 1917, the President made formal announcement of the prices which had been fixed by negotiated agreement on the basic raw materials of the iron and steel group. These prices served as the basis for all price fixing within that group. They were announced as effective immediately and subject to revision January 1, 1918, as follows: †

Commodity.	Basis.	Price.
Iron ore	Lower Lake ports	$5.05 per gross ton.
Coke	Connellsville	$6 per net ton.
Pig iron		$33 per gross ton.
Steel bars	Pittsburgh-Chicago	$2.90 per 100 pounds.
Shapes	....do	$3 per 100 pounds.
Plates	....do	$3.25 per 100 pounds.

† *Editor's Note:* January, 1940, prices were: iron ore, $4.75 per gross ton; coke, $5.75 per net ton; pig iron, $24.00 per gross ton; shapes, $2.10 per 100 pounds; and plates, $2.15 per 100 pounds.

In contrast with the meteoric rise in prices from 1914 to September, 1917, present-day prices have been very well maintained—reflecting the common understanding that the Government would act quickly to fix steel prices if they got out of hand as they did then.

It is interesting to note that Mr. Replogle's division, in fixing the price of bars and shapes and plates in 1917, established a common Chicago-Pittsburgh base price. The steel people strongly objected to the elimination— even for the duration of the war—of the Pittsburgh-plus pricing system, terming it revolutionary. Yet eventually, in the early 1920's, the U. S. Steel Corporation voluntarily abandoned the Pittsburgh-plus system.

As part and parcel of the announcement and the agreement, three principles of policy were stated: First, that there should be no reduction in the present rate of wages; second, that the prices above named should be made to the public and to the Allies as well as to the Government; and, third, that the steel men had pledged themselves to exert every effort necessary to keep up the production to the maximum of the past, so long as the war should last. At the same time the President directed the War Industries Board to take such measures of control over distribution as would be required as a corollary to price control.

Coke was reduced from $12.75 to $6; pig iron from $60 to $33; steel bars from $5 to $2.90; shapes from $6 to $3; and plates from $22 to $3.25. It will be remembered that many contract prices prevailing in September were much lower than the open-market prices quoted here, and others were materially higher, plates having sold as high as $15 per 100 pounds. It was quite as much the object of the Government to stabilize the market at a point which would effect a maximum of production as to scale down prices from higher levels. While the fixed prices averaged considerably above prewar normal, they were not above the average advance in the prices of commodities and they were far below the prices paid by the Allies and by industries before we entered the war.

This agreement between the War Industries Board and the steel manufacturers resulted in an enormous saving in the war program, which some authorities estimate in excess of a thousand million dollars a year.

Following the same general procedure, on October 11, 1917, prices were fixed on intermediate products—blooms, billets, slabs, sheet bars, wire rods, shell bars, and skelp. In the meantime an important reorganization took place in respect to the committees through whom the Government control was to be administered. The old iron and steel committee of the Council of National Defense was succeeded by the American Iron and Steel Institute, which became the formal and authoritative spokesman of the industry, representing the interests of the industry and not the Government in all cases of negotiation and agreement. The steel manufacturers formed committees under the Iron and Steel Institute for the purpose of furnishing information to the War Industries Board, and for the purpose of negotiating with the Board in behalf of the industry, these committees not representing nor acting for the Government in any capacity, although working in close cooperation in helping to meet the demands as given through the director of steel supply.

The prices for intermediate steel products were worked out by the two parties to the case conferring among themselves and with each other, and thus the agreement of October 11 was reached.[5] On November 5, 1917, maximum prices were fixed on finished steel products.[6] It will be noted that these prices were for basic products only.

In order to control fully the prices in this industry, a very large schedule of differentials, or prices for products which vary from the basic types, had to be worked out. The problem of calculating these was assigned to the industry itself, and the work was accomplished by a committee of the American Iron and Steel Institute. These differentials were promulgated by the committee directly to the industry, but when once announced they were given the same application in all policies as those prices fixed specifically by the President through the War Industries Board or later through the price-fixing committee. It should be noted that the great bulk of the basic price fixing of iron and steel during the war was done by the War Industries Board before the price-fixing committee got started in March, 1918. While several revisions were later made, relatively few changes of significance were necessary. The original prices were renewed every three months after considerable discussion between the Government and the industry.

Production during 1918, under fixed prices, fell a little below production in 1917. But it can hardly be said that price fixing was a significant cause. The iron and steel industry, in common with all industries, suffered during the winter from the transportation tie-up. The decline of $4\frac{1}{2}$ per cent in the output of pig iron can be traced to the interruption in the movement of ore and coke. Steel ingots increased about 2 per cent over the previous year. This was accomplished through the use of more scrap and the closer paring down of pig-iron stocks usually carried over.

The transportation difficulties were having such an adverse effect on the operations of war industries, that they were the subject of many conferences between the Railroad Administration and the War Industries Board. The director of steel supply finally, to eliminate cross-hauls, rearranged many contracts, some of which had been placed directly with the steel manufacturers at varying prices on a strictly competitive basis by the nations at war and naturally placed with-

[5] See Appendix XV for prices of intermediate steel products as fixed October 11, 1917.

[6] See Appendix XVI for the schedule of prices on finished steel products fixed November 5, 1917.

out regard to the transportation factor. To illustrate: A Buffalo steel manufacturer was making an enormous tonnage of projectile steel to be shipped in bar form to a Cincinnati forge plant to be forged into projectile forgings, which were in turn to be shipped back to Buffalo for machining into the finished projectile. A steel plant within 50 miles of Cincinnati was making projectile bars which were being sent to Buffalo for forging and machining. The differential in price of the several contracts was very great, but after a number of conferences which the director of steel supply had with the various manufacturers involved, arrangements were made to have the steel bars rolled in Buffalo shipped to a near-by plant and machine shop for finishing, and in turn the Cincinnati forge man was supplied by the steel mills in his district.

There were hundreds of changes of this character, which, while difficult of solution, were fully justified by the transportation situation, which had become a very important factor in our war program. Many millions of ton-miles and an enormous amount of money and time were saved by these transfers.

The natural corollary of price fixing, where demand exceeds supply and the price fixing is resorted to chiefly to prevent high prices, is control over distribution. When demand greatly exceeds supply and purchasers are not able by paying higher prices than their competitors to buy the right to have their orders filled first, because maximum prices are fixed, the result is a reversal of the ordinary processes of salesmanship and distribution, and a confusion results in which personal elements and ambitions are likely to play an important part. Unified direction is necessary if anything like efficiency is to characterize the processes of distribution and production.

The earlier War Industries Board made its first attempt to control distribution by the process of priorities on September 21, 1917, when it issued (1) priorities circular No. 1, directing the sequence in which orders for iron and steel and their products should be filled, and (2) priorities circular No. 2, explaining the method of obtaining and using priorities certificates for expediting manufacture on war orders. The problems of assisting in securing transportation and fuel and in relieving special situations as they arose, together with continuous studies of possible further control, which might be necessary to meet the situation as it developed, engaged the attention of the director of steel and his staff during the winter. By July of 1918 it had become clear that very rigid and far-reaching control over the distribution of steel was necessary.

The meaning and use of priorities and priority certificates, as explained elsewhere, not only as applied to the iron and steel industry, but to all industries in which there was a real or threatened shortage, had become current by this time. But the far-reaching and complex nature of the civilian needs and the indirect war needs for iron and steel, combined with the increasing shortage due to the increasing war program, brought on a situation requiring further control than the first application of the priority principle could accomplish.

It became a question either of eliminating industries from the bottom of the list until enough material could be turned to the satisfaction of the war need, or of rationing so as to preserve all industries at least in skeleton form. The rationing principle was adopted, and on July 22, 1918, to carry out the policy of the Board, the priorities commissioner issued circular No. 5, which summed up the situation and completed the system of regulations which made the iron and steel trade in effect a Government-controlled industry.

Priorities Circular No. 4, issued July 1, 1918, restated all rules and regulations governing priority in production and superseded all previous regulations on the subject, except outstanding priority certificates. The system of ratings to be used in the priority certificates was set forth and each class defined. Then a list of automatic classifications was set forth and explained. Such a system was found necessary in order to relieve the Board of the work involved in issuing an impossible number of priority certificates. The form and effect of the priority certificate was explained, and an application blank, as well as a blank form of the certificate, was printed in the circular.

The meaning of the priority classification of an order was explained to the effect that a manufacturer should give to an order marked AA only such precedence over orders of a lower classification as might be necessary to insure delivery on the date specified in the order; that it did not mean that work should cease on orders of a lower classification or that the order should be completed and delivery made in advance of orders taking a lower classification if this was not necessary to effect delivery within the time specified. "The one to whom a priority certificate is directed or with whom the order taking an automatic classification is placed should make his own production plans, so as to get the maximum of efficiency out of his operations, making all deliveries at the times contracted for, if possible, and where this is not possible, giving precedence to the orders taking the higher classification." When two orders have the same priority classification, the date of delivery contracted for will control, unless this should operate to delay the delivery required by an earlier order of the same class, in which event the earlier order will have precedence in delivery. The dates of the orders and not the dates of the certificates are controlling.

On July 3, 1918, a joint circular [7] was issued to the steel industry by the priorities commissioner and the director of steel supply, setting forth instructions for administering a resolution passed by the War Industries Board on June 6, 1918. This resolution confirmed an agreement which had been reached as a result of several conferences between the Steel Division and the American Iron and Steel Institute. That agreement provided that no pig iron or steel manufactured products should be shipped or delivered except (1) on priority certificates, or (2) after orders, covered by priority certificates, should have been taken care of, producers might utilize their facilities to fill orders of their customers not covered by certificates, provided such orders were embraced within the classification of purposes entitled to preference treatment, as determined by the Priorities Board,[8] and further that, after orders of these two classes had been taken care of, producers might ship other orders to other customers "subject to the approval in writing of the director of steel supply first had and obtained."

The joint circular provided a method of applying for the approval in writing of the director of steel supply. It explained that it was not the purpose of the resolution of June 6 to completely postpone all orders under "classification of purposes" to all priority orders, but that they might be given such place as would not interfere with the filling of priority orders. Priority certificates were issued at this time in classes AA, A, and B. Orders falling within the "classification of purposes" clause were now designated as class C, and could be filled without a certificate of rating. All other orders were designated by this circular as class D, and required the written approval of the director of steel supply.

In line with what has been said above, it was not the purpose of the Board to cut off all orders falling in class D. This would have been equivalent to elimination of certain industries for the rest of the war period. Instead it was decided to ration these industries, but the resolution of June 6 placed all such industries in the position of plaintiff before the Board. They would have been automatically

---

[7] See Appendix XVII for copy of joint circular signed by Parker and Replogle.
[8] See Appendix VIII for this classification of purposes, which is explained more fully in chap. 4, Part 1.

ruined without the help of the Board, for there was not steel enough to go around.

In order that the director of steel supply might not be burdened with more applications than he could give attention to, this circular gave automatic approval in class C of all orders not exceeding 5 tons, requiring, however, that manufacturers filling such orders should certify to him once a month that they believed that it was in the public interest that such orders should be filled. For all other orders in class D, the manufacturer was required to file an application in duplicate to the director of steel supply on blanks which he furnished. The director would indorse on the bottom of the application the word "Granted" or "Declined," and return one copy to the applicant. If granted, the manufacturer was allowed to ship on such terms and under such conditions as might be imposed by the director of steel supply.

The circular also provided rules for the jobbers. Orders from jobbers were rated as class B–4, and a pledge was exacted from each jobber, upon his placing an order with the manufacturer, to the effect that he was not hoarding the stocks, and further that the stocks, which this order was to replace, had been sold for essential uses, as defined by the Priorities Division.[9]

Priorities Circular No. 5, July 22, 1918, set forth the program for rationing iron and steel to those less essential industries whose existence depended upon their getting at least a portion of their normal supply of this commodity. The nature of the plan is best explained in the words of the circular itself:

Sec. IV. *Rationing industries.*—As it is obviously impossible to supply all industries utilizing iron and steel in their activities with their normal supply, the War Industries Board, through its Priorities Division, cooperating with the commodity section dealing with the particular industry or product involved, with the Conservation Division and representatives of other interested Government agencies, has inaugurated a system of industrial hearings in which committees representing the entire industry appear and present, (a) the normal requirements of such industry for iron and steel, (b) their reasonable requirements under war conditions, (c) the stocks now on hand in each plant, and (d) the fuel consumed, and all other pertinent facts.

A portion at least of the product of nearly every industry may be properly classed as a direct or indirect war requirement or essential to the civilian population, but in many the percentage of nonessentiality predominates. On the

---

[9] See Appendix XVII for the rules applying to the purchases of jobbers, as contained in the joint circular of July 3, 1918.

other hand, nearly every industry, including so-called war industries, has a percentage of nonessentiality in its production.

It is the policy of the War Industries Board, through the hearings mentioned, to take counsel with each industry, determine the extent to which it can and should as a war measure curtail its production—and particularly curtail its consumption of iron and steel—limiting its output to essential uses as far as practicable, but without destroying or unnecessarily injuring any industry or legitimate business. On these hearings the chairman of the Conservation Division or his representatives give the industry the benefit of their expert knowledge and research into methods of standardization and substitution, and cooperate with the industry in (a) reducing needless lines, varieties, and sizes of products, thereby securing economy in manufacture and reducing the volume of stocks which the manufacturer, wholesaler, and dealer are required to carry, (b) through the elimination of wasteful styles, models, and methods, greatly conserving materials, and (c) through the substitution of products or materials not needed for those that are needed for war work, conserving the latter without unnecessarily reducing the output of the industry.

When the maximum conservation of materials and products has been attained through these processes of standardization, substitution, and curtailment, the representatives of the War Industries Board participating in these conferences indicate to the industry their views as to the maximum consumption by the industries of the materials and products in question, treating the industry as a unit where such a course is practicable.

The chief of the commodity section dealing with the particular industry then prepares a schedule apportioning such indicated maximum of materials or products to each plant on a basis which will enable each member of the industry to procure the same per cent of his normal production as all other members, taking into account the existing stocks of each. When this has been done, each plant places its orders for the amount apportioned to it with its regular sources of supply, and such orders take a class C rating.

The war-service committees of those industries which have not as yet participated in such hearings will be given an appointment on application to the priorities commissioner or to the chief of the appropriate commodity section of the War Industries Board.

Following this announcement, and pursuant to its terms, a series of prolonged conferences was held with each industry of the less essential class requiring iron and steel in important amounts. The industries were usually represented by their war service committees, but any individual member was privileged to appear, and frequently did appear in person. The hearings were conducted by Edwin B. Parker, priorities commissioner, or by Rhodes S. Baker, assistant priorities commissioner. At these hearings appeared also the chairman of the Conservation Division, the chief of the Labor Section, the chief or chiefs of such commodity sections as were interested, and other representatives of the Government as their interests appeared. After the facts had been fully developed at one of these hearings and from such other sources as was necessary, and after a tentative agreement had been reached with the representatives of the trade, a brief memorandum of the essential facts and of the recommendations was presented in conference to the industrial adjustment committee of the Priorities Board. Messrs. Parker and Baker were members of this committee. The representatives of the industry were asked to remain in Washinton until the committee should act, in order that they might give their approval to the regulations before the circular of instructions, embodying the regulations, was issued to the trade.

The industrial adjustments committee was composed of one member each from the War Trade Board, the Food Administration, the Railroad Administration, the Fuel Administration, the Shipping Board, the War Labor Policies Board, and the Treasury War Loan Staff, together with the priorities commissioner.[10] As soon as this committee ratified a program of curtailment or rationing, the chief of the appropriate commodity section would prepare, under the direction of the Priorities Division, a circular addressed to all firms engaged in the trade, embodying the regulations which had been agreed upon. It was then the duty of such section to see to it that the regulations were carried into effect. These regulations represented, in form at least, an agreement between the Government and the industry.

As has been pointed out, the Government was coming to have a stronger position in the negotiation of a bargain. With the distribution of fuel, transportation, and iron and steel definitely in the hands of the Government, few factories could function except by the grace of the Government. Thus it was that, in return for the privilege of securing steel, fuel, and transportation, any industry or individual firm would readily agree to abide by such regulations as the Government saw fit to impose.

Under this procedure rationing and curtailment, involving substantial savings of iron or steel, was instituted during the summer and fall of 1918, over such industries as passenger automobiles, pianos, cutlery, stoves, enameled ware, refrigerators, clothes wringers, corsets, metal beds, boilers, radiators, baby carriages, gas stoves and appliances, tin plate, talking machines, agricultural implements, farm tractors, bicycles,

---

[10] The minutes of this committee give a very concise and satisfactory record of the series of resolutions, by which a large number of industries were rationed or curtailed. They are contained in the files of the War Industries Board, but have not been published.

electric heating apparatus, oil stoves, watches, watch cases, sewing machines, metal stamps, electric fans, safes and vaults, lawn mowers, pottery, padlocks, builder's hardware, scales and balances, sporting arms, cash registers, rat and animal traps, talking machine needles, ice cream freezers, vacuum cleaners, road making machinery, cast iron boilers and radiators.

The makers of passenger automobiles had unbalanced stocks in their factories and could not go forward with their production without aid in filling them out. On August 14, they were put on a rationing schedule for the six months ending December 31, 1918, which provided for a production not exceeding 25 per cent of production during the calendar year 1917. The manufacturers pledged themselves to limit their purchases of supplies to such as were absolutely necessary to match up their stocks on hand; they pledged themselves, also, to release, on request of the War Industries Board, to other manufacturers such surpluses of particular stocks as were not necessary for production as limited or for war work. Sworn reports of stocks had been rendered before the meeting, and further sworn reports were provided for in the agreement. These reports were used as a basis for calculating the savings and for determining particular cases of distribution, when such determination should be necessary on the part of the Steel Division.

On September 17, following the report by the priorities commissioner that a tentative agreement had been reached in conference with the manufacturers of farm implements and tractors, the following resolution was passed by the industrial adjustments committee:

Be it resolved, that effective October 1, 1918, on a 12-months schedule, the agricultural implement and farm tractor manufacturers be curtailed in their use of iron and steel to 75 per cent of their consumption for the calendar year ending September 30, 1918.

These are typical examples of the action of the industrial adjustments committee with regard to the long list of commodities mentioned above. The first step in the administration of such resolutions was the issuance of circular after circular to all the members of each trade. These circulars, after reciting that an agreement had been reached with the representatives of the particular industry, to which each was addressed, would set forth the conditions under which priority certificates would be issued to any manufacturer to aid him in obtaining the raw materials necessary to accomplish the limited production which had been agreed to. They were signed by the priorities commissioner.[11]

---

[11] All circulars were printed and copies may be found in the files of the War Industries Board.

Some 30 circulars of this character were issued to manufacturers of commodities whose chief constituent materials were iron and steel. In many cases these industries became problems of sufficient importance to require separate commodity sections in the War Industries Board to supervise their activities. In such cases, there will be further comment in this report in the chapters dealing with those sections.

The iron and steel industry was, on the whole, one of the most important centers of approach to the control over the vast number of manufacturing industries which the progress of the war was making necessary. The difficulty and complexity of the undertaking was realized by no one more fully than by those who were engaged in it. It is possible that mistakes might have been made. But it is believed that central control, involving as it did an almost impossible amount and quality of work on the part of those at the apex, resulted in advantages of far greater importance than the individual cases of loss and distress which might have accompanied it.

CHAPTER 3

Copper and Brass

COPPER

SECOND ONLY to steel in its importance, as a basic metal required for war, is copper. And in the spring of 1917 the copper market pointed just as unerringly as that of steel to the necessity for some kind of Government control. Electrolytic copper sold around 16 cents a pound before 1914. It was selling at 35.74 cents in March, 1917. The rise had been steady except during the short period in 1916 when an early peace seemed probable.

This country controls the bulk of the copper in the world. Demand, due to war requirements of the Allies, was far outrunning supply for two years before we entered the conflict. And it was evident that the situation would grow steadily worse as our participation in the war was enlarged. Maximum production was of extreme importance. Thus it was that copper became one of the first problems to engage the attention of Mr. Baruch when he came to Washington early in March, 1917, to take charge of raw materials as a member of the advisory commission of the Council of National Defense.

There were two schools of thought touching the question. The one argued that, as increase of production was the essential factor, the rise in prices should not be interfered with, but the accumulation of undue profits should be taken care of through excess profit taxes; the other, which included Messrs. Summers, Meyer, and Baruch, believed that there was a limit to which high prices would be effective in stimulating production, and that, if advances in this and other commodities were allowed to take their course, not only would the readjustments incident to peace bring catastrophe with them, but it would also be next to impossible to finance the war. They believed that control over prices and excess profit taxes were both necessary.

Their first action was an appeal to the large producing and smelting interests direct. This appeal resulted, on March 20, 1917, in an understanding by which the Army and Navy were enabled to purchase their requirements, estimated at that time to be 45,510,000 pounds, to be delivered quarterly for a year, at 16.6739 cents a pound. This represented the actual average selling price obtained by the United Metals Selling Co. over a period of 10 years, 1907 to 1916. The market quotations for that date were 35.74 cents per pound, and sales were being made as high as 37 cents. The copper industry was the first one to come forward with its offer in the industrial preparedness campaign. This early offer of the copper trade, followed rapidly as it was by several other trades, to sell to their own Government its war needs at prewar prices had an important psychological effect upon prices generally. Eugene Meyer, jr.,[1] originally proposed the arrangement, and it was Daniel Guggenheim and John D. Ryan who brought about the agreement on the side of the copper trade. Market prices began to decline from this date, but they did not fall rapidly.

Meanwhile war broke out and the increasing copper requirements found the market with scarcely enough copper to meet contract needs, even by calling reserve stocks into use, watching supplies, and carefully conserving every pound. The necessity for stimulating increased production seemed paramount. The Federal Trade Commission was asked to examine into the current costs of production.

Another order for 60,000,000 pounds was placed on June 27 by the War Department for early delivery, with the open market standing at the time at 32.57 cents. After much discussion the price determination was left until the Federal Trade Commission should report on costs. Shortly afterward the Secretary of the Navy announced that he would pay down for Navy copper 75 per cent of 25 cents a pound, leaving the other 25 per cent for adjustment when the cost of production should have been determined.

The announcement of this policy, which was interpreted in some quarters as the price the Government intended to fix, gave concern to the markets. Strikes or threatened strikes at the mines in Arizona pointed to serious curtailment of production. The miners were being paid on a sliding wage scale, adjusted to the price of copper.[2] Their

---

[1] Eugene Meyer, jr., an investment banker widely regarded as one of the best-informed men in "The Street" on copper, first went to Washington as one of Mr. Baruch's aides in the raw materials division of the Council of National Defense. He later became chairman of the War Finance Corporation—an agency which, to a large extent, served as a guide when Mr. Meyer, as its first Chairman, set up the Reconstruction Finance Corporation under Herbert Hoover in 1932. He is, today, the publisher of the Washington *Post*, and member of the National Defense Mediation Board.

[2] These sliding scales provide for the minimum wages of $3.50 per day of eight hours for miners and men employed underground, and $4.50 for mechanics, with many higher classifications where skilled labor is necessary; the minimum to apply

wages were based on 27-cent copper at this time. They threatened to strike if these wages should be reduced, and did strike wherever they were reduced.

The producers continued to supply copper to the Government, but refused to bill it at 18¾ cents. The indebtedness of the Government to producers soon ran into millions of dollars. Refineries were short of blister and were running at only 60 to 75 per cent capacity, but the curtailment was not due to the delayed payments.

In the meantime the War Industries Board, upon which were representatives of the Army and Navy, had been created and in its examination of price problems became convinced that 18¾ cents would curtail production. The Board agreed to advance 22½ cents to the producers and to leave the difference between 22½ cents and 25 cents to the findings of the Federal Trade Commission.

The demands of the Allies were an equally important consideration at this time. During 1916 England and France had purchased over 660,000,000 pounds of copper in the United States in blocks so large as to be featured in the trade news. In September, 1916, 448,000,000 pounds were purchased at 27 cents. This had reduced stocks everywhere to lowest level and caused a highly speculative market. While their purchases in the spring of 1917 were in less dramatic quantities, they still continued to take such copper as they could secure.

In August, while the discussion of prices and production was at its height, it was officially made known to the War Industries Board that the French and British were in the market for 60,000,000 pounds. The Board decided to call the producers into conference and, bearing in mind their firm offer to the Government of copper for 25 cents per pound, make them a tentative offer of 20 cents for this quantity. This offer was made at a meeting on August 7, but it was agreed that the price should be subject to revision, upward or downward, later.[3] After the representatives of the trade withdrew from the meeting, it was moved that if the copper producers refused to enter into this agreement the Government would proceed to commandeer the necessary supply. When the joint meeting was resumed it appeared that the opposition of the industry to the 20 cents, and indeed to sales at a memorandum price at all, was very determined,

---

when copper sells below 15 cents per pound, and 25 cents additional per day to every man employed to be paid for each 2-cents advance in the price of copper above 15 cents. The result had been that for over a year wages were based on a price of copper at 27 cents and above, so that miners were receiving $5 to $5.25 per day, and all mechanics $6.25 to $6.50 per day.

[3] See War Industries Board Minute Book, August 7, 1917.

and the arguments in support of the opposition seemed worthy of most serious consideration. On August 8 the Board passed the following resolution:

That as the copper emergency requires immediate action necessary to secure a supply for our Government and our allies, the Board endeavor to secure from the copper interests the needs of ourselves and our allies at a price to be fixed when we shall see the report of the Federal Trade Commission as to the costs and for purposes of payment on account of deliveries, a tentative price of 22½ cents to be fixed with the understanding that this price shall in no way be taken into consideration when the final price is to be determined.

The result of the controversy was that on August 16, 1917, the copper interests agreed to deliver 77,000,000 pounds to the Allies on a memorandum, no price to be paid pending the final fixing of a price after an investigation.

By September 5, 1917, the Federal Trade Commission had made its report on costs of producing copper, the War Industries Board had studied it, and at a meeting that day reached a conclusion to fix the price of electrolytic copper at 22 cents per pound.

In order to acquaint the copper interests with the position of the Board, to try to reach an agreement with them, and to secure their cooperation, their representatives were called to Washington on September 11. The representatives were told that the Board believed that 22 cents per pound f. o. b. New York for refined electrolytic copper, 99.93 per cent pure, was a fair price and would allow the producers a reasonable profit. They were told that the price should hold for a certain period only, and could then be revised upward or downward; further, that it was to be applicable alike to the Government, the Allies, and the public, and that wages to labor should remain the same notwithstanding the sliding scale agreement.

The industry objected. Their position was presented orally at the meeting, and three days later by a long memorandum. They declared flatly that the copper interests could not control the price to the public at a point much below 25 cents, and that, if the Government fixed 22 cents as the price, the small high-cost producers would not voluntarily cooperate in selling at the fixed price. They pointed out that acute labor troubles would result should the sliding scale of rates be disturbed. They showed how impracticable it would be for the Government to commandeer the numerous small high-cost mines. They gave evidence to show that if 22 cents were finally fixed, it would be impossible to obtain the cooperation of the majority of mine owners.

The difficulty was not with the large producers, in whose hands, of course, the bulk of the business is concentrated, but the copper industry also embraces a large number of smaller high-cost producers, whose product was also needed in the extraordinary emergency. Everybody agreed that the considerable output of the small high-cost producers was indispensable.

The copper interests pointed out with particular care the important bearing of wages on copper prices. It is true that there are few raw materials of which so large a percentage of the cost of production goes to pay wages. They pointed out that the average wages of all men in the copper industry had been advanced 50 per cent over those of 1915, and that they could not be lowered without serious consequences. Labor shortage and labor unrest might easily make it necessary to raise them. If wages were to be maintained, the small plants could not keep open on a selling price of less than 25 cents. Their memorandum contained the following proposal:

While some of the low-cost producers will show a large profit at 25 cents, some of the largest and practically all of the small producers cannot show more than the usual peace-time profit at that price, and if depletion of mines is considered, their profit would probably be less than in normal times at average prices. We believe that it would be to the interest of the Government to pay 25 cents per pound and to take all of the production of all of the mines of the country at that price, retaining all the copper which is needed for this Government and for its Allies, and selling the balance at the same price, or approximately the same price, to the public.

Following the conference in Washington of September 11 the leading copper producers met in New York on September 14 and voted to propose to the War Industries Board a compromise price of 23½ cents. In their communication they said:

With one exception those present agreed that if your committee would unanimously recommend a price of 23½ cents * * * we would still be able to get the practical result that we are aiming for, that is, pretty nearly maximum production; therefore, I would say that if your committee would agree to 23½ cents we can pledge the copper industry almost as a whole to use every possible means to secure a maximum production and to maintain the present scale of wages, and I am satisfied we can succeed.

On September 21, 1917, the price of 23½ cents was definitely fixed in the form of an agreement between the Government and the producers. It was approved by the President, subject to revision after four months; the short period being established for the purpose of allowing any producer, consumer, or other interested party to appear and present reasons, if any, for increasing or decreasing the price. It is interesting in this connection to note that while many producers appeared with arguments urging increases, no consumer, public or private, nor official of our own or other Government, appeared to object to the prices as too high. The fact is the fixed price of copper represented a smaller advance over prewar normal than that of perhaps any other commodity. This was the first negotiated price-fixing arrangement ever established by the United States Government. As part of the agreement the producers pledged themselves not to reduce wages; to sell their products to the Allies and the general public at the same price as that to be paid by the Government; to exert every effort to maintain maximum production during the war; and to take the necessary measures to prevent copper from falling into the hands of speculators. The Army, Navy, and other Government agencies interested in the purchase of copper participated in the negotiations.

The industry, though dissatisfied, had finally acceded. They believed that at least it gave them a definite program and would bring stability. But within a week many questions began to arise as to how the new scheme was to be administered. This was a new kind of undertaking both for the Government and the industry.[4]

A letter of inquiry was addressed to the Board October 19, 1917, and its prompt answer contained the Government's solution of several of the most important problems.

(1) That all outstanding bona fide contracts between producers and consumers might be consummated at contract prices. Some of these were at 27 cents a pound. But under the priority agreement our Government had first call and the Allies second, and as these two purchasers consumed nearly all the supply, few high-priced orders could be filled.

(2) The rule was laid down that all contract sales made for delivery after the expiration of the present fixed price (Jan. 21, 1918) should be made at a price subject to any revision which the Board might see fit later to make.

(3) In answer to the complaint that outside dealers and brokers were trading and quoting at 28, 29, and 30 cents for copper, a control

---

[4] The *Wall Street Journal* of September 27, 1917, said in this connection: "Both producers and consumers are 'up in the air' due to lack of details in connection with carrying out of the proposed plans for handling the copper market, and this condition will continue until Washington furnishes more detailed advices as to what can be done and what should not be attempted under the new order of things."

committee or selling agency was established, which by buying and selling at the fixed price was designed to crowd the speculators from the market.

(4) It was urged that differentials be established for modifications from electrolytic copper, and particularly that prices for scrap be fixed. But it was ruled that no other prices would be fixed.

The price of 23½ cents was continued until July 2, 1918, when it was increased to 26 cents and remained at that figure until control ceased. By the spring of 1918, many complaints of hardship were coming to the Board from the numerous small high-cost producers. The Government was requiring about 93 per cent of the output at this time, 49 per cent being consumed by the United States and 44 per cent by the Allies.

Maximum production was absolutely required and the Government could afford to take no risk of causing a reduction. The price-fixing committee voted on May 22, 1918, to continue the 23½ cents until August 15. But a few days later, when evidence had been shown them of advances in freight rates and increases and prospective increases in costs of labor, which were making the smaller producers run at such great loss that they would have to close down, the committee voted that the price should be raised to 26 cents on July 2.[5] A committee, formed to represent 15 of the smaller companies, presented the case at Washington.

The fixing of copper prices, as was the case of steel, brought with it the necessity of control in other directions. Control over the distribution of copper was far less difficult than that of steel. While civilian uses of copper are very numerous and very important, they are not nearly so indispensable, particularly for a short period, as are those of iron and steel. The war required over 90 per cent of the copper which we could produce. This simply meant that civilian use had to be practically suspended, and this was accomplished not so much by priority control in the sense in which that process was used on steel; but it was accomplished through the purchase by the War Department of a high percentage of the copper and its distribution to the manufacturers of armaments as they needed it.

The principal responsibility of the Board, after the market had once been stabilized, was to watch over production and take care that it was not diminished; to guard against speculation; and to keep the small producers encouraged to continue their furnaces. The

---

[5] The cost sheets of the smelting and refining companies showed losses. One and a half cents of the advance went to smelters and refiners, one cent to producers.

copper producers' committee, at the direction of the Board, allocated the various orders.

In October, 1917, Eugene Meyer, jr., was placed in charge of the Board's section on nonferrous metals. He gave particular attention to the problem of maintaining adequate production and the proper distribution of copper, but did not take part in the price fixing. He remained in this position until March, 1918, when he became a director in the War Finance Corporation, and Pope Yeatman [6] succeeded him and remained chief until the end. * * * [7]

Despite many hardships and obstacles, the American copper producers played their part and contributed to the successful prosecution of the war in a way second to no other industry. There are ample grounds for the belief that the prices fixed by the Government worked hardship on many operators; and to add to the distress, the signing of the armistice on November 11 left them, like producers of other raw materials, with very large stocks on hand, produced at the highest costs in the history of the trade, and with no large orders booked.

ZINC

Zinc, commonly known in the trade as spelter, was never a serious problem for the War Industries Board. It has two important war uses. Sheet zinc is used for lining the boxes in which all explosives are packed, and zinc enters about 33 per cent in the manufacture of brass, which was so important in the shipbuilding program, and to a lesser extent in the manufacture of munitions. In normal times the galvanizing industry uses 60 per cent of our total consumption.

Zinc was one of the metals which the commissioner of raw materials took up in March, 1917, as part of the general preparation carried on just before war was declared. An agreement was obtained from Edgar Palmer, president of the New Jersey Zinc Co., to supply such quantities as the Government might need at 12 cents per pound for sheet zinc, the prevailing market price being about 20 cents.

During the war the Conservation Division of the Board relieved the industry of some of its surplus production by suggesting substitutions of zinc for tin, lead, aluminum, and nickel, when shortages ap-

---

[6] Pope Yeatman has been for many years one of the country's best-known mining engineers.

[7] As in the chapter on the Iron and Steel Industry, the deleted material sketched something of the economy of the copper industry. Similar deletions have been made in some other chapters dealing with the commodity sections where, it is felt, they do not detract from the narrative of wartime experience.

peared in the latter metals. Zinc was substituted for lead and copper in the coffin industry—quite a large item. Zinc castings supplanted brass in some instances.

Domestic production, constituting about one-third of the world's output, is more than adequate for our needs. Belgium, Germany, Australia, Austria, and Great Britain are the other producers. When the war broke out in Europe and Germany, Belgium, and Austria were eliminated, large foreign markets were opened for American spelter. In July, 1914, our exports were 157 tons; in September they were 19,045 tons. Considering our total annual production of 700,000 tons, this sudden demand from abroad was reflected extraordinarily in prices. Starting in November, 1914, and culminating in June, 1915, prices rose from 5.08 cents per pound to 22.50 cents, or approximately 350 per cent.

One of the largest low-cost producers closed just as the export demand began, and by the beginning of 1915 the home market was being stimulated by the buying of munitions manufacturers who were getting lucrative contracts from the Allies, and for whom the price of spelter represented such a small percentage that it was of little moment. Galvanizers were almost put out of business. During this period smelters were expanding, extinct coal burning plants were being resurrected, and new works constructed. An over-production soon brought a depression of prices, but they went back to 21 cents again in March, 1916. From this time prices began to fall, and with one exception, about the beginning of 1917, continued to fall throughout the war period.

The vacillations of this industry are largely accounted for by the fact that in the Joplin (Mo.) district, where about 35 per cent of our output is produced, the ore is readily accessible and easily concentrated, so that the miner needs little or no capital. While the larger mines of Montana, Idaho, Colorado, and Utah have well equipped works, the whole industry is affected by the simplicity of the operations at Joplin. The refining plants are easily expanded by erecting additional batteries of retorts, and are easily dismantled. During the war the expansion and contraction of smelting capacity was remarkable. They expanded early with rumors of huge requirements, and contracted in 1917 and 1918 when demand did not meet expectation.

Perhaps the most important work of the section was that of studying the uses for zinc which would conserve other metals more difficult to obtain, and to keep the industry encouraged to maintain high production in anticipation of a time when their product would be more needed. With this second point in mind, and for the purpose of insuring a sufficient quantity of the high-grade product needed for war purposes, in the face of a disintegrated and discouraged industry, price fixing was resorted to. There are four grades of zinc, based on the content of cadmium, iron, and lead. The grades range from the purest, grade A or "high grade," through B or "intermediate," and C or "brass special," to D or "prime western." The high grade is used in making the best quality of brass and for rolling sheet zinc; for galvanizing, the prime western, which is by far the most abundant, is used.

The Navy has always required for its brass cartridge cases a grade A zinc, containing 0.07 per cent of cadmium or less. Cadmium cannot be removed by the ordinary distilling process. Only two companies could produce zinc of this specification, the New Jersey Zinc Co. from a pure ore and the Anaconda Copper Mining Co. by the electrolytic process. These two companies could not produce enough for the cartridge cases required by the Navy and the Army together. The section studied the problem with the Army, and specifications allowing up to one-half of 1 per cent cadmium were adopted for the spelter used in the brass of Army cartridge cases. This spelter came to be known as Army grade A.

On February 13, 1918, a maximum price of 12 cents per pound f. o. b. East St. Louis, was set for grade A zinc. This, with the new Army specifications, made it possible for the various companies to produce enough zinc for all cartridge cases required. Plate zinc was fixed at the same time at 14 cents, and sheet zinc at 15 cents.

After prices had been fixed on sheet and plate zinc, a problem in allocations arose. It was deemed important to keep as many as possible of the mines of the Joplin district running. Through the mediation of the section, the zinc rolling mills agreed to pay the miners $75 a ton base on 60 per cent zinc concentrates, and the mills agreed to distribute their buying proportionately among the mines of the district which produced this grade. The miners formed an association and the section appointed an allocating committee of the association to receive the requirements of the rolling mills and allocate them in due proportion. * * *

BRASS

As brass is a mixture of varying ratios of copper and zinc, together with small quantities of lead, tin, nickel, or other metals, our problem of producing enough of it for the war depended largely on the production of the two metals which have just been studied.

About 70 per cent of the brass industry of the country is concentrated in the Naugatuck Valley of Connecticut, which was part of the congested district during the war. But the equipment and skill required in brass works made it impracticable for the war-time development to take place outside of this district. The number of mixtures used in the composition of brass is very great, but the commonest forms are "high brass," which takes about 67 per cent copper and 33 per cent spelter; "low brass," 80 per cent copper and 20 per cent spelter; and "commercial bronze," 90 per cent copper and 10 per cent spelter. "Muntz" metal is 60 per cent copper and 40 per cent spelter. "Nickel silver," called German silver before the war, takes copper 72 per cent, spelter 10 per cent, and nickel 18 per cent, though the percentage of nickel varies with the purpose. "Cupro nickel" is a mixture of 85 per cent copper and 15 per cent nickel. This last-named metal is used for the jacket of bullets for small arms ammunition. We produced a maximum of 4,000,000 pounds a month of all types during the war.

The most important use of brass for war is in the manufacture of cartridge cases of all sizes up to 4.7 inches, the product coming from the brass mills in the form of disks. Demands for this purpose, including those of our Allies, were estimated in August, 1918, at 885,000 pounds per day. The small arms cartridge program called for 1,235,000 pounds of brass per day, although production never reached beyond one-half of the program.

Brass tubing for condensers for steam engines, both stationary and those used on ships, made heavy demands on the industry. Brass rod was needed in great quantities for the manufacture of time fuses and high explosive fuses for shells. Fine, flexible brass wire was required in great quantities by the Signal Corps for outpost wire. Brass wire is an absolute essential in the paper making industry, where it is used in the form of wire netting, which wears out rapidly.

In September, 1918, the Signal Corps asked for 1,500,000 pounds of outpost wire per month. The supply of this was still a subject of concern when the armistice came. Brass rod for fuses was produced in this country for the Allies in great quantity, and our productive capacity had been so increased that no shortage was felt until July 1, 1918, when our increased military program was announced, and France at the same time asked for new orders to be delivered at the rate of 6,000,000 pounds per month. Plans for meeting this situation were making satisfactory progress when the end came.

The Brass Section of the War Industries Board was formed on

April 6, 1918, with Everett Morss [8] as chief. At that time the only important shortage was in tubing, both brass and copper. The section first set to work to make supply of this product meet war needs. Semi-monthly reports on tubing were obtained from each manufacturer on blanks furnished by the section. These reports showed orders received, shipments made, and orders on hand for eight groups of brass tubing and six groups of copper tubing. They showed the distribution of all these orders between the Army, Navy, Emergency Fleet, and others. They showed, also, the priority class of each order. These figures were posted to ledger accounts for each company, and a general summary was also made for all companies. This record made it possible for the section, when a source of supply had to be found for any kind of tubing, to determine quickly what company could probably take the order with the least embarassment and with the least interference with other orders of importance.

The shortage became so acute that on June 26, 1918, notice was issued to the mills to make no shipments of tubing after July 10, except on such orders as were covered by priority certificates or by permits issued by the section. The demands for tubing by the Aircraft Production Bureau, while not large in tonnage, were very difficult to handle because the specifications were constantly changing. The bureau placed the problem in the hands of one man, who, by constant reference to the section for general information, carried it through successfully by dealing directly with the mills. It was not until later in the summer of 1918 that concern began to be felt over shortages in brass production other than tubing.

On August 29 representatives of all the brass manufacturers met the section in Washington, and a war service committee for brass manufacturers was appointed to replace the earlier tube committee. Owing to the complications due to the variety of products and the large number of mills, the section did not arrange for detailed reports similar to those on tubing, but instead it had daily or weekly reports from several of the large producers, pending the development of a general scheme of reports which would give the necessary information.

On September 24, an order was issued to all mills to make the acceptance of new orders subject to a permit from the section, and the mills were requested not to ship after November 30 without a

---

[8] Everett Morss (deceased) was a prominent Boston manufacturer of brass products.

permit even on orders taken before September 24. On November 1, the Army was asked to make a new survey of its requirements with the idea in mind of making all possible substitutions for brass, but this plan did not need to be carried out.

The brass facilities of the country increased during the war between 50 and 75 per cent. The total production in 1917 was 1,072,000,000 pounds. Formal price fixing was not resorted to. The price of brass normally varies with the price of copper and spelter, and it was felt that control in the prices of these two articles would be sufficient for the regulation of brass, and this in a broad way proved true, although the shortages in the latter part of 1918 were being definitely reflected in advancing prices which would have made price-fixing necessary if the war had not ended.

CHAPTER 4

Other Metals

IN THE COURSE of the war period several other metal industries producing war necessities had to be encouraged or controlled to a greater or less extent in order that their activities might be shaped to the war program. Separate sections were formed to study and supervise the Ferroalloys,[1] Tin, Aluminum, Lead, Nickel, Quicksilver, Antimony, and Platinum.

FERROALLOYS

Considerable work had been carried on in this field by Mr. Summers and Mr. Replogle before the section was formed in March, 1918, with Hugh W. Sanford[2] as chief. Contact with the industry was maintained through the ferroalloys committee of the American Iron and Steel Institute. The principal commodities which presented themselves as problems to the section were manganese, vanadium, tungsten, zirconium, ferrosilicon, and chromite.

Manganese.—Manganese in some form is essential in the steel industry. It is the purifying element used for deoxidizing and eliminating the dissolved oxygen, from 15 to 20 pounds to the ton of steel being required. It can be used in any one of three forms, corresponding to types of manganese ores as they occur.

(1) Ferromanganese, containing 80 per cent[3] manganese and about 10 per cent iron, is produced from ores containing 40 to 50 per cent manganese and the iron.

(2) Spiegeleisen, containing about 35 per cent manganese and 5 to 40 per cent iron.

(3) Manganese pig iron, produced from iron ore, bearing small percentages of manganese.

The ores occur in a continuous series, containing decreasing quan-

---

[1] The Ferroalloys Section functioned as part of the Chemical Division, but its work will be accounted for in this chapter because it relates so definitely to the steel industry.

[2] Knoxville, Tenn., industrialist.

[3] In May, 1918, the American standard was reduced to 70 per cent to increase the use of the domestic product.

tities of manganese with increasing quantities of iron. Varying quantities of silica are also frequently present and detract from the value.

Low-grade ores are found in great quantities in the United States, but the higher grades occur in Brazil, the Caucasus, and India. Spiegeleisen can be used for the Bessemer steel process, but the high-grade ferromanganese is required for the open-hearth process. Before the war our steel producers got most of their high-grade ferromanganese from England, where the ores had been brought from India and the Near East. This country produced only 2,600 tons of high-grade ore in 1914. The shipping situation made the pre-war practice impossible, and the growing use of the open-hearth process in our expanding steel industry brought about a serious situation. Relief was sought in two directions, chiefly by stimulating domestic production, but to some extent by assisting importation from Brazil.

Everything possible was done to aid domestic production. Priority was given on machinery, on labor, and on railroad transportation. Prices had been allowed to take their own course on the theory that it would stimulate production. Still it was clear by May, 1918, that heavy shortages were threatening. Although it involved a hardship on the steel trade, the problem was relieved by reducing the standard of purity from 80 per cent to 70 per cent, and this made available several hundred thousand tons of American ore of a type which had not been in use.

About the same time the American Iron and Steel Institute made an agreement with the American ore producers to increase prices and stabilize them over a period of one year. They were fixed at $1 per unit, which was three times the price in 1915. American mines produced about 310,000 tons of high-grade ore and 650,000 tons of low-grade ore in 1918.

Imports of ore from Brazil were encouraged, but imports of ferromanganese from England were forbidden, in order to save the shipping from India to England. During May coal ran short in Brazil and the railroad bringing the ore to the seaboard was shut down. About the same time the Government ship *Cyclops*, en route to this country with a cargo of ore, was sunk.

Through the efforts of the section, a special license was obtained for 12,000 tons from England to meet the demand, and the Shipping Board consented to send coal to Brazil and made possible a continuation of that source. The price of high-grade ferromanganese was $37.50 per ton in 1914. It went as high as $400 in June and July, 1917, but was stabilized, chiefly through the efforts of the American Iron and Steel Institute, at $250 a ton during the later half of 1917 and during 1918. The shortage of shipping and the ever increasing submarine menace made it necessary to pay this price in order to get American production.

Manganese ore is used also in the fabrication of dry batteries, but the dominating problem throughout the war period was to secure enough of the high-grade product to supply the steel industry.

Ferrovanadium.—Ferrovanadium is used in small quantities in the production of high-speed and cutting-tool steels, automobile steels, and other castings designed to withstand heavy and repeated dynamic stresses. It is a rare metal, worth in normal times about $2.20 a pound, the price rising during the war to $5.50. The principal source is Peru, whence the ore concentrates are brought to this country by the American Vanadium Co. The ore is packed to the seacoast on llamas from mines which are at a very high altitude and inaccessible. The American Vanadium Co. has considered the construction of automobile roads, and at one time during the war they considered the practicability of using airplanes for the transportation of the ore.

A small quantity is produced in this country as a 2 or 3 per cent by-product of carnotite ore, which is mined for the uranium or radium which it contains. A small percentage comes also from roscoelite ore of Colorado. But the world's chief source of supply is Peru and is owned by one company. Shipments from Peru have been very irregular, and there was a great shortage both in England and in this country during the war. In 1914 imports of 14,500 metric tons of 30 per cent ore concentrates were reported, and in 1915, 3,145 metric tons.

The shortage made it necessary for the section to control the distribution of vanadium, and none was allowed except for war requirements either here or abroad. England was supplied with 50 tons a month, although she asked for 100 tons. Stocks were declining rapidly in 1918, consumption exceeding production by about 30 per cent. Nothing could be done to increase domestic production except at forbidding costs. Every effort was made to increase production in Peru, and it is believed that if the war had continued a satisfactory solution would have been found. The situation with respect to this commodity would warrant the attention of the Government in peace times as a measure of preparedness for war.

Tungsten.—Tungsten was used in the war (1) chiefly in high-speed tool steels; (2) in magnet steels; (3) in valve steels for airplane engines; (4) in hacksaw and low-tungsten steels; and (5) in the form of ductile tungsten for (a) incandescent lamps, (b) Röntgen or X-ray tubes, (c) for electric contacts, and other chemical work. The high-speed steel for machine tools not only involved the greatest tonnage, but was the most essential, for no satisfactory substitute could be found.

Tungsten is produced in quantity in the United States, but is also imported from the Far East and the west coast of South America.

The price of tungsten is measured in terms of units of 20 pounds of 60 per cent WO_3 concentrates. In January, 1913, the price was $7.50 per unit. In April, 1916, it reached its maximum at $80 per unit. The advance was due to the enormous demand for high-speed tool steels needed in meeting contracts for making shells and guns for the Allies. The scarcity of domestic metal was relieved by importing more ores, but greater relief came from an economy in the use of tungsten steels in making tools which was discovered. It was found that a weld could be made between a tungsten steel and ordinary steel so that only the cutting edge need be made from the special alloy. Under these influences prices gradually dropped and remained close to $25 per unit from the middle of 1917 to the close of the war. Practically the entire output of the United States was consumed in direct or indirect war work.

About the time the war ended, a world shortage of about 4,000 tons per year seemed to be approaching. Efforts were made to encourage increased production everywhere, and an international pooling arrangement for its distribution was being considered in London.

Zirconium.—In the spring of 1918 a piece of light armor plate was brought to the Board. It was identified as a zirconium steel alloy. Mr. Summers took it up with the Carborundum Co., and they became interested. In July, 1918, the Ford Motor Co. presented the results of an experiment in the use of zirconium as a steel alloy for the armor plate of light tanks. The section investigated the deposits of zirconium in the United States and in Brazil. The Ordnance Department entered into contract for the purchase from Brazil of 1,200 tons of monosite sands from which the metal is extracted. These plans were just reaching fruition when the war closed.

Ferrosilicon.—The section found it necessary to intervene in behalf of the manufactures of ferrosilicon in securing power at Niagara Falls. This commodity has two important war uses. The high grade, 80 to 85 per cent pure, is used for making hydrogen gas for balloons; and the second grade, 50 per cent pure, is used for making steel. There is plenty of the ore in the United States, and the only difficulty expressed by the producers was in securing cheap power.

Chromite.—Chromite is the ore mineral from which chromium or chrome metal is obtained. It has a number of uses which were essential to the war. Thousands of tons entered as an alloy into chrome steels for armor plate and for high-speed tools. Chrome brick is widely used as a refractory material in steel furnaces. Chrome salts, such as the bicromates of soda and potash, are used for tanning leather and also in the textile industries. Before the war the bulk of the American supply came from Australia, New Caledonia, and South Africa. In 1914 the United States produced only 591 tons. But, in order to save the long haul, production was increased in 1918 to 60,000 tons, imports being limited to about 90,000 tons. Every assistance was given to the industry by way of priority on machinery, labor, and transportation to encourage sufficient production in this country, and every possible restriction was placed on its use. In normal times, however, domestic production would not pay.

TIN

The Tin Section of the Board was organized March 6, 1918, when George N. Armsby [4] was appointed chief in charge of tin. The feature work of the section was the organization of the interallied tin executive in London, August 28, 1918. But the section was in control of the distribution, as well as the acquisition, of the country's supply of tin when the war ended.

The United States consumes more than 50 per cent of the world's production of tin, but less than 10 per cent of this is mined here. The principal ore deposits are in the Federated Malay States, whence we get "straights" pig tin. Other sources are Bolivia, Dutch East Indies, Southern China, Nigeria, Cornwall, Australia, and South Africa. The Malay deposits are past the peak of their production, and there is concern about the future of the world's supply.

The American Smelting & Refining Co. arranged in 1915 to make large importations of the Bolivian concentrates which had formerly gone to Germany. They built a plant at Perth Amboy for refining them and turned out more than 20,000,000 pounds in 1918. The Alaska mines for that year produced only 120,000 pounds. We imported 142,000,000 pounds of pig tin that year. The National Lead Co. also imports very large quantities of Bolivian concentrates.

The chief use for tin is in the manufacture of tin plate for containers of various kinds, tin being used as a protective covering for

---

[4] Prior to his service in Washington, George Armsby, a New York financier, had been a vice-president of the California Packing Company, which he helped organize in 1916.

iron and steel sheet to prevent rust. Thirty thousand tons went into plate in this country in 1917. Tin plate was a war essential for packing food for shipment abroad as well as preservation in this country. Second in importance is its use in solder. Large quantities of tin are used in making babbitt and other bearing metals. Tin goes into brass and bronze. Collapsible tubes use 2,000 tons per year, and tinfoil uses 4,000 tons. Tin oxide is required in the manufacture of glass, rubber, and in enamel. Tin tetrachloride is used in dyeing silks and to give them weight. Tin was used also in the war in the production of smoke screens for infantry attacks.

Tin and tin products were practically excluded from export during the war, but the problem of securing sufficient importation and suitable distribution was the serious one. In December, 1917, the War Trade Board appointed the American Iron and Steel Institute sole consignee for all pig tin, tin ore, and tin chloride imported into this country, and the tin was to be released to importers upon their giving such guaranties or agreements as the War Trade Board might require. The activities of Mr. Summers were important in obtaining this ruling.

It was designed to eliminate speculators from the market and to direct the flow of tin into most needed channels. It did not, however, break the rise in prices. The uncertainty with which supplies reached the United States, on account of the uncertainty of shipping, caused prices to fluctuate with the arrival of each cargo. The high record of $1.10 a pound was reached in May, 1918. The normal prewar price was about 38 cents a pound.

During May, 1918, the War Industries Board, having taken over the control of tin from the Food Administration and the War Trade Board, started negotiations, through the British Embassy in Washington, looking to the formation of an interallied agreement to provide for the control and distribution of tin to meet the requirements of the war. At the end of July the section chief and three members, who had engaged in these negotiations, joined the War Industries Board foreign mission and sailed for London. Negotiations were continued there, culminating on August 28, 1918, in an agreement by the United States, Great Britain, France, and Italy to establish an interallied tin executive in London. George Armsby and Lincoln Hutchinson [5] were appointed American members. Sir Leonard Llewelyn, K. B. E., was made chairman.

Under the agreement the tin executive controlled and directed all

---

[5] Lincoln Hutchinson (deceased) was a professor of commerce at the University of California.

purchases of pig tin for the participating countries. It appointed its buying agents in the several producing countries, and our import licenses were granted only for tin purchased by the tin executive. The agreement provided that the allocation of pig tin to the participating countries should be on the basis of the following estimated annual requirements:

	Gross tons
United States	80,000
Great Britain	25,000
France	13,000
Italy	4,500

On the basis of this allocation the activities of the International Tin Executive would have meant a saving in our war purchases for 1919 aggregating not less than $75,000,000.

In September the War Industries Board requested the American Iron and Steel Institute to assume charge of the importation, financing, and distribution of the imports of pig tin under its supervision; and the United States Steel Products Co. was made a medium through which the work was carried out. The company agreed to receive and pay at the source for the tin allocated to the United States under the international agreement, and to distribute this tin at cost to all consumers, jobbers, and dealers in the United States who had first received purchasing licenses from the chief in charge of tin of the War Industries Board. The War Trade Board issued ruling No. 307, restricting importations to this company as consignee.

Applications for licenses to purchase were conditioned upon the filing on the part of the applicant of complete reports on stocks, consumption, etc. The applications were required to state the quantity and brand of tin, the use to which it was to be put, and the time during which the metal would be consumed. Each applicant had to pledge not to sell without express permission of the Board. The buyer was required first to present his application to the supplier, who would indicate the terms under which he would furnish the tin. He would then return it to the section chief for approval. No licenses were required for purchases of less than 5 gross tons.

By the 1st of December, 1918, the tin executive had allocated a lot of 10,169 gross tons of tin to the United States. This consignment was handled by the United States Steel Products Co., being distributed to consumers, jobbers, and dealers in the United States holding licenses at the tentative price 72½ cents a pound ex dock, New York. On the final settlement the price was calculated at 69.46876 cents a pound.

Another important phase of the work of the section was that of encouraging and directing economies in the use of tin and in the recovery of scrap. To accomplish this the Tin Section suggested to the various principal trades using tin that each form a war service committee to represent them. About 12 committees of this kind did very important conservation work.

ALUMINUM

In 1885, 23 pounds of aluminum were produced in the United States; in 1896, 1,000,000 pounds; and in 1918, 130,000,000 pounds. The industry in the United States is in the hands of one concern, the Aluminum Co. of America, which owns numerous plants in the United States and one in Quebec, Canada. It is the sole producer of virgin metal and it controls properties covering practically every step and process in the industry from the mining of bauxite ore through the finished castings and utensils. It controls several hydroelectric power companies and electric transmission companies supplying power to the aluminum smelting plants. Power was the limiting factor in increasing production for the war.

The chief war use for aluminum was in the manufacture of ammonal, which is a mixture of aluminum dust and ammonium nitrate, used in the manufacture of munitions. Other military uses were for fuses, flayers, castings for engines, personal equipment, mess equipment, and as a deoxidizer in steel manufacturing. Its peace-time uses include cooking utensils, castings for engines, automobile bodies and mud guards, electrical transmission lines, paints, and ornaments.

Not enough aluminum could be produced to supply the war needs of ourselves and the Allies and at the same time supply normal civilian requirements. Hence the control to be exercised by the Board had to be directed chiefly to two problems: Control of distribution and control of prices. The Board also assisted the Aluminum Co. of America in securing power for increased production and encouraged the recovery of secondary metal from scrap.

The normal prewar price of aluminum is about 20 cents per pound. When this country entered the war, open-market prices were about 60 cents, while contract prices ranged around 38 cents.[6]

The war requirements for aluminum were being studied by the commissioner of raw materials of the Council of National Defense in March, 1917, and on April 25, 1917, with the market at 60 cents,

---

[6] In normal times the bulk of the aluminum output is sold through contracts which are usually made early in the year and cover deliveries for the entire year.

Mr. Davis, president of the Aluminum Co. of America, offered to provide the United States Government with whatever it wanted for its preparedness campaign at whatever price the Government should put upon it. This offer was accepted for 2,000,000 pounds of aluminum ingots at 27½ cents a pound, and a few days later enlarged to 8,000,-000 pounds, to be delivered before August of that year. In September, 1917, the company agreed with the War Industries Board "to accept direct and indirect orders at the prevailing contract prices" (38 cents), and to refund to the Government any difference which might exist between this contract price and any fixed price which might be decided upon at a later date.

Meanwhile the Federal Trade Commission had been studying the costs of production of the Aluminum Co. of America with a view to furnishing data for price fixing. The data were received by the War Industries Board early in 1918, and a price of 32 cents per pound was recommended on February 28, and approved by the President on March 2. On May 9, the question of renewal of the fixed price was brought before the price-fixing committee. The producers presented facts to show that they had been compelled to enlarge their plants to meet the increasing war needs, and that the large cost involved would warrant an advance of 3 cents per pound to the price schedules which expired on June 1; they showed in particular that the Allies were paying much higher prices from other sources. A compromise was reached at 33 cents, and this was continued until March 1, 1919.

The control over the distribution of aluminum was secured through priority certificates and by a working agreement between the Board and the Aluminum Co. of America, whereby the latter exercised certain discretion in the classification of priorities. All purchases were made directly from the Aluminum Co. at the fixed prices. There was never any real shortage for war requirements during the period, though there were occasional delays in delivery due to railroad congestion and lack of power at the smelting plants. Very close control, however, had to be exercised over the distribution of the output, and many restrictions were imposed on its use for non-essential purposes. Aluminum was handled by the Board in the Nonferrous Metals Division by Pope Yeatman and his assistants.

LEAD

Lead was one of the commodities taken up in the days just before we entered the war by the raw-materials committee and the General Munitions Board of the council. The producers, under the leadership of Mr. Crane of the St. Joseph Lead Co., came forward and offered to sell to the Government such quantities as were needed at a price to be set by the Government.

On the face of things lead should not have been a serious problem. In 1913 the United States produced 32.4 per cent of the world's output. The process of production is simple and inexpensive and supply is normally very responsive to demand. But July 1, 1917, saw lead quoted at 11.17 cents per pound—160 per cent above average prewar prices. This situation was caused by the combined circumstances of a European demand, which was never properly calculated or announced in such a way as to produce a steady flow of the material, together with strike trouble, transportation trouble and indefinite guessing on the part of the trade as to the quantities which the United States would demand for the war. Important reductions, during our period in the war, in the use of shrapnel affected very materially the demand for lead.

In May, 1917, the General Munitions Board considered the question of commandeering supplies for the Government. Discussions with the trade, however, brought about a contract on June 18, 1917, for 8,000 tons, July delivery, and 25,000 tons each for August, September, and October deliveries, at 8 cents a pound. Immediately prices began to fall and reached 6.71 cents in September. Price fixing was suggested in October, but was not found necessary, for by that time there was a large supply of lead in the market and there was little probability of a new inflation of prices.

It seemed desirable, however, to devise a working program by which the Government should not be paying higher than market prices for its lead. The method adopted amounted to a series of four-month agreements between the Government and the various lead producers, arranged through the section and the lead producers committee for war service representing the trade, in terms of which the Government agreed to purchase at average current monthly prices as they appeared in the *Engineering and Mining Journal*, and the producers agreed to supply at these prices from a minimum of 6,000 to a maximum of 12,000 tons each month.

On the 15th of each month the lead producers committee was informed, through the section, of the approximate amounts required by each Government purchasing department for the ensuing month. The last four-month agreement expired November 30, 1918. The price never exceeded 7.75 cents per pound East St. Louis or 8.05 cents New York. The total direct purchases by the Government from July, 1917, to November, 1918, amounted to 150,400 tons.

It was believed in October, 1917, that the definition of Government requirements and method of reaching prices would stabilize the market and insure a steady supply to meet all needs, but the freight congestion of early 1918 upset calculations, and in the spring the increased military program both increased and made speculative the demand. A strike tied up the second largest producer during the greater part of March and April, and labor had become so scarce that it seemed impossible to increase the output during the summer.

The only solution seemed to be to ration lead to all consumers on the basis of their essential needs. The problem was worked out by the Lead Section, with Irwin H. Cornell [7] as chief, acting under the Nonferrous Metals Division, in connection with the lead producers committee for war service, representing the industry. The committee handled directly the control over distribution, subject to the section's supervision and occasional alteration. No priority certificates were used. The committee was warned that the industry must keep prices below excessive levels or price fixing would be resorted to.

On June 14 the committee agreed to sell no pig lead higher than 7.75 cents per pound East St. Louis, or 8.05 cents New York, and the *Engineering and Mining Journal* consented to consider no sales made at a higher figure in computing its monthly average price at St. Louis. Under this arrangement prices remained unchanged until the end.

Sheet-lead production increased from 15,000 tons in 1914 to 33,000 tons in 1918, due to the building and expansion of acid plants working in the manufacture of explosives.

NICKEL

About 75 per cent of the nickel consumed in the United States is used in the manufacture of nickel steel. Nickel steel is used in armor plate, ordnance of all sorts, structural work, bridges, railroad rails, steel castings, engine forgings, shafting, and axles where a steel capable of withstanding repeated and alternating strains is necessary. German silver uses another 10 or 12 per cent of our consumption. This alloy is used as a base for silver-plated ware. Monel metal, an alloy containing 67 per cent nickel, 28 per cent copper, and 5 per cent iron and cobalt, has been found to resist successfully the corrosive effect of salt water, and is used extensively for propellers and propeller shafts of warships and for valve stems and other small metal parts underwater.

The war required directly or indirectly nearly 90 per cent of our

---

[7] Irwin H. Cornell is vice-president and sales manager of the St. Joseph Lead Company.

nickel supply, but the problem of controlling the price and distribution was a very simple one, because the country's production is practically all in the hands of one company, the International Nickel Co. This company brings the raw material, in the form of "matte" and ore, from the Sudbury deposits, Ontario, Canada, and refines them at Bayonne, N. J. A small quantity of matte comes also from New Caledonia and from Tasmania. Perhaps 1 per cent comes as a by-product in the electrolytic refining of copper.

The only severe shortage felt by the Government during the war was in electrolytic nickel, required for the fabrication of cupronickel for bullet jackets. The war demands were met largely by radically curtailing non-essential consumption. The International Nickel Co. was required to submit to the War Industries Board all orders which were not really required for war work. The company frequently declined orders, which they knew would be disapproved, without even submitting them. The company also, under the directions of the priorities commissioner, administered priority of deliveries, and except in a few cases priority certificates were not used.

No formal price fixing was resorted to, because on August 15, 1917, the International Nickel Co. arranged to supply the Government requirement at 40 cents a pound, which was 20 per cent below market quotations and slightly lower than the prewar average. The cost of production was studied during the winter, and on January 8, 1918, the company made an agreement with the War Industries Board to supply the United States and the Allies at the rate of 35 cents per pound for ingot or pig nickel, 38 cents for shot, and 40 cents for electrolytic, f. o. b. Bayonne. These prices remained throughout the war. No prices were fixed to the public, but sales for nonwar consumption were very small. The total output for 1917 is estimated at 63,000,000 pounds.

QUICKSILVER

The most important use for quicksilver, or mercury, in the war was in the production of the chemical salt known as fulminate of mercury, used as the detonating agent in cartridges, shells, and grenades. Another large use, which was developed late in the war, was in the manufacture of cellulose acetate, or "dope," with which airplane wings were painted.

Mercury is marketed in 75-pound flasks. Domestic production increased in the United States from 20,000 flasks in 1913, when it was about 16 per cent of the world's output, to about 36,000 flasks in 1917 and 1918. We imported over 5,000 flasks in 1917 and more in 1918.   The domestic market in peace time consumes about 20,000 flasks.   The war requirement was estimated for 1919 at 31,000 flasks.

Prices of quicksilver fluctuated considerably during the war period. In fact, they were eight times prewar normal at one time in 1916, but they had receded to normal by the spring of 1917.   During 1917 prices rose and were irregular.   Price fixing was considered, but because the war program was absorbing less than 40 per cent of the supply and there was no real shortage, formal price fixing was not resorted to. Stability was obtained when, in April, 1918, the Board, through Mr. Yeatman, called together the producers, and they agreed to sell mercury to the Government at $105 per flask, Mare Island, Calif., and $105.75 Brooklyn, and they further agreed informally not to let the outside market go beyond $125 to $130 per flask.   The Board, through Mr. Yeatman, met the importers a few days later and reached the same agreement with them.   The average price in New York for the year 1913 was $38.85 per flask.

The importers agreed to supply 40 per cent of their product, and the producers contracted for definite amounts, with specified monthly deliveries approximating 40 per cent of the 1917 production.   All supplies were taken over by the Government through the Navy Department.   No further control over distribution was needed.

ANTIMONY

Antimony is used as an alloy to give hardness to other metals. About 70 per cent of the available supply was used in the military program, principally to harden the lead of shrapnel bullets.   Its principal civilian use is in the form of antimonial lead, used as type metal.   Antimony-tin-copper and antimony-tin-lead alloys are familiar as bearing metals.   Only a small quantity has ever been produced in this country, because it is cheaper to import it from Europe and China.   During the war most of our supply come from the Far East in Japanese bottoms.

We produced 2,441 tons and imported 11,286 tons in 1917.   There was no shortage during the war, though the stocks in warehouses decreased.   Prices fluctuated considerably during the period, reaching their peak at 34.66 cents a pound in April, 1917.   Prewar normal was about 6.36 cents per pound.   From July, 1917, onward the trend of the market was steadily downward.   The military demands were not as great as had been expected, there were abundant supplies, and keen competition of importers for Government business kept prices low.   Very little was sold to the public during the period.

PLATINUM

When Mr. Baruch and Mr. Summers began their investigations and discussions in February, 1917, about raw materials essential to the war, whose supply was likely to be a problem, platinum was among the commodities which were given serious consideration.

There are only about eight or ten million ounces of recovered platinum in the world, and Russia is the chief source of supply. Platinum is an essential in the contact process of making concentrated sulphuric and nitric acids. It was going to be needed in the new nitrogen-fixation plants which were contemplated. Platinum is essential for contact points of magnetos used in airplanes, trucks, tractors, automobiles, and gas engines generally. In making big guns exact heats have to be maintained at certain stages of the process, and it has been found that platinum wire in the thermocouple is the only substance yet discovered which can stand up substantially under the severe heat. The metal is irreplaceable in the chemical laboratory.

American dentistry normally consumes about 30,000 ounces annually, and the jewelry trade in prosperous times will consume all that it can get.

The 1913 production in Russia was 250,000 ounces and in Colombia 15,000 ounces. Other places produced a few hundred ounces. By 1916 the Russian output had decreased to 63,000 ounces, and that of Colombia increased to 25,000 ounces. Other production was negligible. The production of platinum in the United States from scrap material increased under the efforts of the War Industries Board from 40,000 ounces in 1914 to 59,000 ounces in 1917. This result was obtained chiefly by conditioning in many instances the release of platinum upon the ability to furnish scrap in exchange.

The prospect of a failure of the Russian supply early in the war pointed to the necessity of Government control over a large part of the platinum already in the country. Through the efforts of Mr. Summers, supported by the Secretary of Commerce, F. W. Draper, brought in 21,000 ounces of platinum from Russia in December, 1917. It had been collected with the aid of other American engineers and the Russian-English Bank of Petrograd.

The exact military and other essential requirements were not definitely known in the earlier period of the war. But it was the object of the Board not only to meet all demands, but gradually to build up an available reserve in case the war should last several years. This importation was an encouraging aid. The stocks were bought by the Government. It was decided in the winter of 1917 and 1918 that requisitions would be required to meet the steady increasing demands of the war. The first requisition order was issued to 14 firms on February 23, 1918.

Platinum was handled by Mr. Summers until March, 1918, when it was turned over to the Platinum Section with C. H. Conner [8] in charge. The first requisition order did not seem to be affording sufficient control of the situation, and on May 1, 1918, order No. 104, addressed to 947 firms, was issued. In this order iridium and palladium were included. The very rare metals, iridium and palladium, are used in small quantities as alloys with platinum to give hardness. These two requisition orders brought 59,690 ounces of platinum under control by June 30. On July 1, 1918, another requisition order, No. 342, was issued to 1,555 firms, supposed to be 90 per cent of all firms doing business in platinum.

The supplies, through the requisition orders, were gradually concentrated in the United States assay office in New York and in the hands of the large refiners. The stocks in the assay office were allocated for direct Government work with little formality. But in order to distribute intelligently to essential industries the rest of the supply, printed forms of application for release and a system of questionnaires were drawn up. Releases were issued on the information contained in these sworn statements. Each application was carefully examined to determine the purpose for which the metals were to be used, and there was further investigation of the facts wherever it was thought necessary. In this way unessential uses were eliminated and economy in essential uses was enforced.

As a further safeguard to the supply of platinum, a licensing system was set up under the explosives act of October 6, 1917, as amended July 1, 1918. The rules and regulations of this system, designed to limit further the sales, possession, and use of the metal, became effective on October 1, 1918. All persons or firms who used any appreciable amount of platinum in their business were required to take out a license, and an inventory of stocks was required to accompany the application for a license. It was estimated that between 150,000 and 200,000 licenses would be taken out and that this system would give a very complete survey of the metal in the country, placing it in a status more or less available for Government use when necessary. Only about 3,000 licenses, however, were issued before the armistice was signed.

---

[8] C. H. Conner is now associated with Flynn, Harrison & Conroy (insurance) of New York City.

The section devoted no little attention to the question of conservation of platinum. The use of any platinum, iridium, or palladium in the manufacture, alteration, or repair of any article of jewelry or ornament was prohibited, although no jewelry was ever requisitioned. Releases were refused for the use of platinum in contact points for magnetos for pleasure cars, for electric bells, for various kinds of clocks, electric signs, and other devices. The use of pure platinum in the dental profession was eliminated, as was the use of alloys containing more than 40 per cent. The substitution of perchloric acid for platinum chloride in the determination of potassium salts was urged. The chemical industry was also requested to substitute a palladium-gold alloy for platinum crucibles and dishes in many instances where the substitute would work. It is estimated that in the summer of 1918 these conservations were enough to offset 50 per cent of the essential requirements.

The normal prewar price of refined platinum was $43.86 per troy ounce. By the spring of 1918 it was selling at $108, and had been over $100 since the beginning of 1917. The rise had been more or less steady since the end of 1915. On May 1, 1918, after a series of conferences with the trade, the following maximum prices were fixed: Platinum, $105 per troy ounce; palladium, $135; iridium, $175. Payments for the requisitioned metals were made through the Ordnance Department. Price fixing expired December 1, 1918. The rapid rise in prices, even before the United States entered the war, was due to two principal causes: The supply from Russia became more and more uncertain and domestic consumption was considerably increased both on account of the construction of new sulphuric and nitric acid plants for the manufacture of explosives for the Allies and because the increasing prosperity of the country was greatly stimulating the demand for platinum jewelry. An international platinum executive was in process of being formed in London when the war came to an end.

CHAPTER 5

Chemicals for Munitions

As EARLY as April, 1917, a chemicals committee, with L. L. Summers at the head, was formed to serve under the Raw Materials Division of the council. In November, 1917, Charles H. MacDowell,[1] a member of the chemicals committee, was requested to handle nitrates and other chemicals for explosives, and a subdivision was organized called the Chemicals and Explosives Section. During the early winter the Chemicals and Explosives Section formed, with the War and Navy Departments, the "joint office on chemical statistics" for the purpose of eliminating duplication in questionnaires and compilation of statistical data. The membership of the section was gradually increased during the winter as new problems arose. In the spring the section was reorganized into the Chemicals Division with numerous subordinate sections in charge of particular chemicals. Charles MacDowell was made Director of Chemicals, and the Director of Chemicals was made a member of the Conservation Division as well as the Requirements Division.

As the work undertaken by this division covers a wide and important field, it will be convenient for the purposes of this report to divide the account into three chapters. One will refer to those chemicals more nearly related to the production of powder and explosives, the other two to such additional chemical industries as had to be brought under control for the purposes of the war.

For chemicals used in explosives the following sections were formed: Nitrate of Soda, Sulphur and Pyrites, Acids and Heavy Chemicals, Alkali and Chlorine, Ethyl Alcohol, and Explosives. The work of the Section on Cotton Linters will also be presented in this chapter, because of its close relation to the other subjects.

NITRATE OF SODA

The world's supply of nitrate of soda comes from deposits in Chile. In normal times about 60 per cent of our importations is devoted to the production of fertilizers. In 1913 we brought in 625,000 tons.

---

[1] Associated with the Armour interests since 1887, Mr. MacDowell retired in 1932 from the presidency of the Armour Fertilizer Works.

But orders of the Allies with American munitions manufacturers had brought this figure up to 1,218,423 tons in 1916. For our country and the Allies, Chilean nitrate was practically the only source during the war for the nitric acid essential to all powders and explosives. Germany produced nitric acid by nitrogen-fixation processes, without which she perhaps could not have carried on the war. America started three fixation plants, but none of them were completed before the armistice.

The problem of nitrate of soda had two aspects, (1) shipping and (2) purchasing in Chile.[2] The Chilean market is small and centralized, and thus with the various Allies and the American importers buying for the Government and private consumption alike, each bidding against the other, prices rose rapidly. They were 57 per cent above the normal in the spring of 1917; by September they had become more than twice the average for 1913. It was clearly necessary to eliminate this haphazard competitive system of buying.

Before the war Germany took about one-third of Chile's output for fertilizer purposes. The German oficinas[3] in Chile were operating on a much reduced scale when we entered the war. During the summer of 1917 an effort was made, through the American importers, to have the Chilean Government seize these plants and reopen them in order to supply the ever-increasing demand. This was not effected. Some of the German oficinas continued to operate, but their production was limited by their inability to secure necessary supplies. Some of the stocks produced by the German oficinas were secured by authorized American importers for shipment to the United States. But even with this added supply the increasing competition among the buyers, together with the shortage of fuel, of sacks, and of rail transportation from the refineries to the coast, kept Chilean prices continuously increasing.

In October, 1917, negotiations began between the United States, England, France, and Italy to pool all allied buying, and purchases in Chile were curtailed during the remaining months of the year while the buying pool was being perfected. Prices for 1917 reached their maximum in October. Buying under the pool began in January, 1918, and continued through the war. The pool took the form

---

[2] See Appendix XX for a more exhaustive account of the solution of the nitrate problem.

[3] An oficina is a plant in which the raw nitrate of soda, as it is taken from the ground, is refined by dissolving it in warm water and allowing recrystallization as the water is evaporated off.

of an appointment of a nitrate executive in London, headed by Herbert Gibbs, of Antony Gibbs & Co.   Robert P. Skinner, United States consul general in London, was appointed American representative on the executive.

The first thought was to have the nitrate executive do all of the buying in Chile with an arrangement for reselling to each participating country.   This plan gave way, however, so far as our country was concerned, to one according to which each of our importers bought, under the sole direction of the nitrate executive, a designated share of the total purchases allocated to the United States by the executive, and all prices were pooled.   This kept the regular American buyers in the market during the life of the pool.   The four principal importers of the country were designated as sole purchasing agents of the nitrate executive for its operations in behalf of the United States, and it was arranged that each should handle the following percentages of the total allocated to us: DuPont Nitrate Co., $33\frac{1}{3}$ per cent; W. R. Grace & Co., $36\frac{2}{3}$ per cent; Wessel, Duval & Co., $11\frac{1}{3}$ per cent; and Anthony Gibbs & Co., through H. J. Baker & Bro., agents, $18\frac{2}{3}$ per cent.

In order to coordinate the work of the American importers, calculate prices, allocate shipping, etc., the nitrate committee of the United States was established in New York with H. Ray Paige, representative of the War Industries Board, as manager.   The committee was composed of two representatives from each of the four importers in addition to Mr. Paige.   After the War Industries Board was dissolved, January 1, 1919, Mr. Paige remained to liquidate the affairs of the committee, functioning as a member of the War Trade Board.

In Washington, Mr. MacDowell was in charge of nitrate for the War Industries Board throughout the war.   He remained chief of the Nitrate Section even after he became director of the Chemicals Division.   As early as April, 1917, the raw materials division made an important move to relieve the nitrate situation, and it will be seen that this importing arrangement was only a consummation of the early plan.   The division announced to all manufacturers about to take contracts for munitions with the United States that they need not cover their nitrates by option or by inquiry, but that the Government would guarantee a sufficient supply at $4\frac{1}{4}$ cents per pound.   This was for the purpose of quieting the market, though a way for making good on it had not yet been worked out.   There was, however, a definite nitrate differential for each kind of powder and explosive, so that should the United States have to pay more than 4¼ cents, it would be only a matter of accounting in the price of powder. As a matter of fact, the Government settled all of these contracts in December with a price of 4⅛ cents, having lowered the Chilean prices.

Under the pooling arrangement the four importers agreed to buy in Chile such quantities of nitrate of soda as were allocated to each, ship it to the United States, and deliver as directed by the War Industries Board (1) to the Government at actual cost plus out-of-pocket expenses and (2) to other consumers at landed cost plus a gross commission of 2½ per cent. Arrangements were made whereby the cost of the nitrate was averaged over each month of purchase. The contract and arrangement with the importers covered the auditing of their accounts from time to time to verify costs and other conditions surrounding importation.

The nitrate executive in London calculated monthly prices in Chile, all purchases being averaged each month. The nitrate committee in New York calculated monthly prices delivered at American ports and warehouses. The Shipping Board established uniform shipping rates from Chile to the United States, which simplified the calculations somewhat. Computation of American prices was very difficult and involved. It was impossible to reach final figures within a reasonable time for the importers to bill their sales. During the first four months of 1918 bills were rendered, some at the tentative monthly price of 4.25 cents per pound, others at 4.35 cents. From May forward a tentative monthly price was fixed by the committee.[4] It was the understanding that refunds would be made, so as to adjust those prices to actual costs, as stated above. Final United States landed pool prices were calculated by the committee and announced from time to time, the work being concluded in the spring of 1919.[5]

Purchases made by the American importers in 1917 for delivery in Chile in 1918 were placed in the pool as to quantity, but not as to price. All purchases made during 1918 were made under the pool. In October, 1917, as a preliminary to the formation of the pool, arrangements were made by which the Department of Agriculture was to get, through the DuPont Co., 109,000 long tons of nitrate of soda for distribution to the farmers during the spring of 1918. Only 67,000

---

[4] See Appendix XVIII for table of tentative United States landed pool prices for nitrate of soda.

[5] See Appendix XIX for table of final United States landed pool prices for nitrate of soda.

tons of this was delivered in the spring, the rest being postponed until fall. Because of the serious shortage of ships during the late winter and spring of 1918, and the shortage of nitrate in France on account of sinkings and other difficulties, some of this agricultural nitrate, as well as other Government nitrate (61,000 tons in all), was diverted to France. Our war stocks became very low at this time; there was only about a 6-weeks' supply on May 1, 1918.

Early in the summer of 1918 a shortage of coal, fuel oil, bags, and railroad equipment began to be felt in the nitrate fields of Chile. This region is arid and produces none of these supplies. The Chilean Government approached the United States Government with a special contract providing for the sale of 680,000 gross tons of nitrate of soda on condition that certain of these supplies would be furnished in return. The Nitrate Section made arrangements through the London executive, the American importers, and the priorities commissioner of the Board to accept this contract and have its terms carried out.

The Nitrate Section of the Board kept in close touch with the nitrate committee in New York and the nitrate executive in London, giving current advices to the nitrate executive on the condition of stocks in the United States: requirements, shipments, stocks on hand, consumption, etc. When the shipping control committee would allocate vessels for the trade, Mr. Paige in New York would arrange to have the vessels assigned to the four importers according to their tonnage requirements for the account of the Army, the Navy, or the importer's own account.

Distribution to munitions plants and to acid plants producing for munitions was carefully watched to see that they were never short, even if private industries had to be curtailed. The section brought before the priorities commissioner the question of securing priority certificates for fuel, machinery, and railroad supplies for the nitrate fields.

The principal war use of nitrate of soda is for the production of nitric acid, which is used in a mixture of 30 per cent nitric acid and 70 per cent sulphuric acid for the nitrating process in the manufacture of powder and explosives. Bleached cotton linters are nitrated with this mixed acid to produce nitrocellulose powder, which is the chief propellant. Toluol is nitrated to produce T.N.T., phenol to produce picric acid, and so on. Nitrate of soda is also required for the manufacture of sulphuric acid by the chamber process, 98,000 tons being consumed in this country in 1917 for this purpose. About 697,000 tons were used in 1917 for the production of nitric acid. The larger powder companies make their own sulphuric and nitric acid at their respective powder and explosives plants.†

SULPHUR AND PYRITES

The sulphuric acid requirement of the United States for 1918 measured in terms of 50° Baumé acid was estimated at 9,000,000 tons. This was more than double normal consumption. But the adjustment in the industry, which the situation required, was even more significant, for prior to 1917 about 60 per cent of the sulphuric acid consumed in the United States was made from pyrites ore imported from Spain, and these importations had to be largely cut off to save shipping. Pyrites ore from Canada continued to come in during the war, in fact its importation was greatly increased.

The main sources of sulphur for this country are (1) imported Spanish pyrites ore, (2) pure brimstone from Louisiana and Texas, (3) Canadian pyrites ore, (4) domestic pyrites ore, (5) waste gases at copper and zinc smelters. With the increasing requirement and the decreasing Spanish supply, the problem of the Board was to develop the other sources. Canadian imports were increased considerably, and the production of domestic pyrites was increased; but the real solution lay in the limitless resources of pure brimstone in Texas and in Louisiana. The attention of the Board was turned chiefly to these sources. There are large deposits of pyrites in California and Colorado, but the sulphuric acid plants of the country are

---

† *Editor's Note:* The steady growth in nitrogen fixation plant capacity in recent years has gone far toward solving the problem of nitrate supply in the current emergency. In 1918, estimated consumption of nitrate of soda —all of it imported from Chile—was 1,800,000 long tons, equal in nitrogen content to roughly 270,000 tons. To meet the requirements for munitions it was necessary, of course, to curtail drastically the use of nitrate of soda for fertilizer.

Already the capacity of nitrogen fixation plants in this country is roughly 250,000 tons of nitrogen annually—220,000 tons being represented by two producers, Allied Chemical & Dye in its plant at Hopewell, Va., and DuPont in its plant at Belle, W. Va. In addition, the Government has ordered construction of three fixation plants, one at West Henderson, Ky., to be operated for the Government by the Solvay Company (Allied Chemical); one near Morgantown, W. Va., to be operated by the DuPont company; and a third near Muscle Shoals to be operated by the Tennessee Valley Authority. The capacity of these plants has not been disclosed.

Though the United States continues to be a heavy importer of Chilean nitrate of soda—having brought in around 680,000 tons in 1940—and though this country still relies upon Chile for a large portion of its needs, it is thus freed from the utter dependence upon Chile that existed in 1917 and 1918.

chiefly in the East, and shortage of transportation made a large development of these properties inadvisable.

Prior to the organization of the Chemicals and Explosives Section, a subcommittee of the chemicals committee of the council handled the distribution of foreign pyrites ore. This committee also, in May, 1917, arranged with the sulphur producers for the shipment of sulphur to fertilizer plants, on approval of the fertilizer subcommittee, at a price of $22 per long ton at mines. No shipments were made to plants having pyrites on hand but, as fast as stocks were used up, sulphur was substituted. The chemicals committee issued a pamphlet showing how to turn pyrites burners to sulphur burning at a minimum of expense and time. When the chemicals committee was discontinued, the Chemical Alliance (Inc.), which followed it, continued to distribute sulphur under this agreement. With the reorganization of the Board in the spring of 1918, the Sulphur and Pyrites Section was organized under the direction of William G. Woolfolk.[6]

The section undertook to make a careful survey of the situation with a view to further control if necessary. The question of commandeering the stocks and plants of the Union Sulphur Co. and the Freeport Sulphur Co. was considered and abandoned. Instead of this, a plan was worked out in a series of meetings, conducted by the section with a committee of the Chemical Alliance (Inc.), and representatives of the Railroad Administration and Shipping Board, under which the production and distribution of sulphur materials should be definitely controlled by the section in conjunction with the committee. A program of shipments to the various acid plants of the country, showing tonnage month by month for the remainder of 1918, was worked out and published August 1.

No prices were fixed formally, but the price of $22 per long ton for Government purchases was continued throughout the year, and the control of supplies and their allocation to essential consumers only had the effect of establishing "contract" prices, though market quotations throughout the year stood around $35 per ton. The normal prewar price of crude sulphur was $22 per long ton, and it remained at that figure until the beginning of 1916.

In exercising its control over sulphur, the section had in mind (1) to conserve and use to the best advantage water and rail transportation facilities by requiring materials of the highest sulphur content; (2) to conserve transportation through the use of sulphur materials available at points nearest points of consumption; (3) to increase

---

[6] A Chicago consulting engineer.

production of properties where it was practicable; (4) to increase the stocks at important Government and private consumers' plants before winter weather should interfere with transportation; (5) to stabilize prices; and (6) to cooperate with the War Trade Board in controlling exports. At the time of the armistice there were heavy stocks at most of the consumers' plants and there was no serious problem on the dockets.†

ACIDS AND HEAVY CHEMICALS

The work of this section was devoted to the question of the production of sulphuric and nitric acids. Statistics were had on muriatic acid, but no control was found necessary. Prices were fixed on both of these acids, and the section made exhaustive studies in this connection. But perhaps the most valuable part of the work consisted of the studies and recommendations made in connection with the development of the sulphuric acid plants of the country. The production of nitric acid was always limited by the supply of nitrate of soda and sulphuric acid, 100 pounds of each being required for every 95 pounds of nitric acid.

The section was formed with A. R. Brunker[7] as chief in April, 1918. * * * Before that time the acid problems were handled for the Board by the Chemicals and Explosives Section in cooperation with the committee on acids of the Chemical Alliance (Inc.). The earliest action was devoted chiefly to economizing in tank cars by ordering acid shipments from the nearest plants irrespective of contracts calling for cross hauls.

The consumption of sulphuric acid in industry in this country, as estimated in the summer of 1918, was as follows: (1) Explosives (directly or indirectly), including phenol and nitric acid, 35 per cent; (2) fertilizers, 27.8 per cent; (3) oil refineries, 11.2 per cent; (4) drugs and chemicals, including hydrochloric acid, nitric acid for purposes other than explosives, and ammonium sulphate, 9.6 per cent; (5) steel pickling and galvanizing, 9.1 per cent; (6) miscellaneous, 7.3 per cent. It is estimated that 1,646,000 tons (calculated as 100 per cent H_2SO_4) were consumed in military explosives in 1918.

The question of the location of new sulphuric acid plants was

---

† *Editor's Note:* Though some pyrite ore is still imported from Canada, sulphur has almost completely displaced pyrites in the making of sulphuric acid. Ample supplies of sulphur are available.

[7] Albert Brunker (deceased) was president of the Liquid Carbonic Company in Chicago.

important. It was much more expensive and troublesome to transport the acid than to transport the raw materials for its manufacture. Hence, the cost of a new acid plant had to be constantly weighed against the importance of having one near an explosives plant. During the first nine months of 1918 additions were made to acid plants at the various works of the DuPont Co., the Hercules Co., the Atlas Co., the General Chemical Co., and various small producers. The Government built acid plants in connection with the smokeless-powder plants at Nashville, Tenn., and Nitro, W. Va.

The total plant capacity of the country increased from 427,000 tons per month (measured as 100 per cent H_2SO_4) on January 1, 1918, to 501,000 tons per month on November 1, 1918. The capacity at Government plants was 55,000 tons, and the remainder, 388,000 tons per month, was in the hands of commercial manufacturers. Plants were under construction for an agrregate further capacity of 37,650 tons per month at Emporium, Pa.; Mount Union, Pa.; Brunswick, Ga.; Little Rock, Ark.; and several other places, principally in connection with the production of picric acid. Plans for accommodating the country's plant capacity to the country's need were very much facilitated by a survey made through personal visits to all plants east of the Mississippi River by A. E. Wells, metallurgist of the Bureau of Mines, who was a member of the section.

Sulphuric acid is manufactured chiefly in three different strengths: 60° Baumé acid, 66° Baumé acid, and 20 per cent oleum. The 60° Baumé acid is produced by the chamber process. Oleum is produced by the contact process. The 66° Baumé acid is produced the more economically in the contact process by simple dilution of the stronger acid, but it can also be manufactured from the weaker acid by the expensive process of concentration by heat or by passing the weak chamber acid through a contact acid plant.

Powder and explosives require the stronger acids, so that every effort had to be directed to increasing the production of oleum and 66° Baumé. A large tonnage of 60° Baumé acid had to be concentrated. Thus when it came to price fixing, the price of 66° Baumé acid had to be placed high enough to warrant the production of this type from the weaker acid by the heat concentration process or by passing it through the contact process plants.

The price-fixing committee did not act on sulphuric acid until June, 1918, but late in 1917, after consultation with the War Industries Board, the War and Navy Departments entered into an agreement with the acid manufacturers under which prices to the Government were fixed for the first and second quarters of 1918 as follows:

	Per ton
60° Baumé	$18
66° Baumé	30
20 per cent oleum	35

These prices applied to direct purchases by the Government only.

During the winter the Federal Trade Commission conducted an investigation of costs of production at a number of representative plants throughout the country, both chamber and contact process. It was quite evident that the productive capacity of the country would have to be stimulated in every possible way, through pushing existing capacity to its utmost limit, building additions to existing plants, and erecting new ones. It was further felt necessary to establish fair and full prices to encourage production, provide for the heavy depreciation of plants when pushed to the extent required, and to obtain the fullest output of even the highest cost producers.

There was a great divergence of conditions and costs at the different plants, due both to the process and to the raw materials used. The older plants used the chamber process, with higher cost; in fact, much higher cost for the stronger acids. But these plants constituted by far the larger share of the country's capacity. Those using the modern contact process would make large profits under a price arrangement which would permit the other plants to function. Some small amount was produced as a by-product from the smelting of zinc and copper ores, but the cost varied also at these plants.

In June, 1918, the price-fixing committee established the following prices for all purchasers:

	Per ton
60° Baumé sulphuric acid	$18
66° Baumé sulphuric acid	28
20 per cent oleum	32

These were reduced in September, 1918, to be effective until December 31, to—

	Per ton
60° Baumé sulphuric acid	$16
66° Baumé sulphuric acid	25
20 per cent oleum	28

These reductions were the result of studies and recommendation by the section. The section felt, indeed, that even the new prices were perhaps higher than necessary in view of the possibility of curtailing the use of acid in many less essential industries, and in view of the coming into production of numerous new Government plants.

The work of this section in connection with the production of nitric acid was never so important as in the case of sulphuric. A much smaller tonnage was required for the explosives program, and the production was always limited by the available supply of nitrate of soda and sulphuric acid, the nitrate of soda being the really limiting factor.

For the first half of 1918 a price of 7½ cents per pound for Government purchases of 42° Baumé nitric acid had been arranged between the War and Navy Departments and the producers. This was considerably lower than the prevailing market price. The situation was studied by the section, and a price of 8½ cents per pound was recommended to the price-fixing committee and became effective July 1, 1918, and was continued to the end. The section calculated the cost of a pound of nitric acid as follows:

To produce 95 pounds, the raw materials required are—

100 pounds nitrate of soda	$4.25
100 pounds sulphuric acid	1.35
Average manufacturing cost (including overhead)	1.18
Total cost of 95 pounds	$6.78
Cost of 1 pound	.0714

It was felt that 8½ cents per pound would allow a fair profit and stimulate production.

It would probably have been necessary in the early part of 1919, had the war continued, to curtail heavily the use of nitric acid in several of the nonwar industries, particularly celluloid, aniline oil, and others. A careful study of these industries was made, and it was thought that the celluloid industry could be curtailed 50 per cent. This uses 10,000 tons per annum, measured as 100 per cent acid.

The production of nitric acid in the United States increased from 78,000 tons in 1914 to 602,000 tons in 1917.

ALKALI AND CHLORINE

The Alkali and Chlorine Section was made a separate unit of the Chemicals Division April 15, 1918, when H. G. Carroll [8] was appointed chief. Prior to this time these commodities were handled by Mr. MacDowell in conjunction with J. D. Pennock, chairman of the alkali

---

[8] H. G. Carroll (deceased) was lately with the Solvay Process Co. of Syracuse, N. Y.

section of the Chemical Alliance (Inc.). Mr. Pennock continued to cooperate throughout the period, and his services were very valuable in maintaining contact between the section and the various firms of the industry.

On most of these commodities price agreements for Government purchases had been arranged with groups of manufacturers before the section took up the work, and Mr. Pennock was handling the allocation of Government orders within each group and he continued to do this. The most important commodities handled by the section were caustic soda (sodium hydroxide), soda ash (sodium carbonate), potash, and chlorine and its compounds.

Caustic soda.—Caustic soda is made either by the electrolytic or Solvay process from salt, ammonia, and limestone. Its production depends principally on plant capacity and labor, for there is no great scarcity of the raw materials. Its chief war uses were (1) in the manufacture of phenol for picric acid; (2) in bleaching cotton linters and textiles; (3) in drugs and dyes; and (4) in soap and glycerin. It has an extensive civilian consumption in the manufacture of soap, lye, dyes, various drugs, in the purification of mineral oils and cottonseed oil, in reclaiming rubber, and many other industries. Soap used 23.1 per cent, oil 10.7 per cent, and textile trades 7.9 per cent of the 1917 output. The Government bought 21.5 per cent for direct war uses.

No shortage was felt until the spring of 1918. In fact, exports to Japan, Canada, and South American countries, on the basis of 100,000 tons per year, were allowed until this time. But the increase in the military program in the spring, particularly the decision to double the county's output of picric acid, raising the annual production from 135,000,000 pounds to 270,000,000 pounds, pointed toward important shortages in caustic soda.

The section made a careful study of production and requirements. The figures obtained led the section to believe that it was necessary to curtail both exports and less essential consumption until plants could be expanded or new ones constructed to meet the added requirements. Two new privately owned electrolytic plants, as well as a new Government plant, were started in the spring and were beginning to get into operation in November, 1918. Exports were curtailed by the War Trade Board, between 3,000 and 4,000 tons per month being allowed. Soap manufacturers were curtailed 20 per cent; cotton finishers 40 per cent; and lye manufacturers 30 per cent. Agreements to put these reductions into effect were reached by direct negotiations with the industries.

The total production of caustic soda for 1918 was estimated at 457,000 short tons. The price for Government purchases was arranged by agreement at $3.50 per 100 pounds for 76 per cent caustic soda, f. o. b. car sellers' plants. Though this price was considerably below the quoted market and below current contract prices, it remained until the end. Some of the smaller high-cost producers complained that, due to increase in cost of labor and materials they were losing money on that part of their product which they were required to sell to the Government. The section held a meeting with the 17 manufacturers who were supplying their allotted shares on the Government requirements; the question of prices was carefully considered; and the meeting agreed that the simplest solution was to relieve the four or five high-cost producers from their obligation to sell to the Government, and to redistribute the requirements to the others. And this was done.

Soda ash.—Less than 5 per cent of the country's total production of soda ash was needed for direct military purposes. Though the industry was greatly stimulated by the war, principally through indirect requirements, and though market prices reached a figure four or five times prewar normal, production, increasing from 935,000 short tons in 1914 to 1,854,000 short tons in 1918, was always sufficient to meet all requirements of the Government, and no curtailment or control over distribution was necessary.

Early in 1918, an agreement was reached with the producers, fixing the Government purchase price at $1.57 per 100 pounds for 58 per cent soda ash in bags f. o. b. sellers' plants. This price was maintained throughout the war, though the market in 1918 was more than $1 per hundredweight above it. The Government's purchases were allocated to the various producers through Mr. Pennock.

Potash.—This country consumed very little potash for war purposes, and only a small percentage of normal for fertilizers and other chemicals during the war period. Our supply has always come from Germany. Prewar prices were about 3.7 cents per pound for potassium hydroxide, 88–92 per cent. In March, 1918, the price was 84 cents per pound.

The work of the section consisted chiefly in considering requests for Government aid in the development of potash properties or processes, and in replying to inquiries relating to the Government's policy toward potash production. A number of projects with considerable promise were submitted. It has been the Government policy to encourage with technical advice and experimentation the development of domestic sources.

Substantial progress was made in production in several parts of the country, though we have not, even at this writing, any firm hope that our plants will be able to compete successfully with the German potash syndicate, which has 200 rich mines fully equipped, and with France, which has several mines in operation. Our largest war-time development was in the production of a 25 per cent potash from certain alkaline lakes in western Nebraska by an evaporation process. The high cost of fuel and transportation handicaps this undertaking. The Solvay Process Co. is producing a 50 to 55 per cent potash from salt beds in Utah. This work is developing. Both the Solvay Co. and the Trona Corporation are producing potash in quantity from brines deposited in a defunct lake in the Mojave Desert, California. This project has had to combat the presence in the brine of borax, which is injurious to crops. A process has now been discovered, however, by which they are producing a potash of low borax content.

A plant producing pure sulphate of potash was opened in Utah in the fall of 1915 by Mr. MacDowell and associates. It was from the product made by this plant that the first technically pure carbonate of potash was secured for the making of optical glass and the first potassium permanganate for gas masks. A semicommercial plant was built in connection with this Utah undertaking by the Armour Fertilizer Works during the latter months of the war to fix nitrogen in the alumina by-product obtained in the manufacture of potash. The work was started at the request of the Government and is now being extended to commercial size. The product is known as aluminum nitride. * * *

Chlorine.—The four chief war uses of chlorine in its various forms were for the manufacture of (1) toxic gases, (2) various chemicals for smoke screens, (3) "dope" for airplanes, and (4) textile bleaching powder. The Chemical Warfare Service was the principal Government consumer and its requirements were not well defined before the early summer of 1918. Guesses as to Government requirements before this time had caused some confusion, particularly in the bleaching powder industry. Studies of the section in June, 1918, brought out the fact that a high percentage of the country's output was going to be needed for the war. In addition to the domestic requirements, the French Government had, during 1918, a standing order with American producers for 300 tons per month.

The four forms of chlorine, which were handled by the section, were liquid chlorine, bleaching powder, carbon tetrachloride, and sulphur monochloride. By the 1st of July studies had disclosed the fact that there was a shortage of at least 20 per cent in liquid chlorine.

The section undertook, through constant conferences with the 12 chief producers, to inaugurate a program of curtailment in use on the one hand, and increase of production on the other, to make up this deficit. This scheme kept the deficit about constant throughout the summer, increasing demands being made up by increasing production. Practically no liquid chlorine was used for nonwar purposes, except for the purification of drinking water. Orders were prepared in October to commandeer the industry, but they were not issued. Much difficulty was experienced in obtaining containers for the chlorine. The situation was met by the War Department which inaugurated the manufacture of 1-ton containers.

Early in 1918, the price was fixed by agreement, for all Government purchases at 7½ cents per pound, in Government-owned containers, f. o. b. makers' plants. The quantity of liquid chlorine produced in the United States in 1917 is estimated at 18,000 tons, and an estimate in July, 1918, indicates a production for that year of 22,000 tons.

Early in the war the Government's requirements for bleaching powder were estimated at 300 tons per day. This was later cut down to a working order with the manufacturers for 42,000 tons. This order was canceled in the early spring of 1918, and only about 6,000 tons had been bought before July 1. War demands then began to become definite and insistent, and requirements were estimated in the summer at 4,000 tons per month, which is 50 per cent of the country's productive capacity. A program of curtailment was put into effect. Its burden fell almost entirely on the pulp and paper industry and the textile industry. Representatives of these two trades were called together and an agreement was reached for curtailments which saved about 50 per cent of the bleach ordinarily consumed by them. Compulsory orders were issued by the Government to the producers during the summer. Prices on Government purchases had been previously fixed by agreement at 2.35 cents per pound, basis 35 per cent chlorine, f. o. b. makers' plants. This price was used for practically all of the orders, though the War Department Board of Appraisers had at one time reduced it to 2 cents. The producers claimed that it cost between 2.35 and 2.50 cents per pound to manufacture the powder. The estimated production of bleaching powder in the United States in 1917 was 100,000 short tons.

Carbon tetrachloride is ordinarily used for fire extinguishers and as a cleaning fluid. The French used it in the manufacture of mustard gas and the British for smoke screens. July, 1918, developed a very severe shortage and commandeering orders were issued to the entire industry, the firms of which gave their cordial support in carrying out the orders. Civilian use was completely suspended. Prices were fixed, as in the other chlorines, at 15 cents per pound for carbon tetrachloride and 17 cents for fire-extinguisher fluid.

Sulphur monochloride caused some confusion. The Chemical Warfare Service had placed contracts for sulphur monochloride in a number of plants where the chlorine was greatly needed for other products, such as liquid chlorine, bleaching powder, and monochlorbenzol. After a careful examination of the facts and a consultation between the section and the Chemical Warfare Service, contracts for sulphur monochloride were placed at 20 pulp mills, where machinery was converted for its production. The price was fixed by the Chemical Warfare Service itself.

ETHYL ALCOHOL

The Ethyl Alcohol Section of the Board was organized in April, 1918, with Mr. Woolfolk as chief. Ethyl alcohol was being used in very large quantities in the explosives program as a solvent in the manufacture of smokeless powder and in the refining of T.N.T.; it was used also in the manufacture of toxic gases, in airplane "dope," and the like. The French Government was getting a large supply here. Alcohol is the principal raw material from which ether, chloroform, acetic ether, nitrous ether, and many other substances are made.

The custom of taxing such alcohol as is usable for beverages has led to the practice of "denaturizing" alcohol for use in the industrial arts. Denatured alcohol is manufactured and sold free of tax. The "completely denatured" alcohol is produced by adding 10 gallons of wood alcohol and half a gallon of benzine (or 2 gallons of wood alcohol and half a gallon of pyridine bases) to 100 gallons of ethyl or grain alcohol. For special uses many other formulæ are permitted for producing "specially denatured" alcohol.

It was considered important to make a careful survey of the country's plant capacity and sources of raw material to determine whether control would be necessary in case of a long war. Ethyl alcohol is produced throughout the country in three types of plants: first, those using grain as the principal raw material; second, those using by-product molasses; and, third, plants originally constructed for the production of whisky and later converted. The first two groups of plants were well organized, but many of the third were in process of being dismantled rather than converted. The section asked the owners not to dismantle the plants, but hold them ready for conversion in case additional capacity should be needed. As a result of studies of the section an improvement in the process of manufacture was brought about which increased the capacity of many plants as much as 20 per cent without increasing labor and equipment. No curtailment in use nor increase in facilities was found necessary.

The capacity of the plants using molasses was calculated at 50,-000,000 pounds per month, those using grain at 83,000,000 pounds per month. Our total war requirements at the time of the armistice were set at 47,000,000 pounds per month. Production from molasses increased threefold during the war while production from grain decreased. The price was never fixed by the Government, but after the cessation of manufacture for beverage purposes in September, 1917, prices declined to a point where they remained steady throughout 1918. Grain alcohol, 190 proof, sold at 61 to 62 cents per gallon and denatured alcohol at about 68 cents per gallon throughout the year.

COTTON LINTERS

Cotton linters are used as the base of nitrocellulose or smokeless powder. While they are not a chemical and the section did not function as part of the Chemicals Division, their important relation to the explosives program will justify placing the account of them in this chapter.

"Cotton linters" is the name given to the fine cotton fiber which sticks to the rough surface of cotton seed as it comes from the gin. The lint is removed by an arrangement of revolving saws at the cottonseed crushing plants. In normal times it is used chiefly for stuffing mattresses, pads, horse collars, etc., in making celluloid, felts, absorbent cotton, and other products where a long fiber is not needed. Mattresses require a better quality of linters than munitions.

The section was formed April 4, 1918, with George R. James [9] as chief. Studies were directed toward the question whether the supply of linters would be sufficient for the rapidly developing smokeless-powder facilities, and it appeared that the average annual production for the past five years had been less than one-half of the requirements estimated for the year 1919. It was estimated further that moderately small stocks would be carried over at the end of the cotton year, July 31, 1918.

A series of questionnaires brought out the fact that substitute materials could be found for all of the industries using cotton linters for other than explosives purposes, and the Ordnance Department

---

[9] A Memphis merchant (deceased), Mr. James was later a member of the Federal Reserve Board.

began experiments in the use of cotton hull fiber and wood pulp as substitutes for cotton linters in the manufacture of nitrocellulose powder. The next step was to arrange not only to stimulate production of cotton linters but to turn all linters into the production of munitions. On April 12, 1918, the section called a meeting of representatives of the cottonseed crushing industry with representatives of the War and Navy Departments. An agreement was reached that after May 2, 1918, all crushing mills would cut nothing but "munitions" linters, producing not less than 145 pounds of linters per ton of seed crushed, and that the Government would take the entire output at $4.67 per hundredweight, f. o. b. points of production, for a period ending July 31, 1919.

For the purpose of carrying this arrangement into effect, there was formed what was known as the Cotton Linter Pool, effective August 1, 1918, to July 31, 1919. The participating members of the pool were (1) the Ordnance Department, through which other agencies of the Government, including the Navy, should receive their supplies; (2) the Canadian Government, acting through the Imperial Munitions Board; (3) the French Government, acting through the French Powder Mission; (4) the British Government, acting through the British War Mission; (5) the Italian Government, acting through the Italian Military Mission; (6) the Belgian Government, acting through the Belgian Commission; (7) American manufacturers having Government contracts for smokeless powder or pyro cotton; and (8) manufacturers of absorbent cotton or other supplies using linters, having Government or Red Cross contracts.

The Ordnance Department undertook to finance the entire project. The DuPont American Industries (Inc.) was appointed purchasing agent for the Ordnance Department at a fee of 26 cents for each bale (500 pounds) of linters purchased. The linters had to be purchased at several thousand plants. A set of rules for the operation of the pool was formulated, covering detailed arrangements by which the participating members would secure their supplies at a uniform price, including freight charges. The respective functions of the Ordnance Department and the Cotton Linters Section in relation to the pool were defined to avoid duplication of effort. The Ordnance Department handled questions relating to (1) production and stimulation of production of linters; (2) requisitioning and commandeering of stocks; (3) all financing; (4) the appointment of the DuPont American Industries (Inc.); and (5) any disputes arising between the purchasing agency and the producers. The Cotton Linters Section handled (1) all allocations to consumers; (2)

storage of such stocks as might be purchased during the height of the crushing season in excess of storage capacity at powder plants; (3) the formulation of specifications for cutting and baling to conform to the requirements of all purchasers; (4) a series of periodic reports from producers showing stocks, current production, and estimates; and (5) all records of stocks, production, requirements, and allocations.

Over 500,000 bales of linters were purchased by the pool before the armistice. When the war was over and the question of liquidating the pool and satisfying the claims of the producers arose, a series of meetings, lasting over a month, was held by the section, representatives of the participating members, and the producers. Numerous plans were proposed and discussed, but the burden and responsibility of liquidating the pool and satisfying the claims of the producers were finally taken by the Ordnance Department.

Through the instrumentality of the pool, the maximum cotton linters capacity of the country was turned directly to war use, but still there would not have been enough cellulose material for the powder programs of ourselves and the Allies. The experiments in the use of hull fiber and wood pulp as substitutes or dilutents promised a large measure of success. In the largest DuPont plant (at Hopewell, Va.) and in the Government plants at Nitro and Nashville, machinery was installed for the use of a combination of cotton linters and hull fiber or wood pulp. The Picatinny Arsenal used old cotton rags successfully. These combined plans would have made possible the full smokeless powder program laid down for 1919.

In addition to the pool discussed above, a "Mattress Linter Pool" was also formed by the Ordnance Department with the DuPont American Industries (Inc.) as purchasing agent. The purpose of this pool was to buy in a few thousand bales of mattress linters which had been cut prior to May 2, 1918, and were still in stock in various parts of the country. These linters were needed for Army and Red Cross mattresses.

Prices were set as follows: Grade A, 10 cents per pound; grade B, 7 cents; grade C, 5½ cents; f. o. b. points of location. All holders were asked to make voluntary sales to the purchasing agent at these prices. In this way 9,888 bales of mattress linters were purchased, perhaps 75 per cent of existing stocks. No commandeering orders were issued. The section made allocations of these to Government consumers.

The section made a study of the industry engaged in bleaching or purifying cotton linters for the powder makers. On July 8, 1918, the price-fixing committee established a maximum price of $6.33 per 100 pounds of bleached material for this service. As it happened the production of linters never reached a rate which strained the bleaching capacity of the country.

During the summer the press-cloth industry appealed to the section for help. Press cloth is essential for the cottonseed crushers and the section was interested in supplying them with anything which would stimulate their operations. Its manufacture had been seriously affected by the suspension of importations of horse, camel, and human hair. Several meetings were held, experiments were made in using flax as a substitute for the hair, but they were not successful. Relief was had through a limited number of import licenses.

EXPLOSIVES

The purpose of control and regulation of these several chemicals and of cotton linters was to insure at fair prices an adequate supply of powder and explosives not only for our own Government but for the Allies as well. For after all is said and done, more than half of the burden of supplying the allied line with explosives and propellants fell throughout the entire war on American industry. The raw materials were principally on this side of the water, and the weight of finished articles varied from one-tenth to one-twentieth of that of their constituent parts. Shipping conditions dictated that manufacturing should be done here, even though our plant facilities were negligible when Europe went to war.

While the real responsibility for formulating and developing the explosives program fell with perhaps more peculiar directness on the Ordnance Department of the Army than did that of many other commodities, yet the very significant part which allied purchases had in it and the general governmental problems which it involved made the relations of the War Industries Board unusually important. Exhaustive attention was given to it from the early days of the council onward. Leland Summers was technical adviser to J. P. Morgan & Co. on British and French purchases of explosives during the years preceding our entrance into the war. He was familiar with the powder facilities which had been developed in this country. He and Charles MacDowell, acting first under the council and then under the Board, were very significant factors in working out our Nation's program. In the summer of 1917, Mr. Summers, Gen. Pierce, and Admiral Fletcher were appointed a special committee to draw comprehensive plans for the whole undertaking. Their report was made the basis of the Government program.

During the winter of 1917 and 1918 the Chemicals and Explosives Division remained a single unit. M. F. Chase [10] worked with Mr. Jackling in the erection of the powder plant at Nitro, W. Va. In July, 1918, he returned to the Board to become director of explosives, and the Explosives Division was made a separate unit. Control of the industry was assumed from the start, though formal price fixing was never resorted to. But in exercising this control it was exceedingly important to take care that we should be a help and not a hindrance to the Allies, who had been depending to such large extent upon our nationals for these supplies before we entered the war.

Constant studies of requirements, not only of the United States, but of England, France, Italy, and Belgium, were carried on, while constant studies of existing facilities and plans for extensions and new construction were directed to a comparison of requirements with capacities and of capacities with possible production of raw materials necessary to keep the plants running. A broad view to guide and minute studies to check were necessary at all times. The explosives industry in the United States jumped from a $50,000,000 output in 1913 to a $500,000,000 output in 1917, which in turn had nearly doubled by November, 1918, and the year 1919 would have seen it more than doubled.

Commercial explosives, which constituted nearly all of our output before the war, remained nearly constant throughout the period, increasing a little in 1917 and 1918 because of the increased activities in mining. Our annual production of commercial high explosives has been about 430,000,000 pounds, and of black powder about 400,000,000 pounds.

Our development of military smokeless powder and military explosives during this period is unparalleled in history. In 1914 our smokeless powder capacity was 450,000 pounds per month. On November 10, 1918, we had facilities in operation producing nearly 2,500,000 pounds per day, and plants were nearly completed sufficient for 3,500,000 pounds per day. The developments in the production of ammonium nitrate, picric acid, and T.N.T., while not quite so great, followed an analogous course. We made a few thousand pounds of each of them before the war.

The problem before our Government was to provide for the American program without robbing the allied program here. In fact, increasing difficulties in shipping were making it necessary for the Allies to close down some of their plants at home and depend upon

---

[10] March F. Chase (deceased) was a St. Louis manufacturer.

America for increasing requirements. The vast plant facilities in this country in the spring of 1917, while they were owned by our nationals, had been built at the expense of the allied Governments. While our Government had a legal right to commandeer their output and use it for the American forces, such action would have been hostile to the common purpose. At the very beginning the President announced the policy that we would assist the Allies in taking full advantage of the properties which they had amortized here.

Prices had been from 100 to 300 per cent above normal during 1915, but had come back almost to a prewar basis by the time we entered the conflict. When $1 per pound was being paid for smokeless powder by the British and French, nearly half of the figure was an amortization charge to cover new facilities. The companies could not afford to invest capital in plants, the demand for whose product might come to an end at any moment, except on conditions which would practically pay for the plant out of the first contract. By 1917 renewal contracts were being placed by the Allies at about 50 per cent of this figure. Our operators had gained considerably in technical knowledge, and increased capacities allowed for the introduction of plant economies.

If the Allies were to be protected in their use of the facilities which they had caused to be created, our country had either to amortize further new plants or to build them at Government expense. The latter course was adopted, and $300,000,000 or $400,000,000 was spent in this work. Under this arrangement the price of powder and explosives continued to decline, all parties purchasing at about the same figures.

For nitrocellulose powder, both the Du Pont and the Hercules companies enlarged their plants, and the Government built two new plants of tremendous size. One at Nashville, Tenn.,[11] constructed by the DuPont Co. as agent, was designed for a capacity of 1,000,000 pounds per day and cost about $90,000,000. It was completely equipped with its own acid plants and other facilities for integrating the process of manufacture in the most economical manner. In November, 1918, it was calculated that smokeless cannon powder was being produced there at an actual cost of 38 cents per pound.

The plant covers an area of 1½ by 3 miles, and is 70 times the size of the largest plant in this country before the war. In full operation it would use 1,500,000 pounds of nitrate of soda, 675,000 pounds of sulphur, 450 tons of coal, and 100,000,000 gallons of water per day.

---

[11] Called Old Hickory plant.

The complete plant would have been composed of nine separate units. When the armistice was signed, it was about 80 per cent finished and was producing at about 500,000 pounds per day.

The other Government plant was being built at Nitro,[12] W. Va., for a capacity of 650,000 pounds per day. It was about 50 per cent completed when construction ceased in November. The Hercules Powder Co., which had undertaken to operate the plant, had already produced a large quantity of pyro cotton there. Plans had been drawn for a third Government plant, but no work on it was undertaken.

Under this program America would have supplied the bulk of the propellent powder used on our side of the lines in 1919. In order to simplify the placing of contracts and the control over the flow of raw materials to the plants, the policy was adopted during the summer of 1918 of having the Ordnance Department purchase the entire American output for 1919, the department to resell in turn to the Allies such quantities as their respective programs required. On this theory a contract for 234,000,000 pounds, to be delivered during the first six months of 1919, was placed with the DuPont Co. on September 24, 1918, at a base price of 43¼ cents per pound. This was the lowest figure at which they had ever sold smokeless powder. This gives a notion of the dimensions of the American program for the production of propellent powder.

Modern warfare requires for high explosives, used as shell filler, a tonnage equal to about 85 per cent of that of the propellants. Raw materials for high explosives weigh about 20 pounds to 1 pound of finished product. While England had some of these materials, France and Italy had practically none. Shipping conditions required that America should take the burden of the manufacture, and she set about to do it.

The three principal high explosives used as shell filler were trinitrotoluol, ammonium nitrate, and picric acid. Our production of all three was limited by our facilities for producing the three coal-tar products, toluol (for T.N.T.), aqua ammonia (for ammonium nitrate), and phenol (for picric acid). The country's development in these industries will be explained in the next chapter in connection with dyes.

The United States had not used T.N.T. for shell filler before the war, but by the spring of 1917 the Allies had developed a monthly capacity of 5,000,000 pounds here. This was, however, still needed by

---

[12] Near Charleston.

them. Our requirements, with theirs, would consume much more than could be produced from the toluol which it was possible to turn out in this country. We had used ammonium nitrate, but the Allies had discovered that a mixture of ammonium nitrate and T.N.T. produced a shell filler which was at once cheaper and more easily procured than the pure T.N.T. In October, 1917, this mixture, called "amatol," was adopted as the American shell filler.

New toluol plants were stimulated all over the country. In many cities gas-stripping plants were built. Beehive coke ovens were supplanted by by-product ovens everywhere. Various T.N.T. plants were enlarged. The DuPont plant at Barksdale, Wis., increased its capacity by 2,000,000 pounds per month, and the Hercules plant at Giant, Calif., by 3,500,000 pounds per month. Contracts were signed for the erection of three Government-owned plants at Racine, Wis.; Giant, Calif.; and Perryville, Md. The Racine plant was under construction, but little more than the plans had been finished for the other two when the armistice came. These plans called for a total monthly capacity of 12,000,000 pounds. The working capacity November 11, 1918, was about 22,000,000 pounds per month. The price of T.N.T. followed a course very similar to that of smokeless powder. We were paying less than 50 cents per pound when the end came.

There are three principal processes for the manufacture of ammonium nitrate. The most direct and economical is the nitrogen fixation process used in Germany and Scandinavia. The common process used in America has been the neutralization process, by which aqua ammonia and nitric acid unite to produce the product. It was because no method was in sight for the production of enough either of ammonia or of nitric acid to meet the ammonium nitrate requirements that the two huge nitrogen fixation plants at Muscle Shoals and Sheffield, Ala., were undertaken. It was expected that these two plants would come into operation by the beginning of 1919. A new plant using the Brunner-Mond process[13] was erected at Perryville, Md., and was producing over 450,000 pounds per day on November 11, 1918.

While the fixation plants were being built it was necessary for immediate purposes to stimulate further extensions of plants using the neutralization process. These had reached a monthly capacity of 15,000,000 pounds before the end came. A shortage of ammonia

---

[13] This process is by a double decomposition of nitrate of soda and ammonium sulphate.

was the limiting factor. This commodity was handled by an inter-departmental committee. The Food Administration took control of ammonia and established a fixed price of 8¼ cents per pound. The Government bought ammonium nitrate at 15 cents per pound, and the price was never higher than 20 cents.

Picric acid was the shell filler used by the French and Italians. We used only a negligible quantity in the manufacture of ammonium picrate for armor-piercing shells, and in our Chemical Warfare Service. It is phenol trinitrated. The price before the war was about 25 cents per pound. It jumped to $1.50 early in 1915, when the French began to buy here, and remained at this price until the early part of 1916, when facilities had been amortized in quantity to meet the demands. It sold at 75 cents in December, 1916.

In the spring of 1918 the annual output of our numerous plants was about 135,000,000 pounds. There were no plans for an increase in consumption by the American forces, though, if the war had con-tinued for a number of years, it might have been necessary for us to adopt it as a shell filler as a supplement to our amatol production. This, however, was not contemplated for 1919.

Shipping conditions at this time were making it impossible for the French and Italians to obtain sufficient phenol, sulphuric acid, nitric acid, and other constituents to keep their plants going at home. They asked this country to double its output of picric acid in order to meet their programs. The plan was that France should take 70 per cent of the new product, Italy 20 per cent, and the United States the remaining 10 per cent. With this understanding, the Government undertook the construction of three large plants at Little Rock, Ark., at Grand Rapids, Mich., and at Brunswick, Ga.

We began at the same time to provide for a sufficient production of phenol (for which a synthetic process of manufacture was al-ready on a commercial basis) and the acids and other materials re-quired. This program was just reaching production when the ar-mistice came. It would have been in full capacity early in 1919. Picric acid was selling at 56 and 58 cents per pound on November 10, 1918, and it was the hope of the Ordnance Department to reduce the price eventually to 45 cents.

It is interesting to note that the principal chemicals used in the manufacture of powder and explosives are also the principal chemi-cals of agricultural fertilizers. For war purposes we needed large crops of the fields—cotton, food, and other things—as well as large quantities of cannon filler. In normal times the fertilizer industry is the largest producer of sulphuric acid and other heavy chemicals. It happened that the sulphuric acid used for fertilizer was the weak chamber process kind, so that production for both purposes could be maintained at a maximum. In the case of nitrate of soda and sulphate of ammonia, the problem was more difficult. There was a direct conflict, and in the latter part of 1918 the fertilizer industry would have suffered severe curtailment had the war continued. The big increase in the production of ammonia from by-product coke ovens, brought about by war needs, has given a surplus to the country and considerable exportation is now going on.

CHAPTER 6

Industrial Chemicals

THE RELATION of explosives chemicals to the chemicals used in the dyeing and tanning industries, for the preservation of wood, and for other industrial purposes is very close. The Board found it important to establish further chemical sections, not only to guard the use of chemicals needed for explosives, but to exercise control in the development of certain of these industries essential in themselves to the war and to the civilian population. The following sections were formed at various times during 1918: Artificial Dyes and Intermediates; Industrial Gas and Gas Products; Creosote; Canning Materials and Natural Dyes; Paints and Pigments; Wood Chemicals; and Miscellaneous Chemicals. The technical and consulting staff, functioning from the beginning, handled with unusual skill a large number of special investigations.

ARTIFICIAL DYES AND INTERMEDIATES

There are two aspects to the way in which the war has brought dye manufacturing to America. When the German supply was cut off, the Americans were challenged to manufacture their own dyes. Prices were high enough to stimulate every effort. At the same time the war was demanding for the manufacture of high explosives the same chemicals in huge quantities which for the most part are the constituent materials of synthetic dyes.

Before the war Germany manufactured more than three-fourths of the world's supply of dyes, and nearly all of the intermediates [1] used in their manufacture. This country had plants producing about 10 per cent of its consumption, but 90 per cent of the intermediates used in these plants came from Germany. Every necessary basic raw material, however, except nitrate of soda, is found in this country in abundance greater than we can use. Many of the processes of manufacture were not known here, and the Germans had fought jealously

---

[1] "Intermediates" is the trade name for coal-tar derivatives used in the manufacture of dyes and explosives.

any development. In 1900 we started to manufacture aniline, but the Germans flooded our markets with aniline at a price so low that our plants never got established.

Commerce in German dyes and intermediates began to be curtailed as soon as the war broke out in Europe, and prices rose 1,500 per cent or more before the end of 1915. Two features affected prices: The fact that the shortage was so much discussed led to an extraordinary amount of speculation; and the fact that the cost of dye enters as such a small percentage of the value of finished textiles, while the dye is itself an absolute essential, made textile manufacturers pay any price in preference to closing their mills.

Artificial dyes, called, also, coal tar, aniline, or synthetic dyes, are to be distinguished from vegetable or natural dyes. Natural dyes can not compete with synthetic dyes in normal times, the latter being produced at a very much lower price. The dry distillation of bituminous coal gives as products coke, ammonia, gas, and coal tar. By fractional distillation and other processes, some 150 different chemicals can be derived from coal tar. The elemental derivatives, chief examples of which are benzol, toluol, creosote oil, solvent naphtha, naphthaline, xylol, anthracine, and carbazol, are called in the trade "crudes." By the chemical processing of crudes, the so-called "intermediates" are derived. Intermediates of higher complexity are also made from intermediates of lower complexity. Some of the best-known intermediates are aniline oil, phenol (carbolic acid), salicylic acid, beta-naphthol, and para-nitraniline. For example, benzol, upon treatment with nitric acid, gives nitro-benzol, an intermediate. Nitrobenzol, upon reduction, gives aniline. Aniline, upon treatment with methyl alcohol, gives dimethylaniline, an intermediate. Some 300 intermediates are used in making the 900 synthetic dyes known to the trade.

Very few intermediates were produced in the United States before the war, but in 1917, 134 different intermediates were made by 118 different firms. The total weight was 287,000,000 pounds, valued at $104,000,000. The synthetic phenol industry was created during the war to meet the demands for this material in the manufacture of picric acid. The synthetic process is, however, too expensive to compete with its production as a coal-tar derivative for the normal market. Synthetic dyes are built up from the intermediates.

This country manufactured dyes to the value of about $3,500,000 in 1914 and $68,700,000 in 1917. The production in 1917 equaled the prewar importation in tonnage, but not in the variety of dyes. The azo and the sulphur dyes were made in largest amounts. Only about

3 per cent of the prewar importation of indigo dyes was produced, and the alizarines were little beyond the experimental stage.

The most difficult period of the war for American dye consumers was late 1915 and 1916. Small amounts were brought in from Germany in exchange for shipments of cotton, but it was done with great difficulty on account of British objection. Importations from Switzerland were two or three times normal. American capital was slow in entering the production industry, and many of the processes were protected by German-controlled patents. On September 8, 1916, a dye-stuff tariff law was passed providing for a duty of 30 per cent plus 5 cents per pound on dyes with certain exceptions, 15 per cent plus 2½ cents per pound on intermediates, and placing crudes on a free list. With the passage of this law capital turned to the industry.

The trading with the enemy act, October 6, 1917, broke the German control of patents. Under its provision the Federal Trade Commission was given authority to issue licenses under patents owned by enemy aliens. With this much protection, but under circumstances in which the manufacture of explosives was demanding every pound of coal-tar derivatives which the country could produce, the dye manufacturers built an industry which was in operation in time to save the textile manufacturing business of the country from the disastrous effects of a dye famine.

Supervision of the dye industry was from the beginning of the council an important part of the work of the Chemicals Division. The Artificial Dyes and Intermediates Section was formed in the spring of 1918, with J. F. Schoellkopf, jr., as chief. When he entered the Army in September, V. L. King succeeded him.[2]

Many of the constituent materials of dyes were placed under Government control during 1918—toluol, phenol, acetic acid, wood alcohol, chlorine, caustic soda, nitrate of soda, ammonia, and others. It became the problem of the section to make careful studies of the exact needs of the dye manufacturers in order to supply them with enough to encourage a development sufficient for the necessities of the textile trade and yet not subtract more than was absolutely necessary from the manufacture of explosives.

A number of programs of conservation and curtailment had to be inaugurated. Among notable examples of these are sulphide of soda, toluol, acetic acid, and nitric acid. The demand for olive-drab cloth for uniforms made the consumption of sulphide of soda abnormal. Orders for olive-drab cloth for civilian use were cut to 25

---

[2] Jacob Schoellkopf, Jr., is a prominent Buffalo manufacturer and financier.

per cent, and an agreement was reached with the trade to eliminate them and to eliminate the use of sulphide of soda for dyeing black hosiery, but the end came before this plan was put into operation. A saving was also effected by a rule requiring sulphide of soda to be shipped in fused form instead of crystal form, which is two-thirds water. A new method was discovered by which the quantity of nitrate of soda used in azo dyes was cut down. The use to some extent of vinegar as a substitute for acetic acid was inaugurated.

It was the purpose of the section also to protect the industry in its relation to foreign trade. Two problems arose. A group of Swiss color manufacturers made overtures to obtain the release of certain scarce raw materials from this country under a promise to furnish finished dyes in return to the United States. This action was opposed by the section and was not carried out.

Nutgalls, imported from China, are manufactured into tannin, gallic acid, and pyro gallic acid. These in turn are use for dyes for developing moving-picture films and other films and for medicinals. Shortage in shipping reduced importations, and it became necessary for the section to allocate all that arrived. In order to do this intelligently it was necessary to study the relative needs of each industry using the product and the proportion of nutgalls which should go into each of the acids, in order that each consumer might have his fair share, as the importance of his product was determined.

The close of the war left the dye industry in a favorable condition for full development. Prices of all the constituent materials were immediately reduced and many of them were a drug on the market. Toluol, which had been commandeered at $1.50 per gallon, sold in December, 1918, at 25 cents per gallon. Phenol fell from 43 cents per pound to 11 and 12 cents. * * *

INDUSTRIAL GASES AND GAS PRODUCTS

Early in 1918, J. M. Morehead [3] came to Washington to take charge of stimulating the production of toluol under the direction of Mr. Summers. In the spring the Industrial Gases and Gas Products Section was formed and Mr. Morehead became chief. The section dealt with a large number of commodities, but its principal activities were in connection with toluol, saccharine, acetylene, and oxygen.

Besides the use of toluol in T.N.T. and in synthetic dyes, saccharine and benzoate of soda are made from it, and it enters into

---

[3] John Motley Morehead, a consulting engineer of New York City, was Ambassador to Sweden from 1930 to 1933.

the fabrication of dope for airplane wings. The stimulation of its production has already been noted in this report. During 1917 the Ordnance Department advanced money for the construction of numerous new plants and built several new Government-owned stripping plants at the works of large gas producers. The entire output of the country was commandeered in February, 1918, and a price of $1.50 per gallon was fixed by agreement between the producers and the Government. This price was confirmed by the price-fixing committee in July, 1918. The section took care of all allocations, the Explosives Division agreeing that 5 per cent of the output might be diverted to nonmilitary uses. The rate of production had reached 25,000,000 gallons per year by December, 1918, and would have reached 35,000,000 gallons in 1919. It is estimated that civilian uses will require only about 1,200,000 gallons per year, but it is suggested that at 25 or 20 cents per gallon it might find a use as a dilutent for gasoline as a motor fuel. Toluol is one of the derivatives of the "aromatic series"—benzol, toluol, xylol, and solvent naphtha. If the last stage of refinement, involving the separation of the series into these constituents, be omitted, a product suitable for diluting gasoline could be produced at a profit at 20 cents per gallon.

Saccharine is used as a substitute for sugar, particularly abroad. The principal domestic use is in chewing tobacco. To save toluol, the manufacture of saccharine was restricted and its export stopped during the war. The section, however, permitted enough to be made to satisfy essential domestic needs.

Acetylene gas is produced by adding water to calcium carbide. The electric power for the manufacture of calcium carbide is interchangeable with the power for the manufacture of ferroalloys. The war demand for ferroalloys resulted in a shortage in the carbide supply. Exports were cut off and domestic use curtailed. The section, however, discovered that it would be necessary to supply certain companies doing important war work in South America, and secured export releases for their benefit.

Oxygen is used in connection with acetylene in many kinds of metal work. It is shipped in steel cylinders. The war brought a greatly increased demand, and one of the plants making oxygen cylinders was diverted to the manufacture of trench mortars. By August, 1918, the shortage in cylinders had become critical. The section called a meeting of the industry and after a long conference it was concluded that the situation could be relieved by establishing a system providing for a more rapid return of cylinders. This was accomplished through the cooperation of the large consumers and the Railroad

Administration. Ninety-two per cent of our oxygen output is manufactured by two companies which use the liquid-air process. More than 30 smaller companies manufacture by the electrolytic process. During the war construction began on 21 new plants, calculated to increase the production of oxygen 25 per cent. Some of these were in operation when the end came. * * *

Creosote is a coal-tar product used as a preservative for wood. The chief problem of the section lay in the fact that not enough creosote could be produced to satisfy the needs of the Railroad Administration, the Emergency Fleet, the Army, the Navy, and the Government-controlled telephone and telegraph companies, even by allowing none for private consumption outside these activities.

The ordinary automatic priority rules gave all of these agencies priority, and it was impossible for the producers to decide to which orders they should give preference, for they could not fill all Government orders. Commandeering the entire output was suggested as a solution, particularly by the producers, but the section and the Railroad Administration both opposed this, and a plan was adopted under which the section allocated all orders of the Army, Navy, and Emergency Fleet, giving first preference to these. A letter, setting forth the program, was approved by the priorities commissioner and sent to the producers October 23, 1918.

The railroads were by far the largest consumers, they having used about 40,000,000 of the 52,000,000 gallons produced in 1917. The Administration estimated that it would need 50,000,000 gallons for 1918; but studies of the section made in July showed that only 24,700,000 gallons had been produced during the first six months of 1918, and that not more than 26,500,000 gallons could be looked for during the last six months.

Investigations were made of possible increased production and possible importation from Japan and England. Replies to a questionnaire, sent out by the section July 19, 1918, to the 26 producing companies, indicated that production could not be materially increased during 1918. The section found that 1,000,000 gallons could be obtained from Japan, and that none could be obtained from England.

The Railroad Administration had been studying methods of conservation in substitution of materials for treating ties, and they adopted a program which cut down their requirement about 20 per cent. This, together with the section's careful control over all other

Government orders through clearances, was meeting the situation when the armistice came.

Four of the 26 producing companies turned out over 85 per cent of the supply, and the Railroad Administration bought about 80 per cent of it, and thus were able to maintain a fair price without formal control. Creosote was not used in any way in the explosives program. Creosote remained at 7 cents per gallon from 1913 through until the beginning of 1918, when it rose to 9 cents and remained at that figure until the end of the war.

The Creosote Section was formed in February, 1918, and Ira C. Darling was chief throughout the period.[4]

TANNING MATERIALS AND NATURAL DYES

The tanning materials and natural dyes industries were affected by the war in two ways: (1) The disturbance of shipping made the importation of raw materials difficult; and (2) the shortage and high prices of synthetic dyes brought the more costly natural dyes to the market as a substitute. Very few natural dyes can compete with synthetic dyes in normal times, because their production is more costly and their use has no particular advantage over synthetic dyes of the same color.

Logwood, for example, may be used for blacks on silk and leather and for dyeing wool and cotton black or blue. But it is no better than coal-tar dyes for the purpose. The increase in its use from 1913 to 1916 by several representative textile firms was given by the Tariff Commission as follows: Cotton, 367 per cent; silk, 447 per cent; and wool, 528 per cent, while the average price paid for logwood increased about 320 per cent.

Both the raw materials and finished products of dyes and tanning extracts come to the United States from all parts of the world. The dyes increased more in price and were more difficult to secure than the tanning materials, while the price and scarcity of both varied with different origins. Divi-divi, coming from tropical America, advanced in price to only 160 per cent, while gambier, coming from Singapore, advanced to 600 per cent. The tanning extracts, like chestnut, hemlock bark, and oak bark, being domestically produced, showed very little advance. In fact, oak-bark extract sold at 3.5 cents per pound in January, 1918, while its average price through 1913 was 8 cents. Quebracho extract, coming from South America, sold during 1918 at only about double normal prices.

---

[4] Ira C. Darling is a member of the firm of Bartholomay Darling & Co. of Chicago.

The section was made a separate unit under the Chemicals Division May 1, 1918, and E. J. Haley,[5] who had been handling tanning materials in the Quartermaster Corps, was made chief. By this time the shortage of tanning materials was so great that the problem of the section was to provide for more importations and to take sufficient control over the distribution of both imported and domestic products that the war needs for leather might be satisfied.

Arrangements were made with the War Trade Board and Shipping Board for bringing in 60,000 tons of quebracho extract from Argentina. Shipping could not be provided for quebracho logs. Practically all imports from distant countries had to be eliminated, but arrangements were made for bringing in limited quantities from Central and South America and the west coast of Africa. In order to insure a distribution of these satisfactory to the war program, the War Trade Board granted import licenses subject to allocation of the material upon arrival by the section. The section also allocated shipping space to the quebracho extract shippers. Each tannery was requested by the section to submit a careful estimate of the quantity and kinds of imported tanning materials to be required for the balance of the year on Government contracts. When this information was compiled, a systematic distribution was made in accordance with the supply available, contracts for leather for war purposes being taken care of before all others.

Domestic production also had to have attention. Prices were high, but the rate of output seemed to be decreasing rather than increasing in the summer of 1918. There were 42 plants in the country, most of which produced tanning extracts entirely from chestnut wood. The supply of wood was very short, due to labor and transportation difficulties. The section called a meeting of the extract manufacturers, and in conjunction with the Railroad Administration a zone system was arranged for the chestnut wood producing districts for the purpose (1) of distributing the wood supply where it was most urgently needed, and (2) of conserving transportation.

No price-fixing became necessary, but the section had to limit distribution almost entirely to direct and indirect Government contracts of the United States and Canada, Canadian needs being put on the same basis as our own.

The control over dyewood and natural dyes was very similar to that over tanning materials. The War Trade Board found it neces-

---

[5] E. J. Haley is now sales manager for International Products Co., New York City.

sary to restrict importations to those coming from near-by ports. An arrangement was reached as the result of a meeting with representatives of natural dye manufacturing plants and of the War Trade Board and Shipping Board, to limit the importation of dyewoods and dyes to certain specified kinds and quantities and to grant licenses upon the condition that the section might allocate all of the materials.[6]

Allocations of dyewoods were made to the several manufacturers on the basis of their relative consumption for the three years—1915, 1916, and 1917. This consumption, incidentally, had been two and one-half times the corresponding consumption of the three years immediately preceding 1915. A very effective dyewood war service committee of five members was organized.

The section also handled wool grease. This was first used for the war as shoe dubbin. But it was discovered early in September, 1918, that a large quantity would be needed for the manufacture of lanoline, used to prevent mustard gas burns. The section called a meeting of the producers, presented the facts, and an agreement was reached under which the Government was to take over the entire output at 16 cents per pound, the section allocating the purchases to the Chemical Warfare Service and the Quartermaster Corps.

PAINTS AND PIGMENTS

The section was organized May 6, 1918, with Russell S. Hubbard, chief. Upon the death of Mr. Hubbard, November 5, 1918, L. R. Atwood succeeded him.[7]

The paint and varnish industry of the United States is much larger than that of any other country. The value of its product in 1917 amounted to $175,000,000. There was never any important shortage during the war nor concern in filling Government requirements. Average prices, however, advanced to about 235 per cent of normal, because many of the raw materials consumed by the industry entered also into war production, while others were imported and involved shipping.

The work of the section was devoted chiefly to conservation and

---

[6] See Appendix XXI for ruling of War Trade Board on dyewoods and dyes, effective October 10, 1918.

[7] Russell Sturgis Hubbard, chief of the Paint and Pigment Section, died in the service of his country on November 5, 1918. He had come to Washington with full knowledge that because of his health his death was not unlikely, and he carried on until the end.

also to keeping the Government agencies advised concerning possible shortages in particular elements so that their specifications for producers might be revised so as to avoid shortages. Very important conservation programs were inaugurated: (1) In the use of tin for cans (several sizes were eliminated); (2) for reducing the number of colors produced; (3) for reducing the output devoted to nonwar uses; (4) for substituting female for male workers in the plants; and (5) for reducing the importations of shellac and varnish gums.

The constituent materials for our paint and varnish industry are derived principally as follows. Pigments are substantially all of domestic origin, but of these 400,000 tons were produced in 1917 by chemical or metallurgical processes and only 40,000 tons by the simple crushing, grinding, and washing of minerals. Linseed oil is produced in very large quantities in this country, but in 1917 one-third of it was from imported seed. Flaxseed competes with wheat for farm land, and with wheat at $2.20 per bushel, flaxseed should sell at $3.54 per bushel.

We also use imported china-wood oil and soya-bean oil, the bean being imported from Manchuria. Linseed oil, however, is by far the most important. The gums for varnish, with the exception of rosin, are all imported. Damar gums are from Batavia, Java, and Singapore. The very important Kauri gums are from New Zealand. The copal gums come from the Congo, Zanzibar, Madagascar, Angola, the Gold Coast, British Guiana, the West Indies, and Manila. Shellac all comes from Calcutta. Shellac is derived from a rosinous encrustation exuded by a scaley insect which infests the fig trees of India.

The waxes are also largely imported. Garnabua wax comes from Brazil, Japan wax from Japan, candelilla wax from Mexico, beeswax largely from Cuba, Brazil, and Chile.

The varnish industry is thus dependent to a great extent upon materials which must be transported long distances by shipping. The paint industry finds its best pigments derived from metals widely used in other industries and related to the war program. Lead is a conspicuous example. And finally linseed oil competes with wheat.

An interesting example of the way in which a conservation program is capable of being used indirectly to control prices, even under adverse conditions, is afforded by the case of linseed oil. The price of linseed oil had almost reached its maximum in July, 1918, when importation of seed was cut off. It rose rapidly. The section then began a series of meetings with the paint industry, and, as soon as they had worked out an agreement for a plan to cut down the number of colors and the number of sizes of cans, the slack in the demand for oil was sufficient to cause the price to recede rapidly. It was $1.90 per gallon in September, and $1.55 by November 1.

The importation of shellac was restricted by the War Trade Board, and the section, in agreement with the war service committee of the shellac importers, allocated whatever quantities came in. The same thing was done with Kauri gum. A war conference committee of the paint, varnish, and allied trades on September 18 asked for a hearing before the section, and presented a request to be given a place on the "preference list." The situation was studied and data furnished to the priorities commissioner, but the end came before the request had been acted upon.

WOOD CHEMICALS

This section was formed in December, 1917, when the Secretary of War commandeered the industry. C. H. Connor was section chief. The so-called wood chemicals are the products obtained from the distillation of hardwood. The primary derivatives are acetate of lime, crude wood alcohol, and charcoal.

Acetate of lime results from the neutralization of pyroligneous acid with lime. From acetate of lime is obtained either acetone or acetic acid. In distilling for acetone, methyl ethyl ketone and acetone oil are obtained. Important derivatives of acetic acid are acetic anhydride, ethyl acetate, and amyl acetate.

From the crude wood alcohol the various grades of wood alcohol and methyl acetone are obtained. Wood alcohol is used largely as a denaturing agent for grain alcohol and to make formaldehyde. Both acetone and acetic acid were used in very large quantities in the manufacture of airplane dope. Acetone was also used by the British in making the high explosive cordite.

War purchases of the Allies in this country before we entered the conflict had stimulated both increased production and advancing prices. The British War Mission alone purchased acetone during this period at a rate greater than 50 per cent of the rate of total production in 1914. The average of all prices of wood chemicals was about 190 per cent of normal in the spring of 1917.

As the American air program developed, it became clear that our Government would have to inaugurate important measures of control in order to insure an adequate supply for ourselves without disturbing the American source for the Allies. In December, 1917, by order of the Secretary of War, all wood chemicals were commandeered for Government use, and control over their distribution was placed in the hands of the section. The following prices were established by agreement with the trade, to take effect as soon as existing supplies should be exhausted, stocks on hand to be disposed of by allocation:

		Cents
Acetate of lime	per pound	4
Crude wood alcohol	per gallon	50
Ninety-five per cent wood alcohol	do	79
Ninety-seven per cent wood alcohol	do	82
Pure methyl alcohol	do	86
Methyl acetone	do	86
Denaturing grade wood alcohol	do	79
Acetone	do	25.5
Methyl ethyl ketone	do	25.5

On February 13, 1918, the following prices for acetic acid were agreed upon:

		Cents
Glacial acetic acid	per pound	19
Commercial 100 per cent acid	do	15.75

These prices were all naked at the plant, and a definite charge for the container was to be made. They were continued throughout the period of the war.

Acetate of lime was the limiting factor. Several new plants were started under Government aid during 1918, but they did not reach production. A number of conservation programs were inaugurated. For example, the use of acetone in the manufacture of chloroform was stopped and denatured alcohol used in its place. Two or three new methods of producing acetone were developed. One, called the Weisman process, by which acetone and butyl alcohol are produced from the fermentation of sour and low-grade corn, would have been of great importance had the war lasted longer. Another process obtained acetone from seaweed; and still another from calcium carbide. The production of methyl acetate was developed and the ingredient was used as a substitute for methyl acetone in the airplane program.

The war requirements for acetone were very large, and well over 50 per cent of all the acetate of lime was used for the production of this solvent. Industrial uses were almost eliminated. The draft on acetate of lime for the production of acetone naturally caused a stringency in acetic acid and acetic anhydride, which were also war necessities. It became an important problem of the section to decrease the nonwar uses of acetic acid and its derivatives, which play a large rôle in the manufacture of dyes, tanning materials, chrome yellow, insecticides, etc., as well as acetates.

In order to be sure that there would be enough acetic acid for war uses and yet that as small an amount as possible of acetate of lime should be used for producing this commodity, a program of control was established. All industries were allowed 100 per cent for their Government orders, but no industries were allowed more than 50 per cent for their ordinary needs, except for making synthetic indigo, salvarsin, and cellulose acetate. Certain industries were allowed 25 per cent of their ordinary needs, and other industries (laundry soap, food products, toilet articles, and millinery) were allowed no acetic acid made from acetate of lime.[8]

This ruling naturally led to the use of substitutes. Vinegar, which contains from 9 to 10 per cent acetic acid, was found to be the most important substitute. It was used in insecticides, in white lead, in the bleaching and cleaning of textiles, etc. Lactic acid, formic acid, and Erusto salts were also important substitutes. The section assisted the insecticide industry in obtaining a sufficient supply of vinegar.

Acetic anhydride is used in making acetyl salicylic acid (aspirin). The influenza epidemic in the fall of 1918 made it necessary to release acetic anhydride to increase the production of aspirin. Only 13 per cent of the acetate of lime produced during the first 10 months of 1918 was available for nonwar industries, while the Allies used the solvents made from 60 per cent of the production.

Wood alcohol was never a serious problem. Civilian consumers were allowed 45 per cent of the production in 1918. Its use as a denaturing agent for grain alcohol was restricted, and other agents were substituted, but other conservation was not found necessary.

The American production of wood chemicals in 1917 has been estimated as follows:

Acetate of lime	pounds..	200,000,000
Acetic acid, 28 per cent	do....	80,000,000
Acetone	do....	27,500,000
Acetone oil	gallons..	450,000
Methyl ethyl ketone	pounds..	1,900,000
Methyl acetone	gallons..	1,400,000
Wood alcohol	do....	8,000,000

The production in 1918 was no doubt considerably greater.

MISCELLANEOUS CHEMICALS

On April 23, 1918, the Chemicals Division formed a Miscellaneous Chemicals Section with A. G. Rosengarten[9] as chief. The section

---

[8] See Appendix XXII for the classification of industries using acetic acid, published for the instruction of the trade and subject to revision upon presentation of suitable evidence.

[9] Retired.

held itself ready to study and control a long list of chemicals or to recommend the formation of new sections as necessities might develop. Particular attention had to be given to five of these chemicals: White arsenic, bromine, camphor, celluloid, and metallic magnesium.

The Food Administration had taken charge of white arsenic on account of its importance in the manufacture of insecticides; but in the spring of 1918 a demand developed for it to be used in the production of toxic gas. Studies showed that the annual production here was between 12,000 and 14,000 tons, 8,000 tons being used for insecticides, 2,500 tons in the glass industry, and the balance in miscellaneous industries. To meet the new war demand, its use in the glass industry was eliminated, and steps were taken to reduce the amount used for insecticides. At the same time the Anaconda Co. began the construction of a new plant with a capacity of 10,000 tons per annum. The price was fixed February 23, 1918, at 9 cents per pound f. o. b. plants.

Bromine was required also for toxic gas. Normal production was about 600,000 pounds per annum. This was increased before the end of the war to 1,600,000 pounds, while an additional plant with a capacity of 750,000 pounds per annum was under construction. The Government was installing some 17 deep wells near Midland, Mich., in connection with the bromine manufacturing of the Dow Chemical Co. Bromine is recovered from the bittern remaining after the extraction of the salt from salt brines. The price of bromine rose to 1,670 per cent of normal right after the first German gas attack. It sold at about 75 cents per pound or 250 per cent of normal while we were in the war.

Camphor comes from the Island of Formosa and is controlled by the Japanese monopoly bureau, whose policy it is to restrict its refining except in Japan. Its largest use is in the manufacture of celluloid. The Du Pont Co. has developed a synthetic process for producing camphor from Savannah turpentine as a base. It would appear to be to the interests of the country to have manufacture by the synthetic process continue. The celluloid industry consumes a large quantity of nitric acid, sulphuric acid, and camphor. There are four large manufacturers in the United States, and it is estimated that 250,000 people are connected with its production and distribution. The section worked out a program of curtailment for this industry and made a recommendation to the Conservation Division, but it never became operative.

Metallic magnesium was used in the war in tracer bullets, as an alloy in shells and castings, as a substitute for aluminum in gas masks, as a flux for nickel and Monel metal, and as a deoxidizer and scavenger. It is produced from magnesium oxide and magnesium chloride. In the light of the war requirement for metallic magnesium, the section made a thorough survey of production. It was found that the country's capacity was about 40,000 pounds per month, and that this would not meet the growing demands of ourselves and the Allies. There were plants at Niagara Falls, Rumford, Me., and Lockport, N. Y. The section recommended that the plant at Rumford, Me., be expanded so as to produce 70,000 pounds per month. The Ordnance Department had prepared a contract for this, which was ready to be signed when the end came.

THE TECHNICAL AND CONSULTING STAFF

This staff was organized in the early days of the Chemicals Division to handle special problems arising anywhere in the work and to take up commodities for which separate sections had not yet been found necessary. The staff consisted for the most part of a group of professors of chemistry. Dr. M. T. Bogert began the work. Profs. H. R. Moody, S. A. Tucker, and T. P. McCutcheon were important factors in it.[10] E. R. Weidlein, acting director of the Mellon Institute, carried on important research in behalf of the staff, turning over the valuable equipment and personnel of the institute's laboratories at Pittsburgh without cost to the Government. He was also frequently in consultation at Washington.

The work centered around special problems arising out of the difficulty of manufacturing certain chemicals needed in unusual quantities for the war. It was in particular devoted to developing substitutions for chemicals not obtainable in sufficient quantities. A substitute for platinum in the equipment for the production of acid by the contact process was developed at the Mellon Institute. In the early days of the Chemicals Division, before there were many commodity chiefs, almost every chemical problem, except explosives and nitrates, was referred to this section for such action as was possible with its limited staff. In this way the consulting staff was the origin of many of the chemical sections. The catalogue of cases referred is too long to print here, but a few examples will give an idea of the field.

---

[10] Dr. Bogert is professor emeritus of chemistry at Columbia University. Dr. Moody is professor emeritus of chemistry at the College of the City of New York. S. A. Tucker is curator of the Chandler Museum of Chemistry, Columbia University. T. P. McCutcheon is a professor of chemistry at the University of Pennsylvania.

One of the first tasks attempted by the staff was a complete survey of hydroelectric power which was or might be devoted to chemical manufacture. This was followed by a study of the bromine situation, which resulted in the sinking of new wells in Michigan and the stimulation of production in Ohio and on the Pacific coast.

A problem on the type of cell most suitable for chlorine production and another on plant locations for caustic soda manufacture led, after the general lines of a solution had been worked out, to the formation of the Alkali and Chlorine Section. The staff gave particular attention to the production of radium and the discovery of stocks in existence needed for the war. Both this country and the Allies needed potassium and sodium permanganate for gas masks in quantities unusual in peace time. A method was found for producing them in quantities larger than needed.

The problem of meeting a shortage in sodium silicate, used for food containers, was presented to the staff early in the war. It was solved eventually by eliminating the use of wall board in Government temporary buildings. There was a conflict in demands for the limited supply of arsenic on the part of the insecticide industry, the tanning industry, and the manufacturers of poisonous gases for the war. The Food Administration interceded in behalf of the insecticide producers. The staff devoted considerable attention to the problem and the shortage was finally relieved by a greatly increased production at Anaconda.

When acetic acid was commandeered for use in the manufacture of airplane dope, there followed a severe shortage for commercial purposes, particularly in the textile industry, in laundries, and for the production of insecticides. The staff worked on the question of substitutes in connection with the Wood Chemicals Section. Vinegar, formic acid, and lactic acid proved to be the most valuable substitutes. The production of lactic acid came into conflict with the Gas Defense Service, for the latter was using clippings of vegetable ivory (the normal source of lactic acid) as a source of carbon for canticles.

The staff made extensive investigation of the possibility of a substitution of other oxidizing agents in place of nitrates in the manufacture of explosives. The perchlorates seemed to offer encouragement. These experiments were still going on when the armistice made them unnecessary.

An analogous investigation was made of the question of producing tetryl from dimethylamine, the latter being produced from the nitrogen compound beetain, obtained from beet-root molasses. The beet-root industry was interested and offered important assistance. No conclusions, however, had been reached when the end came.

The ordinary production of phosphorus, limited to a few uses like the manufacture of matches and vermin poisons, is naturally not large. When the war began to use it to produce smoke screens, a great increase in production was necessary. The technical staff solved the problem.

These are only a few of the cases which came before the staff. Many of the chemical problems discussed in connection with the work of particular sections began with the technical staff, and in not a few instances were assisted to a solution by it. The staff did important work in connection with such diverse problems as producing the materials for charging horse masks for gas defense, in producing tear gas, and in developing domestic production of casein for aircraft glues.

CHAPTER 7

Auxiliary Mineral Products

THERE WERE seven further sections which functioned under the Chemicals Division as follows: Refractories and Native Products, Electrodes and Abrasives, Chemical Glass and Stoneware, Asbestos and Magnesia, Mica, Ferroalloys, and Platinum. The work of the sections handling the ferroalloys and platinum has already been discussed in chapter 4, along with other metals, although the important relation of these metals to the chemical industry is obvious.

REFRACTORIES

The general term "refractories" is applied to fire-clay brick, silica brick, etc.; that is, to all materials used for lining furnaces, coke ovens, and other crucibles where a lining capable of withstanding high temperatures and chemical reactions is needed. Refractories are made from various clays and other minerals, a mixture of several substances being usually necessary to secure the desired resisting qualities. Suitable clays occur in numerous parts of this country, but it was the practice before the war for our brickmakers to import quantities of particular clays whose effect in producing certain specific qualities in the brick was well known, Klingenberg clay from Germany is a marked example of this. Most American manufacturers of crucibles have always felt that they could not make a satisfactory product without having the German clay to mix with local materials. Experiment and study during the war has produced a mixture of American clays, which 12 out of 16 manufacturers of crucibles declare to be quite satisfactory, and the others claim that they are getting fair results from it.

Because of the increased activity in smelting and refining metals, occasioned by the war, the supply of refractory brick became a problem of vital importance. The section was formed early in July, 1918, with Charles Catlett[1] as chief. Steps were immediately taken

---

[1] Charles Catlett, of Staunton, Va., is a consultant chemist and geologist.

to make a careful study of the conditions of manufacture and the relation of possible supply to the need. The section found two important difficulties in the industry, in which improvement from a central point seemed possible: (1) Users were in the habit of buying by "brands" rather than by tests of quality and (2) the number and variety of shapes of brick required by different consumers seemed unnecessarily large.

A system of tests for standardizing specifications for clay fire brick had been worked out by the Mellon Institute in conjunction with the Bureau of Standards. The section published these specifications to the trade, asking for comments and objections with a view to issuing them as standard. The problem was considerably involved, and final specifications had not yet been issued when the armistice came.

Standardization of shapes had been proposed and agreed upon to a large extent by the brick makers, but they had not yet been fully adopted by the users. The section was in the midst of work on this problem when the end came.

No attempt was made to fix prices. In a general way the work of the section with the producers was (1) to get them to improve labor supply by special training and better working conditions, (2) to increase the capacity by the installation of additional machinery, and (3) to improve the quality (a) by a more careful study and test of the materials available, (b) by better manufacturing methods, and (c) by better inspection before shipment. The section worked with the consumers to induce them (1) to confine their requirements so far as possible to standard shapes, (2) to differentiate material by tests rather than by brands or trade-marks, and (3) to study more fully the question of suitability of particular brick for specific purposes.

Ceramics.—Ceramics were handled by H. F. Stanley [2] in the technical and consulting staff. The work, carried on in connection with Mr. Catlett, was devoted to the purpose of investigating possibilities of stimulating the further use of domestic clay in American potteries. Before the war we imported annually about 250,000 tons of selected clays, while not more than 300,000 tons of domestic clays were used for our china, porcelain, paper, and linoleum industries. German clays were, of course, cut off, and the British limited shipments to this country to very small amounts.

Attention was devoted not only to studies in the use of domestic clays at the potteries, but also through the State councils of defense and the State geologists to examinations of sources for new types of

---

[2] H. F. Stanley is with the Bureau of Standards, Washington, D. C.

domestic clay. Assistance was given in finding markets and securing transportation for new developments of the domestic product. The potteries found difficulty in persuading their skilled workmen that domestic clays would give satisfactory results.

Production of pottery was stimulated during the war not only by the needs of the Army, Navy, and Shipping Board, but by the general increase in standard of living throughout the country. The demand is said to have increased 300 per cent, while the production was about 75 per cent of normal.

ELECTRODES AND ABRASIVES

The problems falling in this field were handled by S. A. Tucker in the technical and consulting staff until June, 1918, when a separate section was formed with Henry C. Du Bois as chief.

Electrodes.—Electrodes bear the same relation to an electric furnace or an electrochemical crucible as the carbon or other filament bears to an arc light. Carbon electrodes are used only for electrothermic processes, while graphite electrodes are used in both the electrothermic and electrochemical plants. Refiners were hindered in their work considerably during the war from shortages in the supply of electrodes. Efforts were made to increase production, and the output of graphite electrodes was expanded by a ruling that 20 per cent of American graphite should be used in all construction, because the supply of Ceylon graphite was the limiting factor.

But in the spring of 1918 immediate relief seemed to be promised by a more careful distribution of the commodity among the consumers. It was found that many plants had on hand a supply of electrodes sufficient for 15 or 18 months, while other plants had a week's supply or were closed down because it was impossible to secure any. The section took steps to direct that those who had abundance should sell or loan to those who were short. These directions were enforced when necessary through the priority power.

The section formulated a questionnaire which was sent to each of the 300 users of electrodes in the country, and required that it be answered in full on the 15th of each month.[3]

In the light of the information, which was thus brought together by the section, it was possible to control distribution of electrodes in such a way as to keep all plants in operation during the remainder of the war period.

---

[3] See Appendix XXIII for copy of the questionnaire sent to the users of electrodes.

The producing companies were less difficult to handle, for they were only four in number. They reported also on the 15th of each month on a form sent to them by the section.

It was also very difficult to determine whether a plant was using its electrodes for war purposes or not. The plant might be producing a commodity which entered into the manufacture of another commodity, parts of which were useful for the war. For this reason priority among users was practically impossible to determine.

The large chlorine program of the Chemical Warfare Service gave rise to a suddenly increased need for graphite electrodes. A questionnaire was sent out for the purpose of determining to what extent carbon electrodes could be substituted for the graphite ones in certain industries, and plans were being worked out for inaugurating a program of substitutions when the end came.

Abrasives.—"Abrasives" is the term applied to all substances used for grinding and polishing glass, metals, wood, etc. The high-grade abrasives, particularly emery, corundum, and silicon carbide, used in grinding glass, steel, and other metals, were the only ones in which a shortage requiring attention appeared. Emery is required for grinding optical glass. Turkey was the chief source of supply before the war, though a small quantity of low-grade emery is mined in this country. After Turkey was cut off, the Island of Naxos, Greece, became the sole source of high-grade emery for ourselves and the Allies. The French Government controlled its distribution.

This country experienced great difficulty in getting a sufficient supply to satisfy the newly developing optical glass industry. Work had been carried on for some time to develop a synthetic substitute, and in February, 1918, the Norton Co., at Niagara Falls, began the manufacture of an artificial abrasive which satisfied the tests. Other artificial abrasives were being manufactured at Niagara Falls in great quantities, and the congestion at this point, due to the large number of war industries depending upon the hydroelectric power there, caused a stringency in abrasives, which, in the summer of 1918, was threatening seriously to curtail many lines of war work.

It was impossible to do very much by way of classifying consumers because of their complex relation with so many metal industries. Curtailment was left to the indirect effect of other conservation programs, but to stimulate production the priorities commissioner placed the manufacturers of artificial abrasives on Preference List No. 1, and allowed them to store coal for future use. The section induced the Railroad Administration to give the producers special priorities in carrying their raw materials to Niagara Falls. These measures more than made up for the practical elimination of imports, and they solved the problem. A small amount of emery continued to arrive from Naxos throughout the period, but the importation of corundum from India and South Africa was very small.

CHEMICAL GLASS AND STONEWARE

This section, as well as the section on asbestos and magnesia, was in charge of R. M. Torrence.[4] It gave special attention to glass carboys, chemical stoneware, and laboratory glass.

Glass carboys, particularly the 12-gallon ones, were needed in unusual quantities during the war for shipping and storing heavy acids. A serious shortage was threatened in the spring of 1918. The section discovered that it was not the custom to ship back empty carboys for refilling. When this practice was established, by requiring that a clause providing for the return of empty carboys should be in all acid contracts, used stocks in warehouses were cleared and the situation was very much relieved. The civilian use of 5-gallon water bottles and other glass containers was curtailed. The question of production was examined by the section and steps were taken to stimulate its increase. The Illinois Glass Co. built a plant capable of turning out six 12-gallon carboys per minute by the Owens bottle-machine process. The two large older companies, producing carboys by the blown-glass method, were limited by the supply of the highly skilled labor required. The section took steps to guard against having the labor withdrawn by the draft. Some experiments were made in the production of clay carboys as a substitute, but the substitutes were considered unsatisfactory because of their weight and because of the difficulty of inspecting the acid which they contained.

Chemical stoneware is used in the equipment for the manufacture of acids, explosives, fertilizers, and chemicals of every sort. It is required in hundreds of different shapes and forms: pipes, flanges, pump valves, storage receptacles, conveyers, etc. It must be acid proof, not only in glaze but throughout the structure. Chemical stoneware has largely supplanted lead and glass in acid plants. The section made a complete survey of production and facilities, and held a number of meetings with the manufacturers. With such priority assistance as was given the various plants from time to time, they had no difficulty in expanding to meet the war demands. No imported

---

[4] R. M. Torrence (retired) is living at Roland Park, Baltimore, Md.

raw materials are necessary, though Cornwall stone and English china clay are used in normal times.

In scientific glassware, used in chemical laboratories and medical and metallurgical works, American glass blowers were able during the war to develop a product quite as satisfactory as that imported from Germany in normal times. Production was ample for all needs, and it was not necessary for the section to take any important measures of control.

ASBESTOS AND MAGNESIA

A mixture of 85 per cent magnesium carbonate and 15 per cent asbestos with water produces the material used for the heat insulation of pipes and boilers. The war, in its shipbuilding and plant-building program and its aircraft and motor-truck production, needed great quantities of asbestos and magnesia. Our asbestos comes chiefly from mines in the Province of Quebec, Canada, though in 1918 three new properties were opened in Arizona, where a satisfactory product was obtainable. The mines, however, are too far from a railroad to be able to compete with the Canadian production. Our domestic production of magnesia comes from eastern Pennsylvania and southern California.

The section collected full data on the industry, and a meeting was held before the priorities commissioner July 2, 1918. It was decided that the industry as a whole was a war essential and that individual plants should be placed on the "Preference List." It was decided that individual priorities certificates would not be necessary if the concerns engaged in the industry would pledge themselves to distribute their products on orders bearing the highest priority classifications. The section kept in touch with the firms and saw to it that fuel and transportation were furnished in such a way as to guard the Government program.

MICA

Mica or isinglass is a hydrous silicate of potassium, occurring in natural deposits in various parts of the world. The highest grade, or Muscovite mica, comes to us from India through England. Amber mica comes from Canada. Brazil and Argentina also produce the higher grades in small quantities. Large domestic deposits are found in North Carolina and New Hampshire, but our mines have never turned out high-grade blocks or splittings in quantity.

Block, split, and sheet mica are used for motor spark plugs, for condensers or radio apparatus, for condensers for magnetos of automobiles and airplanes, for phonograph diaphragms, for telephone apparatus, in electric generators, etc. It is also used to make lamp chimneys for gas jets and transparent fittings for stoves. Ground mica is used in the fabrication of decorating paints and various building materials. Mica sheets are either natural or are built up from splittings by the use of shellac and high pressure.

The war demands, direct and indirect, were chiefly for the higher grades of mica, and they made necessary a control over imports. The section was formed in March, 1918. * * * It was reorganized in July and placed under the Chemicals Division with C. K. Leith[5] in control and he remained until the end. Lieut. C. P. Storrs, a mica expert, who joined the Navy, was the most important factor in carrying out the control over imports.

It was clear in the spring of 1918 that war needs would make necessary the continuation or increase in imports of high-grade mica from India. England was controlling the supply; she had fixed prices and placed strict supervision over exportations. The British Government was consulted through the State Department, and consented to allocate shipments to us, provided our Government would control the distribution. The section held a conference of the parties interested, and the use of a Navy commandeering order was agreed upon and issued in June, 1918. A list of the importers, to whom the order was issued, was furnished to the British Government, and the British fixed prices plus fixed costs for importing were established as landed prices in the United States. Lieut. Storrs took charge of the commandeering, dividing his time between the commandeering board in New York and the section here.

Enough mica was actually commandeered to maintain a reasonable emergency reserve and to stabilize prices to the users. It was the purpose throughout simply to act as intermediary between importers and consumers, and not to use the authority of the order more than necessary. The mica importers formed an association to represent their interests. Later in the summer the commandeering order was extended to cover imports from South America in order to stabilize prices, and the question of harmony in allied purchasing in that market was taken up through the Foreign Mission of the Board of

---

[5] Prof. Charles K. Leith, geologist of the University of Wisconsin, was also chairman of the Mineral Committee of the Shipping Board and was an advisor on foreign shipments to the chairman of W. I. B. on foreign shipments. He returned to Washington in 1940 as consultant on minerals to the Council of National Defense, Industrial Materials Division.

London. It was not deemed wise or necessary to extend the order to domestic production.

Domestic production increased considerably during the spring and summer of 1918, and some discontent seemed to be exhibited among the promoters. Pressure was brought to bear to have the Government use a much larger part of the domestic output, and requests for financing enterprises were made. In response to this the section undertook a careful investigation of the situation among our own producers.

The Association of Southern Mica Miners and Manufacturers was formed as a war service committee. After a thorough study by the section and by the association, the following conclusions were reached: (1) Artificial stimulation, either in the form of price fixing or financing of mica mines by the Government, was not warranted because its only result could be an increase in the production of the inferior grades, of which there was abundance; (2) there was little prospect that the Government could use a much larger proportion of domestic mica; (3) the situation did warrant the assistance of the Board in priorities and in retaining skilled labor for the production of the commodity, and in having skilled labor returned so far as possible; and (4) new enterprises should be encouraged to the extent of receiving and advising on conditions and the best means of marketing the output.

Slow progress was made by the section in building up a statistical background because of the immense variety of sizes and grades. No questionnaires were used because it was believed that results obtained in this way would be impossible to analyze. Careful estimates of requirements on the part of Government contractors were used as a basis for judging needs.

Toward the end of the period the shortage in higher grade mica began to look serious, even with the increased supplies which were coming from South America. Steps were being taken to get a larger allocation from England when the end came.† It is difficult to make a statement concerning prices because of the infinite variety in the commodity. Prices in 1918 ran from 50 or 60 cents to $12 or $15 per pound, as compared to a range from 25 or 30 cents to $4 or $5 per pound in 1913. The only method of price fixing used was that under the commandeering orders, where the departments concerned fixed the prices.

---

† *Editor's Note:* There is no shortage of mica currently, and a stock pile is being accumulated as a reserve against future contingencies.

CHAPTER 8

Medical Supplies

THE WORK of the Section on Medical Industry was a continuation of work begun by the committee of American physicians for medical preparedness, which was appointed April 14, 1916, by joint action of the presidents of the five leading national medical associations. This committee was taken over by the Council of National Defense shortly after its organization in December, 1916, and continued as a section of the council, a part of it being made a section of the War Industries Board on May 31, 1918. Lieut. Col. F. F. Simpson, of the Army Medical Corps, was secretary of the committee and became chief of the section under the Board.

The first general survey made by the committee disclosed the fact that the country's productive capacity of surgical instruments amounted to scarcely 20 per cent of current civilian needs. In the matter of drugs and pharmaceutical supplies the unpreparedness for a war emergency was not so critical, but in many of these there were important shortages, and prices were very abnormal. Our medicinals come from all parts of the world. Many of them, particularly those derived from coal-tar products, had been manufactured before the war in Germany alone.

A careful inventory of American hospitals disclosed the fact that enough surgical supplies to equip an army of 1,500,000 to 2,000,000 men could be commandeered, in case a pressing emergency made such drastic action necessary, and the result would not cripple civilian institutions beyond repair.

The Medical Section of the council, however, soon determined that work more important than the taking of inventories could be accomplished by them. They secured the appointment, by the chairman of the council, of a committee on standardization of medical and surgical supplies, whose purpose it should be to eliminate, in so far as possible, individual specifications of the Army, Navy, Public Health Service, Red Cross, and civilian agencies, and thereby bring about economies in raw materials and manufacturing facilities. After preparatory studies, this committee and the Medical Section called together in Washington on April 11, 1917, a meeting composed of representatives of the Army, Navy, Public Health Service, Red Cross, the various medical specialties, and manufacturers of surgical instruments.   An agreement was reached that for the period of the emergency the variety of products should be radically reduced. New catalogues of specifications were agreed upon. The most important economies were effected in the production of surgical instruments. The standard illustrated catalogue of surgical instruments in this country before the war contained about 1,100 pages.   The illustrated catalogue accepted by this conference contained 51 pages.

On April 15, 1917, the section held a meeting with some 250 of the leading manufacturers of drugs, medicines, and surgical supplies, and they agreed to begin at once producing at maximum speed the articles agreed upon and outlined in the several lists accepted as staple by the departments and specialists assembled a few days before.

The section also began promptly to bring about a marked increase in the manufacture of surgical instruments. Numerous plants were converted for this work. Manufacturers of household scissors were induced to make surgical scissors. Makers of pocket knives and butcher knives were encouraged to make surgical knives. Sewing-machine companies and jewelry factories began to make surgical needles and other instruments. Nearly all of the surgical needles used in this country had previously been made in England. England's supply was so short that she could not furnish this country more than 5,000 cases of needles for all purposes in 1917, while our military needs alone amounted to 75,000 cases.   Broken needles had to be resharpened for a short period, but the American manufacturers soon began to meet the need, and needles of the highest quality were turned out. The number of styles of surgical needles was reduced by agreement to 12.

The manufacture of dental instruments was about equal to civilian needs before the war, and the extra war requirement was just about met by the conservation involved in the standardization program.

A shortage arose in suture material. This is made by tanning and sterlizing catgut, made principally from the intestines of sheep. The greater part of this raw material is used in sausage casings and for stringing tennis racquets and musical instruments. A very high type of technical skill is required in the preparation of surgical sutures, so that it was difficult to increase the production in this country. The section made provision for increased importations from Spain and New Zealand.

The production of surgical dressings was enormously increased and the Army was supplied with a superabundance everywhere in Europe. The production of clinical thermometers and hypodermic syringes had to be greatly increased to meet the war needs. Very highly skilled workers are required in these industries, and few men with the technical training were found in this country, most of the instruments having been imported from Germany in the days before the war. The stocks of thermometers were commandeered by the Surgeon General at a fixed price of 40 cents each.

This country was a very large producer of medical and surgical rubber goods before as well as during the war. Europe gets its main supply from us. This industry normally uses about 2½ per cent of the rubber consumed in the country. When the importation of rubber was curtailed, the section took care to see that the makers of rubber surgical supplies should receive their full quota. There was a considerable expansion in the manufacture of sterilizers, but to meet the growing discrepancy between production and needs, a conservation program, under which the number of styles was reduced from 96 to 5, was just going into effect when the end came.

To meet the war need for metal hospital furniture, civilian hospitals were asked to stay out of the market so far as possible, and the manufacturers had agreed to sell for civilian purposes only 50 per cent of their normal output. A portable X-ray apparatus on wheels, and carrying its own power to produce current, was developed by the Surgeon General's Department in conjunction with a committee of manufacturers. Work was also done by way of making substitutions for platinum in X-ray tubes. A shortage developed in artificial eyes. The sale of these for civilian purposes was guarded for a while and steps were taken looking to the expansion of the manufacture of suitable glass for their production.

The principal activities of the section in connection with the manufacture of pharmaceuticals were as follows:

(1) Some synthetic drugs had been made under patents held by German firms and made principally in Germany. Under the provisions of the trading with the enemy act of October 6, 1917, these patent rights were granted to American manufacturers, and the manufacture of such commodities as appeared on the approved lists was rapidly developed.

(2) The enormous demand by the war program for such chemicals as phosphorus, sulphuric acid, acetic acid, chlorine, and many others was in excess of the productive capacity of the country. The work of the section in studying the needs of drug manufacturers for these

chemicals and in conferring with the various sections charged with the control of their distribution was of very great importance. While the percentage of each needed for medicinals was very small, the needs were essential to the welfare of both the Army and the civilian population.

(3) Shortages frequently developed in some of the drug-producing plants which are ordinarily grown only in distant lands. The section conferred with the Department of Agriculture on the question of encouraging the production of some of these plants within the United States. Among these were digitalis and castor-oil beans, produced for the double purpose of use in the air program and the medical industry.

(4) The section secured the cooperation of the National Research Council in developing methods of producing substitutes for local anesthetics, such as cocaine and novocaine. The Research Council also worked on the question of producing aspirin under a substitute name. The Bayer patent on acetyl salicylic acid expired February 29, 1917, but the company claimed that the name "aspirin" was secured by their trade-mark. The production of aspirin had been limited by the wood chemicals section in order to economize in acetic anhydride. The section secured a release of this limitation to meet the influenza epidemic.

(5) When the country was divided into cane-sugar zones and beet-sugar zones, it was necessary for the section, in behalf of drug manufacturers whose plants were in beet-sugar zones, to appeal to the Government for arrangements to have sufficient cane sugar shipped to satisfy their needs.

Just before the armistice the section was engaged in a comprehensive collection of data on the exact capacity of the drug manufacturers of the country and the amount and sources of their supplies of raw materials. The inventory of needs, both civilian and military, was then nearing completion. Work along both of these lines, as it affected particular medicinals, had been carried on by the section throughout the period.

Another comprehensive analysis which the section was engaged in at this time would have shown the flow of labor to communities making war materials. Its purpose was to furnish information to the Public Health Service, so that proper medical equipment and attendants might be provided at these centers as their populations increased or decreased. * * *

The average price of medicinals in this country rose very rapidly from the beginning of the war in Europe. Speculation on reserve stocks began almost as soon as importations were disturbed. The advance in drugs remained almost 100 per cent above the general advance in the cost of living, and the war closed with prices at about 320 per cent of normal.

Some individual commodities showed most remarkable fluctuations. Acetiphenetidin sold at 84 cents per pound in 1914 and $42 per pound in 1916; but America discovered a process of manufacture, and it was selling at $2.75 per pound on November 11, 1918, the average 1918 price being $3.94. Licorice root, with a normal price of 4½ cents per pound, sold at 30 cents in 1918. All our licorice comes from the Near East. On the other hand, menthol, with a prewar normal of $4.175 per pound, sold throughout our period in the war at about $3.30 per pound.

The average price of all drugs in the country advanced rapidly throughout our period in the war, and began to decline rapidly upon the signing of the armistice.

CHAPTER 9

Tobacco

A TOBACCO SECTION was formed April 26, 1918, in response to a growing concern over the price and supply of tobacco not only for the
armed forces but for the civil population. A. I. Esberg [1] was made
chief. The section began immediately the preparation of a statistical
background. Studies were made of the purchases and consumption of
the various armed forces and of the Allies and tables were prepared
showing normal consumption both here and abroad. At the same
time investigations were made of the stocks of leaf, the crops, and
the condition of the manufacturing establishments. Records of these
studies are to be found in the files of the Board.

The consumption of tobacco both in this country and in Europe
increased considerably during the war period. It is estimated that
men in service used on an average of 60 to 70 per cent more than
they did in civil life, and that the civil population, due probably to
increased prosperity, the cutting down in this country of alcoholic
beverages, and the sentiment developed by the various campaigns for
supplying "smokes" to soldiers, used 15 or 20 per cent more tobacco
during the war period than before. The stringency, however, was
probably due more to heavy purchases by the Government agencies
of particular brands than to a real shortage in supply. No important control beyond some conservation in methods of packing was
found necessary, though a price-fixing plan was on the calendar when
the war closed.

The studies in average consumption made by the section were
valuable to the Government purchasing agencies in estimating their
needs. There had been some tendency to overstock with particular
brands.

America supplies herself and most of Europe with tobacco. About
1,500,000 acres are planted each year. And the crop for the past

---

[1] Alfred I. Esberg, who had retired from the General Cigar Company prior to
the War, was a sectional chief of the U. S. Food Administration before going to
the W. I. B.

five years has exceeded 1,000,000,000 pounds of leaf, being 1,340,-000,000 in 1918, valued at the farm at $374,000,000.

The country exports annually more than 400,000,000 pounds of leaf besides large quantities of manufactured products.

The country manufactures annually about 240,000,000 pounds of smoking tobacco, 186,000,000 pounds of chewing tobacco, 33,000,000 pounds of snuff, 8,000,000,000 cigars, and 35,000,000,000 cigarettes. Over 700,000,000 pounds of tobacco leaf are consumed in these. If we assume that about 35,000,000 of our population are tobacco users, these figures mean that our consumers average over 20 pounds per annum each.

The price of tobacco was slow in rising as a result of the war. That of the finished product was slower than that of the leaf. The period between the harvesting of the leaf and the turning out of the manufactured product is a year and a half or two years. The sale of the 1916 crop saw the first significant increase in the price of leaf. The 1917 crop, although it was 100,000,000 pounds larger than that of 1916, brought a still higher price and the 1918 crop sold at considerably over 200 per cent of normal.

The demand from Europe, as well as from our own manufacturers, had continued to increase, and when our producers saw by the fall of 1917 that they could successfully increase the price of their manufactured articles, even in the face of the increased revenue taxes, very high prices for leaf were assured. It was not until the middle of 1917 that the prices of finished products began to rise. This was probably due to the fear of injuring the market for well-known brands, and as the tobacco which was being used had been bought two years earlier on a normal market, they were losing nothing in keeping the prices down. But after a careful advertising campaign, smaller packages at the regular prices began to appear and new-sized packages had advanced prices. The advance was steady and rapid, reaching 200 per cent of normal on many products by September, 1918.

At this time the section referred the tobacco question to the price-fixing committee and studies were begun by the Federal Trade Commission into the cost of production and manufacture. This action was accompanied by a decline in prices. The data for price fixing were about ready when the armistice made action unnecessary.

The exportation of tobacco was licensed during the war, but it was not necessary for the War Trade Board to refuse licenses on the ground of safeguarding our own needs. At no time was tobacco on the export conservation list. It has a very high value for its tonnage and the world had been in the habit of depending upon us for its supply. The actual exports in 1917 fell about 47 per cent below those of 1916, but most of the tobacco represented in this decline was purchased in the country by England, France, and Italy and stored here while it seasoned and until a more favorable time for shipping should arrive.

After May 14, 1918, imports of tobacco were prohibited except from Cuba and the West Indies, but imports from other sources had never been very significant. The tax on tobacco has been increased by two successive war revenue acts, one dated October 3, 1917, the other February 25, 1919. But these increases formed a relatively small part of the increase in price.

The section formed a point of contact for the industry in its approach to the Government for aid in getting fuel, transportation, and supplies. The packing of tobacco requires tin, which is imported and was very difficult to secure during the war. There was a substantial curtailment in the use of tin in the tobacco industry. In 1917 the manufacture of chewing tobacco consumed 53,000,000 pounds of licorice root, all of which comes from southeastern Europe and Persia. The chewing-tobacco industry also uses an important amount of saccharine, which is made from toluol, which in turn was much needed for the manufacture of T.N.T.

CHAPTER 10

Forestry Products and Building Materials

WHILE lumber, paper, cement, brick, tile, and other materials falling in this category, had their places in the war program and important regulations were directed to the meeting of Government needs, on the whole the sections handling these commodities, unlike most sections, had as perhaps their principal function the problem of discouraging maximum or even normal production in order to effect economies in labor, capital, and transportation. The total building operation of the country during the war, including war construction, was less than 50 per cent of normal.[1] Separate sections of the Board were formed to handle Lumber, Building Materials, Wood Products, and Pulp and Paper.

LUMBER

The declaration of war brought an immediate requirement for over a billion feet of lumber for cantonments. The country was easily capable of producing it, but it was clear that, if orders for such a quantity should be placed by a large number of competing buyers for quick delivery, a great confusion in prices would follow and delay in deliveries.

A lumber committee was promptly formed in the Raw Materials Division of the Council of National Defense, and its first work was to organize a scheme by which the Government should be able to purchase its building lumber directly from the sawmills at reasonable prices.

The bulk of the cantonment order would fall to the producers of southern yellow pine, for not only is this the leading construction timber in time of peace, but the pine forests were located nearer the sites selected for the camps than were the forests of Douglas fir of the Pacific Coast.[2] The committee called to Washington representative

---

[1] The Nonwar Construction Section of the Board, referred to on p. 58, was the most important direct factor in bringing this about.

[2] For the construction of cantonments, hospitals, warehouses, etc., the woods used by the Government were 76 per cent southern yellow pine, 10 per cent Douglas fir, 7 per cent hemlock, 3 per cent spruce, 1 per cent oak, and 3 per cent miscellaneous.

producers of southern pine lumber. On June 13, 1917, they agreed to a price of $20 per thousand feet for average lumber used for a standard cantonment, giving a mill run average to manufacturers of about $24.85 per thousand. And for the purpose of distributing all Government orders to the sawmills, that their burdens or benefits might be borne in proportion to the size of each mill, plans were laid down for dividing the producing areas into a series of districts, each district to be handled by a "lumber emergency bureau." Four bureaus were organized to handle southern pine, and as time went on other bureaus were formed to handle other building lumber.

Throughout the war whenever a Government order for building lumber was to be placed, the committee, and later the section, would first allocate it to one or more of these emergency bureaus, and each bureau in turn would allocate its share to the various mills under its jurisdiction. Any sawmill could participate in Government orders by listing its stocks and capacity with the emergency bureau of its district. The committee, and later the section, stood ready at all times to investigate any charges of unfair distribution of orders as between the sawmills. Under this system an emergency order could be placed by telegraph in a few hours. One order for 5,000,000 feet was distributed in Louisiana and Texas in five or six hours, and the materials were all shipped within four days. Over 200,000 carloads of lumber, amounting to about 4,000,000,000 feet, were delivered to the Government under these arrangements.

In September and again in October and November prices were slightly reduced by agreement with the manufacturers, the items of the final schedule, adopted Nov. 11, 1917, giving a mill run average of about $23.20 per thousand. In the beginning of 1918 lumber prices to the trade began to advance, and by May they were $5 to $7 above the prices at which the Government was making its purchases. It was believed that production for civilian purposes ought not to be stimulated by high prices. The Federal Trade Commission had been examining the costs of production, and the Price Fixing Committee granted a hearing to the manufacturers in March. But no change in status was made until further hearings on June 12, 13, and 14, 1918, when, after a special committee appointed by the Price Fixing Committee had discussed the question fully with representatives of the southern yellow pine manufacturers in the light of the figures on cost of production presented by the Federal Trade Commission, the Price Fixing Committee reached an agreement with the manufacturers of yellow pine to fix prices for Government and commercial purchasers alike according to the terms of a schedule which was adopted in conference and which averaged about $4.80 per thousand advance over the previous Government purchase prices. It was estimated that the terms of this schedule would yield about $28 per thousand for mill run standard average production.

The manufacturers agreed at the same time to make commercial sales subject, at any time before delivery, to an option in favor of the Government or a nominee of the section. They agreed further to comply with the directions of the War Industries Board as issued from time to time with reference to filling commercial requirements in the order of their public importance, and they agreed to furnish such information and make such reports as might be required. The usual clause protecting labor against reduction in wages or conditions was included. This price arrangement ran to September 15, and just before its expiration the manufacturers appeared before the price-fixing committee with data to show that a further increase was necessary. The committee decided, however, that the same prices should be continued in effect until December 23, 1918. As time went on prices were fixed and other control was instituted over various other types of lumber.

Besides five or six billion feet of softwoods for cantonments, hospitals, warehouses, and other structures, and for boxes and crating, the Government bought for airplane construction over 100,000,000 feet of spruce, 70,000,000 feet of Douglas fir, and four or five million feet of Port Orford cedar. It bought for airplane propellers mahogany, black walnut, cherry, and birch aggregating 40,000,000 feet. The entire black walnut resources of the country were needed for gunstocks, propeller blades, etc. Artillery wheels and Army vehicles consumed about 120,000,000 feet of hardwood. The Emergency Fleet used over 790,000,000 feet, including 2,142,000 feet of locust, for treenails, required for wooden ships and very difficult to secure. The Navy used about 122,000,000 feet.

The total production of lumber in the United States for 1918 was estimated at 32,925,000,000 board feet. Of this about 38 per cent was southern yellow pine, 16 per cent Douglas fir, 6 per cent oak, with white pine and hemlock in equal amounts. This was about 7,000,000,-000 feet less than the production of 1916. The country imports annually from Canada about 3 per cent of the lumber consumed, and we import small tonnages of mahogany and other rare woods from Central and South America and West Africa. Exports are not large even in normal times. Those for the maximum year, 1913, were about three and a quarter billion feet, or 8.4 per cent of our cut. The volume of 1918 was 35 per cent of that of 1913. Europe has taken little since the war began, and even shipments to South America fell off 39 per cent in 1918. Shipping bulk is, of course, the explanation.

The war purchases of the Allies in this country before the spring of 1917, which brought prosperity and high prices to so many industries, causing the average price of commodities to advance before the end of 1916 to more than 150 per cent of 1913 prices, did not have a like effect upon the lumber industry. In 1916 the prices of oak, maple, and chestnut, for example, were below prewar normal, and the average price of all lumber for the year was not above the average for 1913. The events of the spring of 1917, however, saw the prices of lumber begin to advance rapidly. The price agreement on yellow pine, made shortly after our entrance into the war, has been noted. This had a general effect in steadying most other softwoods, for they are sold in competition with yellow pine. By the spring of 1918 prices to the trade of all softwoods had reached a level considerably above the Government purchase prices.

It was felt by the Board that production of lumber for civilian purposes ought not to be stimulated. The Board decided, therefore, that maximum prices ought to be fixed for the trade and the Government alike, to be accompanied by some control over distribution. The Federal Trade Commission had been studying costs of production. Groups of operators, representing the several divisions of the industry, were called into conference in succession. The price-fixing committee established, by agreement, a schedule of maximum prices for North Carolina pine June 28, 1918.[3] This schedule, with slight changes made October 1, remained effective until December 31, 1918. Douglas fir was sold to the Government at an agreed rate similar to the arrangement for yellow pine until June 15, 1918, when the price-fixing committee set maximum prices for all purchases at an average advance over the Government purchase prices of $2.75 per thousand. These prices were continued, after conferences with the producers in October, until January 15, 1919.

The committee established maximum prices on eastern spruce April 12, 1918. These were adjusted after studies of cost by the Federal Trade Commission and following a hearing of the New England Spruce Emergency Bureau on July 19, an advance averaging $8 per thousand being allowed. The July 19 schedule was continued until December 1, 1918. Pennsylvania hemlock was placed on the control list May 9, 1918, the price schedule to expire August 8. On August 15 a new base price of $29 per thousand was adopted, representing

---

[3] See W. I. B. Price Bulletin No. 43, Prices of Lumber, for price schedules.

an average advance of $2. Following conferences in October, these prices were continued until December 20, 1918.

In the latter part of May, 1917, the lumber committee of the council reached an agreement with the yellow pine manufacturers covering prices for a specific schedule of the yellow pine entering into the construction of wooden ships of the Ferris type at an average rate of $35 per thousand feet. The Shipping Board subsequently placed orders with the Southern Pine Emergency Bureau for one hundred schedules on the basis of that price. The prices for a schedule of this kind were later raised by mutual agreement between the manufacturers and the Shipping Board to an average of $40 per thousand, and later, on account of higher specifications, advanced to $44.72. About the same time the fir manufacturers on the Pacific Coast agreed to furnish a schedule of the Ferris type of ship at $37.50 per thousand, the Shipping Board placing orders on this basis until the schedule was changed to call for much larger timbers, at which time the price was raised to conform to the new requirement.

In July, 1917, the lumber committee of the council held conferences with the spruce producers of Washington and Oregon and representatives of the Aircraft Production Board and of the British, French, and Italian missions. The producers agreed to furnish aircraft spruce of specified quality and size during the remainder of the year at $105 per thousand board feet. On April 10, 1918, the Spruce Production Division of the Signal Corps [4] issued a new schedule of prices for western spruce and Port Orford cedar airplane material. The price for "A" wing-beam stock of western spruce and Port Orford cedar was set at $175 per thousand board feet f. o. b. mill; "B" long clears at $80, and "C" short and thin clears at $45. Western spruce cants for aircraft grade I were set at $90 and grade II at $50. These prices remained throughout the period.

No official price was set on black walnut lumber as a whole, but a fixed maximum was placed on gunstock flitches and propeller grades. On August 10, 1917, the Ordnance Department fixed $1.05 each for gunstock dimension blanks f. o. b. mill. On August 1, 1918, the price-fixing committee raised this to $1.20 each. The Signal Corps set a maximum price of $310 per thousand board feet for airplane propeller stock on January 28, 1918, which was continued throughout the period. On August 1, 1918, the price-fixing committee made an informal agreement, placing the price of 2½-inch black walnut

---

[4] After September, 1917, the Board no longer assisted in negotiating or fixing prices for airplane lumber.

flitch at $80 per thousand, and a similar agreement on August 7 on the prices of walnut logs. These prices were published to purchasers and producers of the logs with the announcement that the prices, which the Government was paying for propeller lumber and gunstocks, were based on the announced prices for logs and would allow only a fair and reasonable profit to the mills. Informal agreements were also made and published to the producers, covering cypress, tupelo, birch, and mahogany. Mahogany was placed at $350 per thousand board feet. The price of all lumber during 1918 averaged about 170 per cent of normal as against an average of about 190 per cent for all commodities.

In connection with administering the fixed prices of softwoods to all consumers, certain wholesalers, who had been in the habit of buying from a large number of small mills for resale, raised the question that they should be allowed to add their profit to the fixed mill price. Under the price-fixing rule it had been contemplated that the Government and other consumers should purchase directly from the mills. These wholesalers claimed that they performed a useful function in collecting lumber from mills too small to bargain for themselves. The price-fixing committee ruled, however, that these wholesalers should look for their profits from the producers and should be required to sell at the fixed price.

In order to carry out more effectively the rulings of the price-fixing committee, it was decided early in July, 1918, to appoint a number of regional lumber administrators. * * * To handle the administration of priority in production and shipment, price rulings, and other matters of control in the Pacific Northwest, where so much ship timber and airplane lumber was being produced, the Fir Production Board was appointed in January, 1918, and maintained by the Government departments interested.

In May, 1918, the Railroad Administration began to place its orders for softwoods through the organization for distributing orders, which had been created and was administered by the section. The first order of this kind was for 278,000,000 feet, and other orders followed. The Railroad Administration placed a representative on the staff of the section.

During the course of the war it was found necessary to limit the activities of various wood-using industries in order to make available to the Government the lumber ordinarily used by them and to divert labor, transportation, and supplies to military purposes. This control was exercised chiefly through the Priorities Division, which from time to time issued orders governing priority in securing fuel, trans-

portation, labor, and materials.   On March 21, 1918, the Board passed
and published a resolution, in part as follows:

That in the public interest all new undertakings not essential to and not
contributing either directly or indirectly toward winning the war, which
involve the utilization of labor, material, and capital required in the production, supply, or distribution of direct or indirect war needs, will be discouraged, notwithstanding they may be of local importance and of a character
which should in normal times meet with every encouragement.

In pursuance of this resolution, the manufacturers of the principal
building materials were requested to sign and file with the Priorities
Division the following pledge, and to exact a similar pledge from
such of their customers as purchased for resale:

The undersigned hereby pledges itself not to use, nor so far as lies within
its power permit to be used, any products of its manufacture now in, or
which may hereafter come into, its possession or control, save (a) for essential uses, as that term has been or may be defined or applied from time
to time by the Priorities Division of the War Industries Board, or (b) under
permits in writing signed by or under authority of such Priorities Division;
that it will make no sale or delivery of such products to any customer for
resale until such customer has filed with it a similar pledge in writing and
that it will use its utmost endeavor to insure that its products shall be distributed solely for essential uses.

The Nonwar Construction Section of the Board watched the effect
of these regulations, and at its suggestion Circular No. 21 was issued
September 3, 1918, to all manufacturers, jobbers, distributors, dealers, and consumers of building materials.   This circular contained the
resolutions and pledges referred to above, together with an interpreta-
tion of them in order that—

all interested in the manufacture and sale of building materials, as well as
those interested in building projects of every character, may have a clear
definition of or a ready means of ascertaining the uses to which such materials
may be put, and be advised of building projects which may be prosecuted
during the war with the approval of the War Industries Board.

It announced that building permits would be required for all construction, except under Government contracts "cleared" by the Board,
repairs not exceeding $2,500, construction directly connected with
mines producing coal or metals, and highway improvements approved
by the United States Highways Council.   A few days later the Board

announced that the ruling did not apply to construction already under way.

Preference List No. 1 was issued by the Priorities Division, April 6, 1918, announcing a list of the industries which should receive preferred treatment by all Government agencies in the supply and distribution of coal. Lumber manufacturing plants were not included in this list, but on it were numerous industries using lumber as raw material. On September 3, 1918, Preference List No. 2 superseded Preference List No. 1 and all its amendments and supplements. The lumber manufacturers were not included on this list either, but class groupings were assigned as follows to industries using wood:

Aircraft, I; farm implements, IV; food containers, IV; public institutions and buildings (maintenance and operation of) other than hospitals and sanitariums, III; public buildings (maintenance and operation of) used as hospitals or sanitariums, I; public utilities, II; pulp and paper plants, IV; ships, I; War Department and Navy Department construction work, II.

A series of conservation programs was inaugurated after conference with representatives of each industry involved. On March 28, 1918, producers of walnut timber agreed to refrain for the period of the war from the manufacture of veneer from walnut lumber other than butts, crotches, or figured material. The musical-instrument industry agreed April 9, 1918, to curtail their output 30 per cent and to make arrangements for the transfer of war work to their factories. The builders of farm wagons and trucks agreed July 26, 1918, to make large reductions in the varieties of their product for the purpose of conserving material. This was directed principally to saving iron and steel, but it also reduced the lumber required.

Conservation plans were discussed with the furniture manufacturing industry August 2, 1918, and an agreement was reached September 16, 1918, to cut down the number of patterns made at least 50 per cent. A conservation program was put into effect September 10 by the cotton spool manufacturers reducing the use of lumber, cardboard, twine, nails, and other materials.

On September 17, 1918, Labor Priority Bulletin No. 1 was issued by the priorities commissioner, and defined priority for employees engaged in the lumber industry. This bulletin explained that the essential nature of the industry as a whole was recognized, even though for special reasons it had not been included in the preference list. The district boards were advised that in passing upon claims for industrial deferment, the lumber industry should be treated equivalent to those which appeared in Class IV on the preference list.

Attention was also called in the bulletin to the heavy Government orders for lumber in certain regions.

On October 25, 1918, the priorities commissioner issued Circular No. 54 to all lumber manufacturers, which read in part as follows:

I. Each manufacturer will conserve to the greatest possible extent materials, fuel, and labor; will so far as is practicable, having due regard to the production of lumber necessary for direct war uses, limit his production of lumber to the current demand therefor; will refrain from unnecessary acquisition of and the hoarding of fuel, supplies, equipment, and materials; and will limit his items and amounts of production for export to those covered by export licenses issued by the War Trade Board.

II. No manufacturer will sell or deliver lumber except for essential uses, as that term may from time to time be defined by the Priorities Division of the War Industries Board, which until further order shall include only the following:

(a) For supplying the requirements of the United States Government, or of any department, agency, or bureau thereof, or of the Allies.

(b) For supplying railroads operated by the United States Railroad Administration.

(c) For supplying to others lumber of primary importance in war work or in essential civilian requirements. Each manufacturer should carefully and conscientiously scrutinize every order received for delivery to a user in order to ascertain that the use to which the lumber is to be put is an essential use. Should the manufacturer be in doubt, he will submit the matter to the Priorities Division, making a full statement of the name of the purchaser, the amount of the order, and the use to which it is to be put. Should the lumber be sold to a customer for resale, the manufacturer will protect himself by obtaining the pledge provided for in Paragraph IV hereof.

Construction projects, neither (a) falling within any one of the seven classes not requiring permits by the terms of Circular No. 21 issued by the Priorities Division, September 3, 1918, as revised October 15, 1918, nor (b) for which no construction permit shall have been issued by the Nonwar Construction Section of said Priorities Division shall not be deemed essential within the meaning of the foregoing paragraph.

The circular also contained new pledges for lumber manufacturers and sellers. These various restrictions were removed or modified on November 11, 1918, and all were removed by December 1.

R. H. Downman [5] came to Washington on April 7, 1917, to take charge of lumber under the raw materials division of the Council. He became director of lumber under the earlier Board and remained

---

[5] R. H. Downman (deceased) was a New Orleans cypress dealer.

in charge until January 1, 1918, when Charles Edgar [6] succeeded him and conducted the work until the end.

The work of the committee on emergency construction, first of the council and then of the Board and the Army, should be mentioned in connection with lumber. Col. W. A. Starrett [7] was chairman throughout the period. This committee did very valuable and far-reaching work in bringing together on a common plan of operation the various agencies of the Government engaged in constructing cantonments, hospitals, warehouses, etc., throughout the country.

BUILDING MATERIALS

The Building Materials Division was formed March 16, 1918, with Richard L. Humphrey [8] as director. The control of building materials, other than lumber and steel, began April 21, 1917, with cement, sand, gravel, and crushed stone being added soon afterward. A committee of the council first took up the work. Then building materials were under the Nonferrous Metals Section of the old Board and later under a section by themselves until the division was formed. Mr. Humphrey was connected with the work from October 7, 1917, until the end.

The attention of the division was devoted principally to Portland cement, brick, hollow tile, gypsum plasterboard and wallboard, and sand, gravel, and crushed stone. The conservation regulations discussed under lumber above applied equally, of course, to cement, brick, structural steel, and other building materials, and they need not be repeated here. The building industry had become very active and prosperous by 1916. The general prosperity made necessary plant extensions, and rising wages encouraged the building of homes; and building activity continued into 1917 even with the advancing prices of materials.

By the summer of 1917, however, the advancing cost and scarcity of labor and materials were beginning to effect curtailment. But throughout 1918, as noticed earlier in this report, the Board found it important to institute regulations for the purpose of curtailing construction not necessary for the war. The normal prewar annual building program for the entire country is estimated at $3,000,000,000. War construction for 1918 amounted to about $1,500,000,000. Nonwar construction for the same period is estimated at $1,000,000,000.

---

[6] Charles Edgar (deceased) was a retired businessman of Essex Falls, N. J.
[7] Col. Starrett (deceased) was a prominent architect of New York City.
[8] Richard L. Humphrey (deceased) was a consulting engineer of Philadelphia.

When it is considered that physical valuations in 1918 were about double prewar normal, it is seen that the aggregate physical building in the country, including war building, was less than 50 per cent of normal.

There was no actual war shortage in any of the materials handled by this section. An abundance of Portland cement is produced in various parts of the country, and this is equally true of common brick and the other commodities. But the unnaturally large Government demands in particular congested localities made a limited control over prices and distribution necessary. The Government used only 11,000,-000 barrels of Portland cement in 1918, out of a total production of over 71,000,000 barrels and from an industry which ordinarily produces more than 90,000,000 barrels per year.

Fixed price schedules for cement were arranged, after investigations by the Federal Trade Commission and hearings with the producers, first in December, 1917, and again in August, 1918. The prices were effective over four-month periods. They applied to Government purchases only, and varied with 30 different producing points, from $1.30 per barrel in Texas, for example, to $1.90 per barrel in California. A slight advance in Government price was made for the four-month period ending August 31, 1918, but no advance for the last period of the war. Prices to the general public ranged about 30 cents per barrel higher than the Government prices. On April 13, 1918, the Fuel Administration, in cooperation with the division, reduced the fuel allotment of the cement mills to 75 per cent of normal on the theory that part of the coal used in this industry could be better employed for other war work. This was part of a general program curtailing the use of fuel in building-material industries. Prices were kept low enough to cause an important curtailment of production, and ordinary civilian purchases were running very low toward the close of the war period.

The Government price fixing of brick was also localized and applied to Government purchases only. It varied from such figures as $9 per thousand for light-burned common brick in Chicago to $15.50 per thousand for the same brick in Philadelphia. Throughout the period only about 108,000,000 brick were allocated at Government fixed prices out of a total production of 5,800,000,000 in 1917 and about 2,500,000,000 in 1918. The production and use of brick were declining very rapidly toward the close of the period.

Local prices for Government purchases of hollow building tile were also fixed by the committee, and 176,000 tons were bought by the Government.

By the spring of 1918, due to the Government demands and transportation difficulties, a shortage in sand, gravel, and crushed stone appeared in the congested district of the East, and it became necessary to fix prices and allocate orders in the Philadelphia, New York, Baltimore, Washington, and Norfolk districts. A total of 2,949,879 tons, valued at over $3,000,000, was allocated.

It was the general purpose of the division and the price-fixing committee to hold down the prices of building materials, because normal production was in excess of all essential war needs, and it was desirable, in the interests of war conservation, to enforce a price low enough to have a tendency to curtail production. Prices fixed for building materials allowed about 7 per cent on investments. The division, however, found one item of building material in which the Government required more than double the normal capacity of the plants. This was gypsum wallboard and plasterboard. It was necessary to take over the entire output of these materials for Government use, and to authorize plant extensions. The material was allocated at tentative prices, and the price-fixing committee acted upon the question February 27, 1919. The Government took about 52,000,-000 square feet, valued at $956,000.

The division did a very important body of work in the direction of conservation by preparing and establishing schedules of standard specifications applicable to war building projects. Standardization was accomplished in the following industries: Carpentry and millwork, composition roofing, slate roofing, clay tile roofing, gypsum wall and plasterboard, fiber wallboard, finishing hardware, door hangers and track, plumbing and gas fitting, heating, electric wiring and lighting fixtures, painting, hollow building tile, magnesite stucco, fire prevention and protection.

The extreme difficulty of the work of this division on account of the wide scope and great diversity of the industries under its control can be readily understood. The work covered 43 industries. The division had a staff of 55 persons, exclusive of the representatives of the War, Navy, and other Government departments, who worked with it. Plans for a wide extension of its activities were in process of execution when the end made them unnecessary.

WOOD PRODUCTS

This section originated in October, 1917, when the demands of the Army for escort wagons, artillery wheels, machine-gun carts, and other vehicles seemed to be disturbing the woodworking industry. E. E.

Parsonage was chief throughout the period. A thorough analysis of the wagon industry and light woodworking plants was made. There was a shortage of dry hardwood. The Government gave aid in constructing adequate dry-kiln facilities. The section assisted in allocating the Army orders to the various wagon, truck, and wheel manufacturers of the country, and assisted in inducing about 125 furniture manufacturers to participate by producing vehicle parts.

As time went on, the principal work of the section was to make plans for so allocating the various Government requirements for wood products that the 12,000 woodworking plants of the country might not be driven out of business; for, in general, facilities greatly exceeded war-time needs. At two separate times in 1918 the Army and Navy purchasing agents reported shortages in wooden handles for axes, picks, etc. The section found, upon investigation, both times that the shortage was more apparent than real, and seemed to be largely due to indiscriminate and competitive buying. Arrangements were made to "clear" orders, and requirements were met.

The supply of black walnut had to be very materially increased to meet the requirements for gunstocks and airplane propellers. This section joined the Lumber Division in a "campaign of education" to bring up production. The Boy Scouts were appealed to and gave real assistance.

PULP AND PAPER

The Pulp and Paper Section was organized June 6, 1918, with W. B. Colver as chief. He was later succeeded by T. E. Donnelley, and on October 1 the section was made a division. Its work was then subdivided under a Manufacturing Section, S. L. Wilson, chief; a Paper Economies Section, I. W. Blanchard, chief; a Newspaper Section, G. J. Palmer, chief; and a Fiber Board and Container Section, H. W. Nichols, chief.[9]

This country manufactures about one-half of the world's output of paper. It consumes about 90 per cent of its own production, and its imports amount to about 8 per cent of the domestic consumption. Domestic production in 1917 was 6,595,637 short tons, of which 30 per cent was boards; 22½ per cent newsprint; 17 per cent wrapping

---

[9] Thomas E. Donnelley is president of R. D. Donnelley Sons Co., 350 East 22nd Street, Chicago. S. L. Wilson (retired) lately was president of American Writing Paper Corp. of Holyoke,, Mass. Isaac H. Blanchard (deceased) was lately president of Isaac H. Blanchard Co. of New York City. G. J. Palmer is with the Houston, Tex., *Post.*

paper; 15 per cent book paper; 6 per cent writing paper; and the rest scattered among building paper, tissue paper, specialties, etc.

Our paper is made of basic raw materials as follows: About four-sevenths is made of wood pulp, two-sevenths of old paper stocks, 6 per cent of old rags, 5 per cent of straw and vegetable fibers, and a little over 1 per cent of rope. Various chemicals, like bleaching powder, sulphur, lime, caustic soda, soda ash, clay, rosin, glue, etc., are also used in large quantities, totaling over 1,000,000 tons per year, for the entire industry. Large quantities of felt and copper wire screening are consumed in the plants.

From a report made to the division by 681 paper mills it was estimated that the annual fuel consumption was 9,375,000 tons, that 4 tons of raw materials would produce 1 ton of paper, that 1,204,000 cars were loaded and unloaded annually with materials and products connected with paper manufacture, that the annual output at 1918 prices was valued at $850,000,000, and that 60 per cent of the mills were located in the congested area of the East.

The paper industry passed through two crises during the World War, one in 1916–17 and the other in 1918. In 1916 and early 1917 increased demands, accompanied by difficulties of production, threw the average price of paper to about 200 per cent of normal, causing newsprint to rise to 250 or 300 per cent. Then prices began to decline and continued to go down through the rest of 1917. And it was not until the summer of 1918 that prices had come back to their high level and seemed to be going higher.

This case could not be solved by an increase of production because there was not only a shortage of coal, labor, and transportation, but many of the other materials essential for paper were more essential for direct war purposes—sulphur, soda ash, chlorine, wood pulp, etc. It was planned for 1919 to withdraw 150,000 tons of wood fiber from the paper industry to be used as a substitute for cotton linters in the manufacture of smokeless powder. The solution, therefore, which commended itself to the division was first curtailment and economy in consumption and to a lesser extent the elimination of wasteful practices in production.

The price advance of 1916, following, as it did, a market which had been practically stationary for over 20 years, was led by newsprint. The war in Europe brought us prosperity, and it furnished us with news which the people wanted to read. Increased business meant more advertising and war news meant more newspaper copy. The result was an enormous increase in the consumption of newspaper print. There was more advertising space in each newspaper, there was more news in each paper, and more people bought papers.

Moreover, as the manufacture of munitions began to cause a scarcity of metals, the use of paper as a substitute in the fabrication of containers of all kinds developed rapidly. At the same time the cutting off of importations of pulp and dyes, together with the general rise in wages, made the cost of production advance.

The first work of the division was to study with the war service committee of each branch of the producing industry plans for eliminating wasteful practices and for curtailing the use of certain chemicals needed for the war. Just before the armistice, paper makers had agreed to give up the use of a large percentage of the chlorine to which they had been accustomed. This was to have been done by reducing the amount of bleaching. It would have changed the quality and character of paper very materially.

The priorities commissioner placed the pulp and paper industry on the preference list for coal and transportation, Class IV, in return for pledges to eliminate wasteful usages and pledges to obey all rules and regulations issued by the Board in respect to distributing to consumers. But the great work of the division consisted in the series of regulations worked out and issued to 36 branches of the industry consuming large quantities of paper.

The paper used by daily and weekly newspapers was reduced 15 per cent; Sunday newspapers, 20 per cent; periodicals and general job printing, 25 per cent. It was planned that the paper used for packing should be reduced to the greatest possible extent, consistent with proper protection for carriage. The war service committees of the various industries were in turn invited to Washington, and to these committees were explained the curtailments thought necessary. Each committee was requested to work out its own methods of accomplishing the savings and to recommend such methods to the division. When these recommendations were acceptable to the division, they were mailed to the entire industry with request for criticism. Then, after the division had given careful consideration to all objections filed, the matter was again taken up with the original war service committees and the final regulations were formulated and issued.

The newspaper publishers were met on June 19, 1918, and certain regulations, designed to eliminate wasteful practices, were issued on July 5. On July 19, 20, and 21, another series of meetings was held with the newspaper publishers. The war service committee recommended that the curtailment ruling should not be applied so as to require each individual paper to reduce exactly 15 per cent for daily and 20 per cent for Sunday papers. It was felt that some publishers were so much more wasteful than others that the general curtailment could best be effected by treating many of them individually. The recommendation also contained a clause requiring that all newspapers should be raised to 2 cents, and on this account the division refused to accept it. The committee met again on August 3, and on August 5 a new set of regulations was issued. An organization was formed to obtain reports upon all newspapers, covering size, circulation, and paper used, for the first six months of 1918, with weekly reports for August and September, 1918, and monthly reports thereafter. Through this system the curtailment program was to be administered. In the same manner the "country" newspapers were taken up through their war service committee.

The periodicals were to suffer a curtailment in the use of paper amounting to 25 per cent. Early in July, after a conference with the war service committees of the periodicals' publishers and the trade journal publishers, a set of questionnaires was sent out with a view to establishing the practicability of certain curtailments and regulations suggested by the committees. The answers of the questionnaires showed that it would work a very great hardship to establish over periodicals the rules applied to daily and Sunday papers, particularly to eliminate the return privilege or to eliminate the giving of premiums as inducements to subscribers. Regulations were issued August 22, making reductions in weight and size and advocating the elimination of wasteful practices. No exact percentage of reduction was established so as to apply equally to each publication. But it was attempted, through a careful watch over reports from each publisher, to see that the industry as a whole should curtail from 20 to 25 per cent, and that the burden should fall where it could be borne with the least disadvantage. Accompanying the regulations was a request for a statement from each publisher of his consumption of paper for the year ending June 30, 1918, and also a statement of his requirements for the 10 succeeding months, based on the reductions established by the regulations. Each publisher was required to sign a pledge that he would not exceed his allotment, which was to be calculated by the division as based on a comparison of all requirements filed with possible production. He was also required to file a report every three months showing the exact amount of paper which he had actually used. Special consideration was given to those publications which, during the last few months, had had a legitimate increase in paid circulation, and consideration was also given to those periodicals of an industrial or scientific character whose size had been increased by the demands of the war program. Restrictions did not apply to export journals. The plan was just going into operation when the end came.

A separate war service committee of agricultural publications worked out a plan under which their use of paper was to be curtailed only 15 per cent. Trade books were taken up through the war service committee of their publishers. It was decided that it would be unfair to curtail publishers by reducing the allotment of paper by a certain percentage of the paper used during any previous year. The business of a book publisher varies materially from year to year on account of "runs" on certain successful books. A curtailment made on the basis of previous years would leave some publishers with more paper than they could use and others with a quantity insufficient for carrying on their business. The plan established curtailed each publisher (1) by reducing the number of new titles to be issued; (2) by reducing the weights of paper, sizes of type, widths of margins, etc.; and (3) by the elimination of certain other wasteful practices.

Regulations governing the publication of school textbooks were issued August 21, 1918. They followed the trade books, with the exception that it was found impracticable to reduce the weights of paper and the sizes of type because of the large number of contracts which various publishers had with State governments to furnish books to conform to samples on file. The reduction in new titles constituted the chief economy.

The publishers of medical books objected to having their product classed with either of the above, and desired that no curtailment should be attempted in their field, because it was very important that accounts of the development of medical science occasioned by the war should be published fully. A separate program was established for these publishers on November 1, but it was very soon withdrawn.

The committee representing mail-order houses met the division in June, 1918, and discussed plans for economies in the use of paper in their catalogues. A questionnaire was issued and a meeting held in September to discuss its results and decide upon the regulations. It was found that the preparation of "spring of 1919" catalogues had by that time already reached a stage of completion which would make curtailment impossible, except in circulation. It was agreed that each house should curtail circulation 10 per cent for the spring of 1919 and establish a system whereby their total consumption of paper for the "fall of 1919" catalogues should be diminished by 20 per cent.

Wallpaper manufacturers were met, but little was accomplished in reducing their consumption of paper. Calendar manufacturers met with the division September 26, 1918. It developed that the designs for 1920 were well advanced and that it was too late to curtail the production of calendars for the year 1920, except by limitations on the weights of paper. It was agreed that no regulations would be issued at that time, but that after the first of the year, when plans were being made for 1921, another meeting would be held.

To cover general book, job printing, and lithographing the war service committee decided that the most important economies could be accomplished by limiting the weights of paper at the source and by reducing margins and the number of blank pages. The United Typothetae of America, an association of master printers, held their convention on September 24, 1918, and explained to the trade the desires and the regulations of the War Industries Board, pointing out to all printers the importance of their consulting with their customers with a view to accomplishing the curtailment plan.

On October 2, 1918, the division held a conference with various agencies of the Government for the purpose of developing a plan for eliminating wasteful practices in the use of stationery. Instructions and suggestions were issued to the various Government departments, boards, and commissions. A publicity bureau was organized in the Paper Economies Section of the division. It issued suggestions concerning the unnecessary wrapping of merchandise and other practices in the use of paper and they were circulated among retail merchants throughout the country. "Don't-waste-paper" window cards were broadly distributed. The effect of these various regulations in accomplishing the general purpose of equalizing supply and demand cannot be fairly measured, because few of them had been operating long enough to show results, when the need for such regulation came fortunately to an end.

The division did no direct work on the question of price control and prices were regulated on only one commodity in this field, namely, newsprint. The price which this article had reached by the spring of 1916 caused both Houses of Congress to begin an investigation. A resolution, dated April 24, 1916, requested the Federal Trade Commission to examine into the cost of producing newsprint and the reasons for its high prices. The commission reported June 30, 1917, recommending $3.10 per hundredweight as a fair and reasonable price for newsprint. After a number of appeals and hearings, a base price of $3.10 was established on April 1, 1918. On September 25, 1918, the United States Circuit Court for the Southern District of New

York gave a decision as arbiter that $3.50 per hundredweight was a fair and reasonable base price from April 1, 1918, forward. On October 18, 1918, the Federal Trade Commission, after a series of hearings, decided that the base price should be increased to $3.63¼ per hundredweight to become effective May 1, 1918, to account for the wage increase; and that to account for the freight increase, becoming effective July 1, 1918, an additional amount should be allowed, making the total base price $3.75¼ per hundredweight. On October 30, 1918, the division adopted plans for controlling and allocating all newsprint tonnage to go into operation November 15, 1918, but the order was rescinded before it became effective.

CHAPTER 11

Textiles

THE WAR brought with it a very distinct disturbance in the various textile industries. In clothing alone it became necessary to provide at once entirely new and unusual outfits for a prospective army of 5,000,000 men, and further to prepare for a reserve of four spare outfits for each of these men. Hospital supplies in unheard of quantities, knapsacks, gun covers, hosiery, blankets, overcoats, duck, tarpaulins, tents, shoe linings and innumerable articles requiring textiles had to be provided for at the expense of civilian needs. In a word, it was necessary to direct to war use over 70 per cent of the textile products of this country, and in many cases to create new sources of supply or adapt machinery to new uses. The extent of the undertaking can be appreciated when it is realized that this country's average production of textiles at normal prices aggregates in value between four and five billion dollars per year.

At the same time the shortage of ocean tonnage was causing a shortage in wool. Dyes were almost impossible to obtain. Labor was leaving the factories to go to war or to work in munitions plants, and coal and transportation were becoming hard to secure. Heavy buying by separate agencies of the Government caused unstable markets. The textile industry is old and well established. The mills are controlled by many individual owners, each plant has its specialties, and competition is keen.

The textile problem was taken up by the committee on supplies of the council as soon as we entered the war. War service committees were formed in the summer of 1917 for various branches of the industry. The committee brought together the separate purchasing agencies of the Government, so that they dealt in a group to lay out production programs in consultation with the several war service committees. Many of the members of the textile committee of the council joined the forces of the Quartermaster General in the spring of 1918. Then separate sections of the War Industries Board were formed for the particular branches of the trade.

John W. Scott [1] was director of the Textile Division, which operated under the direction of George N. Peek, Commissioner of Finished Products.

COTTON GOODS

The Cotton Goods Section of the Board, with Spencer Turner [2] as chief, was organized in the summer of 1917. The section inherited a body of information from its predecessor and continued as an information bureau and point of contact between producer and Government purchaser, indicating sources of supply, making allocations, and securing the cooperation of the cotton-goods industry in turning over its production to the Government at reasonable prices. By way of routine, 1,150 questionnaires were used to verify and complete the Government's information concerning equipment and facilities, 2,100 monthly reports from manufacturers were received and classified, 1,733 orders were cleared, and 1,752 priority certificates were recommended and handled by the section.

The heaviest demands of the Government on the cotton-goods trade, and those which strained it most, were for duck, denim, and twills. The shortage in duck and methods for overcoming it had been studied from the beginning of the war. Many carpet and tire-fabric mills converted their machinery for the manufacture of heavy duck, specialty mills for shelter-tent duck, and fine-goods mills for airplane and balloon cloth. But with all that could be done by way of increased facilities the summer of 1918 faced both a present and anticipated shortage in this fabric.

The condition naturally stimulated speculative purchasing and hoarding as well as high prices. Army duck, ordinarily sold at 15½ cents per yard, was bringing 34 cents. Sail duck, normal at 20 cents per yard, brought 52 cents. To combat this, cotton duck was made a "controlled" industry. The manufacturers were called together, and after conference they agreed to sell their product only on permits issued by the section. Under this agreement 1,330 permits were issued.

For the cotton-goods industry as a whole, the question of prices and the advisability of price fixing was a problem continuously before the section. A careful study was made of the condition and recent history of the industry, the sources and condition of the supply of

---

[1] John W. Scott (deceased) was a member of the department store firm of Carson, Pirie, Scott & Co., in Chicago.

[2] Spencer Turner (deceased) was a member of the textile firm of Turner-Halsey Co., in New York City.

raw materials, and the machinery of production, as well as a comparison of war needs with ordinary peace-time consumption. The representatives of the industry itself were for a long time strongly opposed to price fixing. It seemed to them a dangerous departure from the theory on which the business had always been conducted.

The United States grows more than three-fifths of the world's supply of cotton. We export in normal times between 6,000,000 and 8,000,000 bales of 500 pounds each, from a total production of 11,000,000 to 16,000,000 bales. We import only a few thousand bales of the long-staple Egyptian variety for special uses. It happened that our 1914 crop was very large—2,000,000 bales more than usual—while disturbance of manufacturing conditions in Europe, combined with the difficulties of shipping, cut down our exports by more than 1,000,000 bales. This left a surplus to be carried over to the 1915 season of over 3,000,000 bales in addition to the normal surplus of about 1,500,000 bales. The natural result was a great depression in the price of cotton. The "Buy-a-bale" movement was instigated in order to relieve distress among the smaller cotton growers of the South, who were unable to convert their sole source of revenue into money, and for the purpose of improving prices.

By January, 1915, the price began gradually to rise, and continued until the fall of 1916, when the German peace proposal caused uncertainty again. On February 3, the day after diplomatic relations with Germany were severed, the price began to rise sharply and the advance continued until the spring of 1918, when Government price regulations were threatened and later inaugurated. For the greater part of the period from July 27, 1914, until February 3, 1917, prices were below normal.

The crops of 1915, 1916, and 1917 were all below normal, and the consumption abroad, as well as the ability to ship, proved more favorable to sellers than the trade had anticipated. As a matter of fact, less than 250,000 bales of cotton were actually lost at sea during the entire war. The fear, however, that it might be lost, together with the shortage of bottoms, caused a marked decrease in exports. Throughout the war there was always a surplus of raw cotton in the country and this section never found it necessary to control either prices or distribution of the domestic fiber. The Egyptian fiber was imported under the direction of the War Trade Board and the section indicated its distribution.

As soon as the United States entered the war, the prices of cotton fabrics, cotton yarns, and raw cotton all began to rise rapidly—the fabrics more rapidly than the yarns and the yarns more rapidly than the raw cotton. The explanation for this can be found in the very urgent demand for finished fabrics, which had to be met at any cost. To satisfy the increased demand, manufacturing costs were increased both by the use of inferior machines and the conversion of machines to the production of new commodities, and by the expense of breaking in untrained workmen, as well as by increased wages. In addition to these substantial reasons the very urgent war demand, combined with the decentralized purchasing methods in use during the first few months of the war, gave much incentive to speculators and dealers to profit at the expense of the Government.

In the spring of 1917 the cotton goods section of the committee on supplies of the Council of National Defense undertook to recommend to the trade prices which the committee considered as fair and reasonable for a number of fabrics especially needed in war. These prices were accepted by many influential manufacturers and served as a guide to Government purchasing agents in placing contracts.

The war service committee of the cotton manufacturers was organized in September, 1917, with subcommittees on denim, cotton duck, flat duck, outing flannels, tire fabrics, gingham, and ticking. These committees served as points of contact between the manufacturers and the section. They represented the interests of the trade before the section, discussing suggestions, furnishing information, predicting tendencies, etc. For a long time they fought Government price fixing.

Finally, however, a majority of the representatives of the trade were persuaded that price fixing would be necessary in order to prevent profiteering and to insure reasonable prices not only to the Government but to civilian consumers as well. On July 8, 1918, at a meeting of the price-fixing committee with representatives of the cotton industry, maximum prices on certain basic fabrics were agreed upon.[3] Further lists of prices were to be issued as soon as they could be prepared and agreed upon, and accordingly additional schedules came out during July, August, September, and October. The first schedule was to expire October 1, and meetings were held in September for the purpose of agreeing upon a revision, but as no agreement was reached the original prices remained effective until January 1, 1919. All of these fixed prices were maximum net prices at the mills to the United States, the allied Governments, and to the American

---

[3] See Appendix XXIV for schedule of fixed prices for cotton goods, July 8, 1918.

public. They covered primary sales made after June 8 for delivery after October 1 and all primary sales made after June 21. They included brokerage and commission for selling.

A special committee * * * was appointed by the President in the spring of 1918, to study and report on the advisability and feasibility of fixing the price of raw cotton. After an extended investigation the committee reported unanimously against such action.

As a result of the activities of the council and Board, the cotton manufacturers, along with a number of other industries in which vigorous competition had been the rule, have learned some significant new habits. The exigencies of the war impelled the formation of various associations within the industry, in order through cooperation to accomplish war purposes which would have been impossible otherwise. This was all done under closest Government supervision. These associations exchange trade information and will very likely in the future show the effects of cooperation in pursuance of common purposes. This may not result in advantage to the public if it is accompanied by no public control.

WOOL

The chief war problem of the wool industry, unlike that of cotton, lay in the supply of raw material. We now import two-thirds of our raw wool—that is to say, we did in 1917 and again in 1918—and we consumed nearly twice as much wool during those years as we did before the war in Europe began.

The trade enjoyed a season of great prosperity during the years immediately preceding our entrance into the war in spite of the 1913 tariff reductions, which were more than compensated by the economic conditions of Europe. While our people had few war orders for woolen goods, European manufacturers were prevented from producing the surplus which we had ordinarily bought. There was, moreover, a marked increase in the consumption of woolen goods in this country, due, no doubt, to general prosperity and high wages, enabling a larger number of people to use woolen garments.

The annual consumption of raw wool in the United States increased steadily from about 450,000,000 pounds in 1913 to 752,000,000 pounds in 1918. Our domestic production was about 290,000,000 pounds a year. Thus, our imports have more than tripled since 1913. As the period of production from raw wool to clothing varies from six months to a year, it can be seen how a prospective demand for large and prompt deliveries of cloth, such as the war brought about, together with a shortage of wool in sight and a suitable supply of shipping in doubt, would stimulate speculation to the highest pitch unless some control could be devised. Prices rose 65 per cent during the first few months of 1917, and that on top of an already high market, although there was no real shortage of wool in the country at that time.

The first act of the Government in the direction of control was the setting aside in July, 1917, of $25,000,000, to be used in the purchase of wool; and 6,000,000 pounds were immediately purchased by the committee on supplies of the council. This was held through the year, ready to dump in case the market should fluctuate too radically. But it soon became evident that Government buying for actual use was going to be necessary, not only as a price-control measure but in order to make sure of securing a sufficient supply of wool for the war requirements.

In 1916 the British Government contracted with the Australian and New Zealand Governments for their entire output of wool year by year during the war. Our merchants had been obtaining in normal times over 150,000,000 pounds a year from these sources. During 1917 practically no wool came to us from Australasia on account of shortage in shipping. In order to cover the deficit, the War Department on October 10, 1917, arranged to purchase 247,000 bales (123,-500,000 pounds) of this wool from the British Government for delivery in 1918, at the British "civil issues" prices. The British had been able to purchase this wool at very low prices by taking the entire clip and in this way insuring the producers against a shortage of bottoms which might leave them out of contact with the world markets. They resold the wool under two schedules of prices, namely, "military issues," which represented cost plus transportation, and "civil issues," which represented cost plus transportation plus a margin to cover insurance and the overhead incident to the whole wool purchase, the last being divided evenly between the British Government and the respective selling Governments. On November 9, 1918, another purchase of 325,000 bales of Australasian wool was made, but only 110,000 bales were delivered, the rest being canceled without payment of indemnity by the United States, indemnity being waived in consideration of payment by the United States of "civil issues" prices for both lots of wool.

Three other important steps were taken by the Government for the purpose of turning raw wool into direct war-industry channels. In November, 1917, wool was put on the list of materials for which an import license was required, and on December 15 the War Trade Board announced that any applicant for an import license for wool purchased after that date would have to comply with the following regulations:

1. No imported wool should be sold to any person other than a manufacturer without the consent of the War Industries Board.
2. The United States Government should hold an option on all wool imported, for 10 days after the customhouse entry, and thereafter on any unsold part until the whole amount had been disposed of. * * *

The price for Government purchases was fixed on the basis of the Boston exchange price of July 30, 1917, less 5 per cent. It was not, however, until March 1, 1918, that the Quartermaster Corps began to exercise the option to purchase all imported wools.

About this same time the estimates of Army requirements were increased. The available supplies of stocks were studied and found very short. It was decided, therefore, on April 5, 1918, that the Government would purchase all stocks held by wool dealers, and a few days later it was further decided that the Government would purchase the entire 1918 domestic clip. At the request of the Quartermaster General, prices for both transactions were set by the price-fixing committee to be those prevailing on July 30, 1917, or, if wool had cost a dealer more than that, then the July 30 price plus 5 per cent. This placed the Government in complete control of all raw wool in the United States.

Machinery was set up for handling the business. The office of wool administrator, Quartermaster Corps, created in March, 1918, took care of receiving the wool under all three of the purchasing arrangements. The domestic clip was handled through ordinary business channels under the guidance of "regulations" issued by the Wool Division of the War Industries Board on May 21, 1918.[4] On the other hand, the wool distributor parceled out these wools to the manufacturers holding Government contracts as they were needed.

There remained one more problem in connection with the purchase of wool. South America and South Africa were open markets where the Allies and private merchants were competing with each other in making purchases. For the purpose of eliminating competition between American traders and the American Government, an import regulation was made effective July 28, 1918, restricting licenses to the Quartermaster General only. In order to handle the purchases in South America for the Quartermaster General, the South American

---

[4] See Appendix XXV for copy of "Government Regulations for Handling Wool Clip of 1918," issued May 21, 1918, by Wool Division, War Industries Board.

Wool Purchasing Syndicate, consisting of six large importers, was formed under the supervision of the War Department and operated from July 23 until October 10, when the wool purchasing commission superseded it. Under this arrangement 44,500 bales of wool were brought in.

Lewis Penwell was chief of the Domestic Wool Section of the Board throughout the period of control and was responsible for this important work.

It will be seen that from the beginning of the summer of 1918 no new stocks of raw wool became available for civilian uses in the country. At the same time only about 45 per cent of the looms were engaged on war work. This presented a very serious problem, in view of the fact that it was then thought that the war might extend over a period of several years. For the purpose of studying means of relieving this situation, as well as to serve as an information bureau and point of contact for all parties interested in wool manufactures, the Woolen Goods Section of the Board was formed on June 1, 1918, with Herbert E. Peabody as chief.

The Woolen Goods Section sent out questionnaires to determine how much privately owned wool remained in the possession of manufacturers throughout the country. It also, through the war service committees, and through individuals, made a study of the condition of clothing stocks, both wholesale and retail. It was clear that important steps by way of conservation would have to be inaugurated if none of the Government stocks of wool could be diverted to civilian use for months to come, and this appeared to be the case. Instructions were issued to cut off the dyeing of wool and the spinning of yarn for hand-knitting purposes; but at the same time, in order to assist the American Red Cross to obtain its requirements of hand knitting yarns, an appeal was issued to spinners and dealers throughout the country to turn over all stocks on hand to that organization.

A careful study was made of methods of conserving woolen cloth in the manufacture and distribution of clothing. The Conservation Division of the Board, working through the industrial adjustments committee and the priorities commissioner, reached an agreement with the trade and issued instructions designed to cut down the number of styles and to eliminate certain features which required an extravagant use of cloth in the manufacture of men's, women's and children's suits and overcoats. A great saving was effected, both in cloth and in baggage space, by reducing the dimensions of samples carried by traveling salesmen and by reducing the number of sample suits allowed to a given house. It was estimated that several million yards of cloth would be saved annually by these means.

As the shortage of wool began to be anticipated, and actually felt, in the mills manufacturing for civilian consumption, the demand for rags and reworked wools began to be very sharp and the prices advanced rapidly. Very little of this material was used in Government work, so that it was not considered wise to have the Government purchase the stocks. As an alternative, Government control was exercised by means of price fixing, and a rag administrator, A. L. Gifford, was appointed to supervise the application of prices and regulate the distribution of materials.

With no wool in sight for civilian use, speculation began in woolen piece goods in some of the larger markets of the country during the late winter and spring of 1918. In June the Board requested the Federal Trade Commission to make an investigation of the situation in New York. Many pieces of goods, whose sales were traced from the woolen mill through the hands of jobbers and cutters, had changed hands as many as eight times. The presence of Federal Trade Commission agents in the field abated speculation somewhat, though prices continued to climb throughout the year. By fall the privately owned stocks had become so low that persistent demands were made by manufacturers that Government wool be allocated for civilian cloth. The section made a careful survey of available stocks and it was decided that this could probably not be done before April 1, 1919, without encroaching upon necessary military supplies.

The close of hostilities naturally left very large stocks of raw wool in the hands of the War Department because there had been necessity for preparing for the future. On December 30 they amounted to some 313,000,000 pounds plus 70,000,000 pounds in the hands of dealers yet to be taken over. Total purchases by the wool purchasing quartermaster up to March 20, 1919, were 612,450,168 pounds, valued at $436,781,206. There had been sold to manufacturers 235,349,628 pounds, worth $193,347,536. The 1918 domestic clip had amounted to 298,000,000 pounds. Imports for the year were 450,000,000 pounds.

For some months following the armistice the trade was full of misgivings as to how the Government would dispose of these immense stocks. A multitude of suggestions came in. A plan was suggested by the War Industries Board, but it was not adopted. The program was finally announced that sales by auction would be conducted from time to time, such quantities being offered at each auction as the trade was in the habit of absorbing. The auctioneers were given an unannounced minimum price. Sales were suspended during that period of 1919 in which the domestic crop was being marketed.

KNIT GOODS

The Army purchased knit goods to the value of $304,630,850 during the war. It was made by an industry whose product, prior to the war, was mostly cotton, but which under the guidance of this section was quickly transformed for the production of woolen materials suited to military requirements.

There are 1,622 knitting mills of all sizes in the United States, many of them being very small; in fact, less than 5 per cent have an annual production valued at over $1,000,000. It has never been possible to form large combinations in this industry, due partly to the small capital required to start a new plant, partly to the individual quality of many products, and partly to the type of men who have been the leaders in the trade.

Our war orders caused upheaval in the industry almost as soon as they began, first, because they were large and urgent; and, second, because they called for a much higher percentage of shirts and drawers than our mills had been accustomed to producing. While American-made knitting and spinning machinery is considered the best in the world and is exported everywhere, we had been getting many of our knitting needles from England and Germany and our dyes from Germany. Shortages soon developed in needles, dyes, trimmings, and fuel, all aggravated by increasing delays in transportation. Wages increased 100 per cent. The Government had taken control of raw wool, and other raw materials were hard to get. Prices advanced during 1917 from 110 per cent to 280 per cent of those of 1913. It was necessary, as time went on, to convert more and more of the machinery to war work.

In order to cope with all of these problems, the Knit Goods Section was organized on June 10, 1918, with Lincoln Cromwell [5] as chief. He and the men whom he brought in to assist him had been buying knit goods for the Army since the beginning of the war. It had been necessary to draw revised specifications for Army knit goods in order to put into immediate use the machinery which the industry possessed. These men had been instrumental in drawing the revised specifications.

The section served as an information bureau for both the manufacturers and for the purchasing agents of the Government. It com-

---

[5] New York financier, long identified with the commission house of William Iselin & Co.

pleted a census of the underwear materials of the country, showing the weekly production, machinery equipment, and kinds of garments made. A similar census was made of hosiery mills. A census was taken of the knit goods in the hands of jobbers in order to ascertain the condition of the civilian stocks and to determine the steps necessary to protect consumers from unfair prices.

The section was able to arrange with the knitting and yarn mills to eliminate a great deal of useless transportation in the delivery of yarns. Statements of capacity, unfilled orders, and requirements of materials furnished monthly by spinners and knitters enabled the section to guide and control the industry in purchasing yarns and other supplies. All French spun worsted yarns were reserved for the underwear manufacturers. Some Bradford spinning was allotted to the hosiery makers but most of it went to the weavers.

The section, of course, passed on all requests for priorities by members of the trade and made their recommendations to the Priority Division. The section suggested and supervised the conversion of most of the mills from civilian to war work. Factories famous for fine silk hosiery were adjusted to produce woolen stockings. Women's underwear mills were converted by the exchange of machinery to larger sizes to the production of men's heavy woolen underwear. Something like 1,200 stocking machines were specially built to supply the heavy worsted socks for the Army. There was, of course, a shortage of woolen yarns. The section supervised experiments which culminated in the use of a low-grade South American wool (whose usefulness had been limited) for the production of a successful hosiery yarn. The woolen stocking production was developed from practically nothing at the beginning of the war to 8,000,000 pairs per month at its close.

By way of conservation, a program was worked out for eliminating packing boxes in the shipment of knit goods. The materials were baled in place of being boxed. Thus both shipping space and packing materials were saved. A program was worked out for the standardization of colors and models in sweaters, but was not put into effect on account of the armistice.

There was no price fixing in this industry, though there had been a continuous rise since 1915. The Government was buying a high enough percentage of the product to have an important effect in establishing prices and the section worked with the Quartermaster Corps in establishing maximum prices beyond which no Government contracts would be placed. The section secured cost sheets from all mills and analyzed them before bids were requested on any new requirements. It was made known to the manufacturers that no bids would be received for prices in excess of 10 per cent of cost to the low-cost producers.

About 75 per cent of the cost of knit goods is contained in the cost of yarns. It was, therefore, by controlling the price of yarns and in guiding the distribution of raw wool to spinners working exclusively on Government contracts that the section did its most effective work in securing knit goods for the Government departments at reasonable rates.

FELT

The felt industry in its various branches depends principally upon wool, cotton, and to a lesser extent upon rabbit fur for its raw materials. When the Government took control of wool the problem of distributing it suitably to the large number of felt manufacturers became a serious one.

The Army had direct requirements for large amounts of felt for hats, for padding coats, and for the manufacture of armaments, particularly gas-defense equipment. But on the whole this industry was marked by the multitude of indirect requirements for its products, and on this account the work of the section was peculiarly important and difficult. Felt was required for canteens, gas masks, helmets, clothing, hats, caps, splints, shells, fuse boxes, chevrons, surgical uses, packing, shipbuilding, airplane construction, percussion caps, motor trucks, and in small quantities for hundreds of places in all kinds of machinery. Paper makers cannot function without a large supply of felt, which must be constantly renewed in their machines.

When the war began the felt industry was in a prosperous condition with a moderate but remunerative export trade, so that when war bids began to be requested the response was not at all satisfactory. To overcome this, the Council of National Defense established the Felt Section early in the war, and there began the work of studying requirements, advising on specifications in the light of facilities in existence, and of assisting the mills in procuring raw materials, as well as bringing together the various purchasing agencies of the Government. At the beginning the section did a great deal of work in studying specifications, recommending blends and mixtures, and testing finished samples. It also used its knowledge of the industry in advising purchasing agencies regarding costs and fair selling prices for the product.

The Felt Section, under Sylvan I. Stroock [6] as chief, in the form in which it had been effective under the council, continued under the Board, and after the Government took control of wool in the spring of 1918, its work was greatly increased. There was no difficulty involved in passing upon the allocation of wool to factories engaged on direct war orders, but the number and variety of indirect requirements and the number and variety of factories producing felt, some of which was on order from factories producing war materials in whole or in part and some being produced for the open market, rendered the problem of the allocation of raw wool very complex. Arrangements were made with the wool distributor to have all such allocations pass through the Felt Section.

A severe shortage in "textile felts" was showing itself by the spring of 1918. The new Government requirements seemed to show a demand for several times the capacity of the country, while the demands of the allied Governments for both military and civilian use were also very great. The section called together all the manufacturers for a conference. An appeal was made to them to eliminate all sales for civilian uses until the emergency should pass. They agreed to do this and to place the control of both the production of their mills and the sale of their goods in the hands of the War Industries Board. This control was exercised by a system of applications and permits. The manufacturers would submit their orders and contracts to the Felt Section for approval before accepting them. The applications were required to show precisely what types of wool, noils, waste, etc., and what quantities, were required to produce the felt, and to show further what specific Government contract or contracts would later use the felt. In this way felt novelties of all kinds and many other non-essential or less essential products were done away with, in spite of the fact that their manufacture would have carried much higher profits for the mills. A tabulation of the reports of all felt mills for the first seven months of 1918 showed an average profit of but 6.3 per cent. The mills were willing at all times to show the Government their cost sheets for each item, and they accepted such prices as the Government considered fair.

The problem of the factories which required felt in the production of some entirely different Government requirements, direct or indirect, received attention by the section. These factories would apply for permits to purchase felt and for instructions regarding possible sources. In this way it was possible so to direct buyers that various felt mills

---

[6] Member of the firm of S. Stroock & Co., New York City.

were able to make large and long runs of a few varieties of felt and thereby important economies were effected.

It frequently occurred that manufacturers of certain less essential felt products did not possess "trade secrets" necessary to enable them to produce goods required by the Government. At the request of the section many mills gave unhesitatingly of their knowledge to prospective competitors. Methods of conservation and of substitution of other fabrics for felt were matters of continuous study by the section. In a number of those cases the substitutions have worked so well that the use of felt was abandoned until normal times.

Felt cutting is a special industry. The cutters purchase the felt and sell a great variety of small objects like percussion caps, fuse caps, gaskets, buffers, bumpers, oil rings, mats, pads, etc. It was necessary for the section to parcel out felt to the cutters on their individual agreements that the product would be sold for essential uses only.

The sheet felt makers turn out a product ordinarily used in pianos, for dental and surgical work, and for polishing and buffing wheels. These factories proved to be the most suitable for the production of the felt required in gas masks, and their facilities, except those used for surgical and dental felt, were entirely converted to the production of this new war need.

The felt-hat industry brought several problems to the section. Large quantities were needed for the Army, and there was naturally a great falling off in capacity of production for civilian use. Wool and rabbit fur were needed. Rabbit fur comes chiefly from Australasia; and in an effort to force ships from Pacific trade to the Atlantic, an embargo was placed on this commodity along with many others on May 23, 1918. A lot of fur found its way into the country in violation of the embargo, but the Government would not release it on the theory that it would only encourage further violations. The section worked with the War Trade Board and Shipping Board to obtain its release. A program of conservation for the felt-hat industry was worked out by the section. The number of styles and types of hats were reduced considerably, and restrictions were placed on imports, making them conform to domestic specifications in such a way that fair competition should not be destroyed. An elaborate program was worked out for conservation of materials for packing hats. It was designed to save 50 per cent of the shipping space ordinarily required and large quantities of packing material.

The wool felt hat manufacturers were assisted by the section, not by supplying them with wool so that they could continue in their usual pursuits, but by supervising the conversion of their plants to the manufacture of felt for gas masks.

A plan for extensive conservation in the straw-hat industry was also worked by the section. Under it the number of styles and shapes were greatly reduced and plans for shipping and handling samples made more economical. It was put in effect in October, 1918, and canceled shortly afterwards.

There was one special problem which the section worked over in behalf of the manufacturers of paper-makers' felt. They had had a large export business before the war. The paper mills of some foreign countries depend entirely on our felt makers. Thus, when the wool restrictions stopped the export of this commodity, a great struggle began both on the part of the countries who had been accustomed to receiving our felt and on the part of the makers. The section finally worked out a solution which provided for a certain amount of export, all shipments being conditioned on the shipment to this country in return of a corresponding supply of raw wool.

In conjunction with the pulp and paper section, the section conducted experiments looking to a more efficient use of felt in the paper mills, and a set of instructions embodying the results was sent to each paper mill.

Woven felts, used in lithographic work, for newspaper presses, in textile mills, filtering apparatus, etc., presented a problem very similar to that of the paper-makers' felt, and solutions were worked out by the section along the same lines.

SILK

Owing to the comparatively small diversity in the large quantity of silk fabrics required for war work, the difficulties encountered by the industry were intensive rather than extensive. The articles manufactured consisted of cartridge-bag cloth, silk parachute flares, cartridge-igniter cloth, cartridge-bag lacing cord, ballastite rings, taffeta-line, cotton webbing, cap ribbons, cravats, neckerchiefs, spool sewing silks, and banner silk. But there were two principal products involved in the war program; first, the cartridge-bag cloth, a heavy natural silk fabric, and, second, a light-weight pure silk taffeta cloth, used for parachute flares. The cloth most adaptable for these flares was Japanese habutai, but the available stock of this was soon exhausted. To meet the deficiency a similar fabric was woven by American mills and gave complete satisfaction.

But the problem of securing the millions of yards of coarse silk required to make the bags in which all propellent powder for large guns is loaded was a more difficult one. Experiments were made looking to a substitution of cotton cloth chemically treated, but they failed. Silk is the only fabric which is known to be completely consumed in burning, never leaving hot ashes in the gun after firing.

During the first few months of the war, orders were placed by the Ordnance Department for 7,000,000 yards of cartridge-bag silk, and this seemed to absorb the facilities of the country, so that in November, 1917, when a further 10,000,000 yards was needed, new facilities had to be developed. All of the raw materials come from the Far East. To meet the situation the American silk spinners were called together to discuss ways and means. The meeting resulted in the formation of the Allied Silk Trading Corporation, composed of the seven American manufacturing companies, each contributing in proportion to its normal output. This corporation took a contract for the 10,000,000 yards at cost plus 7½ per cent. This 7½ per cent was later voluntarily reduced to 1 per cent. A further contract for 20,000,000 yards was placed with the corporation on July 12, 1918.

Production was just about meeting the program on November 11. A great many cotton and woolen looms were converted to the production of this silk. The corporation itself did much of the buying of raw material abroad, but as the demand was so searching speculation by American jobbers naturally began to creep in. To cope with this, the War Trade Board, at the request of the War Industries Board, made a ruling empowering the Government to take over any importations of raw materials entering into cartridge cloth at foreign cost plus 2 per cent.

The Silk Section of the Board was not formed as a separate unit until August 2, 1918. William Skinner [7] was chief. The section had numerous smaller problems connected with the purchasing, handling, and testing of silk.

FLAX PRODUCTS

The war problem of the flax industry was handled from the beginning by one man, George F. Smith,[9] who came to Washington in June, 1917, as advisor to the Ordnance Department on linen thread. In the autumn he was attached to the Council of National Defense and the following spring was made a section chief of the War Industries Board.

---

[7] William Skinner has been for many years the head of William Skinner & Sons of Holyoke, Mass., and New York City.

Linen thread is required for sewing all kinds of leather goods and canvas equipment. It is quite superior to cotton both on account of its strength and durability and because moisture causes it to swell and fill out the hole made by the needle in sewing. This country imports most of its flax. The 1913 tariff reduction weakened the industry. It had scarcely recovered when we entered the war, and a greatly increased supply was required to meet the increased demand for finished leather goods. A shortage was anticipated from the start, and experiments were conducted for the purpose of finding a suitable substitute or method of diluting the base material. An admixture of hemp to the flax was tried and to a limited extent was successful. Cotton thread was used as a substitute, also with limited success. The use of flax for linen cloth was practically eliminated during the war.

The problem of the section was to assist in getting a suitable supply of flax into the country, to guide in its distribution to the thread trade, and so to control the distribution of the linen thread itself that various war orders could be met.

England controls the world's trade in flax, which is raised chiefly in Russia, Belgium, Holland, Ireland, France, and Canada. Russian flax is of an inferior quality and has to have an admixture of Irish or Belgian fiber to produce a good thread. There was throughout the war a struggle with the British to obtain from them enough of the Irish product for this country.

On February 25, 1918, a system of control over the distribution of thread by licenses was established. From that date forward no orders were accepted nor shipments made by the trade to any destination, military, naval, or civilian, without first obtaining a license from the Board. A list was secured from each manufacturer of all unfilled orders on his books. These were examined and blanket licenses issued for most of them and then all new orders had to be submitted for approval.

Restrictions in the civilian use of flax gave rise to several interesting problems. All fine gill fishing nets have to made of linen because it gives strength without bulk and is much less visible to a fish than cotton or other line. A great shortage in fishing nets developed toward the autumn of 1918. The Food Administration took a hand in the matter and carried on a correspondence with the British Government looking to a release of nets. About the time of the armistice the nets began to arrive.

The section worked out a program for distributing flax seed through the Department of Agriculture with a view to encouraging and fostering the cultivation of fiber flax in this country, but the plan was never made effective. This country produces a moderate share of the flax-seed consumed here in the manufacture of linseed oil, but the same plant is not available for the double purpose, because fiber flax has to be harvested before the seeds are ripe.

JUTE, HEMP, AND CORDAGE

This section was formed May 16, 1918, with E. C. Heidrich, Jr.,[8] as chief. The two largest problems in this field had to do with (1) jute, which comes from India and produces burlap and gunny cloth, and (2) henequen or Mexican sisal, which comes from Yucatan and is the source of more than 85 per cent of the world's supply of binder twine.[9]

The section also dealt with Manila fiber, kapok, coir yarn, linoleum, cork, and bristles. But none of these involved problems so difficult as burlap and binder twine, though they or their constituent materials are practically all imported into this country.

Upon the declaration of war, cordage and twines of all descriptions, from wrapping cord and linen thread to the heaviest marine cordage, were in immediate demand in extraordinary quantities. Japan increased her shipbuilding rapidly. Our Shipping Board required marine cordage for the emergency fleet. Our navy yards increased their supplies of cordage, jute products, and oakum about 80 per cent. Immense quantities of fiber products of all kinds were consumed in the packing of materials for transportation from the United States to France.

In June, 1918, the Army abandoned crating in wooden boxes because it required too much shipping space, and burlap coverings were in part substituted. The coverings were required to be cut in certain sizes, to be used later in France as sandbags in trench warfare. The British controlled both the jute fiber and the burlap manufactured from it in the mills at Calcutta, India, and Dundee, Scotland.

In 1917 this country imported 325,000,000 yards of burlap, 125,-000,000 pounds of jute cordage, and 196,000,000 pounds of raw jute. We have 554 importers or manufacturers and 2,919 companies which consume large quantities of jute products. One hundred and fifty-four million pounds of gunny cloth are used annually in baling cotton. Sugar, flour, meal, rice, potatoes, nuts, beans, grain, seeds, coffee, wool,

---

[8] E. C. Heidrich, Jr., is vice-president of the Peoria Cordage Co. of Peoria, Illinois.

[9] The Food Administration handled the principal problems relating to binder twine. It also dealt with burlap until September 1, 1918.

fertilizer, nitrate of soda, etc. are packed in burlap for shipping. Meat is wrapped in it for shipment.

In June, 1916, the British Government placed an embargo on the exportation of jute and jute products. They required that all licenses for export into the United States would have to be approved by the British Embassy at Washington and the material purchased through the Textile Alliance (Inc.). Prices were practically fixed at Calcutta by the jute merchants, the British Government taking the position that it was not willing to interfere with the course of a trade of such importance to India. On October 4, 1918, the Board, through the section, secured a voluntary agreement with our importers establishing maximum prices for burlap based on 16 cents per yard Pacific coast for 40-inch, 10½-ounce material, the open market being 21 cents at the time. The agreement further stipulated that these prices should not affect contracts made before October 3, 1918, and that any cancellation of contracts or repudiation of agreements made before that date would be regarded with disfavor.

On October 5 it was further resolved that no licenses should be granted for the importation of burlap or jute without the joint approval of the Board and the Food Administration. At the same time further freight space for the Calcutta-United States burlap trade was secured, so that rates were reduced from 400 to 300 shillings per ton. Buying in the Calcutta market was held up for a short time, so that prices fell from 22.69 cents per yard in September to 15.05 cents per yard by late October, 1918. The January, 1915, price was 4.45 cents per yard. English restrictions were removed February 1, 1919. An international jute executive was under discussion in London when the end came. The Board's foreign mission was negotiating with the Indian Government to have a study made of costs of production with a view to price fixing, which would have effected enormous savings in our purchases.

Referring to the henequen or sisal of Yucatan, there was an abundance produced for all needs; but the fiber is controlled by a Mexican monopoly, the Reguladora. Practically the only substitute for henequen in the manufacture of binder twine is Manila hemp, and not enough of this could be brought into use to combat successfully the power of the monopoly to raise the price of henequen. The problem was solved by the Food Administration buying of the Reguladora on behalf of all American interests at a price fixed by negotiation.

Manila hemp, the chief material for heavy marine cordage, oil-well cables, transmission rope, and similar line, is raised exclusively in the Philippines. Manila hemp sold at 11.19 cents per pound at New

York in January, 1913. It had declined to 7 cents by December, 1914. It then began to rise and reached 15.75 cents in January, 1917, from which point it rose rapidly to 28.25 cents by the beginning of 1918. It continued at this figure until April, when the War Trade Board fixed a minimum price at Manila of 17 cents per pound and a maximum price at New York of 26 cents per pound, with $15 per bale ocean freight rate, to continue for four months from date. In June, 1918, Gov. Harrison, of the Philippines, issued an edict declaring the fixed price null and void after July 25, 1918.

On July 22 the War Industries Board fixed a price on Manila hemp of 14 cents at Manila and 26 cents at New York. In August, the price-fixing committee, at the urgent request of the governor of the Philippines, discontinued price fixing. The purpose of the price fixing had been to steady the market. It was the intent to prevent the too great fluctuations in price which tended to accompany the uncertainty of shipping.

Kapok comes from Java and is used for life preservers, mattresses, pillows, etc. Import and export embargoes were placed upon it, and the Navy commandeered all stocks in the United States.

As a measure for conserving linseed oil, cork, and burlap, the manufacture of linoleum was curtailed to 40 per cent of the 1917 production. The Navy substituted koko mats made from coir yarn as floor coverings and the section took control of the distribution of the latter for Government use.

While the consumption of cork was curtailed by cutting down linoleum manufacture, its use for refrigerators at sea and in the various Army storage plants gave rise to more than normal demands. The section gave aid in securing supplies from Spain, Portugal, and Algiers.

The shortage in bristles did not become apparent until October, 1918, and the plan which the section worked out for revising Army and Navy specifications for brushes and conserving the use of bristles in other ways was never put into effect.

CHAPTER 12

Leather and Rubber

HIDES, LEATHER, AND LEATHER GOODS

The United States manufactures more leather than all the countries of Europe combined. This country is also the largest consumer of leather in the world, the largest item of export being from 15,000,000 to 25,000,000 pairs of shoes per annum. We import raw hides in great quantities. Thirty-four per cent of the cowhides and kips, 72 per cent of the calfskins, 88 per cent of the horsehides, 99 per cent of the goat and cabaretta skins, and 67 per cent of the sheepskins tanned in the United States are imported.

In 1914 we made 292,000,000 pairs of shoes, valued at the source at over $600,000,000, and our product leads the world both in quality and quantity. The war brought new and tremendously increased demands for leather goods. Our shoe manufacturing industry had to produce 20,000,000 pairs of a new type of shoes for the Army in 1917 and 29,000,000 pairs in 1918. Saddles and harness were required in such quantities that a decadent trade had to be brought back to heavy production. More than 3,500,000 leather jerkins and more than 7,000,000 pairs of heavy leather work gloves were actually delivered to the Army. Belting leather and specialties of various kinds were required in extraordinary quantities. These requirements were faced under conditions in which the shipment of raw hides and tanning materials to the United States was becoming increasingly difficult, while the industry was hindered by the common shortage of labor, transportation, and fuel.

The price of hides and leather, however, never reached the high average of all commodities during the war. It advanced rapidly in 1916 until December, when the British inaugurated a system of price fixing, which had a remarkable effect in stabilizing the prices on this side of the water. In December, 1916, our prices averaged about 165 per cent of prewar normal, and they never went beyond 175 per cent throughout the period. Some particular commodities, however, varied from the general average, sheepskin for leather jerkins reaching 350 per cent at one time.

Leather problems were first handled under the council by the leather equipment committee and the shoe committee. The War Trade Board early took control over the importation of hides. In February, 1918, a hide and leather control board was formed, with C. F. C. Stout as chairman. This board functioned in very close cooperation with the Quartermaster Corps, which maintained a large force of field men who did inspecting and collecting of information. In the spring of 1918 the control board was reorganized into the Hide, Leather, and Leather Goods Division of the War Industries Board. The division as constituted during the summer and fall of 1918 had C. F. C. Stout as director and was composed of nine sections, as follows: Hides and Skins, O. C. Howe, chief; Sole and Belting Leather, H. W. Boyd, chief, succeeded by T. Cover; Upper Leather, F. A. Vogel, chief; Harness, Bag, and Strap Leather, F. A. Vogel, chief; Sheepskin and Glove Leather, E. C. Shotwell, chief; Boot and Shoe, C. D. P. Hamilton; Harness and Personal Equipment, C. A. Rogers, chief; Belting, C. B. Rowbotham, chief; and Gloves and Leather Clothing, H. J. Lewis, chief.[1]

With the increasing demands of an increasing Army, prospects for 1919 pointed to Government requirements equal to or exceeding in some branches of the industry our entire productive capacity. These conditions were faced at a time when imports of raw hides had to be cut down in order to economize shipping space, and in light of the fact that hides are a by-product of an industry aimed at producing food, so that domestic output could not be greatly increased. Systems of economies and curtailments in civilian uses seemed to offer the only hope of relief, and it was felt that these should be accompanied by price fixing.

The period of manufacture through the various stages from raw hides to finished articles is so long (six months or a year or more) that plans had to be laid down on an elaborate scale and had to extend over a long period. The problem required a vast amount of organization and a vast amount of study before effective steps could be taken. The numerous branches of this industry involved an invested capital of nearly $2,000,000,000. The purpose of the division was to build up a coordinate scheme of control from the take-off of

---

[1] Owen C. Howe is a partner in the firm of Sands & Leckie, Boston, Mass. Henry W. Boyd is president of Armour Leather Co., Chicago. F. A. Vogel (deceased) was formerly general manager of Pfister-Vogel Leather Co., Milwaukee. C. D. P. Hamilton (deceased) was formerly president of International Shoe Co. of St. Louis. C. F. C. Stout (retired) is a former partner of John R. Evans & Co., Philadelphia. T. C. Shotwell (deceased) was a member of the firm of S. H. Shotwell & Sons, Gloversville, N. Y. T. Cover (deceased) was a partner in Cover & Co. of Philadelphia.

the raw hide to the last stitch of the finished leather product. Steps were taken to eliminate wasteful practices in taking off the hides and in preserving them during the marketing processes. Elaborate plans were worked out for simplifying the manufacture and distribution of certain articles for civilian uses, in order to save leather for the military program without causing a leather-goods famine in the country.

Hides and skins.—The first commodity over which the division inaugurated a control was sheepskins for leather jerkins. The Army demands had caused the price of these to advance to 250 per cent of normal, and the Army needed virtually the entire domestic output, estimated at 1,000,000 pelts per year. On March 20, 1918, the various packers and wool pullers producing these pelts were called together at Washington. The meeting resulted in an agreement whereby the wool pullers promised to give to the tanners of jerkin leather an option on all picked sheepskins at a maximum price of 14 cents per square foot, while the tanners in turn agreed to dress these skins for the Government at a fee of 4 cents per square foot. The arrangement amounted practically to a contract by the Army to take over all pelts of this description at a fixed price for the period ending June 7, 1918.

This made no provision for prices to civilian purchasers, and toward the expiration of the period it was thought best not to renew the contract but to place the whole matter before the price-fixing committee. Data were presented by the industry and by the division, and on June 7 the price-fixing committee adopted a schedule of maximum prices for various grades of sheepskins, ranging from 8 to 18 cents per pound, to be effective for the period ending August 1, 1918. These prices were later extended through October, 1918, when with a slight downward revision they were reissued, effective until the end of January, 1919.

On April 26, 1918, the producers, importers, and distributors of cattle hides met the price-fixing committee for the purpose of discussing a price agreement. The price of cattle hides at this time was declining slightly, but the division had under consideration with the Shipping Board and the Food Administration a plan for curtailing importations in order to economize in shipping space, and it was felt necessary to do something to steady the market before putting this program into effect.[2]

The committee representing the industry presented to the price-

---

[2] These restrictions became operative June 15, 1918, and limited importations of raw hides to certain heavy cattle hides from South America, to hides coming by rail, and to hides coming as back haul from Europe.

fixing committee a schedule calculated on the basis of the average level of prices for the period April 1 to 24, 1918. This was about 10 per cent above current market quotations. The price-fixing committee objected on the ground that it was contrary to their policy to raise existing prices, and the livestock producers objected on the ground that in their opinion no emergency existed sufficient to justify the Government in fixing prices. The committee, nevertheless, issued two schedules of maximum prices on April 30, 1918. Both were calculated on the basis of hides from heavy native steers No. 1, and differentials were applied for other types. A price of 29 cents per pound was set for all stocks on hand April 30, and a price of 33 cents per pound for the domestic take-off during the months of May, June, and July and for imported hides shipped before July 31.

On July 19 another meeting was held with representatives of the industry for the purpose of continuing or revising these schedules. Complaints were made of the impracticability of these fixed prices. It was claimed that the committee had placed an artificial price on hides; that the better grades were being purchased by the Government at the maximum price, thereby keeping the figure up, while the cheaper grades, for which there was little demand, were selling below the fixed maxima. The committee suggested as a solution a reduction in the schedule, but this was objected to on the ground that a change in prices at that time would inject an element of doubt into the market and diminish production. The price-fixing committee, however, after appointing a board made up of members of the trade and of the division to study and draw a new price schedule, established a series of prices based on 30 cents per pound for No. 1 native steer hides, to be effective until November 1, 1918. This schedule was in turn revised downward in October, 29 cents being made the basis for November-December prices and 28 cents for January, 1919, at the end of which period price fixing ceased. The various price schedules were administered by the Hides and Skins Section. The task was difficult and enormous.

There are several thousand junk dealers, hide dealers, and tanners who collect hides throughout the country. Prompt action was taken by the section whenever violations of the schedules were reported, but it was only the good will of the trade as a whole which made a successful administration of the program possible. A set of regulations designed to standardize the taking off of hides and their handling and curing after being taken off was published by the division. Before the end of the war reports were beginning to indicate that these regulations were having an important effect in preventing waste in the branch of the industry producing what are known as "country hides." These regulations were simply an effort to bring up the standard of the small butchers to that of the great packing houses in the handling of hides.

The end came before it was found necessary for the section to allocate domestic stocks. But the rules of the War Trade Board required that all applications for import licenses after June 15 should be accompanied by allocation certificates issued by the section, In this way all imported hides were applied to war purposes.

Sole and belting leather.—Army shoes require a particularly heavy and strong quality of sole leather, and by the spring of 1918 shortages were being felt. On May 18 the section issued instructions to all tanners, sole cutters, strip and block cutters, and shoe manufacturers restricting them in the sale and use for civilian trade to such sole leather as was not suitable for Government shoes. In administering this plan the section required weekly reports from all tanners that it might direct the distribution of accumulated stocks to shoemakers having Government contracts. Weekly reports were also required from shoe manufacturers and sole cutters.

This section had at its disposal a field force which visited tanners for the purpose of guiding the industry in the manufacture of leather meeting the Army specifications. A protracted study was made of the cost of tanning this leather before price fixing was inaugurated.

After this policy was adopted, there was no trouble in supplying the manufacturers with sufficient quantities and quality leathers to cover all Government contracts. At the same time the domestic market was amply supplied with leather of good quality, but of slightly lighter weight than was used in Army shoes. Tanners cooperated to the very fullest extent and it was not necessary at any time to use priorities to get them to do so.

Upper leather.—The term "upper leather" is applied to all types of leather used for the sides or upper parts of shoes. It is made variously of calfskin, kip,[3] sheepskins, goatskins, cabaretta, kangaroo, and horsehide. These depend largely on imports, and as was natural their price advanced to a higher point than that of any other leather during the war.

In addition to the system of weekly reports from tanneries and shoemakers, by which the section was able to assist in a fair distribution of materials and to bring about further standardization in the industry, the section carried through two very large and impor-

---

[3] Kips are hides from young cattle weighing from 25 to 50 pounds per hide.

tant tasks, (1) in connection with the production of upper leather for the new "trench shoe," and (2) the preparation of data for the price fixing of upper leather.

Early in March, 1918, the American Expeditionary Forces decided that our Army shoes were not heavy enough to be suitable for trench service. The British were using a shoe made of bark-tanned India kip, finished flesh out in the natural color. It was a shoe of this character which Pershing's staff decided that we wanted. We had been using a lighter chrome-tanned calfskin. The shoe committee of the Quartermaster Corps designed specifications for the American trench shoe and the section undertook to get the American tanneries to turn out a sufficient quantity of upper leather meeting the new specifications. The standard required was a bark-tanned or chrome-retanned "bend," [4] of kip or calfskin of proper weight.

A great deal of work was done in connection with the plan to fix maximum prices for all purchases of upper leather. This work was closely connected with the work which was going on at the same time in preparation of the price fixing and conservation program to be applied to shoes. The tanners of both the eastern and the western group were called together and formulated recommendations. The Federal Trade Commission carried out a long and painstaking investigation of costs. The differences in the various findings were discussed by the section with various representatives of the trade and were finally, in October, 1918, reconciled. The section, together with representatives of the trade, appeared before the price-fixing committee and recommended a schedule of maximum prices, which was adopted November 1, 1918. The armistice came, however, before it was announced.

Harness, bag, and strap leather.—A schedule of maximum prices for black harness leather to all consumers was established by the price-fixing committee June 25, 1918. It was calculated on the basis of 70 cents per pound, grade A, and reached by the usual procedure. No fixed prices were established for russet harness, bag, or strap leather, though studies had been made and the schedules were prepared when the end came.

The important work of the section was in bringing about a better distribution of leather from tanneries to the harness makers. This was done through a system of periodical reports from both groups. The data thus collected put the section in a position to direct both

---

[4] A bend of leather is a tanned hide with the flanks and other undesirable portions trimmed off.

purchasers and sellers in such a way as to keep up a steady supply of the limited stocks of leather to Government contractors and others.

Sheepskin and glove leather.—This section was active in administering the leather jerkin price-fixing arrangement referred to under hides and skins above. It also had charge of sheepskin shearlings required for saddles and for aviators' boots.

Perhaps the most important work of this section related to the supply of horsehide leather for Army gloves. It appeared in the summer of 1918 that the Quartermaster Corps had authorized purchases of gloves exceeding the country's entire supply of horsehide leather. Through the instrumentality of the section a substitute in the form of cowhide splits was used for the heavy mittens. All horsehide and cowhide split leather was allocated to Government contractors.

Boots and shoes.—This section undertook one of the most ambitious programs attempted by the Board. Its work was the first step in a general plan to reduce the cost of wearing apparel which was undertaken by the chairman of the Board with the approval of the President. A committee representing the retail merchants of the country was called to Washington and notified that immediate steps must be taken to reduce the price of wearing apparel. The director of the division took an active part in the program designed to regulate the price of shoes, as did the Conservation Division and the Priorities Division. The plan was to put the entire industry, including the manufacturers, distributors, and retailers of shoes for civilian use on a controlled basis. The first step in this direction was taken on June 29, 1918, when the Conservation Division issued a set of regulations broadly outlining a scheme for cutting down the number of styles, colors, and lasts of shoes and eliminating certain styles which required an extravagant use of leather. The section administered these regulations.

In order to make these regulations more effective the priorities commissioner on August 7, 1918, issued circular No. 10, requiring of each manufacturer of boots and shoes a pledge to practice the economies outlined in return for a place which the priorities commissioner gave such manufacturers on the preference list for fuel and transportation. Each manufacturer was required to exact a like pledge from those who purchased from him for resale. The trade was instructed that any firm which failed to carry out the terms of the regulations in good faith would receive no aid in procuring coal and transportation.

From this time forward elaborate studies were being carried on, and many conferences were held with every branch of the shoe industry for the purpose of developing a plan for much more rigid conservation and for control over prices including retail prices. A number of plans were suggested. The idea of producing a single type to be called the "liberty shoe" was given careful consideration. It was proposed that nothing but black leather be allowed. Women's styles at this time required a different colored glazed kid shoe for each gown. The price of glazed kid was 350 per cent of normal, and it was hard to get. It was proposed that the wholesale price be stamped on the sole of every shoe, but the industry objected strenuously to this.

After a long series of conferences with representatives of more than 50 per cent of the producing companies involved, an agreement was reached and a schedule of regulations issued on September 30, 1918, to be applicable until June 1, 1919. Colors of shoes were limited to black, white, and one shade of tan. Heights were limited. The introduction of new lasts was stopped. The production of certain styles requiring an extravagant use of leather was forbidden. Manufacturers were required to reduce the variety of their product by about two-thirds.

All shoes were reduced to four classes which the trade agreed to sell at retail as follows: Class A, $9 to $12 for high shoes, $9 to $11 for low shoes; class B, $6 to $8.95; class C, $3 to $5.95; class D, any price below $3. Each shoe was to be stamped with a number and a key to the numbers was to be provided so that the purchaser would be able to determine by whom the shoe was made and in which class it belonged. This last regulation represented a compromise on the question of printing the wholesale price on the sole.

A system of pledges was required of manufacturers, jobbers, and retailers. Retailers were required to exhibit a card explaining the scheme in a conspicious place in their stores. It was contemplated that this plan in its entirety should be applied for the spring season of 1919. After the armistice the pledge and price-fixing elements were rescinded, but the trade voluntarily retained some of the conservation features. This plan would have reduced enormously the amount of leather stock carried by the various agencies all the way from the tannery to the retail store. One tanner, who had been turning out leather in 81 colors and shades, was able to simplify his plant to produce only three colors, and thus he was saved the necessity of carrying in stock raw hides and leather to the value of many thousands of dollars. Retail stores were enabled to reduce their lines and thus reduce the total quantity of stock carried and the risks of loss on left-over ends of particular styles. It is estimated that under this program the industry would have been freed from the burden of carrying materials to the value of more than $100,000,000 per year. All parties in interest were convinced that all branches of the industry would have reaped reasonable profits and the price to consumers would have been far below what has been recently paid.

Harness and personal equipment.—This section, formed June 12, 1918, devoted its attention principally to the inauguration of a conservation program. In cooperation with the war service committees and the Conservation Division a plan for eliminating about 75 per cent of the styles and types of harness and saddles was developed. Near the close of the war the manufacture of light harness was entirely suspended. There had been 60 styles of horse collars. The program limited them to 15. Heavy team and farm harness was limited to 12 types. Styles of riding saddles were reduced from 200 to 36. The Army demand for saddles, particularly McClellan saddles, caused a shortage of saddle trees. At first an attempt was made to allocate the production, but this was abandoned and the section set about to encourage the production of saddle trees by the numerous small woodworking plants throughout the country. All prices of harness and saddles as well as all contracts for their purchase were made by the appropriate Army bureaus before the formation of the section.

Belting.—In the fall of 1918 the shortage in the supply of russet harness leather for the Army made it necessary to form a section to control the distribution of belting leather. Sales were restricted to Government contractors from October to the end. The section used a questionnaire and established a system of monthly reports.

Gloves and leather clothing.—This section was formed late in the summer of 1918 and devoted most of its attention to the preparation of a conservation program for the glove industry. The work was not yet completed when the end of the war made its adoption unnecessary.

RUBBER AND RUBBER GOODS

The United States leads the world in the manufacture of rubber goods, producing about seven times the output of Great Britain, the next largest manufacturer. Our production has increased very rapidly in recent years. In 1906 we consumed 24,113 tons of crude rubber. In 1917 this had increased to 157,371 tons, the finished product that year being valued at $896,000,000. In 1914 we made 8,021,000 pneumatic tires, while in 1917 our output amounted to 25,835,000 tires.

Over 70 per cent of the rubber consumed in the United States goes into automobile tires and tubes, about 14 per cent into mechanical rubber goods of various kinds, 8 per cent into boots and shoes, 2 per cent into druggists' and stationers' sundries, of which we produce the bulk of the world's supply, and the rest goes into miscellaneous articles.

Priestley discovered the first use to which rubber was put in 1770 when he found it would "rub out" lead pencil marks.

The Amazon Basin was the original source of rubber and is still the principal source of wild rubber, though 80 per cent of the crude material which reaches the United States comes from the rubber plantations of Asia, Ceylon, and the East Indies. There are 60 types of rubber plants, but the industry depends mainly upon two trees—the Heva Braziliensis and the Castilloa. Besides the crude rubber, which enters every year into our product in a quantity exceeding 150,000 tons, we use about 90,000 tons of reclaimed rubber annually. We also use about 11,000 tons of rubber substitutes.

The Rubber and Rubber Goods Section was not formed until August 5, 1918, though the War Trade Board took control of rubber imports in December, 1917, and other important measures for regulating the industry were put into effect before that time. H. T. Dunn [5] was chief of the section.

Crude rubber is, perhaps, the only important staple which did not experience an increase in price during the period of the World War. The price during 1915, 1916, and even 1917 and 1918 was, with the exception of two short periods, considerably below that of 1912, 1913, and 1914. The price of rubber products followed quite closely that of crude rubber without showing the sudden fluctuations. The average price of all rubber products during 1917 and 1918 ranged from 70 to 80 per cent below the average relative price of commodities in general.

The important reason for the low-price levels of rubber during the war was that while the world consumption increased continuously over the period, the production increased still more rapidly. The plantations of the Far East were reaching the "bearing" age. In 1904 these plantations produced 43 tons of rubber; in 1913, 47,618 tons; in 1917, 204,348 tons; and in 1918, about 240,000 tons. At the same time Germany, which uses from 15,000 to 20,000 tons per year, practically dropped out of the buying market; and in 1917 and 1918 Russia, with a consuming capacity of more than 20,000 tons per year, also ceased buying. This left heavy surpluses in the plantation countries.

---

[5] Harry T. Dunn, of New York City, was president of Fisk Rubber Company and Federal Rubber Company until 1932. He is now with the New York brokerage firm of J. R. Timmins & Co.

The only problem for us was one of shipping. The first regulation of the War Trade Board was issued December 7, 1917, and was aimed to prevent rubber from reaching the Central Powers, who were greatly in need of it. No restrictions were placed on amounts, but the regulations provided for the licensing of imports, for the consignment of shipments to the Rubber Association of America, and for the submission of guaranties by importers and manufacturers that they would not sell any rubber directly or indirectly to any country at war with the United States nor to any person unless satisfied that he had no intention of exporting without an export license.

By the spring of 1918, as part of the program to force shipping from the Pacific which was needed on the Atlantic, it was felt that the situation necessitated a curtailment of the amount of rubber to be imported. The War Trade Board held conferences with representatives of the rubber industry and the Shipping Board, and on May 8 issued regulations restricting the quantity of rubber to be licensed for import during the three-month period May, June, and July, 1918, to 25,000 long tons, which represented a rate of importation about two-thirds that of 1917. The restrictions did not apply to shipments which had left the foreign ports before May 8, and, as they had been anticipated by the trade, there was heavy buying in April, so that 55,000 tons actually reached the United States during this three-month period.

The war requirements of rubber were for motor vehicles, airplanes, gas masks, medical supplies, etc. It was estimated that about 30,000 tons would go into direct war work in 1918. This meant that heavy curtailments would have to take place in other industries, particularly automobile tires. The various manufacturing concerns were classified, and imports were allocated to them on the basis of a definite percentage of their 1917 and early 1918 consumption. The manufacture of motor cars for civilian use was curtailed under a separate program, and the use of motors cars for pleasure was discouraged. This naturally led to a decrease in the demand for tires. Toward the end of the period a program was worked out for greatly reducing the number of types of automobile tires, and this in turn was designed to reduce the consumption of rubber by making it unnecessary for manufacturers and dealers to carry large stocks.

The section carried on the usual routine of collecting information and discussing problems involved in adjusting the industry to war conditions. A series of 27 questionnaires was issued to the trade through its War Service Committee. Data were collected and conferences held in preparation of the regulations issued September 21, 1918, by the Priorities Commissioner in the form of Circular No. 24, which placed the rubber trade in the list of controlled industries. This circular, following the usual form, instructed the industry that in order to conserve the supply of rubber in the United States, as well as to save labor, fuel, and transportation, it would be necessary for the various firms to cut down their production of rubber goods to the greatest possible extent. It suggested that unnnecessary and undesirable types, sizes, and styles of articles be eliminated, that production be kept as near to current demand as possible, and that nothing should be produced or delivered except for such essential uses as were designated by the Board. The circular provided that the production of pneumatic automobile tires and tubes should be cut down during the last three months of 1918 to three-twelfths of 50 per cent (measured both by units and amount of rubber consumed) of the annual production of each firm, estimated on the basis of the 18 months ending June 30, 1918. The ruling on tires did not apply, however, to direct orders from any agencies of the United States, and no restrictions were placed on solid tires.

The manufacturers were required to file a pledge in which they promised (1) not to use any product of their manufacture except for essential purposes, (2) to make no sale to any customer for resale until such customer should have filed a similar pledge to do his best to insure the distribution of his products for essential uses only (this was not to apply to tires), and (3) to observe the production program set forth in the circular and make such reports concerning production and activities as might be required. The industry, in turn, was placed on the Preference List for fuel and transportation, and was given an automatic class C rating.

On October 1, 1918, there was issued through the War Service Committee of the industry a set of regulations defining more fully the program of control outlined in Circular No. 24. Manufacturers were to be guided in their work by the following four general classes of articles, rated according to their importance to the war:

Class I. Articles to be supplied on direct orders received from governmental departments, railways, express companies, telephone and telegraph companies, the Red Cross, and Allied Governments. Production was limited only by orders in hand, and the crude rubber consumed in filling these orders was to be replaced under the War Trade Board plan of issuing allocation certificates.

Class II. Articles to be supplied for use in industries approved by the War Industries Board. Production of articles in this class was authorized in quantities sufficient to supply essential requirements of those engaged in industries on the preference list and individual manufacturers who had been given preferential treatment.

Class III. Articles for general use. They were to be produced only to the extent necessary to meet current demands, unless otherwise specified.

Class IV. Non-essential articles—so considered by the War Industries Board. Their production was absolutely prohibited.

A list of the preferential industries, as well as of the various articles coming within each class, was furnished to the trade, and the regulations became effective upon receipt of the list.

During October the Board issued a revised circular of instructions containing only three classes and naming, so far as possible, the articles in Class II. Class I continued to include direct Government orders. The new Class II became (1) a list of articles which were included without comment and could be produced in sufficient quantities to meet current needs, (2) another list of articles the production of which was limited to a certain percentage of 1917 production, and (3) a list of articles which could be produced only for designated purposes. The new Class III was a list of articles whose production was prohibited. All regulations were rescinded shortly after the armistice, except rules of the War Trade Board prohibiting exports to the Central Powers.

CHAPTER 13

Machinery and Tools

THE PROBLEMS arising in the machinery and tools industries related in many respects, particularly during the later period of the war, to the work of the Resources and Conversion Section. But it was found necessary as early as 1917, in some of these trades, to establish sections of the board to handle special situations. Sections were formed for machine tools; forgings, ordnance, small arms, and ammunition; hardware and hand tools; cranes; chains; and military optical glass and instruments.

MACHINE TOOLS

"Machine tool" is the name given to a piece of machinery used to produce other machines, implements, factory equipment, or tools. It is evident that the development of new facilities for the manufacture of guns, shells, powder, and other supplies, directly needed in newly enlarged quantities by the war, occasioned the manufacture or conversion of machinery for the rapid equipment of many new plants. In most cases it was necessary for the management of a new munitions factory to know the design of the product which was to be turned out before it could place orders with machine tool manufacturers for the equipment of the factory. The integration necessary to make this process go forward with dispatch could hardly be expected without the assistance of such an agency as the War Industries Board.

Thus it was that the Machine Tool Section was formed October 1, 1917, and G. E. Merryweather,[1] who had come to Washington in March and in association with the Munitions Board had worked on the problem of securing machine tools for the War Department, was made chief of the section. He had 14 assistants besides the coordinating members representing various departments of the Government.

The first work of the section was to prepare a careful inventory of production and facilities. Manufacturers were asked to submit a

---

[1] George Merryweather (deceased) was a prominent Cleveland machine-tool manufacturer.

complete report of their shop schedules, giving the output of their plants in detail per month and indicating the sold and unsold portions of the output. These figures were supplied monthly from October, 1917, to February, 1918, and when tabulated under types and sizes they indicated which machines were being produced in sufficient quantities, which ones were overproduced, and which underproduced. As a result of this inventory the section was able to advise the various departments of the Government in the placing of contracts and to advise the War Trade Board in the modification of its conservation list. By comparing estimated requirements of the Government with existing facilities it was possible to work out and suggest plans for expansion and conversion.

Cincinnati is the greatest machine tool manufacturing center in the world. In 1913 the total value of the annual product of the United States was only about $50,000,000. During the war period preceding our entrance, our productive capacity was more than double, but the expansion took place largely in the output of small and medium-sized machines—machines for the production of shells, rifles, bayonets, fuses, etc.—for the Allies were not ordering the larger and heavier types of ordnance materials in this country in great quantities. The shipping question was a deterrent to the production of heavy artillery on this side of the water both before and after the entrance of the United States into the war. Economy required that as a general policy, smaller parts should be manufactured here and heavier parts abroad. As the pressure of increased demands developed, however, plans were made for producing large quantities of heavy parts also in this country.

On July 1, 1917, the export of machine tools, consigned to countries other than England, France, Italy, and Japan, was stopped. As a result the section found, when it began its inventories, that there were about 6,000 machines valued at approximately $5,000,000 standing at various ports consigned to forbidden countries. Some of them had been sold and part payments had been made. Most of them were waiting in idleness for possible shipment. Some were being speculated on. The section made arrangements to have them purchased, or, if the title was doubtful, commandeered by the Secretary of War, and installed in the factories of Government contractors.

It was clear in the latter part of 1917 that an important shortage of larger machine tools was likely to be felt if the war should continue over a long period. With a view to discovering what could be done in case it should become necessary to commandeer machinery of this type in use in private plants, the section made a survey of all available machine tools of the larger sizes. Manufacturers were requested to submit lists of all the larger machines which they had produced for periods ranging from 10 to 20 years prior to 1917. This information was tabulated, the list comprising approximately 50,000 machines. It did not become necessary to commandeer many of these machines, but the lists were frequently consulted when the question of placing contracts for heavy machinery was being considered.

The section did not a little in arranging for the conversion of factories making wood-working machinery, etc., into the manufacture of metal-working machinery. It also assisted several concerns in securing patterns, drawings, and other information needed to develop machine tool plants. The producing capacity of the country was kept carefully tabulated so that prompt instructions could be given showing by what plant and in how long a period any certain order of machine tools could be produced.

A new method of manufacturing certain heavy machine tools was developed. This method used reinforced concrete for the construction of the principal parts, with the wearing surfaces provided with metal facings. There were two features of economy in this: (1) There was a saving in time, labor, and materials; and (2) large machines were not needed for the construction.

The question of conservation by limitation of types and styles was studied. It was not felt, however, that a general policy of reducing designs and models could be applied to the manufacture of machine tools, owing to the varied nature of the requirements. Furthermore, the manufacturing equipment of most of the machine tool plants was so balanced for the production of machines of various sizes and types that a curtailment of any individual size or type would not, as a rule, tend to increase, relatively, the output of others. In a few cases, however, this thing was done by appeals made through the editorial columns of trade journals.

The indirectness of the requirements for machine tools was a source of great difficulty in calculating quantities needed. When an ordnance program was laid down, it was necessary to know the speed at which a given machine could turn out a given article in order to determine the number of machines required to carry out the program. This section secured for the Ordnance Department a number of experts in the use of machine tools, who devoted their attention to time-studies in the calculation of requirements.

To cover a shortage which developed in testing-machines, the section sent out a questionnaire and appeal to the colleges, universities, and technical schools, which uncovered the fact that sufficient testing machines could be spared from various laboratories to satisfy the Government need.

On account of the characteristic indirectness of war requirements for machine tools, the administration of priorities was particularly difficult. At first the industry was not placed on the preference list for fuel, labor, and transportation, but it was soon found expedient to give the industry an automatic rating of A-6. In order to assist the priorities committee in issuing certificates covering orders for the machines themselves, a card record system was installed by the section. Manufacturers were requested to report every order placed for machines, deliveries of which were more than 30 days removed. A card showing the nature of the order was sent to the section and a duplicate retained by the manufacturer in his files until the machine was completed, diverted by priority, or the order cancelled, when notation was made on the duplicate card and it was sent to the section so that the section's file could be corrected. The card showed the customer's order number, date of order, promised date of delivery, size and type of machine, manufacturer's name, and grade of priority. Some 20,000 orders were recorded in this way, giving a complete running inventory.

This industry developed during the period of the war from a capacity represented by an annual output of about $50,000,000 to that of an output estimated at nearly $400,000,000 in 1918.

FORGINGS, ORDNANCE, SMALL ARMS, AND AMMUNITION

The field contemplated by this section fell so peculiarly within the province of the war-making agencies themselves that the work of the section was perhaps more indirect and less exhautive than that of many of the other commodity units. The section was not formed until June 1, 1918, when S. P. Bush [2] was made chief, though much work in advising and assisting the War and Navy Departments in laying down their ordnance programs was carried on throughout the earlier period by a committee of the Council with S. M. Vauclain [3] as chairman.

The principal functions of the section were to study and allocate the resources needed for the production of forgings, ordnance, ordnance ammunition, small arms, and small arms ammunition; to bring information concerning facilities to the various Government

[2] See page 42.
[3] See page 43.

departments; to coordinate the demands of the several departments and of the Allied Governments so that the needs of each might be supplied to the fullest possible extent; and to study the distribution of new facilities in the light of industrial conditions in various parts of the country.

The section kept itself carefully informed on the questions of power, transportation, labor, and fuel in their relation to the production of ordnance. The section did nothing with reference to designs and specifications. It acted only in a broadly advisory character in the matter of creating new facilities, pointing out in respect to projects the availability of power, transportation, labor, and fuel.

The function of "clearing" purchase orders submitted by the various agencies of our Government and the Allied Purchasing Commission constituted an important part of the duty of the section. When a request for clearance was made, the section would study it in the light of conditions in the locality where the order was contemplated and in the light of the success of the plant designated. It would then either clear the proposal as made or return it with a recommendation suggesting another place and manner believed to be more suitable for accomplishing the order.

Prior to the war the production of the implements and munitions of war was restricted to a very small number of plants situated in the eastern part of the country on or near the seaboard. Small arms and ammunition were produced by a few companies in Connecticut, Rhode Island, Massachusetts, and New York, and ordnance was produced principally by the Bethlehem and Midvale Steel Cos., with a small quantity being turned out by Government arsenals. The instruments of trench warfare had never been produced in this country and no one was familiar with the processes of their manufacture.

The production of all munitions which were manufactured in this country was surrounded by more or less secrecy and few people outside of the regular establishments knew anything about the work. Obviously when necessity arose for unprecedented quantities of all of these articles, the Allies and later the United States turned naturally for their requirements to those comparatively few establishments which were familiar with the work. Time was of the essence, and expansion of these establishments seemed to promise the quickest method of supplying the need. In many respects the eastern section of the country was more suited for work of this character as well as for other manufacturing essential to the war.

The general result was that by the spring of 1918 the congestion in the eastern manufacturing district had become very serious. If there had been a central control over distribution of orders, this need never have occurred. There was a shortage of power, fuel, and transportation. Nearly all work was far behind the ambitious program which had been laid down. The heart of the manufacturing center of the country was declared by the Board a restricted area, and all hands, particularly the Ordnance Section, gave careful study to the question of directing expansion of war work in other centers wherever the peculiar nature of the product to be turned out made the use of facilities in other parts of the country possible.

The conservation agreements which were reached by the Board during the summer of 1918, as well as the general application of the priorities system which was diverting materials and the use of transportation from many of the less essential industries, were gradually producing a condition in which many well-organized factory managements and plants were functioning at a very low ebb. As needs arose it was the purpose of the section, in close conference with the Resources and Conversion Section, so to direct the placing of orders involving developments as to utilize managements and plants already in existence and which could be turned to the new work with a little encouragement and instruction.

The Ordnance Section did not always attempt to allocate in detail the various facilities required, but by refusing clearance to some proposals, where resources were known to be inadequate, and by indicating localities in which resources were available, and by constantly presenting the importance of avoiding congestion, it did much to equalize the burdens and benefits of direct war contracts. This was particularly true when the plan for the enlarged Army was adopted, and a great expansion of our production was undertaken.

HARDWARE AND HAND TOOLS

This section dealt with a large number of industries manufacturing small finished products made of metal—sewing machines and needles, horseshoes, fire extinguishers, bedsteads, plumbers' supplies, gauges, twist drills, pneumatic tools, woodworking tools, precision machinery, and the like. In most of these industries the war requirements represented a very small percentage of normal output, and they were industries in which curtailment for the purpose of releasing metal, labor, capital, and factory organization for war work was possible.

Fourteen industries supervised by this section were placed on a ration basis. Most of the plants were located in the congested area, and the industry as a whole has always been on a highly competitive basis. A great deal of prosperity was being enjoyed at the time this country entered the war, due partly to the elimination of German-made products from the markets in this country and South America.

The section was first organized in April, 1918, and was reorganized and enlarged so as to contain a number of subdivisions in charge of particular commodities on June 1, with Murray Sargent as chief. One of the few commodities under the section, in which there was a serious shortage for war purposes, was textile needles of all kinds. These had been manufactured largely in England and Germany; and this country, before the war, was in the habit of importing practically its entire supply, in face of the fact that this is the leading country of the world in the production of textile machinery and sewing machines. Facilities were rapidly developed by construction or conversion for the manufacture of these articles, and before the war was over all needs were being satisfactorily met.

A shortage occurred also in saddlery hardware. This industry had been rapidly declining before the war, and the new demands were accompanied by very high prices. Meetings were held with the manufacturers, and studies were made in the cost of production with a view to fixing prices; but while this activity was going on, a better system of distribution of orders had so cleared the situation that price fixing was not resorted to.

The manufacture of fire extinguishers came into conflict with the production of toxic gas for the Chemical Warfare Service, carbon tetrachloride being needed in quantities greater than were available for both purposes. The price of fire extinguishers began to advance rapidly. At the suggestion of the section, the Navy sent an accountant to the plant of the Pyrene Co. to study costs, and later a price agreement was reached for Government purchases at $4.25 each for 1-quart Pyrene fire extinguishers and 90 cents for refilling one.

A difficulty arose in connection with the purchase of horseshoes by the several Government departments. The industry organized and insisted on dealing as a unit. There was no shortage, and the departments preferred to buy on a competitive basis. The section called the representatives of the industry to Washington and explained the situation, calling attention to the fact that only a small percentage of the output would be needed for Government purposes, that the departments preferred to purchase on a competitive basis, and that no prices would be fixed.

A shortage occurred in ships' hardware. The most important action in relief of this was an agreement brought about by the section between the War Service Committee of the industry and the Emergency Fleet for a set of standard specifications. Steps were taken to develop a similar arrangement between the Navy and the industry, but the work had not been completed when the end came.

The Engineer Corps of the Army brought to the attention of the section the fact that it was unable to place business with individual manufacturers of hydrants and valves for the reason that all inquiries were referred to a single representative of the manufacturers in Washington. Attention was also called to the fact that the prices quoted by this representative were higher than prices quoted by the various manufacturers for analogous materials not being sold to the Government. Investigation showed that this process of representing the industry through a single channel had been established early in the war at the request of the council, but it was clear that such a method of purchasing could not be satisfactory without its corollary, price fixing. There did not seem a sufficient shortage to warrant price fixing, and therefore it was requested that the centralized selling method be broken up and selling be put on a competitive basis, which was done.

Metal beds were another problem. Their manufacturers had been put on a 50 per cent ration basis by the Priorities Commissioner. The influenza epidemic brought on a severe shortage. Plans were immediately projected to have wooden beds manufactured as substitutes. The Army and Navy, however, objected to them on sanitary grounds.

Builders' hardware was put on a ration basis, and soon a shortage began to appear in the supply for the housing program. A list of standard articles was drawn up and plans were made for allocating the business so as to draw on existing stocks as far as possible and not to require new manufacture. It was arranged that each program involving $5,000 or more should be cleared through the section.

Toward the end of the period a great many concerns, who were operating on a ration basis, were beginning to find that their priority rating was so low that they would have to close shop unless they could get Government orders, bringing with them higher ratings. They were flocking to Washington and seeking contracts at whatever prices they could get in order to secure higher priority ratings for the supply of raw materials. This is an interesting comment on the effect of the priority system on prices. There are two sides to the matter, however. It is likely that, if the war had continued for two or three more years, the priority system would have developed further refinements designed to give more complete protection to the industries which it was putting on a skeleton basis. The end came while the development was in process.

CRANES

The crane industry depends upon the activities of railroads, contractors, blast furnaces, steel mills, ore docks, coal companies, shipyards, etc. This country manufactures all the cranes needed for its own use, and exports to England, France, Germany, Chile, Brazil, Japan, China, India, annd other countries. The business was below normal until the beginning of 1915 when the war demand appeared and increased steadily through to the end.

The most important shortage occurred in locomotive cranes. The section was formed November 12, 1917, with Alexander C. Brown [4] as chief. By that time the direct Government requirements for locomotive cranes had reached a point which indicated the possibility of an acute shortage in the near future, making a general survey of the situation necessary. Data were collected covering the available output of the builders whose plants could be easily converted to the production of locomotive cranes. Builders of steam shovels were the most important on the latter list.

In normal times the delivery period for locomotive cranes is only two or three weeks, because, while orders are by specifications, nearly all of the constituent elements are standard and are held in reserve stock by the builders. But by the summer of 1917, the demand for these cranes had been so great that reserve stocks were practically exhausted and delivery periods began to grow longer and longer.

The section took over the administration of priorities both in the delivery of cranes and of raw materials for their manufacture. On July 1, 1918, materials for the construction of locomotive cranes were placed on the list entitled to automatic priority. It was necessary to make very careful studies of the relative importance of the needs of those who came to buy the limited supplies. But price fixing never became necessary.

The section made a careful study of existing cranes and current output, as well as present and prospective requirements of the various Government agencies. Quite satisfactory figures were received on future requirements, so that the section was able to arrange in advance for sufficient capacity to turn out the required cranes. The seven regular builders who were producing cranes when the section was formed increased their production 50 per cent during our period

---

[4] Alexander Brown, Cleveland industrialist and director in numerous corporations, was president of the Brown Hoisting Machine Co. before going with the Government.

in the war, and in addition 11 other plants were converted to crane production to meet the war program. By October, 1918, capacity to produce standard locomotive cranes had been developed to provide for 140 cranes per month as compared to a maximum monthly output in 1913 and 1914 of from forty to fifty cranes. The production of special designs of the locomotive cranes type brought up the total capacity of the country to 240 standard and special cranes per month. The 1918 output was nearly all purchased for direct Government use.

The production of electric traveling cranes was always sufficient to meet all war needs; and, while they were placed on the list of commodities requiring clearance of orders, they never involved a serious problem. In December, 1917, the Army purchased 60 gantry cranes for use on the docks in France. They were shipped to our ports early in 1918 and stood there all through the spring and early summer, while plans in France seemed not to be requiring them. The section took steps to have them released for use in loading vessels on this side, but in August it was arranged to have them shipped to France.

In September, 1918, the A. E. F. asked for a new and enlarged supply of cranes. In order to expedite production to meet this special demand, the Priorities Committee arranged for special priority to be given to what was termed the "Pershing crane program," and the requirement was promptly take care of.

CHAINS

This section was formed April 11, 1918, on account of the shortage of anchor cables brought on by the shipbuilding program. The section found it necessary to deal also with sprocket chains, and it administered the conservation and rationing program applied to trace chains. John C. Schmidt was chief of the section. He witnessed a test of a new type of anchor chain made of cast steel at the factory of the National Malleable Castings Co., Sharon, Pa., and made a favorable report on the results of the test. This process seemed to present the solution of the chain shortage.

The Emergency Fleet placed an order with the company for 150 suites of chain at a very satisfactory price. The company had great difficulty, however, in getting its factory built, and no important deliveries had been made by the time of the armistice. A sample of the chain, however, has been used on one of the buoys in New York Harbor since August 8, 1918, and inspections show that it is resisting corrosion as satisfactorily as the welded wrought-iron chain attached to the same buoy.

Manufacturers of anchor chain were encouraged by the section to increase their output and new manufacturers were brought into the work. The output was increased also by the abrogation during the war of a number of the highly technical rules which the skilled labor of these shops was in the habit of observing. With all that could be done, however, not enough chain could be produced to equip ships as rapidly as they were being turned out by the Emergency Fleet Corporation. As a temporary expedient the American Bureau of Shipping agreed that for the period of the war the requirements of the length of ships' cables might be reduced 25 per cent.

The section was asked by the Army to make a comparative study of chain tire grips. Samples were secured and an exhaustive report made, touching weight, prices, and suitability for particular services. The section also prepared a complete descriptive and illustrated catalogue of every known make and type of chain.

No prices, except those included in the Iron and Steel Institute's schedule, were ever fixed in this industry. The price of the basic raw material having been fixed, it was possible by the exercise of the priorities system so to control the output that further fixing of prices did not seem necessary.

MILITARY OPTICAL GLASS AND INSTRUMENTS

Before the war this country produced practically no optical glass and comparatively few optical instruments. Europe, particularly Germany, supplied us. By the time the United States entered the war, reserve stocks were largely exhausted and little progress had been made in the production of glass, though many instruments were being made and fitted with imported lenses. The Army and Navy needed great quantities of field glasses, cameras, fire-control instruments, sextants, surveying instruments, microscopes, and the like. There was a strong demand for moving-picture machines.

The period from April, 1917, to about June, 1918, was one of experimentation and development. Glass formulæ had been secret and well guarded. The difference between the kinds of glass used for the various types of lenses lies in the basic constituents required to produce different densities. While formulæ were being discovered and developed, it was necessary to train workmen in the art of making and grinding glass. A school was established at Rochester, N. Y., under the supervision of the Mechanics' Institute, where skilled mechanics were given a special course to fit them for this work. The

Geophysical Laboratory, under the personal direction of Col. Fred E. Wright, gave valuable assistance in determining the materials suitable for optical glass, sending a staff to the Bausch & Lomb Optical Co., where the scientific problems connected with optical-glass manufacture were solved and the product turned out on a commercial scale. The proper pot for melting glass presented a serious difficulty, credit for the solution of which is due to Prof. Bleininger of the Bureau of Standards.

The Government gave assistance to the Pittsburgh Plate Glass Co., and they became the largest producers of optical glass. The Spencer Lens Co. was given a Government contract which necessitated the erection of a new plant. Dr. Morey of the Geophysical Laboratory was stationed at this plant and there discovered, in the summer of 1918, a method by which the period required for making glass was reduced from 40 to 24 hours. The Mount Wilson Observatory, aided by the Ordnance Department, entered the field of grinding precision optical glass. One new concern, Keuffel & Esser Co., built a plant at Hoboken, N. J., for the manufacture of optical glass.

By June, 1918, the country was producing glass of a quality comparing favorably with the product of Europe, and was producing in quantity almost sufficient for current demands. When a little later Dr. Morey's discovery reduced the period of manufacture, capacity became sufficient for all essential needs.

The section was formed early in March, 1918, with George E. Chatillon [5] as chief. On March 27 the entire industry was notified that it had been placed under the supervision of the War Industries Board, and that no company could accept orders without the approval of the Board. Labor was controlled by placing restrictions upon shifting from plant to plant. Prices were left entirely to the Government purchasing agencies. By a system of permits the section controlled the distribution to the various Government departments and to manufacturers having direct Government contracts.

Requests for priority on raw materials, including steel and brass, were passed upon by the section. In conjunction with the War Trade Board, the section passed upon a number of applications for both import and export licenses for materials affecting this industry.

Practically the entire available capacity for optical instruments was occupied with Government orders. Production increased from month to month during 1918. The total number of orders placed by the Government amounted to more than $50,000,000, of which

---

[5] Geo. E. Chatillon is president of John Chatillon & Sons, New York City.

about $15,000,000 went to the Navy. It is believed that the productive capacity brought about by the war is considerably in excess of the normal commercial demand of the country. There is no tariff to protect the industry from foreign competition, and our manufacturers will likely have difficulty in maintaining the position which they have gained during the war.

CHAPTER 14

Transportation and Power

THE SECTIONS falling within the scope of this chapter handled Automotive Products, Railroad Equipment and Supplies, Stored Materials, Fire Prevention, Power, Electrical and Power Equipment, and Electric Wire and Cable.

AUTOMOTIVE PRODUCTS

C. C. Hanch[1] was made chief of the Automotive Products Section on June 19, 1918, when the section was reorganized to conform to the final form of the War Industries Board. The work of supervision in this field began, however, June 4, 1917, with the formation of the Automotive Transportation Committee of the Council, this committee consisting of representatives of the industry itself. * * *

The section had jurisdiction not only of the automobile industry but also of the other lines of production in which the automobile industry engaged; for example, airplane engines, tanks, marine gas engines, armored cars, motorcycles, and bicycles. The automobile factories supplied for the most part the engineering skill and the skilled workmen which carried forward the vast airplane program of the war. In addition, some of these manufacturing establishments converted a part of their equipment to the production of gun carriages, gun recoil mechanisms, escort wagons, water carts, artillery wheels, litters, shells, depth bombs, mine anchors, grenades, torpedo directors, balloon winches, and other military equipment. It is estimated that the automobile industry took contracts for direct and indirect war work to the amount of nearly $1,000,000,000.

The section did a vast amount of work making clearances of purchases of the various Government departments and of the Allies. It studied and recommended sources of supply and allocated orders where that was found necessary. It made investigations for the

---

[1] Charles Hanch has been identified with automobile industry since 1894, when he became treasurer of the old Nordyke & Marmon Company in Indianapolis. He is today a consulting expert on finance and taxation to numerous companies.

Priorities Commissioner. But perhaps the most important and difficult work of the section was the administration of the program under which the automobile industry was curtailed to 50 per cent of normal production during the latter half of 1918.

This industry has had a phenomenal growth during the past two decades. This country produced during 1917 passenger automobiles to the number of 1,740,791 and trucks 128,157, aggregating in wholesale selling value $1,238,979,891. Approximately 300,000 men were employed in automobile and truck factories and another 320,000 in factories making component parts and accessories. High-grade steel and other metals were being consumed by the industry at the rate of more than 2,000,000 tons per year in 1917.

Of course, the war requirements represented only a small percentage of this capacity. The requirement for trucks, however, was such that that branch of the industry had to be assisted by favorable priorities on materials and transportation throughout the period. About 40,000 trucks went to England, France, and Russia before the United States entered the war. About 200,000 trucks and ambulances were ordered by our Army and Navy, and 54,343 were shipped to Europe. It was thus that, in the spring of 1918, when industrial conditions were such that the Conservation Division and the Priorities Division began to examine the different industries for the purpose of determining which could be most satisfactorily curtailed for the purpose of saving materials, labor, and capital the automobile industry was one of the first to be taken into consideration.

Early in March representatives of the industry were called into conference by the Board and, after full discussion, it was agreed that a 30 per cent reduction in the current manufacturing schedules of passenger cars could be made without undue disturbance; and that this curtailment, effecting economies in metals and skilled labor, was of the utmost importance. The manufacturers consented to effect this curtailment in their respective plants from March 1 to July 31, 1918. Under this plan only manufacturers having Government orders got a high priority rating, and, as time went on, the vast majority of makers were becoming less and less able to secure materials for continuing their work. The shops began to be short of stocks of particular parts of a finished machine and to have vast surpluses of other parts. They were unable to turn out more than a small percentage of their usual production.

Further conferences were held in July, and some dissatisfaction was expressed. It was finally agreed that preference would be given to each manufacturer of passenger automobiles who would subscribe to a pledge the essence of which was as follows: "That its production of passenger automobiles and of repair parts therefor shall not, for the six months ending with December 31, 1918, exceed 25 per cent of its production for the calendar year 1917." This pledge meant that passenger-automobile manufacturers were permitted—in fact, aided—to operate on a 50 per cent basis during the last six months of 1918. It was believed that this basis would support the organizations of the various plants until such time as they could convert their facilities, so far as practicable, for the production of direct and indirect war requirements. The attention of the manufacturers was called to the urgent war requirements for iron and steel and to the possible necessity of eliminating the manufacture of passenger automobiles after January 1, 1919, if the war should continue.

The arrangement to curtail was contained in a letter from the Priorities Commissioner to the industry, dated August 24, 1918. The administration of the plan was turned over to this section. The section began by requiring the manufacturers (1) to submit sworn inventory figures showing value of materials on hand and value of materials required to balance their stocks; also tonnage of principal classes of steel and the number of principal units on hand, with the tonnage and number of units required to balance the stocks on hand; (2) to submit a statement showing the number of finished cars which could be built from the above inventory when the stocks had been balanced, and the time required to build them; and (3) to submit sworn production figures separately for the years 1916, 1917, and the first half of 1918. Upon receipt of the foregoing information, the section certified to the Director of Steel Supply the requirements of each manufacturer for the principal classes of steel in tons and the principal units necessary to balance stocks on hand and to produce the number of cars allotted under the manufacturer's pledge.

Each manufacturer was then notified that he was privileged to build his specified number of cars and that materials therefor might be obtained by filing in triplicate with the Director of Steel Supply applications for "permit to purchase." The manufacturer's copy of application for "permit to purchase," when granted, constituted the necessary authority for the seller to fill the manufacturer's order. In case the supplier or manufacturer of parts was not the original source of supply of the raw materials required, he in turn made application for "permit to purchase" in like form as that required from the maker of passenger automobiles. Under this procedure the section certified to the Steel Division the requirements of 95 manufacturers covering the production of 295,468 cars during the last half of 1918.

The control of the industry under the arrangements made with it was accomplished by monthly reports of operation, submitted by the manufacturers containing the following information: (1) Number of finished cars on hand at beginning of month; (2) number of cars produced during the month; (3) number of cars delivered to United States Government during month; (4) number of cars delivered to Allied Governments; and (5) number of cars delivered for civilian use. A total of 186,178 cars were produced during the third quarter, and on November 11, 1918, a circular was issued which removed 50 per cent of the restrictions; and this was followed a short time afterward by a complete removal.

The manufacturers of accessories and spare parts were also dealt with by means of the system of "permits to purchase." No definite ruling was made as to what allowance of materials could be made to individual factories, but each concern was advised to make application for "permit to purchase" and each application was considered on its merits, a general ruling allowing each manufacturer sufficient materials to carry him through a period of from 60 to 90 days at a rate of production of about 50 per cent of normal being applied.

The manufacturers of motor trucks were treated separately on the theory (1) that a large percentage of their output was needed for direct war work, and (2) that trucks were an important transportation medium in essential civilian industries so that curtailment should be avoided as far as practicable. Circular No. 11, dated August 8, 1918, was sent to truck manufacturers by the Priorities Commissioner and explained the conditions under which fuel and steel would be furnished the industry. The circular said: "It appears, however, that there exists in this industry, as in many others, factors of non-essentiality which must, as a war measure, be eliminated." A pledge was required with a view to eliminating these factors of non-essentiality, and the creation of new facilities was discouraged. The pledge bound the manufacturers and dealers to sell no motor trucks except for essential uses; to sell to no user an unnecessary number of trucks, even for essential uses; to discourage the purchase of any truck to replace a usable truck already in service; to give maximum encouragement to the repair of trucks; and to make monthly reports to the section.

Instead of issuing individual priorities certificates to truck manufacturers for each purchase of parts and materials the section recommended that an "industry priority certificate" be issued to each manufacturer, under which he could order his materials in the usual way by attaching the prescribed form of affidavit to his purchase orders. This plan facilitated procurement and avoided an enormous amount of clerical work.

RAILWAY EQUIPMENT AND SUPPLIES

This section was formed July 30, 1918, with J. Rogers Flannery [2] as chief. During the earlier period, the Advisory Committee on Plants and Munitions had been doing very important work in aiding the Railroad Administration and the United States Military Railways in standardizing types of cars and locomotives and following up their production. But in July so many conflicting orders were being received for cars and locomotives from the different branches of this Government and from the Allies, and manufacturers were having so much difficulty in securing materials, that a central channel for the distribution of orders and for laying down a plan of delivery of the products was decided upon.

The two large problems related to (1) locomotives and (2) freight cars. The former was on account of the limited productive capacity as well as the difficulty in securing sufficient iron and steel; the latter lay chiefly in the iron, steel, and lumber supply.

Locomotives.—There are only three builders of locomotives in the United States, besides a few companies which turn out smaller engines. The Railroad Administration ordered 1,415 large steam locomotives in April, 1918, and was very anxious for speedy delivery. On July 23, 1918, the United States Military Railways ordered 510 standard-gauge locomotives from the Baldwin Locomotive Works and insisted upon immediate prosecution of the order. The Railroad Administration was extremely anxious that the military locomotives should not interfere with its order. It was understood that further orders would come from the A. E. F. Plans were considered for adding to the facilities of the Baldwin and American companies at Government expense to the amount of $25,000,000.

A general meeting was held of locomotive builders and representatives of our Government and of the Allied Governments. A requirement of about 9,000 locomotives to be supplied between July, 1918, and December, 1919, appeared. This was clearly greater than existing capacities could fulfill. But the delays inevitable in the construction of new plants under circumstances as they were at that time pointed to the fact that no relief could be hoped for earlier than the middle of 1919 under a new facilities plan.

---

[2] John Rogers Flannery, of Pittsburgh, president of the Flannery Bolt Company and the American Vanadium Company, was assistant to chairman of the U. S. Shipping Board before going with the War Industries Board.

There were about 65,000 engines in use in the country. It was suggested that the Railroad Administration wage an aggressive campaign of general repair work at all shops, that old locomotives might be returned to service and the administration's demand for new ones be considerably reduced. This plan was carried out. No new plants were started, and the "Pershing engine program" was given a high preference. It was decided that the Baldwin Works should concentrate on the military standard-gauge engines and that the American and Lima companies should turn out administration engines exclusively. Under this plan the Baldwin Works was turning out the standard military engines at the rate of 256 per month before the end of the war period. For the week ending October 26, 1918, the Baldwin Works turned out 87 engines. The British and French were taking whatever production was not required by the A. E. F.

The Italian Government was unable to adopt our standard military engine because it was too heavy; but they eagerly desired to place a large order for locomotives here. The American Locomotive Co. had built Italian engines and possessed patterns, but for several weeks it could not devise a way to find facility space for the Italian order. The Baldwin Co. offered to take over the patterns and undertake the work, and plans were under way for doing this when the American Co. came forward with an offer to construct them at its Montreal plant, and the order was finally placed that way.

The war brought out a demand for hundreds of narrow-gauge steam locomotives and large gasoline locomotives. The larger companies, particularly the Baldwin Works, had experts and drawings for this work. But because their plants were filled to capacity with orders for standard engines, most of this business had to be distributed among the builders of small mining and industrial engines. Drawings and specifications, as well as skilled workmen, were turned over by the larger companies to the smaller ones in order to facilitate this work.

Freight cars.—There were 30 car builders in the country capable of turning out freight cars for the Railroad Administration and for the American Expeditionary Forces. December, 1917, when the Railroad Administration took control of the roads, saw this industry running at very low ebb. In April, 1918, the administration ordered 100,000 standard-gauge freight cars, distributing the order among 16 builders. Great difficulty was experienced in procuring the raw materials and in rehabilitating the organizations. Orders were placed with all the car companies at the same time, and efforts were made by all of the concerns to get simultaneous deliveries of the various materials. By the time deliveries were beginning, the United States Military Railways placed orders with the same companies and 14 additional companies for 30,000 freight cars. An A–5 priority was obtained for the military cars, which gave them preference over orders for administration cars, which rated only a B–1 priority.

A schedule of deliveries for the military cars calling for rush work was outlined. This naturally retarded the building of the administration cars. But to make matters worse for the Railroad Administration orders came on September 26 that military operations in France necessitated that the previous schedule of deliveries should be anticipated by at least 30 to 60 days. The section telegraphed all builders and arranged to expedite delivery of steel to meet the new schedules. A few days later the United States Military Railways brought forward additional orders for 40,915 standard-gauge cars and 4,000 narrow-gauge cars. The section called a meeting of representatives of the branches of the Government interested for the purpose of determining the distribution of the new orders. The Railroad Administration recommended that orders be placed in Canada for as many as possible of the new requirement; but the representative of the military railways objected to this on the ground that too much time would be lost in shipping the raw materials to Canada and that labor conditions were not good there. Finally a schedule of distribution of the new order and a new schedule of deliveries for all orders was drawn up and approved by both parties.

In order to assist the manufacturers of cars and locomotives in securing their materials as quickly as possible, this section, with the approval of the Steel Division and the Lumber Section, handled all requests for allocation of steel and lumber to these manufacturers. Standard forms for requesting allocations were sent to all builders. Immediately upon receipt of the request for allocation the section would carefully check it, approve it, number it, and send three copies to the Director of Steel Supply or to the Lumber Section. These requests were followed closely by the section until they were returned with suitable allocations, when the manufacturer was immediately notified and requested to place his order.

Standard forms were adopted by the section on which the railroad equipment manufacturers reported at the beginning of each month delivery of materials required for the following month; and from these data the section furnished the Director of Steel Supply with a statement of the steel tonnage required by each manufacturer from month to month. By this method orders which had been allocated were followed through to delivery.

Definite monthly schedules of shipments from the steel manufacturers were arranged for in order that the railway equipment manufacturers might lay out their programs of work with some certainty of receiving materials. The manufacturers of specialties, who furnished their product to the builders of cars and locomotives, were required to follow the same procedure as the car and locomotive builders themselves. Under this system a certain percentage of the steel tonnage of the country was set aside for railroad purposes each month, the amount being determined upon by conference between the section and the Steel Division. The section kept a close watch on the production of both cars and locomotives throughout the country by a system of weekly reports of output from each builder. The entire routine had just become established and seemed to be working well when the armistice made its further application unnecessary.

STORED MATERIALS

In the winter of 1917–18 it was discovered that a great many warehouses throughout the country contained heavy stores of supplies, many of them seeming to be held by their owners for speculative purposes and others held up by export regulations or by trade difficulties of some nature. In January, 1918, a stored materials section was formed, with John F. Wilkins as chief, for the purpose of securing an inventory of these stores, that they might be turned, where necessary, to war uses. The section gathered information showing the character, quantities, and owners of stored merchandise everywhere and transmitted it to the particular bureaus of the Government or to the commodity sections of the Board interested in the different supplies. Officers representing the Army and Navy in the section brought constant advices as to the Government's needs, and searches for supplies to satisfy them would follow. Constant contact was maintained with the several Government intelligence agencies, with fire insurance companies, exporters, shipping brokers, and many manufacturers.

The section not only accomplished its main purpose in bringing forth important quantities of different supplies which current regulations or appeals had failed to effect, but it was able also, through its several contacts, to lend incidental assistance to other war agencies. It gave the War Trade Board information concerning goods destined for consignees on the enemy-trading list. It gave the Alien Property Custodian information about enemy-owned goods. It collected and maintained an important body of information showing congested conditions in certain warehouses, docks, and railroad terminals. In

September, 1918, the section undertook the operation of a plan devised by the conservation division of the Board to create an interdepartmental clearing house for all classes of inactive Governmental materials.   Under this plan quantities of materials, which one Government agency had bought, but on account of some change of program could not use, were inventoried and made available for some other department which needed them.

FIRE PREVENTION

Following the establishment of the War Risk Insurance and the Government Marine Insurance, there was much discussion of a proposal to inaugurate Government fire insurance for plants having war orders.   Congress did not find this step necessary or advisable.   The danger, however, which was involved in less than fully adequate fire inspection and protection in such plants was called to the attention of the President, and the Chairman of the War Industries Board was advised to organize a section to take care of this important work. The Fire Prevention Section was organized on April 5, 1918, with W. H. Merrill [3] as chief.   An advisory committee consisting of representatives of the leading insurance organizations was formed to cooperate in the work, and the section itself developed a staff of 31 experts exclusive of representatives of the War, Navy, and other regular departments.

The purposes of the section were carried out by means of inspections followed by recommendations to the Government departments concerned, the inspections being made either by experts from the section or by the use of various insurance organizations.   The first effort was to cover only plants where the work was most needed, then later a program was laid down for the inspection of all plants having Government contracts exceeding $100,000 in value.   At the beginning, the work of the section on any plant ceased after it had completed an inspection and drafted a recommendation to the War or Navy Department, but after a few months it was felt that delay would be prevented if the section could take its recommendations directly to the owners of the plants.   Such an arrangement was made with the Army and Navy representatives, and, during the summer and fall of 1918, the work was carried on in this way, the proper military or

---

[3] W. H. Merrill (deceased) for many years was president of Underwriters Laboratories in Chicago.

naval authorities being advised of the action in each case.   Questions
in connection with the production and distribution of fire-prevention
apparatus were also handled by the section.

POWER

During the years immediately preceding 1917 there was a rapid
and wholesome growth of the central station power business throughout the country, both on the part of new and of old industries, many
of the latter changing from a system of isolated plants to electric
power taken from large central sources.

The work of the Power Section began in December, 1917.   A shortage in power had appeared before this time at Niagara Falls, and
the situation had been taken in charge by the Secretary of War,
who appointed Gen. Charles Keller, Engineer Corps, and R. J. Bulkley
to represent him in handling the power situation.   Gen. Keller secured
the assignment of a number of Engineer officers to assist in the work.
Upon the reorganization of the Board, Frederick Darlington was
made chief of the Power Section and Gen. Keller maintained an informal Consultation Committee.[4]   Later, when the power shortage
became acute in certain localities, Charles K. Foster, vice-chairman
of the Priorities Committee, was made Director in Charge of Preferential Power Distribution, acting under the Priorities Division, and
certain Army Engineers attached to the section were assigned to work
with Mr. Foster.

On October 7, 1917, the priorities commissioner issued Circular No.
45,[5] embodying rules and regulations for the guidance of light and
power companies in the distribution of electric energy, which enabled
the companies in most instances themselves to make priority distribu-
tions in the event of a shortage without reference to Mr. Foster, the
Director of Power.

The general purpose of the section was to gather information to
give a broad picture of the power situation of the country and to
establish specifically the localities which had a surplus and those
which had a shortage.   The early attempts of Government agencies
to locate national plants were necessarily made with incomplete
knowledge of the total power situation.   There was a tendency to
build power plants without sufficient reference to existing plants and
available equipment.   Before the formation of the Facilities Division

---

[4] Robert J. Bulkley, Cleveland attorney, later U. S. Senator from Ohio, was
also in charge of the legal section of W. I. B.

[5] See Appendix XXVI.

it was the duty of this section to review the projects contemplating the commandeering or building of power plants. Advice was given both as to best methods of obtaining power in localities selected and as to selection of localities for particular projects. The principal work of the section came to be to notify the various commodity chiefs and departments of the Government as to where there was a shortage of power in order to avoid the placing of orders or the erection of new facilities where no power was available.

With the assistance of material prepared by the section the Priorities Commissioner advised with the Capital Issues Committee upon request as to the war need of electrical power projects in cases where application had been made to that committee for the issue of securities. Advice was likewise given to the War Finance Corporation concerning the need of extensions for which loans had been requested. The section also consulted frequently with the Electrical and Power Equipment Section concerning schedules of supplies. It made frequent recommendations to the Priorities Committee in behalf of companies needing materials for new construction, repairs, and replacements.

The growth of power plants was naturally irregular during the war on account of the impossibility of so anticipating the development of war needs as to keep them distributed proportionately over the country. Many current projects for the construction of central station electric power services were halted by the war emergency and held in abeyance on account of the high costs involved in completion. If other conditions had made it possible to so place war orders that these facilities could have been completed in the normal way, no power shortage need have developed and much of the power constructed for war purposes and not economical in peace times would not have been built. Some of this unnecessary expenditure of wealth could, perhaps, have been averted by an earlier establishment of such control as the War Industries Board was exercising at the close of the period. Much extravagance in this direction was averted.

The generating capacity of the country in 1917 was approximately 13,693,000 horsepower. Over 2,000,000 horsepower was added during the war period. The most troublesome shortages occurred in districts where power is abundant but where war industries happened to be concentrated in the most unusual amounts. Assistance was rendered by the section to relieve the situation in the Pittsburgh district, New Jersey district, Georgia district, and Philadelphia district during the summer of 1918. It was in these districts that the special priority director and his assistants were called upon to direct the distribution of power in aid of the war program.

ELECTRICAL AND POWER EQUIPMENT

This section was established November 14, 1917. Walter Robbins [6] was made chief and remained in charge through the reorganization of the Board and until the section was disbanded. Three subdivisions were created in the section, having charge, respectively, of (1) electrical apparatus and supplies, (2) steam turbines, and (3) boilers, condensers, and analogous equipment.

Electrical apparatus and supplies.—No very great difficulty arose in connection with electrical supplies, with the exception of electric wire and cable, for which a separate section * * * was formed late in the period. The Wire Section allocated Government orders from the middle of August forward. This action was necessitated by the general shortage in copper and by the confusion which arose when the Signal Corps announced a requirement of 65,000 miles of outpost wire. In general there were heavy reserve stocks of electrical supplies throughout the country, and the war did little more than reduce these to a point far below normal. Studies were made of the locations and conditions of these stocks, and 24 War Service Committees were formed to guide the industry in its relation to war work, but no important steps on the part of the Board had yet been found necessary when the war ended.

The problem of electrical apparatus was different. Important shortages and threatened shortages were evident from the start. A general War Service Committee with 11 subcommittees was organized, and with the aid of this committee the section made a survey of the country to locate and list the available stocks. The record thus obtained was kept up to date by semi-monthly reports from manufacturers and others. War requirements in this industry were very difficult to handle because most of them were indirect. But the section soon found itself possessed of sufficient information about supplies and requirements to indicate where shortages and surpluses were occurring and thus to guide shifts in production. The section was frequently able to point out existing equipment or facilities suitable for conversion to some war need, and through this service many new construction projects were shown to be unnecessary. The section was in several instances able to anticipate shortages in certain stocks and encourage sufficient manufacture to prevent them. Adjustable speed motors for the manufacture of machine tools and pyrometers required

---

[6] Walter Robbins was chairman of the board of the General Cable Corporation from 1929 to 1938. He joined the British Purchasing Commission in February, 1940.

in unusual numbers for testing and recording heat in the manufacture of munitions were taken care of in this way.

Commencing January 1, 1918, all applications for priority certificates for electrical apparatus were referred to this section for recommendation before consideration by the Priorities Committee. Much attention was given to applications involving apparatus going into the "restricted area" or into centers where power shortage existed. Occasionally when investigation revealed that certain of the equipment called for could not be produced under any grade of priority within the time required, substitutions or altered methods were suggested by the section for accomplishing the desired results. Sometimes second-hand equipment located by the section was found to serve as a temporary or even permanent solution.

Applications for priority came in gradually increasing volume up to the period when automatic ratings were put into effect. The section received as many as 300 applications in one day. About 29,000 in all came before the section and their disposition is recorded in the files. The section "cleared" 1,257 orders from various agencies of our Government and 112 orders from the Allied Governments.

It devoted a great deal of work to the problem of standardization in this industry, particularly standardization in Government requirements. The War Department appointed a committee of Army engineers to work on the question, and this section obtained for the Army contact with the general War Service Committee and its 35 subcommittees. It was the purpose of the Army committee to adopt for its standards such stocks as had reached a reasonable state of standardization for industrial uses and not to attempt to establish new standards. The War Service Committee had been working for a year on a very comprehensive program of standardization, directed to the conservation of raw materials, labor, and transportation.

Curtailment agreements were arranged with the manufacturers of electric heating devices and of fan motors, and the section administered the plans. In August, 1918, the Priorities Commissioner held a meeting with the jobbers of electrical apparatus and supplies. It was determined that the jobbers should be recognized and given an automatic priority rating Class B–4 upon their pledge to police the industry for the observance of all priority rulings.

Steam turbines.—By the time the section was formed, an extreme shortage in steam turbines was evident. The creation of new facilities for their manufacture is a long process. Hence the first studies of the section were devoted to the question of the relative importance of the various needs with a view to determining a proper sequence of deliveries. The first work was on the larger size land type, because both the Navy and the Emergency Fleet maintained in the turbine shops a corps of production experts whose duty it was to direct the sequence of production of orders of the marine type. To take care of companies producing both types, an agreement was reached, after conference of the parties, that the following sequence should, in the absence of express directions to the contrary, hold: (1) Navy, (2) Emergency Fleet, (3) Army, and (4) private companies.

The section prepared a schedule of all Government requirements for land-type turbines with date of delivery required. It then called all manufacturers together to discuss the possibilities of meeting the requirements. There seemed to be no available finished stocks on account of acute congestion. The delivery period for new orders was estimated at 7 to 10 months for smaller sizes and 18 to 24 months for larger sizes. The only solution seemed to be to divert turbines under order. The manufacturers were requested to submit a tabulation of all units then under order in sizes of 10,000 or more kilowatts, and at a later meeting a shipping schedule for Government requirements was arranged, diversions being made only after giving full consideration to the relative importance of the various needs. The requirements of the large public-service corporations were next studied by the section. Following this the manufacturers were asked to extend their schedules of information on production to include all turbines of 1,000 or more kilowatts, and a similar production and shipping schedule covering such smaller units was arranged.

As the spring of 1918 approached, the situation was becoming gradually worse. It seemed to be impossible to establish a fixed schedule of deliveries, because of constant changes in the war program, and new difficulties in securing raw materials. On May 27, 1918, following the usual series of conferences, steam turbine production was made a controlled industry. All schedules of deliveries of both finished products and materials going to the plants were placed under the control of the Board, with detail management in the hands of a special joint committee representing the Navy, Emergency Fleet, Army, and the division.

A difficulty arose in regard to large forgings. The only plants available for this work were fully occupied with gun forgings for the Army and Navy on an A–1 priority rating. The matter was taken up with the Army and Navy and an agreement reached that a certain share of these facilities should be relieved for the production of turbine forgings. The section conferred frequently with the Power Section with a view to reducing as much as possible the requirement for new turbines by the exercise of greater care in locating projects devoted to war manufacture.

Boilers, condensers, and similar equipment.—The third subdivision of the section handled the problems arising in this general field. The surface pipe steam condenser industry was taken under complete control by the Board and much attention had to be given to the production of steam boilers. By June, 1918, it was clear that the war requirement for iron and steel would soon be in excess of the country's productive capacity. In line with the general program of conserving iron and steel, the section made investigations with a view to withholding priority assistance for the delivery of new boilers wherever old ones could be repaired or used boilers substituted.

It was pointed out to the Railroad Administration that many old locomotive boilers might be used temporarily for stationary power and heating purposes. A protest was entered against the use of Scotch marine boilers because their manufacture requires an unusual amount of metal. Steps were taken to prevent the expansion of shop facilities for their production.

All important steam power plants, whether on land or afloat, must be equipped with condensers of one of the three standard types: jet, barometric, or surface. Jet and barometric condensers can be used on land, but surface condensers are required for ships. Recently the tendency has been to install surface condensers on land, particularly in large turbine units. The essential distinguishing feature of a surface condenser is the large amount of non-ferrous tubing with which it is filled. By the spring of 1918 it became clear that the demands of the Navy and the Emergency Fleet for brass tubing could not be met if the installation of surface condensers on land plants was allowed to go unchecked. The manufacturers were called to Washington for conference and study of the situation, and in August an agreement was reached that the distribution of surface condensers should be completely controlled by the Board. No sales could be made unless the buyer should present a "purchase permit" issued by the Board. The Brass Section took control at the same time over the distribution of non-ferrous tubing. Efforts were made to have seamless steel tubes substituted for non-ferrous tubes wherever contact with salt water did not make this substitution impracticable.

An interesting question arose in connection with automatic mechanical stokers. The demand for this equipment increased very rapidly during the war. The Fuel Administration was encouraging the installation of these stokers under existing boilers with a view to conserving fuel. It became a question of balancing the saving in fuel and operating labor, resulting from the installation of a stoker, as against the metal and productive labor required in manufacturing one. The section studied each important proposed installation, conferring with the Fuel Administration and the War Service Committee of the stoker manufacturers in an endeavor to adjust the demand to production.

Much the same problem arose in connection with the production of superheaters and economizers. The general conclusion reached with regard to them was that their production should be discouraged on the theory that, for the time being, the saving of metal and labor was more important than the saving of fuel.

The section made studies also in connection with the distribution of raw materials to manufacturers of conveying apparatus, fans and blowers, small engines, transmission machinery, water heaters, pumps and compressors, refrigerating machinery, and other analogous equipment.

Not very much important work was done by way of standardization of machinery, though steps in this direction had been taken in several instances. If the war had lasted several more years, standardization in all lines of machinery would have become a necessity and would have been one of the deciding factors in the adjustment of possible production to the requirements of the war. Important economies were effected by the section through the use of priority power so as to divert materials and effort from less essential to more essential purposes.

APPENDICES†

APPENDIX I.

SECTION 2 OF THE ARMY APPROPRIATION ACT, APPROVED AUGUST 29, 1916.

SEC. 2. That a Council of National Defense is hereby established for the coordination of industries and resources for the national security and welfare, to consist of the Secretary of War, the Secretary of the Navy, the Secretary of the Interior, the Secretary of Agriculture, the Secretary of Commerce, and the Secretary of Labor.

That the Council of National Defense shall nominate to the President, and the President shall appoint, an advisory commission, consisting of not more than seven persons, each of whom shall have special knowledge of some industry, public utility, or the development of some natural resource, or be otherwise specially qualified, in the opinion of the council, for the performance of the duties hereinafter provided. The members of the advisory commission shall serve without compensation, but shall be allowed actual expenses of travel and subsistence when attending meetings of the commission or engaged in investigations pertaining to its activities. The advisory commission shall hold such meetings as shall be called by the council or be provided by the rules and regulations adopted by the council for the conduct of its work.

That it shall be the duty of the Council of National Defense to supervise and direct investigations and make recommendations to the President and the heads of executive departments as to the location of railroads with reference to the frontier of the United States, so as to render possible expeditious concentration of troops and supplies to points of defense; the coordination of military, industrial, and commercial purposes in the location of extensive highways and branch lines of railroad; the utilization of waterways; the mobilization of military and naval resources for defense; the increase of domestic production of articles and materials essential to the support of armies and of the people during the interruption of foreign commerce; the development of seagoing transportation; data as to amounts, location, method, and means of production, and availability of military supplies; the giving of information to producers and manufacturers as to the class of supplies needed by the military and other services of the Government, the requirements relating thereto, and the creation of relations which will render possible in time of need the immediate concentration and utilization of the resources of the Nation.

That the Council of National Defense shall adopt rules and regulations for the conduct of its work, which rules and regulations shall be subject to the

---

† *Editor's Note:* Certain deletions have been made in the list of appendices, including all yearly production schedules and lists of imports and exports which are readily available.

approval of the President, and shall provide for the work of the advisory commission, to the end that the special knowledge of such commission may be developed by suitable investigation, research, and inquiry and made available in conference and report for the use of the council; and the council may organize subordinate bodies for its assistance in special investigations, either by the employment of experts or by the creation of committees of specially qualified persons to serve without compensation, but to direct the investigations of experts so employed.

That the sum of $200,000, or so much thereof as may be necessary, is hereby appropriated, out of any money in the Treasury not otherwise appropriated, to be immediately available for experimental work and investigations undertaken by the council, by the advisory commission, or subordinate bodies, for the employment of a director, expert and clerical expenses and supplies, and for the necessary expenses of members of the advisory commission or subordinate bodies going to and attending meetings of the commission or subordinate bodies. Reports shall be submitted by all subordinate bodies and by the advisory commission to the council, and from time to time the council shall report to the President or to the heads of executive departments upon special inquiries or subjects appropriate thereto, and an annual report to the Congress shall be submitted through the President, including as full a statement of the activities of the council and the agencies subordinate to it as is consistent with the public interest, including an itemized account of the expenditures made by the council or authorized by it, in as full detail as the public interest will permit: *Provided, however,* That when deemed proper the President may authorize, in amounts stipulated by him, unvouchered expenditures and report the gross sum so authorized not itemized.

Appendix II.

ADVANTAGES OF WAR SERVICE COMMITTEES REPRESENTING INDUSTRIES.

[As set forth in pamphlet of United States Chamber of Commerce, Feb. 28, 1918.]

I. They provide an organized method by which the Government can quickly present to all the factors in an industry its needs in a particular line and receive dependable information as to how they may be met and what facilities are available for use. Necessary publicity as to Government needs thus presented simultaneously to all interests in a line prevents the possibility of unfair advantage through the presentation of information of this character to separate firms or individuals.

II. They can arrange promptly for gathering figures as to cost of production and from time to time report to Government agencies changes in conditions which affect such cost. Such cost sheets can, of course, be checked independently by Government authorities.

III. They can aid effectively in the distribution and conservation of raw material essential for war output.

IV. They provide organized machinery to collect information and advise the Government as to what the needs of industry will be to meet the future requirements of the Government, and as a result comprehensive plans may be made well in advance for any necessary readjustments of industry.

V. When committees are chosen by the industries themselves, so that they are representative of all interests in each industry, the appointment of the ablest and best posted men in each line is assured, and the basis for any allegation of favoritism in selection or preferential treatment by Government agencies is eliminated.

VI. The possibility of complaints that business men chosen by the Government for committee work are in a position to influence privately the placing of contracts with concerns in which they are financially interested is likewise removed.

VII. If committees are organized by the industries themselves, the Government is in no way responsible for them, and is free to consult with them as their merits may justify.

VIII. The committees are able to advance rapidly the process of standardization and to eliminate in manufacturing lines unnecessary sizes, styles, and shapes, thus conserving raw material, labor, and capital.

IX. The committes can bring to the attention of the Government unemployed facilities which may readily be adapted to the production of supplies needed by the Government and thus avoid the misuse of money, material, and labor involved in extension of existing plants. The saving of time in this process is also of great advantage.

Utilization of the committees has these advantages:

1. A committee chosen by an industry having the confidence of all the factors in the line, and for which the industry is responsible, is available at all times on call of the Government to meet with Government agencies for conference with reference to any Government needs or policies.

2. It can give to Government agencies complete information as to all the individuals, firms, and corporations in the line, with facts as to their facilities and management.

3. If the Government places its needs before such a committee in planning a certain purchase, the raw material market can be protected and inflation prevented.

4. The committee can have cost figures prepared on the commodity or merchandise desired and place before the Government cost sheets, on the basis of which the Government may fix prices fair to all.

5. The committee can make recommendations as to the distribution of orders to prevent bad location, railroad congestion, and labor disturbance.

6. The Government experts can check the cost sheets submitted and the recommendations as to distribution and make their own decisions, which industry will gladly accept if reached in an orderly way.

7. Each factor in an industry will have to take its share of Government business where full production is required, and advantage to some will be prevented.

8. The Government may be constantly advised by the committee in an authoritative way as to changing conditions, and plans may be made systematically to anticipate emergencies and meet future needs.

9. Individual applications for priority have in the past greatly complicated operations of the priority system. In many lines priority applications can be cleared through the committees of the industries and much better results thereby secured.

10. Such committees may likewise be utilized to great advantage in dealing with the fuel, transportation, labor, reconstruction, foreign trade, and similar problems where an industry as a whole should be considered rather than a part of it or individuals in it.

APPENDIX III.

THE OVERMAN ACT.

[Approved May 20, 1918.]

AN ACT Authorizing the President to coordinate or consolidate executive bureaus, agencies, and offices, and for other purposes, in the interest of economy and the more efficient concentration of the Government.

Be it enacted by the Senate and House of Representatives of the United States of America in Congress assembled, That, for the national security and defense, for the successful prosecution of the war, for the support and maintenance of the Army and Navy, for the better utilization of resources and industries, and for the more effective exercise and more efficient administration by the President of his powers as Commander in Chief of the land and naval forces, the President is hereby authorized to make such redistribution of functions among executive agencies as he may deem necessary, including any functions, duties, and powers hitherto by law conferred upon any executive department, commission, bureau, agency, office, or officer, in such manner as in his judgment shall seem best fitted to carry out the purposes of this act, and to this end is authorized to make such regulations and to issue such orders as he may deem necessary, which regulations and orders shall be in writing and shall be filed with the head of the department affected and constitute a public record: *Provided,* That this act shall remain in force during the continuance of the present war and for six months after the termination of the war by the proclamation of the treaty of peace, or at such earlier time as the President may designate: *Provided further,* That the termination of this act shall not affect any act done or any right or obligation accruing or accrued pursuant to this act, and during the time that this act is in force: *Provided further,* That the authority by this act granted shall be exercised only in matters relating to the conduct of the present war.

Sec. 2. That in carrying out the purposes of this act the President is authorized to utilize, coordinate, or consolidate any executive or administrative commissions, bureaus, agencies, offices, or officers now existing by law, to transfer any duties or powers from one existing department, commission, bureau, agency, office, or officer to another, to transfer the personnel thereof or any part of it either by detail or assignment, together with the whole or any part of the records and public property belonging thereto.

Sec. 3. That the President is further authorized to establish an executive agency which may exercise such jurisdiction and control over the production of aeroplanes, aeroplane engines, and aircraft equipment as in his judgment may be advantageous; and, further, to transfer to such agency, for its use, all or any moneys heretofore appropriated for the production of aeroplanes, aeroplane engines, and aircraft equipment.

Sec. 4. That for the purpose of carrying out the provisions of this act, any moneys heretofore and hereafter appropriated for the use of any executive department, commission, bureau, agency, office, or officer shall be expended only for the purposes for which it was appropriated under the direction of such other agency as may be directed by the President hereunder to perform and execute said function.

Sec. 5. That should the President, in redistributing the functions among the executive agencies as provided in this act, conclude that any bureau should be abolished and it or their duties and functions conferred upon some other department or bureau or eliminated entirely, he shall report his conclusions to Congress with such recommendations as he may deem proper.

Sec. 6. That all laws or parts of laws conflicting with the provisions of this act are to the extent of such conflict suspended while this act is in force.

Upon the termination of this act all executive or administrative agencies, departments, commissions, bureaus, offices, or officers shall exercise the same functions, duties, and powers as heretofore or as hereafter by law may be provided, any authorization of the President under this act to the contrary notwithstanding.

Appendix IV.

ORGANIZATION AND FUNCTIONS OF REQUIREMENTS DIVISION OF WAR INDUSTRIES BOARD.

(Circular Creating Requirements Division.)

In order that the responsibilities which the President has laid upon the chairman of the War Industries Board, as outlined in his letter of March 4, 1918, may be discharged, there has been created a "requirements division" of the said board, to which each supply division of each department of this Government and the Allied Purchasing Commission shall furnish "as far in advance as possible" statements with as much detail as practicable of their "prospective needs" of raw materials and finished products. The President has decreed that the chairman is to be constantly and systematically informed of all contracts and purchases in order that he may have always before him a schematized analysis of the progress of business in the several divisions of the Government in all the departments, and in order that this may be accomplished, the statements above mentioned will include not only those commodities, materials, or products of which a present or threatened shortage exists, but also those of which the supply is ample, and will also include not only commodities, materials, and products required by several different departments or nations but also those required by one department only.

In the procurement of materials and finished products in which no shortage exists and where no allocation seems necessary or desirable the requirements division will so advise the department presenting the requirements, which will thereupon proceed with the purchase in pursuance with their established practices.

SECTION 1. *Notice of requirements.*—The statements above mentioned will, from time to time, and as far in advance as possible of the date required, be presented to the requirements division by the member or members thereof representing the department in which the requirements originate or by the representative of the Allied Purchasing Commission. Where the requirements are novel or unusual, either with respect to the amount of the proposed expenditure, quantities involved or location proposed, or where the requirements division for any reason deems it desirable that the project be considered in conference between the head of the department in which it originates and the chairman of the War Industries Board, the matter shall be immediately called to the attention of the chairman of the War Industries Board, and also submitted to the board at its next meeting, without, however, delaying reference to and consideration by the appropriate commodity section.

SEC. 2. *Commodity sections.*—The chairman of the War Industries Board shall utilize existing sections and, where necessary, create additional sections to handle raw materials and finished products of which there is an actual or threatened shortage, or the price and production of which should be controlled, in order that the United States Government, its Allies, and the civilian population may be protected as far as possible. These sections shall be designated "commodity sections," and each shall be in charge of an executive officer to be designated "chief" of such section.

Each section chief shall create and maintain such organization and keep such records as may be prescribed by the authority appointing him.

SEC. 3. *Members of commodity sections.*—Each commodity section shall be composed of the section chief and representatives (hereinafter called members) of each of the supply departments of the Government interested in the commodity in question. Each member shall be named by his department head. Since each member will have regular duties to perform in connection with the supply department which he represents, he need give to the commodity section to which he is attached only so much time as may be necessary to perform the duties herein prescribed, and will not be charged with the executive conduct of the business of the section, but will have access to all data and information collected by the section and will in turn supply the section with all information he may have or can procure pertaining to the commodity in question.

SEC. 4. *Duties of commodity sections.*—Upon receipt from the requirements division of statements embodying the requirements of any department of this Government or of its Allies, it shall be the duty of the chief of the section to carefully study and consider same and procure from all available sources information and data which will be helpful in the allocation of such requirements. Meetings of each commodity section shall be called by the chief thereof at such times as will interfere as little as possible with the other duties of the members. At such meetings the requirements referred to the section shall be considered, and wherever possible the allocation of material or facilities to meet such requirements shall be determined. In the event any member is dissatisfied with the decision reached he may at his election file a protest with the section chief and also with the head of his division or department. The latter may at his election appeal to the chairman of the War Industries Board, whose decision, after giving all interested parties an opportunity to be heard, shall be final, subject only to modification by agreement between the chairman of the War Industries Board and the respective Secretaries of War and the Navy and the Chairman of the Shipping Board to the extent of their respective interests. A record of each meeting will be preserved in the office of the chief of the section, the decisions reached at meetings will be reduced to writing in a succinct form, and a copy thereof will be transmitted to (1) the chairman of the requirements division; (2) to each member of the section; (3) to the director of Army purchases; (4) to the Paymaster General of the Navy; (5) to the vice president and general manager of the Emergency Fleet Corporation; (6) to the priorities commissioner; and (7) to such other official or officials as may be from time to time designated by the chairman of the War Industries Board.

Each commodity section will also from time to time consider the necessity for expansion of existing sources of production or the creation of new facilities, and the disclosing, if necessary, the opening up of additional sources of supply and the conversion of existing facilities to new uses.

Each section chief will be charged with the responsibility of collecting from the several departments of the Government, from the manufacturers and producers, and from the committees representing them, and especially from the war-service committee or committees created under the supervision of the Chamber of Commerce of the United States, and from any and all other reliable and available sources information concerning the production of the particular commodity or commodities with which his section has to deal, including available supplies, new sources of supply, methods for increasing production, etc. These data and information will at all times be available to the several interested departments, the price committee, the priorities committee, and any other agency that may be designated by the chairman of the War Industries Board.

Each commodity section shall consider market conditions pertaining to the materials or commodities over which it has jurisdiction, and shall, where deemed advisable, recommend purchase plans to the several purchasing departments. In cases where it becomes necessary to control an industry in whole or in part by means of allotments, the appropriate section will determine the allotments of materials, commodities, and facilities to the several departments of this Government and to its allies, and also the extent to which manufacturers and others, whether serving the civilian population or engaged in the manufacture of war supplies, shall be rationed.

SEC. 5. *Special commodity section.*—Where the requirements deal with a commodity listed, where a shortage exists, or where an allocation seems desirable, but for which no regular section has been established, such requirements will be considered by a special section created for such purpose by the requirements division, which shall perform the same functions as are performed by the regular commodity sections.

SEC. 6. *Priorities.*—When a commodity section comes to make its final report on the allocation of any specific requirement the chief of such section shall notify a member of the priorities committee, to be designated for such purpose by the priorities commissioner, who shall, with the section chief and the member, consider and tentatively determine the priority rating which such requirements shall take when orders therefor shall have been placed. Such tentative rating shall be observed by the priorities committee in connection with all applications for priority on orders covering such requirements unless the priorities committee should (because of conditions changing in the time intervening between the time of the fixing of the tentative rating and the application for priorities, or other good cause) conclude such rating to be improper, in which event the section chief and each member of the section fixing the tentative rating shall be notified and have an opportunity to be heard before such rating shall be changed. In the event a change is made the section chief or any member may appeal from such decision in the manner prescribed by that portion of the organization plan of the War Industries Board governing priorities.

SEC. 7. *Inspection and production.*—It shall be no part of the task of the War Industries Board to make inspection of products for which orders have been placed, to keep in touch with production or to follow up delays, which duties devolve upon the several governmental supply departments. Each supply department, however, will promptly and fully advise the requirements division whenever serious delays in deliveries or shortages in requirements occur or are threatened.

SEC. 8. *Membership.*—The requirements division shall be composed of Mr. Alex Legge, chairman; Mr. James Inglis, executive secretary; Mr. Edwin B. Parker, priorities; Mr. George N. Peek, finished products; Mr. J. Leonard Replogle, iron, steel, and steel products; Mr. L. L. Summers, chemicals and explosives; Mr. Pope Yeatman, nonferrous metals; Mr. J. A. Carr, representing Allied Purchasing Commission; one or more representatives of the War Department; one or more representatives of the Navy Department; a representative of the Marine Corps; one or more representatives of the United States

Shipping Board, Emergency Fleet Corporation; and a representative of the Railroad Administration.

The chairman of the War Industries Board shall from time to time agree with the Secretary of War, the Secretary of the Navy, and the chairman of the Shipping Board, respectively, as to the number of representatives from their respective departments, and when the number shall have been determined such representatives shall be selected by the Secretary of War, the Secretary of the Navy, and the chairman of the Shipping Board, respectively.

The Fuel Administrator, the Food Administrator, and the American Red Cross shall each designate a representative who shall attend meetings of the requirements division whenever they are prepared to present plans or projects under consideration, the consummation of which will require materials, supplies, facilities, electrical power, fuel, or transportation affecting the industries of the United States.

Sec. 9. *Meetings.*—Meetings of the members of this division shall be held in the office of its chairman at 9 a. m. each day, at which all advices of requirements received since the preceding meeting and all other matters affecting requirements in which the members of the division as a whole shall be interested will be considered, after which the statements of requirements shall be segregated as far as need be and referred by the executive secretary to the appropriate commodity section.

Appendix V.

LIST OF THE WAR INDUSTRIES BOARD PRICE BULLETINS, NOS. 1 TO 57.

1. Summary.
2. International price comparisons.
3. Government control over prices.
4. Prices of foods.
5. Prices of clothing.
6. Prices of building materials.
7. Prices of chemicals.

FOOD.

8. Prices of feed and forage.
9. Prices of wheat and wheat products.
10. Prices of corn and corn products.
11. Prices of oats, rice, buckwheat, and their products.
12. Prices of barley, hops, rye, and their products.
13. Prices of sugar and related products.
14. Prices of vegetables and truck.
15. Prices of edible vegetable oils.
16. Prices of fruits, nuts, and wine.
17. Prices of spices and condiments.

18. Prices of tea, coffee, and cocoa.
19. Prices of tobacco and tobacco products.
20. Prices of livestock, meats, and fats.
21. Prices of poultry and dairy products.
22. Prices of fish and oysters.

CLOTHING.

23. Prices of cotton and cotton products.
24. Prices of wool and wool products.
25. Prices of silk and silk products.
26. Prices of hides and skins and their products.
27. Prices of hatters' fur and fur felt hats.
28. Prices of hair, bristles, and feathers.
29. Prices of buttons.

RUBBER, PAPER, FIBER.

30. Prices of rubber and rubber products.

RUBBER, PAPER, FIBER—continued.

31. Prices of paper.
32. Prices of fibers and fiber products.

METALS.

33. Prices of iron, steel, and their products.
34. Prices of ferroalloys, nonferrous and rare metals.

FUEL.

35. Prices of coal and coke.
36. Prices of petroleum and its products.
37. Prices of matches.

BUILDING MATERIALS.

38. Prices of clay products.
39. Prices of sand and gravel.
40. Prices of quarry products.
41. Prices of cement.
42. Prices of glass.

43. Prices of lumber.
44. Prices of paints and varnishes.

CHEMICALS.

45. Prices of mineral acids.
46. Prices of heavy chemicals.
47. Prices of miscellaneous inorganic chemicals.
48. Prices of fertilizers.
49. Prices of soaps and glycerin.
50. Prices of essential oils, flavoring and perfumery materials.
51. Prices of wood-distillation products and naval stores.
52. Prices of natural dyestuffs and tanning chemicals.
53. Prices of coal-tar crudes, intermediates, and dyes.
54. Prices of drugs and pharmaceuticals.
55. Prices of proprietary preparations.
56. Prices of explosives.
57. Prices of miscellaneous organic chemicals.

The above bulletins—if available—may be obtained from the superintendent of documents, Government Printing Office, Washington, D. C.

Appendix VI.

(1) PRIORITIES CIRCULAR NO. 1.
(September 21, 1917.)

DIRECTIONS AS TO PRIORITY.

During the war in which the United States is now engaged, all individuals, firms, associations, and corporations engaged in the production of iron and steel and in the manufacture of products thereof are requested to observe the following regulations respecting priority, viz.:

CLASSES PRESCRIBED.

1. All orders and work shall be divided into three general classes, Class A, Class B, and Class C, with various subdivisions of Classes A and B, indicated by a suffix number, thus: Class A1, A2, A3, A4, etc., and Class B1, B2, B3, B4, etc.

PRECEDENCE OF CLASSES.

2. Orders and work in Class A shall take precedence of orders and work in both Class B and Class C, and orders and work in Class B shall take preced-

ence of orders and work in Class C, irrespective of the date the orders were received; and orders and work in Class A1 shall take precedence of orders and work in Class A2, etc., and Class B1 shall take precedence of Class B2, etc.

CLASS A DEFINED.

3. Class A comprises war work; that is to say, orders and work urgently necessary in carrying on the war, such as arms, ammunition, ships, etc., and the materials required in the manufacture of same.

CLASS B DEFINED.

4. Class B comprises orders and work which, while not primarily designed for the prosecution of the war, yet are of public interest and essential to the national welfare, or otherwise of exceptional importance.

CLASS C DEFINED.

5. Class C comprises all orders and work not embraced in Class A or Class B, and no certificate of the priorities committee will be required therefor. Any order for work or material not accompanied by a certificate in substantially the form set forth on page 3 of this circular, to the effect that the work or material falls within Class A or Class B, should be treated as an order for work in Class C.

MATERIALS CLASSIFIED.

6. All materials required in the manufacture of an article or in the prosecution of any work will be entitled to take the class of such article or work unless otherwise specified in the certificate covering the same.

CERTIFICATES OF PRIORITY.

7. Certificates in the form set forth on page 3 of this circular will be issued by the priorities committee upon application therefor specifying the classification of the order or work, and priority should be given accordingly in producing and furnishing the material or supplies or in manufacturing and delivering the article. Certificates of a subsidiary nature will be issued upon request for the furnishing of material and articles required in manufacturing the article or prosecuting the work ordered.

CLASSIFICATION OF EXISTING ORDERS.

8. All orders placed prior to the date hereof by or on behalf of the War Department or Navy Department of the United States or the United States Shipping Board Emergency Fleet Corporation should be classed as subdivision A–1 of Class A unless otherwise ordered by the officer placing the order or by the priorities committee, and all orders for arms, ammunition, and other military supplies and equipment placed prior to the date hereof by or on be-

half of the nations associated with the United States in the war in which it is now engaged should be classed as subdivision A–2 of Class A unless otherwise ordered by the priorities committee.

CLASSIFICATION OF FUTURE ORDERS.

9. All orders placed after the date hereof should be classed as Class C unless covered by certificates of the priorities committee or other written directions of the said committee.

EXECUTION OF CERTIFICATES.

10. Certificates or other documents signed by the chairman or any member of the priorities committee shall be deemed to have been authorized by said committee and by the War Industries Board of the Council of National Defense.

> ROBERT S. LOVETT,
> *Chairman of the Priorities Committee.*
> COUNCIL OF NATIONAL DEFENSE,
> By NEWTON D. BAKER,
> *Chairman.*

Approved:
  NEWTON D. BAKER,
    Secretary of War.
  JOSEPHUS DANIELS,
    Secretary of the Navy.

APPENDIX VII.

PRIORITIES CIRCULAR NO. 4.
(July 1, 1918.)

RULES AND REGULATIONS GOVERNING PRIORITY IN PRODUCTION.

These rules and regulations governing priority in production will supersede all directions, rules, and regulations heretofore promulgated by this committee. All priority certificates heretofore issued and now outstanding shall remain in full force and effect according to their original terms.

During the war in which the United States is now engaged all individuals, firms, associations, and corporations engaged in the production of raw materials and manufactured products (save foods, feeds, and fuels) are requested to observe the following regulations respecting priority, namely:

CLASSIFICATIONS.

1. *Classes prescribed.*—All orders and work are divided into five general classes: Class AA, Class A, Class B, Class C, and Class D, with subdivisions of

Class AA, Class A, and Class B, indicated by suffix number, thus: Class AA–1, Class AA–2, etc.; Class A–1, Class A–2, etc.; and Class B–1, Class B–2, etc.

2. *Class AA defined.*—Class AA comprises only emergency war work of an exceptional and urgent nature.

3. *Class A defined.*—Class A comprises all other war work; that is to say, orders and work necessary to carry on the war, such as arms, ammunitions, destroyers, submarines, battleships, transports, merchant ships, and other water craft, airplanes, locomotives, etc., and the materials or commodities required in the production or manufacture of same.

4. *Class B defined.*—Class B comprises orders and work which, while not primarily designed for the prosecution of the war, yet are of public interest and essential to the national welfare or otherwise of exceptional importance.

5. *Class C defined.*—Class C comprises all orders and work not covered by priority certificates issued by the priorities committee or not taking an automatic rating, in accordance with the provisions of sections 7, 8, and 9 hereof, which orders and work are to be utilized in furtherance of one or more of the purposes embraced within the "General classification of purposes demanding preference treatment" promulgated by the priorities board, appearing on page 17 of this circular, as same may be from time to time amended or substituted; or which orders and work are placed by or are to be utilized in connection with an industry or plant appearing on Preference List No. 1, promulgated and published by the priorities board under date of April 6, 1918 (as set forth on pp. 18–19 of this circular), and all amendments or substitutes therefor. No Class C certificates shall be issued.

6. *Class D defined.*—Class D comprises all orders and work not embraced in Class AA, Class A, Class B, or Class C, and no certificates will be issued therefor. All orders for work or materials not covered by priority certificates or not taking an automatic classification in accordance with the provisions of sections 8 and 9 hereof, and not taking a Class C classification under the provisions of section 5 hereof, will fall within Class D.

7. *Automatic classifications.*—Each order placed after June 30, 1918, by a duly authorized officer of the War Department or of the Navy Department of the United States, or of the United States Shipping Board Emergency Fleet Corporation, which falls within Class A as defined in section 3 hereof, shall by virtue of this rule, upon the placing of the order, automatically be classified as A–5, provided said order carries an indorsement personally signed by the officer placing the order, reading:

"Unless rerated by express order in writing by the priorities committee of the War Industries Board this order is by authority of said priorities committee rated as Class A–5, and its execution shall take precedence over all your orders and work of a lower classification to the extent necessary to insure delivery according to the date specified herein, as prescribed by Circular No. 4, issued by the priorities division of the War Industries Board, of date July 1, 1918, and all amendments thereto."

8. Each order for materials, equipment, or supplies for the purposes or uses

hereinafter in this section mentioned shall, by virtue of this rule, automatically take a classification as herein prescribed, namely:

(a) For the manufacture of turbines (all classes) A–4
(b) For the repair or construction of steam railroad locomotives for use on the railroads under the jurisdiction of the United States Railroad Administration A–4
(c) For the production of electrodes A–5
(d) For the manufacture of rope wire and of wire rope A–5
(e) For the building of ships or other water craft for and under direct contracts with the United States Shipping Board Emergency Fleet Corporation A–5
(f) For the building of all cargo water craft (but not pleasure craft) save such as are under construction by or for the United States Shipping Board Emergency Fleet Corporation A–6
(g) For the manufacture of machine tools for working both metal and wood; of machinists' tools, of small tools, of hand tools, and of mining tools, machinery, and equipment A–6
(h) For the manufacture of steam railroad materials, equipment, and supplies (other than locomotives) for use on the railroads under the jurisdiction of the United States Railroad Administration B–1
(i) For the manufacture of locomotive cranes and traveling cranes B–1
(j) For the manufacture of electrical equipment other than turbines (but not electrical supplies as distinguished from equipment) B–2
(k) For the manufacture of farm implements B–2
(l) For the manufacture of textile machinery B–2
(m) For the manufacture of tools, implements, machinery, and equipment required for the production, harvesting, distribution, milling, canning, and refining of foods and feeds B–2
(n) For the manufacture of binder twine and rope B–2
(o) For the manufacture of oil-well supplies or equipment—by which is meant supplies for the production of petroleum and natural gas— but not including pipe lines, storage tanks of 1,000 barrels capacity or over, tank cars, or refineries B–2

No order shall take an automatic classification under the provisions of this section 8 save where the person intending to use the materials, equipment, or supplies ordered states under oath in writing that they are to be used for one or more of the purposes mentioned in this section and for no other purpose; which affidavit shall be indorsed on or attached to the order and shall be in the form following:

"Unless rerated by express order in writing by the priorities committee of the War Industries Board, this order is by authority of said priorities committee rated as Class—under and by virtue of subdivision—of section 8 of Circular No. 4 issued by the priorities division of the War Industries Board of date July 1, 1918, and all amendments thereto.

"For the purpose of securing the said rating I do solemnly swear—

"(1) That I have taken and filed whatever pledge is required by the War Industries Board from the industry of which I am a member; and

"(2) That the materials, equipment, or supplies covered by this order are intended for use, and will be used, for the purpose or purposes mentioned in the said subdivision or subdivisions of said section 8, and for no other purpose."

9. Each order for materials, equipment, or supplies for such purposes or uses as fall within Class C, as defined in section 5 hereof, will automatically be classed as Class C; provided the person intending to use the materials, equipment, or supplies ordered shall file with and as a part of said order an affidavit in writing in the form following:

"Unless rerated by express order in writing by the priorities committee of the War Industries Board, this order is by authority of said priorities committee rated as Class C under and by virtue of section 9 of Circular No. 4 issued by the priorities division of the War Industries Board of date July 1, 1918, and all amendments thereto.

"For the purpose of securing the said rating I do solemnly swear—

"(1) That I have taken and filed whatever pledge is required by the War Industries Board from the industry of which I am a member; and

"(2) That the materials, equipment, or supplies covered by this order are intended for use, and will be used, for the purpose or purposes mentioned and referred to in section 5 of said circular, and for no other purpose."

10. Where the party placing an order under sections 7, 8, or 9 hereof conceives it to be in the public interest that the order should take a higher classification than the automatic classification prescribed herein, then in such event an application for such higher classification setting forth the reasons therefor may be filed and same will be considered by and promptly acted upon by the priorities committee. No such application should be made, however, save in cases where the automatic rating will not secure delivery on or near the date required, and such application must disclose facts evidencing that the public interest requires an earlier delivery of the order than can be secured under the existing automatic rating. The application must be made on the regular priorities committee Application Form PC 15.

11. *Class D orders.*—All orders save such as are automatically classed under the provisions of sections 7, 8, and 9 hereof shall be automatically classed as Class D unless covered by certificates or other written directions issued in accordance with the rules and regulations embodied in this circular or amendments thereto.

PRECEDENCE OF CLASSES.

12. *Rules of precedence.*—Orders and work in Class AA shall take precedence of orders and work in all other classes; those in Class A shall take precedence of those in Classes B, C, and D; those in Class B shall take precedence of those in Classes C and D; those in Class C shall take precedence of those in Class D; all irrespective of the dates the orders were placed.

Orders and work in Class AA–1 shall take precedence of orders and work in Class AA–2 and all lower classes; those in Class A–1 shall take precedence of those in Class A–2 and all lower classes; those in Class B–1 shall take precedence of those in Class B–2; etc., etc.

Where work is in progress on several classified orders the rules of precedence set forth in sections 13 and 14 hereof will be observed.

13. *Orders in different classes.*—The classification of an order simply means

that it shall be given such precedence over orders of a lower classification as may be necessary (and only such as may be necessary) to insure delivery on the date specified in the order. It does not mean that work should cease on orders of a lower classification or that the order should be completed and delivery made in advance of orders taking a lower classification if this is not necessary to effect delivery within the time specified. The one to whom a priority certificate is directed or with whom an order taking an automatic classification is placed should make his own production plans, so as to get the maximum of efficiency out of his operations, making all deliveries at the times contracted for, if possible, and where this is not possible, giving precedence to the orders taking the highest classification.

14. *Orders in same class.*—As between orders in the same subdivision of a class (as A–1), save where otherwise specifically requested by the committee, the date of delivery contracted for will control unless this will operate to delay the delivery required by an earlier order of the same class, in which event the earlier order will have precedence in delivery. For example: Two orders, Order X and Order Y, are both covered by A–1 certificates. Order X is dated October 1, 1918, and calls for delivery February 1, 1919. Order Y is dated November 1, 1918, but calls for delivery January 1, 1919. As between these two orders preference will ordinarily be given to Order Y, because it calls for an earlier delivery date. If, however, such delivery will delay the completion of Order X, then preference should be given Order X, because it is the earlier order. If possible, both orders will be completed on the delivery dates called for. The dates of the certificates are not controlling.

15. *Doubtful cases.*—In case of doubt as to which certificate or order should have precedence, the matter should be laid before the committee by correspondence or in conference, so that the committee may give specific instructions.

APPLICATIONS.

16. *Form of application.*—Applications for priority certificates must be made on the form of application prescribed by this committee. (See form set out at pages 14 and 15 of this circular.)

17. *Who may apply.*—As a general rule, where an application is necessary it should be made by the one intending to use the materials, equipment, and supplies.

18. *United States Government.*—If the order has been placed by some purchasing officer of the United States Army, Navy, Shipping Board Emergency Fleet Corporation, or any other branch or department of the Government, the application should be made by and in the name of the department or official for whose account the order has been placed.

19. *Allied Governments.*—If the order has been placed for export to the territory of an allied Government or for delivery to an allied Government or to some person for account thereof, the application must be made to this committee through and with the written approval of the War Mission which

is representing said Government in the United States and also with the written approval of the Allied Purchasing Commission.

20. *A Government contractor.*—One who has a contract with the Government or with the Allies, and who needs priority assistance to obtain the materials, commodities, or work to fill such contract may make application direct to this committee. In some instances the committee will have already issued a priority certificate against such contractor directing him to give priority to the filling of his Government contract or contracts. In other instances such certificates will not have been issued. In either event, however, one who is working on Government contracts may make application direct if he needs priority assistance. While it is not necessary for such applications to be made through or with the approval of the Government official placing the contract, it is desirable that this course should be pursued where it will not involve substantial delay. Where this course is not pursued, such applicant's connection with the Government work and the correctness of his representations will be verified and checked by the committee.

21. *Government subcontractors.*—Those who may be one or more times removed from a direct contractor with the Government or with the Allies, but who are furnishing materials, supplies, or commodities to be used in connection with the fulfillment of such direct contract, may make application direct to the committee for such assistance as they may need to obtain such materials, commodities, or supplies. Such applications need not be approved by either the principal contractor or by the agency of the Government or the Allies placing the original order, but the representations of the applicant will be verified by the committee.

22. *Applicants not engaged directly or remotely on Government contracts.*—One who has placed an order for any material, commodities, or supplies which fall within Class B, as defined in section 4 hereof, and who requires priority assistance to procure reasonably prompt delivery thereof, may make application direct to the committee. In such cases the paragraphs in the application seeking to elicit information with respect to the applicant's connection with the Government or Allied contracts may be disregarded.

23. *Against whom applications may be made.*—Applications for priority should be made against the actual producer or manufacturer. The committee will not—save in exceptional cases, where the issuance of a certificate will clearly expedite the filling of an important order—administer priority against jobbers, brokers, or middlemen. When an order is placed through a third person, his name should appear in paragraph 4 of Application Form PC 15 (see pp. 14 and 15 of this order).

24. *Premature deliveries.*—In placing orders care should be exercised in determining the date that delivery will actually be required. The contractor should not ask to have delivery made before he will be prepared to use the articles. A rigid adherence to this rule will greatly facilitate timely deliveries of urgent orders and prevent needless interference. The application must state the date of delivery promised by the producer.

25. *Form and effect of certificates.*—When the committee shall approve an application and give it a rating, it will issue a priority certificate in the form set forth on page 16 of this circular. The one to whom the certificate shall be directed will, in fulfilling the contract or order mentioned in the certificate, give to it such precedence or priority as it may be entitled to under the classification specified in the certificate and the rules of this circular.

26. *Priority classifications supersede other instructions.*—Priority classifications, whether evidenced by certificates or automatic ratings as prescribed in sections 7, 8, and 9 hereof, shall supersede any and all previous instructions, by whomsoever issued, with respect to priority in production and delivery of the contract or order covered thereby, except commandeering orders and special priority directions issued in pursuance of section 28 hereof.

27. *Execution of certificates.*—Certificates or other documents signed by order of the priorities committee (printed) and countersigned in person by any person whose name appears thereon as one of the persons authorized to countersign shall be deemed to have been authorized by said committee, the priorities commissioner, and the War Industries Board.

28. *Special priority directions.*—That unusual emergencies may be promptly met and cases of great urgency provided for, the priorities committee may, by an order in the form of a letter, a special certificate, or otherwise, signed personally by the priorities commissioner, direct that a particular contract or order shall have priority over other contracts or orders covered by existing certificates or automatic ratings, or may in the same manner reclassify or regrade existing contracts or orders covered by outstanding certificates or automatic ratings.

29. *Delivery of certificates.*—Unless requested to the contrary, the priorities committee will forward direct to the applicant the original and one copy of the certificate, if issued, that the applicant may send the original to the one to whom it is directed, retaining the copy for his files. If the applicant desires, and so expressly states, the certificates, if issued, will be forwarded to the one to whom directed. Should the committee decline to approve the application, prompt notification of such action will be sent direct to the applicant.

SCOPE OF WORK.

30. The committee undertakes where necessary to administer priority in the production of all raw materials and finished products save foods, feeds, and fuels.

31. *Fuel.*—The production, supply, and distribution of fuel is under the supervision of the United States Fuel Administrator, who, in the distribution of fuel to industries and plants, is guided by the preference list, in so far as it classifies such industries and plants according to their relative importance. The preference list is compiled and promulgated by the priorities board, of which the priorities commissioner is chairman and H. G. Phillipps is secretary. While the priorities committee does not administer priority in the production of fuel, should those engaged on orders covered by priority certificates, auto-

matic classifications, or special priority directions experience difficulty in securing a fuel supply to the extent of interfering with the production covered by such priority, they may apply for a place on the preference list on Application Form PL-1, which will be furnished to them by H. G. Phillipps, secretary, on request. Such applications will be investigated and appropriate recommendations will be made to the Fuel Administrator, to the end that all orders to which this committee has accorded priority in production may not be unnecessarily delayed for lack of fuel.

The committee will also consider applications by fuel producers for priority assistance to procure materials, tools, equipment, or supplies required for the production of fuel.

32. *Foods and feeds excluded.*—The committee does not distribute foods or feeds, over the production, supply, and distribution of which the United States Food Administrator has supervision. Requests for assistance in purchasing foods and feeds or in expediting deliveries thereof should be addressed to the United States Food Administrator, Washington, D. C.

The committee, however, will consider applications from producers of foods and feeds for priority assistance to procure materials, tools, equipment, or supplies required for their production.

33. *Transportation.*—This committee does not administer priority in transportation. The United States Railroad Administration in furnishing transportation service is guided by the preference list mentioned in section 31 hereof, defining the relative importance of industries and plants. Should those engaged on orders covered by priority certificates, automatic classifications, or special priority directions experience difficulty in arranging for the transportation of materials, equipment, or supplies to the extent of interfering with the production of said orders, representations to this effect addressed to the Manager of Inland Traffic, War Industries Board, Washington, D. C., setting forth such facts in detail, duly verified by affidavit, will be carefully considered and in proper cases certified to the United States Railroad Administration to the end that all orders to which this committee has accorded priority in production may not be unnecessarily delayed for lack of transportation. Special application forms for this purpose may be secured from the manager of inland traffic, War Industries Board.

This committee will also consider applications of transportation companies for priority assistance to procure materials, equipment, or supplies required in their operations.

34. *Export and import licenses excluded.*—The committee does not issue export or import licenses. All applications for such licenses should be addressed to the War Trade Board, Washington, D. C.

35. *Prices and purchases excluded.*—The committee does not fix or assist in fixing prices. Neither does it make or assist in making purchases.

36. *Regrading of schedules.*—When it appears that a large per cent of the capacity of any plant is covered by certificates or automatic ratings of the same subdivision of a class, the priorities committee will, when it appears desirable so to do, arrange, through conference between it, the authorized rep-

resentatives of such plant, and those placing the orders covered by such certificates or automatic ratings, for the reclassification thereof or the rearrangement and regrading of the schedules within each subdivision of a class, so as to insure the most urgent orders having precedence without unnecessarily interfering with the efficient management and operation of such plant.

INSTANCES WHERE APPLICATIONS SHOULD NOT BE MADE.

37. *Orders not within Class AA, Class A, or Class B.*—No application should be made for priority in any case which does not fall within Class AA, Class A, or Class B, as defined in sections 2, 3, and 4 hereof.

38. *Before order is placed.*—Applications should not, save in very exceptional instances, be made for priority assistance unless an order is actually placed for the materials, commodities, or work.

39. *Where no shortage exists.*—Save in very exceptional cases priority assistance is only required where the demand exceeds the supply.

40. *Where no delay is expected.*—Although there may be a general shortage in a given product, the particular producer or manufacturer with whom the order is placed may be prepared to make delivery on scheduled time. Inquiry should first be made of him to ascertain if there will be a delay. In all cases the application should state when delivery is needed and when delivery is promised.

THE TEST.

41. The paramount purpose of priorities is the selective mobilization of the products of the soil, the mines, and the factories for direct and indirect war needs in such a way as will most effectually contribute toward winning the war. In requesting priority the petitioner should join with the committee in applying the test: To what extent, if at all, will the granting of this application contribute, directly or indirectly, toward winning the war; and if at all, how urgent is the need?

Conclusion.—The sole object of this division is to render a very real service to the Government and to the Nation, within the scope of its activities, and to that end invites and confidently hopes to receive the wholehearted cooperation of every department of the Government and of all others with whom it has to deal. Careful and painstaking consideration will be given all applications for priority, and decisions will be promptly rendered thereon.

EDWIN B. PARKER, *Priorities Commissioner.*

WASHINGTON, D. C., *July 1, 1918.*

Approved:

BERNARD M. BARUCH, *Chairman War Industries Board.*
NEWTON D. BAKER, *Secretary of War.*
JOSEPHUS DANIELS, *Secretary of the Navy.*
U. S. SHIPPING BOARD,
By EDWARD N. HURLEY, *Chairman.*
U. S. SHIPPING BOARD EMERGENCY FLEET CORPORATION,
By EDWARD N. HURLEY, *President.*

(1) GENERAL CLASSIFICATION OF PURPOSES DEMANDING PREFERENCE TREATMENT.

For the guidance of all governmental agencies in the production, supply, and distribution of raw materials, finished products, electrical energy, fuel, and transportation by rail, water, pipe lines, and otherwise, the priorities board has adopted the following general classification of purposes demanding preferance treatment:

Ships.—Including destroyers and submarine chasers. Including all necessary raw materials, partially manufactured parts, and supplies for completion of products.

Aircraft.—Munitions, military and naval supplies, and operations. Building construction for Government needs. Equipment for same. Including all necessary raw materials, partially manufactured parts, and supplies for completion of products.

Fuel.—Domestic consumption. Manufacturing necessities named herein, including all necessary raw materials, partially manufactured parts, and supplies for completion of products.

Food and collateral industries.—Foodstuffs for human consumption and plants handling same. Feeding stuffs for domestic fowls and animals, and plants handling same. All tools, utensils, implements, machinery, and equipment required for production, harvesting, and distribution, milling, preparing, canning, and refining foods and feeds such as seeds of foods and feeds, binder twine, etc. Products of collateral industries, such as fertilizers, fertilizer ingredients, insecticides, and fungicides. Containers for foods and feeds, collateral products. Materials and equipment for preservation of foods and feeds, such as ammonia and other refrigeration supplies, including ice. Including all necessary raw materials, partially manufactured parts, and supplies for completion of products.

Clothing.—For civilian population. Including all necessary raw materials, partially manufactured parts and supplies for completion of products.

Railroads.—Or other necessary transportation equipment, including water transportation. Including all necessary raw materials, partially manufactured parts and supplies for completion of products.

Public utilities.—Serving war industries, Army, Navy, and civilian population. Including all necessary raw materials, partially manufactured parts and supplies for completion of products.

EDWIN B. PARKER,
Chairman, Priorities Board.

WASHINGTON, D. C., *March 27, 1918.*

---

(2) PREFERENCE LIST NO. 1.

In pursuance of a resolution unanimously adopted by the priorities board, at a meeting held April 6, 1918, the following preference list of classes of industries, whose operation as a war measure is of exceptional importance, is promulgated and published for the guidance of all agencies of the United States Government in the supply and distribution of coal and coke, and in the supply of transportation by rail and water for the movement of coal and coke to said industries.

The priorities commissioner shall, under the direction of and with the approval of the priorities board, certify additional classes of industries, and also certify individual plants whose operation as a war measure is of exceptional importance, which industries and plants when so certified shall be automatically included in this preference list, which shall be amended or revised from time to time by action of the priorities board to meet changing conditions.

No distinction is made between any of the industries or plants which are or may be included in this preference list, and no significance should attach to the order in which the industries or plants appear in the list.

Aircraft.—Plants engaged exclusively in manufacturing aircraft or supplies and equipment therefor.

Ammunition.—Plants engaged in the manufacture of ammunition for the United States Government and the Allies.

Army and Navy cantonments and camps.

Arms (small).—Plants engaged in manufacturing small arms for the United States Government and the Allies.

Chemicals.—Plants engaged exclusively in manufacturing chemicals.

Coke plants.

Domestic consumers of fuel.

Electric equipment.—Plants manufacturing same.

Electrodes.—Plants producing electrodes.

Explosives.—Plants manufacturing explosives.

Farm implements.—Manufacturers exclusively of agricultural implements and farm-operating equipment.

Feed.—Plants producing feed.

Ferro-alloys.—Plants producing.

Fertilizers.—Manufacturers of fertilizers.

Fire brick.—Plants producing exclusively.

Food.—Plants manufacturing, milling, preparing, refining, preserving, and wholesaling food for human consumption.

Food containers.—Manufacturers of tin and glass containers and manufacturers exclusively of other food containers.

Gas.—Gas-producing plants.

Gas.—Plants manufacturing exclusively gas-producing machinery.

Guns (large).—Plants manufacturing same.

Hemp, jute, and cotton bags.—Plants manufacturing exclusively hemp, jute, and cotton bags.

Insecticides.—Manufacturers exclusively of insecticides and fungicides.

Iron and steel.—Blast furnaces and foundries.

Laundries.

Machine tools.—Plants manufacturing machine tools.

Mines.

Mines.—Plants engaged exclusively in manufacturing mining tools and equipment.

Newspapers and periodicals.—Plants printing and publishing exclusively newspapers and periodicals.

Oil.—Refineries of both mineral and vegetable oils.

Oil production.—Plants manufacturing exclusively oil-well equipment.

Public institutions and buildings.

Public utilities.

Railways.

Railways.—Plants manufacturing locomotives, freight cars, and rails, and other plants engaged exclusively in manufacture of railway supplies.

Refrigeration.—Refrigeration for food and exclusively ice-producing plants.

Seeds.—Producers or wholesalers of seeds (except flower seeds).

Ships (bunker coal).—Not including pleasure craft.

Ships.—Plants engaged exclusively in building ships (not including pleasure craft) or in manufacturing exclusively supplies and equipment therefor.

Soap.—Manufacturers of soap.

Steel.—Steel plants and rolling mills.

Tanners.—Tanning plants, save for patent leather.

Tanning extracts.—Plants manufacturing tanning extracts.

Tin plate.—Manufacturers of tin plate.

Twine (binder) and rope.—Plants producing exclusively binder twine and rope.

Wire rope and rope wire.—Manufacturers of same.

Edwin B. Parker,
Chairman, Priorities Board.

Washington, D. C., *April 6, 1918.*

———

Appendix IX.

PRIORITIES CIRCULAR NO. 20.—PREFERENCE LIST NO. 2.

FOREWORD.

The President has placed upon the chairman of the War Industries Board the responsibility for determining and administering all priorities in production and delivery. The determination of the relative importance of all industries and plants for both production and delivery by a single agency renders it possible to reasonably maintain a well-balanced program with respect to the several factors entering into production, which include (*a*) plant facilities, (*b*) fuel supply or electric energy, or both, (*c*) supply of raw materials and finished products, (*d*) labor, and (*e*) transportation by rail, water, pipe lines, or otherwise. Without all of these, speaking generally, production is impossible.

In compliance with the directions of the President that plans be formulated whereby there may be "common, consistent, and concerted action" in carrying into effect all priority policies and decisions, the chairman of the War Industries Board has created a Priorities Board, with the priorities commissioner of the War Industries Board as chairman, consisting of (1) the chairman of the War Industries Board, (2) the priorities commissioner, (3) a member of the Railroad Administration, (4) a member of the United States Shipping Board Emergency Fleet Corporation, (5) a member of the War Trade Board, (6) a member of the Food Administration, (7) a member of the Fuel Administration, (8) a representative of the War Department, (9) a representative of the Navy Department, (10) a member of the Allied Purchasing Commission, and (11) the chairman of the War Labor Policies Board.

The decisions of the Priorities Board are subject to review only by the chairman of the War Industries Board and by the President.

For the guidance of all governmental agencies and all others interested in (1) the production and supply of fuel and electric energy, (2) in the supply of labor, and (3) in the supply of transportation service by rail, water, pipe lines, or otherwise, in so far as such service contributes to production of finished products, the accompanying designated Preference List No. 2 has been adopted by the Priorities Board superseding Preference List No. 1, adopted April 6, 1918, and all amendments and supplements thereto.

Where advisable, industries, as such, have been classified and listed. In numerous instances individual plants have been found to be entitled to preference, although the industries to which they belong are not; and in other instances where an industry, as such, has been accorded a degree of preference, particular plants in such industry have been placed in a higher class. This has necessitated classifying and listing not only industries as such but to a limited extent individual plants, some of which are not embraced within any listed industry, while others are accorded a higher rating than that accorded the listed industry to which they belong.

The preference list is made up of industries and plants which in the public interest are deemed entitled to preferential treatment. The inclusion of these industries and plants on this list does not operate as an embargo against all others, but the effect is to defer the requirements of all other industries and plants until the requirements of those on the preference list shall have been satisfied.

In the compilation of this list, industries and plants have been divided according to their relative importance into four classes, viz.: Class I, Class II, Class III, and Class IV. In determning such relative importance consideration and weight have been given not solely to any one but to all of the following factors: (1) The intrinsic importance of the product itself for use during the war, and the urgency, as measured by time, of the demand or of the use to which it is to be put; (2) the necessity for maintaining or stimulating and increasing the total quantity of production, which in turn depends largely upon the relation of the supply to the demand for essential uses; (3) the proportion of the capacity of the industry or plant which is devoted to the production of the essential product.

Where it is imperative not only to maintain but to stimulate and increase production to satisfy abnormal demands created by war requirements, a high rating is necessary, even though the intrinsic importance of the product may be less than that of other products placed in a lower classification due to the fact that the supply of such other products equals the demand without the stimulus of high priority. Where it is necessary to speed the production of a particular product required at a particular time to carry into effect an important program, a high priority is given, although changing conditions may thereafter suggest and demand a reclassification. Certain plants produce commodities of great relative importance, but at the same time produce other commodities of less relative importance, and under such circumstances consideration and weight is given to the ratio of production between the more important and less important commodities. Instances occasionally arise where individual plants are given preference so long as they are rendering, and so long as it is in the public interest that they should render, a particular service, even though, taking the country as a whole, the supply of their product is ample to meet all demands.

No distinction has been made between any of the industries or plants within any one class, and no significance attaches to the order in which industries and plants are listed within any class.

The industries and plants grouped under Class I are only such as are of exceptional importance in connection with the prosecution of the war. Their requirements must be fully satisfied in preference to those of the three remaining classes.

Requirements of industries and plants grouped under Class II, Class III, and Class IV shall have precedence over those not appearing on the preference list. As between these three classes, however, there shall be no complete or absolute preference. The division into classes is for the purpose of presenting a composite picture of the relative importance of the industries and plants embraced within each group. It is not intended that the requirements of Class II shall be fully satisfied before supplying any of the requirements of Class III, or that those of Class III shall be fully satisfied before supplying any of those of Class IV. The classification does, however, indicate that the industries and plants grouped in Class II are relatively more important than those in Class III, and that those in Class III are relatively more important than those in Class IV. It will often happen that after satisfying the requirements of Class I the remaining available supply will be less than the aggregate requirements of the other three classes, in which event such supply will be rationed to the industries and plants embraced within those classes. In determining a basis for such rationing, the relative importance of each industry and plant, according to its class rating, must be considered. It has been found impracticable to prescribe for rationing purposes any general and uniform rule or formula, but the priorities board will, from time to time, after conference and in cooperation with each of the several governmental agencies charged with the distribution thereof, determine particular principles, values, and methods of application which may be followed in allocating fuel, power, transportation, and labor, respectively, to the end that proper recognition and weight may, as far as practicable in each case, be given to the relative importance of Class II, Class III, and Class IV.

Each plant listed as such shall not later than the 15th of each month file with the secretary of the priorities board, Washington, D. C., a report on P. L. Form No. 3 (a supply of which will be furnished on application) covering its activities during the preceding month. Any plant failing to file such report will be dropped from the preference list.

Priorities in the supply and distribution of raw materials, semifinished products, and finished products shall be governed by Circular No. 4 issued by the priorities division of the War Industries Board under date of July 1, 1918, and all amendments and supplements thereto or substitutes therefor.

The term "principally" as used in listing industries shall be construed to mean plants whose output is not less than 75 per cent of the products mentioned.

This preference list shall be amended or revised from time to time by action of the priorities board to meet changing conditions. The priorities commissioner shall, under the direction of and with the approval of the priorities board, certify additional classes of industries and also certify additional plants whose operations as a war measure entitle them to preference treatment, which industries and plants when so certified shall be automatically included in the preference list.

EDWIN B. PARKER,
Priorities Commissioner.

Approved:
    BERNARD M. BARUCH,
        Chairman War Industries Board.
WASHINGTON, D. C., *September 3, 1918.*

INDUSTRIES.

Listed alphabetically.

[The term "principally" means 75 per cent of the products mentioned.]

	Class
Agricultural implements.—*See* Farm implements.	
Aircraft.—Plants engaged principally in manufacturing aircraft or aircraft supplies and equipment	I
Ammunition.—Plants engaged principally in manufacturing same for the United States Government and the Allies	I
Army and Navy.—Arsenals and navy yards	I
Army and Navy.—Cantonments and camps	I
Arms (small).—Plants engaged principally in manufacturing same for the United States Government and the Allies	I
Bags.—Hemp, jute, and cotton.—Plants engaged principally in manufacturing same	IV
Blast furnaces.—Producing pig iron	I

Class

Boots and shoes.—Plants engaged exclusively in manufacturing same...... IV

Brass and copper.—Plants engaged principally in rolling and drawing copper, brass and other copper alloys in the form of sheets, rods, wire, and tubes II

Buildings.—*See* Public institutions and buildings.

Chain.—Plants engaged principally in manufacturing iron and steel chain III

Chemicals.—Plants engaged principally in manufacturing chemicals for the production of military and naval explosives, ammunition and aircraft, and use in chemical warfare... I

Chemicals.—Plants, not otherwise classified and listed, engaged principally in manufacturing chemicals... IV

Coke.—Plants engaged principally in producing metallurgical coke and by-products, including toluol... I

Coke.—Plants, not otherwise classified and listed, producing same......... II

Copper and brass.—*See* Brass and copper.

Cotton.—Plants engaged in the compression of cotton.................... IV

Cotton textiles.—*See* Textiles.

Cranes.—Plants engaged principally in manufacturing locomotive cranes... II

Cranes.—Plants engaged principally in manufacturing traveling cranes..... III

Domestic consumers.—Fuel and electric energy for residential consumption, including homes, apartment houses, residential flats, restaurants, and hotels I

Domestic consumers.—Fuel and electric energy not otherwise specifically listed III

Drugs.—Medicines and medical and surgical supplies.—Plants engaged principally in manufacturing same.................................... IV

Electrical equipment.—Plants engaged principally in manufacturing same.. III

Explosives.—Plants engaged principally in manufacturing same for military and naval purposes for the United States Government and the Allies..... I

Explosives.—Plants, not otherwise classified or listed, engaged principally in manufacturing same III

Farm implements.—Plants engaged principally in manufacturing agricultural implements and farm operating equipment...................... IV

Feed.—Plants engaged principally in preparing or manufacturing feed for livestock and poultry I

Ferroalloys.—Plants engaged principally in producing ferrochrome, ferromanganese, ferromolybdenum, ferrosilicon, ferrotungsten, ferrouranium, ferrovanadium, and ferrozirconium...................................... II

Fertilizers.—Plants engaged principally in producing same................ IV

Fire brick.—Plants engaged principally in manufacturing same............ IV

Foods.—Plants engaged principally in producing, milling, refining, preserving, refrigerating, wholesaling, or storing food for human consumption embraced within the following description: All cereals and cereal products, meats including poultry, fish, vegetables, fruit, sugar, sirups, glucose, butter, eggs, cheese, milk and cream, lard, lard compounds, oleomargarine and other substitutes for butter or lard, vegetable oils, beans, salt, coffee, baking powder, soda and yeast; also ammonia for refrigeration.......... I

Foods.—Plants engaged principally in producing, milling, preparing, refining, preserving, refrigerating, or storing food for human consumption not otherwise specifically listed (excepting herefrom plants producing confectionery, soft drinks, and chewing gum)................................ III

Food containers.—Plants engaged principally in manufacturing same...... IV

Foundries (iron).—Plants engaged principally in the manufacture of grey iron and malleable iron castings....................................... **IV**

Fungicides.—*See* Insecticides and fungicides.

Class

Gas.—*See* Oil and gas; also Public utilities.

Guns (large).—Plants engaged principally in manufacturing same for the United States Government and the Allies............................ I

Hospitals.—*See* Public institutions and buildings.

Ice.—Plants engaged principally in manufacturing same.................. III

Insecticides and fungicides.—Plants engaged principally in manufacturing same IV

Laundries IV

Machine tools.—Plants engaged principally in manufacturing same........ II

Medicines.—*See* Drugs and medicines.

Mines.—Coal I

Mines.—Producing metals and ferroalloy minerals...................... II

Mines.—Plants engaged principally in manufacturing mining tools or equipment III

Navy.—*See* Army and Navy.

Navy Department.—*See* War and Navy Departments.

Newspapers and periodicals.—Plants engaged principally in printing newspapers or periodicals which are entered at the post office as second-class mail matter... IV

Oil and gas.—Plants engaged principally in producing oil or natural gas for fuel, or for mechanical purposes, including refining or manufacturing oil for fuel, or for mechanical purposes................................... I

Oil and gas.—Pipe lines and pumping stations engaged in transporting oil or natural gas... I

Oil and gas.—Plants engaged principally in manufacturing equipment or supplies for producing or transporting oil or natural gas, or for refining and manufacturing oil for fuel or for mechanical purposes.............. III

Paper and pulp.—*See* Pulp and paper.

Periodicals.—*See* Newspapers and periodicals.

Public institutions and buildings (maintenance and operation of).—Used as hospitals or sanitariums... I

Public institutions and buildings (maintenance and operation of).—Other than hospitals and sanitariums..................................... III

Public utilities.—Gas plants producing toluol........................... I

Public utilities.—Street railways, electric lighting and power companies, gas plants not otherwise classified, telephone and telegraph companies, water-supply companies, and like general utilities........................... II

Public utilities.—Plants engaged principally in manufacturing equipment for railways or other public utilities................................. II

Pulp and paper.—Plants engaged exclusively in manufacturing same....... IV

Railways.—Operated by United States Railroad Administration........... I

Railways.—Not operated by United States Railroad Administration (excluding those operated as plant facilities)........................... II

Railways (street).—*See* Public utilities.

Rope.—*See* Twine and rope.

Rope wire.—*See* Wire rope.

Sanitariums.—*See* Public institutions and buildings.

Ships (maintenance and operation of).—Excluding pleasure craft not common carriers I

Ships.—Plants engaged principally in building ships, excluding (*a*) pleasure craft not common carriers, (*b*) ships not built for the United States Government or the Allies nor under license from United States Shipping Board I

Soap.—Plants engaged principally in manufacturing same................. IV

Class

Steel-making furnaces.—Plants engaged solely in manufacturing ingots and
steel castings by the open-hearth, Bessemer, crucible, or electric-furnace
process, including blooming mills, billet mills, and slabbing mills for same   I
Steel-plate mills   I
Steel-rail mills.—Rolling rails 50 or more pounds per yard................   II
Steel.—All plants operating steel rolling and drawing mills exclusive of
those taking higher classification......................................   III
Surgical supplies.—*See* Drugs and medicines.
Tanners.—Plants engaged principally in tanning leather..................   IV
Tanning.—Plants engaged principally in manufacturing tanning extracts...   IV
Textiles.—Plants engaged principally in manufacturing cotton textiles, in-
cluding spinning, weaving, and finishing............................   IV
Textiles.—Plants engaged principally in manufacturing woolen textiles, in-
cluding spinners, top makers and weavers............................   IV
Textiles.—Plants engaged principally in manufacturing cotton or woolen
knit goods...   IV
Textiles.—Plants engaged principally in manufacturing textile machinery..   IV
Tin plates.—Plants engaged principally in manufacturing same...........   III
Tobacco.—Only for preserving, drying, curing, packing, and storing same—
not for manufacturing and marketing................................   IV
Toluol.—*See* Coke, also Public utilities.
Tools.—Plants engaged principally in manufacturing small or hand tools for
working wood or metal..   III
Twine (binder) and rope.—Plants engaged principally in manufacturing
same   IV
War and Navy Departments.—Construction work conducted by either the
War Department or the Navy Department of the United States in em-
barkation ports, harbors, fortified places, flood-protection operations,
docks, locks, channels, inland waterways, and in the maintenance and
repair of same...   II
Wire rope and rope wire.—Plants engaged principally in manufacturing
same   II
Woolen textiles.—*See* Textiles.

[Grouped by classes and listed alphabetically.]

CLASS I.

Aircraft.—Plants engaged principally in manufacturing aircraft or aircraft supplies
and equipment.
Ammunition.—Plants engaged principally in manufacturing same for the United
States Government and the Allies.
Army and Navy.—Arsenals and navy yards.
Army and Navy.—Cantonments and camps.
Arms (small).—Plants engaged principally in manufacturing same for the United
States Government and the Allies.
Blast furnaces.—Producing pig iron.
Chemicals.—Plants engaged principally in manufacturing chemicals for the pro-
duction of military and naval explosives, ammunition, and aircraft, and use in
chemical warfare.
Coke.—Plants engaged principally in producing metallurgical coke and by-prod-
ucts, including toluol.
Domestic consumers.—Fuel and electric energy for residential consumption, in-
cluding homes, apartment houses, residential flats, restaurants, and hotels.
Explosives.—Plants engaged principally in manufacturing same for military and
naval purposes for the United States Government and the Allies.

Feed.—Plants engaged principally in preparing or manufacturing feed for live-stock and poultry.

Foods.—Plants engaged principally in producing, milling, refining, preserving, refrigerating, wholesaling, or storing food for human consumption embraced within the following description: All cereals and cereal products, meats including poultry, fish, vegetables, fruit, sugar, sirups, glucose, butter, eggs, cheese, milk and cream, lard, lard compounds, oleomargarine and other substitutes for butter or lard, vegetable oils, beans, salt, coffee, baking powder, soda, and yeast; also ammonia for refrigeration.

Gas.—See Oil and gas, also Public utilities.

Guns (large).—Plants engaged principally in manufacturing same for the United States Government and the Allies.

Hospitals.—See Public institutions and buildings.

Mines.—Coal.

Navy yards.—See Army and Navy.

Oil and gas.—Plants engaged principally in producing oil or natural gas for fuel, or for mechanical purposes, including refining or manufacturing oil for fuel, or mechanical purposes.

Oil and gas.—Pipe lines and pumping stations engaged in transporting oil or natural gas.

Public institutions and buildings (maintenance and operation of).—Used as hospitals or sanitariums.

Public utilities.—Gas plants producing toluol.

Railways.—Operated by United States Railroad Administration.

Sanitariums.—See Public institutions and buildings.

Ships (maintenance and operation of).—Excluding pleasure craft not common carriers.

Ships.—Plants engaged principally in building ships, excluding (a) pleasure craft not common carriers, (b) ships not built for the United States Government or the Allies nor under license from the United States Shipping Board.

Steel-making furnaces.—Plants engaged solely in manufacturing ingots and steel castings by the open-hearth, Bessemer, crucible, or electric-furnace process, including blooming mills, billet mills, and slabbing mills for same.

Steel-plate mills.

Toluol.—See Coke, also Public utilities.

CLASS II.

Brass and copper.—Plants engaged principally in rolling and drawing copper, brass and other copper alloys in the form of sheets, rods, wire, and tubes.

Coke.—Plants, not otherwise classified or listed, producing same.

Copper and brass.—See Brass and copper.

Cranes.—Plants engaged principally in manufacturing locomotive cranes.

Ferro-alloys.—Plants engaged principally in producing ferrochrome, ferromanganese, ferromolybdenum, ferrosilicon, ferrotungsten, ferrouranium, ferrovanadium, and ferrozirconium.

Gas.—See Oil and gas.

Machine tools.—Plants engaged principally in manufacturing same.

Mines.—Producing metals and ferro-alloy minerals.

Navy Department.—See War and Navy Departments.

Public utilities.—Street railways, electric lighting and power companies, gas plants not otherwise classified, telephone and telegraph companies, water supply companies, and like general utilities.

Public utilities.—Plants engaged principally in manufacturing equipment for railways and other public utilities.

Railways.—Not operated by United States Railroad Administration (excluding those operated as plant facilities).

Rope wire.—*See* Wire rope.

Steel rail mills.—Rolling rails 50 or more pounds per yard.

War and Navy Departments.—Construction work conducted by either the War Department or the Navy Department of the United States in embarkation ports, harbors, fortified places, flood protection operations, docks, locks, channels, inland waterways, and in the maintenance and repair of same.

Wire rope and rope wire.—Plants engaged principally in manufacturing same.

CLASS III.

Buildings.—*See* Public institutions and buildings.

Chain.—Plants engaged principally in manufacturing iron and steel chain.

Cranes.—Plants engaged principally in manufacturing traveling cranes.

Domestic consumers.—Fuel and electric energy not otherwise specifically listed.

Electrical equipment.—Plants engaged principally in manufacturing same.

Explosives.—Plants, not otherwise classified or listed, engaged principally in manufacturing same.

Foods.—Plants engaged principally in producing, milling, preparing, refining, preserving, refrigerating, or storing foods for human consumption not otherwise specifically listed (excepting herefrom plants producing confectionery, soft drinks, and chewing gum).

Gas.—*See* Oil and gas.

Ice.—Plants engaged principally in manufacturing same.

Mines.—Plants engaged principally in manufacturing mining tools or equipment.

Oil and gas.—Plants engaged principally in manufacturing equipment or supplies for producing or transporting oil or natural gas, or for refining and manufacturing oil for fuel or for mechanical purposes.

Public institutions and buildings (maintenance and operation of).—Other than hospitals and sanitariums.

Steel.—All plants operating steel rolling and drawing mills, exclusive of those taking higher classification.

Tin plates.—Plants engaged principally in manufacturing same.

Tools.—Plants engaged principally in manufacturing small or hand tools for working wood or metal.

CLASS IV.

Agricultural implements.—*See* Farm implements.

Bags.—Hemp, jute, cotton.—Plants engaged principally in manufacturing same.

Boots and shoes.—Plants engaged exclusively in manufacturing same.

Chemicals.—Plants, not otherwise classified or listed, engaged principally in manufacturing chemicals.

Cotton.—Plants engaged in the compression of cotton.

Cotton textiles.—*See* Textiles.

Drugs—Medicines and medical and surgical supplies.—Plants engaged principally in manufacturing same.

Farm implements.—Plants engaged principally in manufacturing agricultural implements and farm operating equipment.

Fertilizers.—Plants engaged principally in producing same.

Fire brick.—Plants engaged principally in manufacturing same.

Food containers.—Plants engaged principally in manufacturing same.

Foundries (iron).—Plants engaged principally in the manufacture of gray iron and malleable-iron castings.

Insecticides and fungicides.—Plants engaged principally in manufacturing same.

Laundries.

Newspapers and periodicals.—Plants engaged principally in printing newspapers or periodicals which are entered at the post office as second-class mail matter.

Paper and pulp.—*See* Pulp and paper.
Periodicals.—*See* Newspapers and periodicals.
Pulp and paper.—Plants engaged exclusively in manufacturing same.
Rope.—*See* Twine and rope.
Soap.—Plants engaged principally in manufacturing same.
Surgical supplies.—*See* Drugs and medicines.
Tanners.—Plants engaged principally in tanning leather.
Tanning.—Plants engaged principally in manufacturing tanning extracts.
Textiles.—Plants engaged principally in manufacturing cotton textiles, including spinning, weaving, and finishing.
Textiles.—Plants engaged principally in manufacturing woolen textiles, including spinners, top makers, and weavers.
Textiles.—Plants engaged principally in manufacturing cotton or woolen knit goods.
Textiles.—Plants engaged principally in manufacturing textile machinery.
Tobacco.—Only for preserving, drying, curing, packing, and storing same—not manufacturing and marketing.
Twine (binder) and rope.—Plants engaged principally in manufacturing same.
Woolen textiles.—*See* Textiles.

APPENDIX X.

MINUTES OF MEETINGS OF INDUSTRIAL ADJUSTMENTS COMMITTEE OF PRIORITIES BOARD.

Early in June, 1918, the President appointed Messrs. Vance C. McCormick, Bernard M. Baruch, Herbert C. Hoover, and Harry A. Garfield to investigate industries and report which were nonessential, to the point that they should, in public interest, retire from business during the war.

This committee in turn formed a committee with Mr. C. M. Woolley as chairman and Messrs. Edwin B. Parker, T. F. Whitmarsh, Edward Chambers, P. B. Noyes, and Edwin F. Gay as members.

This committee, after a careful investigation and consideration, made its report under date of June 22, 1918, as follows:

"After careful study of the statistics gathered especially for the purpose, and upon mature consideration of the facts, your committee is unanimously of the opinion—

"First, that no industry should be absolutely prohibited, and

"Second, that a plan of general curtailment can and should be devised broad enough to remove the present conflict between the necessities of war and non-war industries in the matter of raw materials, fuel, transportation, and labor.

"We do not recommend absolute prohibition, because, granting the possibility of selecting from all the products of industry those items which could be agreed upon as of relatively slight importance to the consuming public, the benefits to be derived for the war program by the total and sudden prohibition of the industries producing such commodities would be trifling to the economic loss during and after the war.

"A searching analysis of all our industries revealed 25 which might fairly be classified as producers of nonwar commodities, and therefore worthy of consideration for complete prohibition. We found that the aggregate capital employed by this particular group of industries was $733,000,000. The aggregate number of persons employed was 283,518. The aggregate fuel consumption per annum was 1,701,000 tons.

"The conservation of fuel, the lessening of the burden placed upon the railroads of the country, and the releasing of labor and materials being the principal objects to be attained in setting up a complete prohibition against these industries, it will be seen that the relief thus afforded would be negligible. For example, while the consumption of coal for power, as estimated by the Fuel Administration for the current calendar year will be 554,000,000 tons, the coal consumed by the nonwar industries above specified is but 1,701,000 tons. The saving in so far as fuel is concerned would, therefore, be only three-tenths of 1 per cent of the year's supply. The relief to the railroads would be somewhat greater, but not of sufficient moment to constitute an appreciable alleviation of their burdens.

"The brewing industry, considered as a possible nonwar industry, is the subject of a separate communication.

"Contrasting the degree of relief afforded with the hardships necessarily imposed upon a part of the community, your committee has reached the conclusion that it would be inadvisable to adopt direct industrial prohibition to accomplish the desired end. It would not only result in inequalities and thus engender intense dissatisfaction on the part of those affected but it would also create grave apprehension throughout the entire industrial community. This might weaken the morale of the Nation and, in the final analysis, cause actual harm rather than positive benefit.

"We also invite your attention to the fact that a sudden dislocation through complete prohibition of any industry involves the disintegration of entire organizations, including the workers, foremen, superintendents, and managers. Such organizations in most cases are the cumulative result of many years of constructive effort, and it is obvious that with the ending of the war the prohibited industries would be obliged to go through the pioneer process of recreation. This would, in the opinion of your committee, augment the embarrassment of post-war industrial readjustments.

"It should also be noted that some of the industries affected center in a single town, where they are the only source of its support. We might cite in illustration the case of jewelry, the production of which centers at North Attleboro, Mass. Total prohibition would inflict a heavy blow upon that town; trade would be ruined; the deposits in savings banks withdrawn, and a disastrous state of affairs precipitated throughout the entire district.

"While jewelry is perhaps one of the most obviously nonwar products, it nevertheless has an economic value to a moderate extent, to establish credits in those countries where the normal currents of trade continue to show an adverse balance against the United States. The conscious utilization of this and various other so-called nonwar industries to assist in correcting adverse trade balances abroad obviously will offer benefits that should not be overlooked.

"A plan for the curtailment of nonwar industries should be prepared at once, that men and materials may be released and transportation relieved for the more efficient prosecution of the war. Sufficient notice of proposed curtailments of nonwar industries should be given, that they may anticipate such changes and effect the necessary reorganization of their business either to engage in the production of war necessaries or to accept the curtailment which will follow. It is obvious that industries not engaged in production of direct value to the war program must make such sacrifices as may be necessary that essential war industries may be in no manner impeded, but on the contrary may attain their maximum output.

"We beg to point out that the nonwar industries are already being restricted by forces which will continue to operate with increasing pressure, such as the Army conscription with its selective processes, the imposition of heavy taxation, the restriction of imports, the regulations of the war administrations, such as fuel and food, and the priorities committee, indeed, of every agency of the Government. The operation of these upon industry, however, as now proceeding, is unduly slow and irregular. The curtailment of nonwar industries as proposed by the committee, based upon a scientific study, would not only hasten the necessary adjustment to war needs and reduce friction as among the industries, but would be welcomed, we believe, by business men as tending to lessen their present uncertainties.

"Unless advised that your wishes lie in a contrary direction your committee will undertake the preparation of a plan for the systematic curtailment of nonwar industries.

"Respectfully submitted.

> "Edward Chambers,
> "P. B. Noyes,
> "Edwin B. Parker,
> "Edwin F. Gay,
> "Theo. F. Whitmarsh,
> "Clarence M. Woolley,
> > *"Chairman."*

On June 24 this committee made a separate report with reference to the brewing industry as follows:

"Your committee herewith makes a brief separate report on the brewing industry, which it has considered among the possible nonwar industries for which complete prohibition has been proposed.

"Although the savings in fuel and transportation, in foodstuffs and man power which such a prohibition would effect, are greater than for most of the other industries studied, and although in many States of the Union prohibition is already in operation, nevertheless the general conclusion reached is similar to that in the main report. The policy of curtailment, rather than complete prohibition is recommended as appropriate for administrative action.

"The Census Bureau of the Department of Commerce estimates that on the basis of the 1914 census, the direct fuel consumption of this industry was 3,320,000 tons, or six-tenths of 1 per cent of the total annual coal supply. By regulation of the Food Administration the consumption of grain for the manufacture of beer, ale, and porter has been reduced, by reducing the alcohol content, from 72,000,000 bushels per annum to the rate of 47,000,000 bushels. At a recent conference with the industry, and as a result of it, the Fuel Administrator has given consideration to the subject of reducing by 50 per cent the coal supplied that industry. Such action, if taken, would result in further reduction of the amount of grains used and the coal consumption would be reduced to 1,662,161 tons per annum. The carloads which will be moved by the railroads, both for food grains and coal, and also for the finished produce, are estimated at 215,984 per annum.

"The committee believes that this industry should be classed as a nonwar industry, but, while fully recognizing the savings which might be made by complete suppression of the industry by administrative order, holds that this measure is not to be recommended for the following reasons:

"First. As set forth in the main report, the gain from prohibition is more than offset by the losses and irritation caused by summary action, and

"Second. The social habits and political prejudice associated with this trade are still deep-rooted, though steadily weakening, that entire prohibition should be the result of deliberate legislation rather than an administrative decree which might savor too much of arbitrary power.

"A considerable curtailment, obviously in the interest of conservation, has already been accepted by agreement with the industry. Your committee recommends that the total output in barrelage of the brewing industry (alcoholic and nonalcoholic) be reduced to 50 per cent of the amount produced during the corresponding months of 1917. In view of the cut made by the reduction in alcoholic content this would reduce the grain consumed to the rate of less than 30,000,000 bushels per annum from the previous 72,000,000, and would reinforce the proposal to reduce coal by 50 per cent and effect a saving of 1,660,000 tons of coal per annum. As the amount of malt in process is considerable, this will be even more effective as the stocks of malt are sufficient to last some months without further purchases of barley. The saving on transportation should amount to even more than 50 per cent, as the grains used are in larger proportion than this owing to the reduction in alcoholic content. At a later date, with the progress of the war and with public approval, a further curtailment may be made.

"Respectfully submitted.

> "CLARENCE M. WOOLLEY,
> "P. B. NOYES,
> "EDWIN B. PARKER,
> "EDWARD CHAMBERS,
> "THEO. F. WHITMARSH,
> "EDWIN F. GAY."

Both of these letters were signed by the entire committee.

On July 3 Mr. Hoover, at the request of the committee, of which he was a member, addressed the President as follows:

"In accordance with your instruction that we should prepare for you a recommendation in connection with the systematic curtailment of nonwar industries, we have asked a special committee, comprising Messrs. Clarence M. Woolley of the War Trade Board, Edward Chambers of the Railway Administration, Edwin F. Gay of the Shipping Board, P. B. Noyes of the Fuel Administration, Theodore F. Whitmarsh of the Food Administration, Edwin B. Parker of the War Industries Board, to make a detailed study as to the general policy to be pursued in connection with such industries. The conclusions of this committee, to which we unanimously agree, except in those relating to the brewing industry, upon which subject we are seeking further information, pending possible action by Congress, are:

"That the approach to curtailment of nonwar industries should be made by way of systematic and scientific reduction in their activities rather than by total and initial annihilation. They do not find that there are any industries which should be instantly cut off, but there are many which should be reduced in activities at the earliest possible moment. These gentlemen are all members of the priorities board of the War Industries Board. This problem, in certain phases, lies outside the present conception of priorities in the use of material.

"As to further action in the matter, we recommend that the above committee be constituted a special committee of the priorities board to study each industry from the aspect of what can be curtailed and what is a desirable curtailment, and to make such recommendations to the priorities board from time to time, and that the priorities board should advise the various departments of the action of the board and the departments which will effectuate the conclusions of the board.

"The committee has furnished us with a recommendation that the brewing industry should be curtailed to 50 per cent of the normal barrelage. A copy of this report we inclose herewith. We have asked the committee to further consider whether, in addition to the curtailment at once of 50 per cent, the industry should not be notified that no further foodstuffs are to be purchased and that, with the exhaustion of their present materials in process, they are to cease operation.

"We are also asking the committee to make a further report, if possible, on the reduction that we recommend in connection with other nonwar industries.

"Yours, faithfully,

"HERBERT HOOVER.

"O. K'd.   W. W."

This letter was presented to the President by Messrs. Hoover, Garfield, Baruch, and McCormick, and O. K'd by the President, and forms the charter under which the industrial adjustments committee is operating.

EXTRACT FROM REPORT OF PRESIDENT'S MEDIATION COMMISSION.

Among the causes of unrest familiar to students of industry the following stand out with special significance to the industrial needs of war:

(a) Broadly speaking, American industry lacks a healthy basis of relationship between management and men. At bottom, this is due to the insistence by employers upon individual dealings with their men. Direct dealings with employee's organizations is still the minority rule in the United States. In the majority of instances there is no joint dealing, and in too many instances employers are in active opposition to labor organizations. This failure to equalize the parties in adjustments of inevitable industrial contests is the central cause of their difficulties. There is a commendable spirit throughout the country to correct specific evils. The leaders in industry must go further; they must help to correct the state of mind on the part of labor; they must aim for the release of normal feelings by enabling labor to take its place as a cooperator in the industrial enterprise. In a word, a conscious attempt must be made to generate a new spirit in industry.

(b) Too many labor disturbances are due to the absence of disinterested processes to which resort may be had for peaceful settlement. Force becomes too ready an outlet. We need continuous administrative machinery by which grievances inevitable in industry may be easily and quickly disposed of and not allowed to reach the pressure of explosion.

(c) There is a widespread lack of knowledge on the part of capital as to labor's feelings and needs, and on the part of labor as to problems of management. This is due primarily to a lack of collective negotiation as the normal process of industry. In addition, there is but little realization on the part of industry that the so-called "labor problem" demands not only occasional attention, but continuous and systematic responsibility, as much so as the technical or financial aspects of industry.

(d) Certain specific grievances, when long uncorrected, not only mean definite hardships; they serve as symbols of the attitude of employers and thus affect the underlying spirit. Hours and wages are, of course, mostly in issue. On the whole, wage increases are asked for mostly in order to meet the increased cost of living, and such demands should be met in the light of their economic causes. Again, the demand for the 8-hour day is nation wide, for the workers regard it as expressive of an accepted national policy.

Repressive dealing with manifestations of labor unrest is the source of much bitterness, turns radical labor leaders into martyrs and thus increases their following, and, worst of all, in the minds of workers tends to implicate the Government as a partisan in an economic conflict. The problem is a delicate and difficult one. There is no doubt, however, that the Bisbee and Jerome deportations, the Everett incident, the Little hanging, and similar acts of violence against workers have had a very harmful effect upon labor, both in the United States and in some of the allied countries. Such incidents are attempts to deal with symptoms rather than causes. The I. W. W. has exercised its strongest hold in those industries and communities where employers have most resisted the trade-union movement and where some form of protest against unjust treatment was inevitable.

The derangement of our labor supply is one of the great evils of industry. The shockingly large amount of labor turnover and the phenomenon of migratory labor means an enormous economic waste and involves an even greater social cost. These are evils which flow from grievances such as those we have set forth; they are accentuated by uncontrolled instability of employment. Finally, we have failed in the full use and wise direction of our labor supply, falsely called "labor shortage," because we have failed to establish a vigorous and competent system of labor distribution. However, means and added resources have been recently provided for a better grappling with this problem.

It is then, to uncorrected specific evils and the absence of a healthy spirit between capital and labor, due partly to these evils and partly to an unsound industrial structure, that we must attribute industrial difficulties which we have experienced during the war. Sinister influences and extremist doctrine may have availed themselves of these conditions; they certainly have not created them.

In fact, the overwhelming mass of the laboring population is in no sense disloyal. Before the war labor was, of course, filled with pacific hopes shared by nearly the entire country. But, like other portions of the citizenship, labor has adjusted itself to the new facts revealed by the European war. Its suffering and its faith are the suffering and faith of the Nation. With the exception of the sacrifices of the men in the armed service the greatest sacrifices have come from those at the lower rung of the industrial ladder. Wage increases respond last to the needs of this class of labor, and their meager returns are hardly adequate, in view of the increased cost of living, to maintain even their meager standard of life. It is upon them the war pressure has borne most severely. Labor at heart is as devoted to the purposes of the Government in the prosecution of this war as any other part of society. If labor's enthusiasm is less vocal, and its feelings here and there tepid, we will find the explanation in some of the conditions of the industrial environment in which labor is placed and which in many instances is its nearest contact with the activities of the war.

(a) Too often there is a glaring inconsistency between our democratic purposes in this war abroad and the autocratic conduct of some of those guiding industry at home. This inconsistency is emphasized by such episodes as the Bisbee deportations.

(b) Personal bitterness and more intense industrial strife inevitably result when the claim of loyalty is falsely resorted to by employers and their sympathizers as a means of defeating sincere claims for social justice, even though such claims be asserted in time of war.

(*c*) So long as profiteering is not comprehensively prevented to the full extent that governmental action can prevent it, just so long will a sense of inequality disturb the fullest devotion of labor's contribution to the war.

RECOMMENDATIONS.

The causes of unrest suggest their own means of correction:

1. The elimination to the utmost practical extent of all profiteering during the period of the war is a prerequisite to the best morale in industry.

2. Modern large-scale industry has effectually destroyed the personal relation between employer and employee—the knowledge and cooperation that come from personal contact. It is therefore no longer possible to conduct industry by dealing with employees as individuals. Some form of collective relationship between management and men is indispensable. The recognition of this principle by the Government should form an accepted part of the labor policy of the Nation.

3. Law, in business as elsewhere, depends for its vitality upon steady enforcement. Instead of waiting for adjustment after grievances come to the surface there is needed the establishment of continuous administrative machinery for the orderly disposition of industrial issues and the avoidance of an atmosphere of contention and the waste of disturbances.

4. The eight-hour day is an established policy of the country; experience has proved justification of the principle also in war times. Provision must, of course, be made for longer hours in case of emergencies. Labor will readily meet this requirement if its misuse is guarded against by appropriate overtime payments.

5. Unified direction of the labor administration of the United States for the period of the war should be established. At present there is an unrelated number of separate committees, boards, agencies, and departments having fragmentary and conflicting jurisdiction over the labor problems raised by the war. A single-headed administration is needed, with full power to determine and establish the necessary administrative structure. (Since this report was written the direction of the labor administration for the war was delegated to the Secretary of Labor.)

6. When assured of sound labor conditions and effective means for the just redress of grievances that may arise, labor in its turn should surrender all practices which tend to restrict maximum efficiency.

7. Uncorrected evils are the greatest provocative to extremist propaganda, and their correction in itself would be the best counter propaganda. But there is need for more affirmative education. There has been too little publicity of an educative sort in regard to labor's relation to the war. The purposes of the Government and the methods by which it is pursuing them should be brought home to the fuller understanding of labor. Labor has most at stake in this war, and it will eagerly devote its all if only it be treated with confidence and understanding, subject neither to indulgence nor neglect, but dealt with as a part of the citizenship of the State.

APPENDIX XII.

PRINCIPLES TO BE OBSERVED.

[From Labor Conference Board Report, Mar. 29, 1918.]

There should be no strikes or lockouts during the war.

RIGHT TO ORGANIZE.

1. The right of workers to organize in trade-unions and to bargain collectively through chosen representatives is recognized and affirmed. This right shall not be denied, abridged, or interfered with by the employers in any manner whatsoever.

2. The right of employers to organize in associations of groups and to bargain collectively through chosen representatives is recognized and affirmed. This right shall not be denied, abridged, or interfered with by the workers in any manner whatsoever.

3. Employers should not discharge workers for membership in trade-unions nor for legitimate trade-union activities.

4. The workers, in the exercise of their right to organize, shall not use coercive measures of any kind to induce persons to join their organizations, nor to induce employers to bargain or deal therewith.

EXISTING CONDITIONS.

1. In establishments where the union shop exists the same shall continue and the union standards as to wages, hours of labor, and other conditions of employment shall be maintained.

2. In establishments where union and nonunion men and women now work together, and the employer meets only with employees or representatives engaged in said establishments, the continuance of such condition shall not be deemed a grievance. This declaration, however, is not intended in any manner to deny the right or discourage the practice of the formation of labor unions, or the joining of the same by the workers in said establishments, as guaranteed in the last paragraph, nor to prevent the War Labor Board from urging, or any umpire from granting, under the machinery herein provided, improvement of their situation in the matter of wages, hours of labor, or other conditions, as shall be found desirable from time to time.

3. Established safeguards and regulations for the protection of the health and safety of workers shall not be relaxed.

WOMEN IN INDUSTRY.

If it shall become necessary to employ women on work ordinarily performed by men, they must be allowed equal pay for equal work and must not be allotted tasks disproportionate to their strength.

HOURS OF LABOR.

The basic 8-hour day is recognized as applying in all cases in which existing law requires it. In all other cases the question of hours of labor shall be settled with due regard to governmental necessities and the welfare, health, and proper comfort of the workers.

MAXIMUM PRODUCTION.

The maximum production of all war industries should be maintained, and methods of work and operation on the part of employers or workers which operate to delay or limit production, or which have a tendency to artificially increase the cost thereof, should be discouraged.

MOBILIZATION OF LABOR.

For the purpose of mobilizing the labor supply with a view to its rapid and effective distribution, a permanent list of the number of skilled and other workers available in different parts of the Nation shall be kept on file by the Department of Labor, the information to be constantly furnished—

1. By the trade unions.

2. By State employment bureaus and Federal agencies of like character.

3. By the managers and operators of industrial establishments throughout the country.

These agencies should be given opportunity to aid in the distribution of labor, as necessity demands.

CUSTOM OF LOCALITIES.

In fixing wages, hours, and conditions of labor, regard should always be had to the labor standards, wage scales, and other conditions prevailing in the localities affected.

THE LIVING WAGE.

1. The right of all workers, including common laborers, to a living wage is hereby declared.

2. In fixing wages, minimum rates of pay shall be established which will insure the subsistence of the worker and his family in health and reasonable comfort.

APPENDIX XIII.

LABOR PRIORITY BULLETIN NO. 1.

To United States Employment Service and all industrial advisers:

Section 80 of the Revised Selective Service Regulations among other things provides:

Such industrial advisers may place before the district board at its meetings, or at such other time as the board may request, all facts and information in their possession as to the preference lists issued by the priorities division of the War Industries Board. Such lists shall not be regarded as binding upon the district board in its conclusions as to whether or not any particular industry, occupation, or employment, including agriculture, is a necessary industry, occupation, or employment within the meaning of the law and regulations, nor shall such lists prevent the district board from holding as necessary any industry, occupation, or employment, including agriculture, not contained therein.   Such preference lists and other facts and information in the possession of such advisers will supplement the information in possession of the district boards and will also be used to assist the district boards in dealing with specific cases.

The "preference lists" referred to in the regulation quoted are those embraced in Circular No. 20, issued by the priorities division of the War Industries Board under date of September 3, 1918, embodying "Preference List No. 2" and such amendments, supplements, or substitutions therefor as may from time to time issue.   A careful study of the "Foreword" to Circular No. 20 is invited and attention is particularly directed to the concluding paragraph thereof, reading:

"This preference list shall be amended or revised from time to time by action of the priorities board to meet changing conditions.   The priorities commissioner shall, under the direction of and with the approval of the priorities board, certify additional classes of industries and also certify additional plants whose operations as a war measure entitle them to preference treatment, which industries and plants when so certified shall be automatically included in the preference list."

From time to time it may become necessary to certify to you additional industries, or additional plants, entitled to preferential treatment in their supply of labor, and this will be accomplished through labor priorities bulletins, of which this is No. 1.

Attention is particularly invited to the fact that no attempt has been made to embrace within the preference list all essential industries, but only such as, taking into account the urgency of the demand and the relation of the supply to the demand, in the public interest as a war measure require the artificial stimulus of priority over other essential industries.   It should be constantly borne in mind that there are industries and plants which, measured by this test, may not require general preferential treatment, which are, nevertheless, essential industries and an important part of the industrial fabric.

THE LUMBER INDUSTRY.

It is deemed of immediate importance that information as to the essential character of the lumber industry and the degree of consideration which should be given the industry with respect to its labor requirements should be furnished to you for your guidance in the administration of the labor-recruiting program and to the district boards for their guidance in the matter of claims for industrial deferment.

It will be noted that the lumber industry as such does not appear on the preference list, and the comparatively few plants whose names appear thereon were listed to assist them in securing fuel to operate their logging roads.   As a general rule it has been deemed in the public interest that lumber manufacturing plants should use wood as a fuel in order to conserve coal in those districts where the coal supply is less than the demand (although there are necessary exceptions to this rule), and this is one of the reasons why it was not deemed proper to accord to the industry as a whole preferential treatment for its supply of fuel.

Taking into account its very heavy tonnage, coupled with the necessity of applying special priority regulations for the movement of Government timbers and lumber, as well as the necessity for placing embargoes from time to time on commercial shipments into congested territory, it was not deemed proper to accord to the industry as a whole preferential treatment for its transportation service.

The essential nature of the industry as a whole is, however, recognized and a large per cent of the present lumber production of the United States is required, directly or indirectly, in the prosecution of the war.

To guard against the action of the priorities board being misunderstood because of so important an industry being omitted from the preference list, it is proper to advise you that in the opinion of the priorities board the district boards may, in passing upon claims for industrial deferment made by or on behalf of "necessary" employees of lumber manufacturing plants supplying lumber "necessary to the maintenance of military establishments, or to the effective operation of the military forces of the United States or its allies, or to the maintenance of national interest during the emergency," give to such claims consideration substantially equivalent to that which would be given them if they appeared in Class IV on the preference list. The suggestion is made that when such claims for industrial deferment arise, the registrant or the plant interested be given an opportunity to present evidence in such form and manner as may be indicated by the district boards, that it is to some substantial extent supplying lumber, through direct or indirect orders, to the Government or some of its agencies (including railroads operated by the United States Railroad Administration), or supplying to others lumber of primary importance in war work, or in essential civilian requirements.

Attention is particularly invited to the fact that for some time to come many of the lumber manufacturing plants in the district east of the Mississippi River and south of the Ohio and Potomac Rivers, and also in Louisiana and Texas and in the Pennsylvania hemlock district in eastern Pennsylvania will be largely engaged in filling heavy orders for the War Department and for the Emergency Fleet Corporation, as well as for the Railroad Administration, while many mills in the States of Washington and Oregon will be largely engaged in supplying spruce and fir for aircraft production, as well as ship timbers.

Attention is invited to the accompanying copy of Circular No. 21, issued by the priorities division of the War Industries Board under date of September 3, 1918, dealing with "nonwar construction." The curtailment of all building operations which can and should be deferred until after the war shall have been won will, to a considerable extent, automatically curtail the production of lumber not required for essential uses.

The request is made that this bulletin have your careful consideration, and that it be called to the attention of the several district boards.

Yours truly,

EDWIN B. PARKER,
Priorities Commissioner.

WASHINGTON, D. C., *September 17, 1918.*

REPORT OF J. L. REPLOGLE ON THE IRON AND STEEL SITUATION, SEPTEMBER 14, 1917.

In compliance with your request, I inclose herewith a memorandum showing my ideas as to prices on various iron and steel products. Whatever prices are determined upon should be put into effect at the earliest possible date, as conditions in the steel line are in an extremely chaotic condition, and I believe many manufacturers in anticipation of what they consider very low prices to be established on steel products, are giving right of way in their mill operations to the more profitable products, such as are purchased by the automobile manufacturer, who is willing to pay the exorbitant prices asked if he can secure delivery, with the result that too much steel is going into non-essentials and entirely too little into war necessities.

Certain manufacturers * * * have given us every cooperation, while others have shown a very indifferent attitude. Despite the fact that the output of * * * is only about 50 per cent of the total capacity of the country, they have taken approximately 70 per cent of all the orders placed by the United States Government and in many cases the prices were far below their competitors', and in all cases where asked to do so, they have taken orders subject to the Government prices to be established, based on the Federal Trade Commission report as to cost. When prices are established and priority schedules are out, I believe most of the others will fall into line.

Products most essential to war.—The products most essential to the war and on which we must have the maximum production are coke, pig iron, sheared plates, shell steel billets and rounds. I believe on the products most needed that it would be well to establish a stimulating price, as in most cases a steel manufacturer has a finishing capacity far in excess of his ingot capacity, this being due to the fact that in normal times one line or another may be inactive and the demands on other products will be such that he can work up through other lines his entire ingot production.

The situation on the various products is about as follows:

Coke.—The total production of coke in 1916 was approximately 54,000,000 tons, about 35,000,000 tons or 65 per cent of which was Beehive coke and about 19,000,000 or 35 per cent being made in by-product ovens. Owing to the insufficient car supply and shortage of labor, the production of Beehive coke has fallen off in a very serious way during the past five or six months, with the result that the price has gone as high as $17 at the ovens, as compared to an average price of about $2.20 during the past 10 years. The Connellsville ovens are now runing at the rate of about 70 per cent capacity, and are losing about 20 per cent of their output on account of labor shortage and 10 per cent on account of car service and other causes. Coke will be, I think, the limiting factor in our iron and steel production, although the shortage of iron ore may also be a contributing element.

Iron ore.—On September 1, the shipment to lower lake ports was about 3,000,000 tons less than the same time last year, this being largely due to the late opening of lake navigation and insufficient vessel capacity and more particularly, inadequate car service at lower lake points. This matter is receiving every consideration by the ore committee, but I strongly recommend that the movement to take about 86 vessels from the Great Lakes for use in ocean traffic be dropped, as the boats are badly needed for the ore-carrying trade. In order to take them through the Welland Canal and make them serviceable, an enormous amount of labor and money would be necessary to cut them in half and repair them, and even after this was done they would not be suitable for ocean traffic. I understand that of the 86 boats under consideration, 37 of them are packet boats which can be spared. The ore consumption in 1916 was approximately 57,000,000 tons, and the annual capacity now with about 19 new furnaces in blast is about 64,000,000 tons, and if the 86 boats are taken from the lake trade, it would cut their tonnage to the extent of probably 3,500,000 tons annually, which would seriously cripple the industry.

Pig iron.—The output for 1916 was approximately 39,500,000 tons, but the production of iron in the first half of this year was considerably under the previous six months, this being largely due to the shortage of coke and labor. Most of the furnaces make iron, of course, only for their own use, and the average monthly production for sale during the first six months of this year was about 940,000 gross tons. The sales obligations of the various manufacturers on July 21, 1917, were 8,233,130 tons, of which about 250,000 tons were for export largely to Canada, Great Britain, Italy, and Japan. From this you will note that the merchant furnace production of the country is sold up for a little over nine months. There has been a great increase in steel-making capacity, but the production of iron has not kept pace with it. A number of our Allies, particularly Italy, are in the market for very heavy tonnages, and I think their necessities are such that they cannot be denied.

Plates.—Supplementing my letter of the 30th ultimo, I consider plates about the weakest link in our chain. The total production of sheared and universal plates in 1916, which was a record year, was 3,687,384 tons, of which 1,224,234 tons were universal mill plates not adaptable to any great extent for ship construction. As a matter of fact, the production of sheared plates one-fourth inch or over was 1,865,642 tons. The sales obligations of the various plate manufacturers as of July 21 last total about 2,300,000 tons and the requirements of the Shipping Board and of the Navy and Army to the end of 1918 will approximate 1,750,000 tons, so that it is plain that we have fully two solid years' maximum operation now in sight, without taking into consideration the needs of our Allies, which will be very heavy. The British war mission is now trying to secure right of way on a plate specification; the Italian mission informs us that their requirements will also be quite heavy, and Japan wants an enormous tonnage. Of the 425,556 tons of plates for export on the books of the plate manufacturers July 21 last, 292,000 or about 68 per cent were for shipment to Japan, and about 70,000 tons for shipment to Canada. If we continue to permit the export of plates, it is plain that the output of our own shipyards will be restricted. I cannot too strongly impress upon you the grave situation in this particular line. There was considerable new plate capacity under serious consideration some months ago; in fact, some of the work on the mills had already been started, when for some reason construction was called off at the time Government prices on plates were discussed by representatives of the Government and the manufacturers.

If the demand for pipes and tubes can be reduced by discouraging building construction and all nonessential work of this character, these skelp mills could be used to very great advantage on ship plates. I think that this is one of the greatest possibilities we have and it must promptly be taken advantage of by someone in authority.

In view of the above conditions, which I consider most serious to our war program, I believe a stimulating price on plates would be advisable to encourage the mills in exerting every possible influence for maximum tonnage from their existing mills, and also to influence new construction.

Projectile steel.—The situation in this line is equally as bad as on plates. The requirements of this Government for the next year will approximate 1,600,000 tons. The British war mission advise us that they have approximately 700,000 tons now on order with various plants in this country which have not yet been delivered, and their requirements will be at least 1,000,000 tons additional. Italy wants about 40,000 tons and Belgium about 28,000 tons, making a total of 3,368,000 tons. I have not yet been able to get the requirements of France and Russia, but I assume that there will be a tremendous tonnage required by them.

Prior to the war there was comparatively little of this tonnage rolled and there are practically no mills in this country adapted particularly for this character of product, as the ordinary bar mill is designed more particularly for bars of one-fourth inch to, say, 2-inch diameter, and the shell steel in this country is largely rolled on rail mills and heavy structural mills, and the rolling of this tonnage on these mills displaces a very much heavier tonnage of the products for which the mills were designed.

We have had the greatest difficulty in placing a small requisition for about 30,000 tons for the Ordnance Department, as all the mills are filled up largely on foreign orders. The British, Italian, and Belgian missions are all pushing us for deliveries on their requirements in this line, and to place additional tonnages, which we cannot see any possibility of their getting, without a serious shortage in our own requirements. We are giving this subject a lot of detailed study, but we cannot see any possible chance of meeting our requirements in this line, unless something is done promptly to prevent the manufacture of the enormous tonnage of steel going into nonessentials.

I believe on the larger shells we will have to go to the steel casting companies, although I understand the War Department is not very favorable to this. This has been done by some of the foreign governments in an emergency, and I believe we will have to come to it here, which will help the situation to some extent, but not greatly.

A very serious complication is the closing of shell factories in Canada, where they have a capacity of 400,000 shells per day, which is considerably in excess of the output in this country. I have talked with three of the Canadian munition manufacturers, who state they propose to change their factories to other lines of product, as they cannot get additional shell orders from the British Government, which insists that Canada must finance their own requirements in this line, which they state they are unable to do, and according to the terms of the United States Government's loan to Great Britain, this money can only be used for purchases in this country, with the result that they are trying to divert this Canadian business to us. They have been consuming 225,000 tons of shell steel monthly in Canada, about 190,000 tons of which was supplied by the Canadian steel plants, and approximately 35,000 tons imported from this country.

I certainly feel that some arrangement should promptly be made to continue the manufacture of shell steel and finished shells in Canada, and understand that negotiations are now on with this object in view.

Summary.—As previously advised, coke, pig iron, plates, and projectile steel will be the most serious factors in the steel situation. The situation on structural steel, pipe, and tubes, wire products, rails, merchant bars, etc., is approximately as reported in my letter of the 30th ultimo. These lines will all have to be materially curtailed in order to meet the absolute war necessities. I again recommend that the leading steel manufacturers be called to Washington at the earliest possible date for a full discussion of the serious condition, with the hope that immediate action will be taken to improve it, as we cannot continue on the present basis without most serious results.

Appendix XV.

STEEL PRICES AS FIXED OCTOBER 11, 1917.

Commodity.	Basis.	Price.
Blooms and billets, 4 by 4 inches and larger	Pittsburgh-Youngstown	$47.50 per gross ton.
Billets, under 4 by 4 inches	....do	$51 per gross ton.
Slabs	....do	$50 per gross ton.
Sheet bars	....do	$51 per gross ton.
Wire rods	Pittsburgh	$57 per gross ton.
Shell bars:		
3 to 5 inches	....do	$3.25 per 100 pounds.
Over 5 to 8 inches	....do	$3.50 per 100 pounds.
Over 8 to 10 inches	....do	$3.75 per 100 pounds.
Over 10 inches	....do	$4 per 100 pounds.
Skelp:		
Grooved	....do	$2.90 per 100 pounds.
Universal	....do	$3.15 per 100 pounds.
Sheared	....do	$3.25 per 100 pounds.

STEEL PRICES AS FIXED NOVEMBER 11, 1917.

Sheets: Per 100 pounds.
    No. 28 black sheets f. o. b. Pittsburgh $5.00
    No. 10 blue annealed sheets f. o. b. Pittsburgh 4.25
    No. 28 galvanized sheets f. o. b. Pittsburgh 6.25

The above prices to apply to both Bessemer and open-hearth grades.

Pipe: On ¾-inch to 3-inch black steel pipe, discount 52 and 5 and 2½ per cent f. o. b. Pittsburgh.

Cold-rolled steel: Seventeen per cent discount from March 15, 1915, list f. o. b. Pittsburgh.

Scrap (f. o. b. consuming point):   Per gross ton.
    No. 1 heavy melting... $30.00
    Cast-iron borings and machine-shop turnings........................ 20.00
    No. 1 railroad wrought... 35.00
Wire, plain wire f. o. b. Pittsburgh, per 100 pounds...................... 3.25
Tin plate, coke base, Bessemer and open-hearth, f. o. b. Pittsburgh, per 100-pound box 7.75

JOINT CIRCULAR—PARKER AND REPLOGLE, JULY 3, 1918.

To all producers and consumers of iron and all manufacturers and consumers of iron and steel products:

In order that misunderstandings which have apparently arisen in some quarters as to the practices to be observed in the distribution of pig iron and of iron and steel manufactured products may be removed, we invite careful consideration to the following:

1. All pig iron and steel manufactured products are now being shipped and delivered by the producer or manufacturer in accordance with the resolution of the War Industries Board adopted June 6, 1918, copy of which resolution, marked for identification "Exhibit A," is hereunto attached and made a part hereof.

2. *Priority orders.*—It will be noted that under the resolution of June 6, 1918, all orders covered by priority certificates shall be first provided for or filled and thereafter orders embraced within the schedule of purposes entitled to preferential treatment as determined by the priorities board may be filled without other specific priority instructions and without the further approval of any governmental agency.

The purpose was to permit deliveries of pig iron and of steel-manufactured products under the schedule of purposes not only after orders covered by priority certificates shall have been filled but at any time to the extent that such deliveries will not interfere with the filling when and as required of orders covered by priority certificates.

The priorities committee is now issuing certificates of three classes, namely, Class AA, Class A, and Class B. One effect of this resolution is to put all orders not covered by priority certificates, but embraced within the schedule of purposes entitled to preference treatment, in a fourth class, which we will designate Class C, and to give such orders priority and precedence over all other orders not covered either by priority certificates or embraced within the said schedule of purposes, which other orders will be designated Class D.

If reasonably satisfactory delivery can be secured on Class C orders, no application for a higher priority rating need or should be made to the priorities committee.

3. *Class D orders—permits to ship.*—Orders falling within Class D may be filled from surplus stocks, if any remain, after orders covered by priority certificates or falling in Class C have been provided for or filled, subject, however, to the approval in writing of the director of steel supply first had and obtained.

In order to avoid delays in the filling of small orders urgently required for essential civilian uses, the director of steel supply does hereby approve in writing the filing of such orders falling in Class D on the conditions following:

(*a*) That the order in the aggregate shall not exceed in quantity 5 tons;

(*b*) That the manufacturer shall, on or before the 10th of each month, report to the director of steel supply all orders filled during the preceding month under this authority; and shall certify that he believes that it was in the public interest that such orders should be filled.

Applications for permit to manufacture or ship Class D orders which cannot be shipped under the foregoing authority must be filled out and mailed in duplicate to the director of steel supply on blanks which will be forwarded to each manufacturer; such applications must be made by the manufacturer only and not by the purchaser. Upon receipt of such application it will have prompt and careful consideration at the hands of the director of steel supply, who will indorse on the bottom of the application in a space provided therefor the word "Granted" or the word "Declined" and return one copy to the applicant. If granted, the manufacturer may ship on such terms and under such conditions as may be imposed by the director of steel supply.

4. *Allocations.*—The direct war requirements of iron and of iron and steel products of all departments and agencies of the United States Government and of its Allies will be allocated to the various manufacturers by the director of steel supply.

All other orders for direct and indirect war requirements for iron and iron and steel products should be placed by the consumer with his regular source of supply. In the event a consumer is unable to find a producer or manufacturer who will accept his order, application for allotment should be made to the director of steel supply only when supported by strong evidence in writing that the public interest requires that such order shall be placed and filled.

5. *Jobbers' stocks.*—It is in the public interest that jobbers dealing in plates, sheets, bars and shapes, structural shapes, tubular products, wire and wire products, tin plate, heavy hardware, farm implements, mining tools, ma-

chinery and equipment, oil-well supplies, and similar products should be permitted to maintain reasonable stocks from which Government agencies, war industries, and the civilian population may draw to meet essential requirements. The jobbers recognize the necessity for rigidly restricting all iron, steel, and tin products to essential uses and have pledged their whole-hearted cooperation to a program to prevent hoarding on the part either of the jobbers or of their customers, and to reduce to an absolute minimum both jobbing and retail stocks. On the faith of this pledge on the part of the jobbers a plan has been adopted, as follows:

(a) Each jobber shall, not later than the 5th of each month, file with the director of steel supply, on forms to be furnished by him, a certified statement covering shipments made by the jobber during the preceding month.

(b) To the extent that such shipments fall within priority Class AA, Class A, Class B, or Class C, as hereinbefore defined, or by permits issued by the director of steel supply, the jobber shall be entitled to place with the manufacturer or manufacturers constituting his regular source or sources of supply, orders for the replacement of shipments so made; provided the total tonnage or quantity of each commodity ordered for replacement shall not be in excess of the amount of such commodity shipped by him during the previous month and embraced within the priority classes mentioned.

(c) The manufacturer will, upon receipt of such order, scrutinize it carefully in the light of the other demands made upon him and in the light of the then relation of the demands to the supply generally, and the particular requirements and demands for the products ordered in the territory served by the jobber placing the order, to guard against hoarding or an inequitable distribution of the supply available to meet all demands for essential uses. The Government is depending upon the experience and patriotism of the manufacturers to assist it in securing an equitable distribution of all products and their restriction to essential uses.

(d) All orders for stocks placed in accordance with the foregoing rules shall be and are hereby rated as Class B–4 and entitled to priority and precedence accordingly; conditioned, however, upon the jobber placing the order having first filed with the priorities committee and also with the director of steel supply a pledge in writing as follows:

"I do hereby pledge myself not to use or, so far as lies within my power, permit the use of any stocks now in or which may hereafter come into my possession or control, save (1) for essential uses as that term may be defined from time to time by the priorities division of the War Industries Board, or (2) under permits in writing signed by the director of steel supply; that I will make no sale or delivery from such stocks to any customer or retailer before his filing with me a similar pledge in writing; and that I will use my utmost endeavor to prevent the hoarding of stocks and to insure that they be distributed solely for essential uses."

Where such pledge has been once filed in accordance with the above paragraph the jobber should so certify to the manufacturer when placing his order, and the order shall not be accepted by the manufacturer in the absence of such certification.

6. *Exports.*—No application for a license to export iron or iron and steel products (save on direct orders of the United States and its allies) should be made to the War Trade Board unless the orders are (1) covered by priority certificates Class AA, Class A, or Class B, or (2) covered by a permit signed by the director of steel supply.

All communications with respect to priority matters dealt with herein should be addressed to the Priorities Committee. All communications with respect to all other matters dealt with herein should be addressed to the Director of Steel Supply.

EDWIN B. PARKER,
Priorities Commissioner.
J. LEONARD REPLOGLE,
Director of Steel Supply.

Approved:
B. M. BARUCH,
Chairman War Industries Board.
WASHINGTON, D. C., *July 3, 1918.*

[Exhibit A.]

The War Industries Board on June 6, 1918, adopted the following resolution:

Be it resolved by the War Industries Board that the following agreement, reached as a result of several conferences between a committee of this board and the American Iron & Steel Institute, be and the same is hereby, ratified, confirmed, and approved, to become effective at once.

The agreement follows:

Whereas a careful study of the sources of supply in connection with the present and rapidly increasing direct and indirect war requirements for iron and steel products has convinced the War Industries Board of the necessity for (1) a strict conservation of the available supply of iron and steel products, on the one hand, and (2) the expansion of existing sources and development of new sources of supply of iron and steel products, on the other hand; and

Whereas the producers of iron and of iron and steel products in the main concur in this conclusion reached by the said board and have expressed their willingness to whole-heartedly cooperate with the said board in its efforts to provide for promptly meeting the direct and indirect war requirements of the United States and its Allies for iron and steel products.

Now, therefore, it is understood and agreed by the committee on steel and steel products of the American Iron & Steel Institute and the War Industries Board that no pig iron or steel manufactured products shall be shipped or delivered, except as follows:

(1) By priority certificates issued by the priorities division of the War Industries Board; or,

(2) After orders covered by priority certificates shall have been provided

for or filled, then producers of pig iron and of steel manufactured products may utilize such raw materials and manufacturing capacity, if any, as they may have available, to fill orders of their customers not covered by priority certificates, provided such orders are embraced within the schedule of purposes entitled to preference treatment as determined by the priorities board, as follows:

Ships.—Including destroyers and submarine chasers. Including all necessary raw materials, partially manufactured parts and supplies for completion of products.

Aircraft.—*Munitions, military and naval supplies, and operations.*—Building construction for Government needs. Equipment for same. Including all necessary raw materials, partially manufactured parts and supplies for completion of products.

Fuel.—Domestic consumption. Manufacturing necessities named herein. Including all necessary raw materials, partially manufactured parts and supplies for completion of products.

Food and collateral industries.—Foodstuffs for human consumption, and plants handling same. Feeding stuffs for domestic fowls and animals, and plants handling same. All tools, utensils, implements, machinery, and equipment required for production, harvesting, and distribution, milling, preparing, canning, and refining foods and feeds, such as seeds of foods and feeds, binder twine, etc. Products of collateral industries, such as fertilizers, fertilizer ingredients, insecticides, and fungicides. Containers for foods and feeds, collateral products. Materials and equipment for preservation of foods and feeds, such as ammonia and other refrigeration supplies, including ice. Including all necessary raw materials, partially manufactured parts and supplies for completion of products.

Clothing.—For civilian population.

Railroad or other necessary transportation equipment, including water transportation.

Public utilities serving war industries, Army, Navy, and civilian population. Including all necessary raw materials, partially manufactured parts and supplies for completion of products.

Provided, however, That whenever the priorities board shall have promulgated and certified for observance to the producers of pig iron and steel-manufactured products a revised preference list, no surplus material or capacity after filling or providing for all orders covered by priority certificates shall be used to fill nonpriority orders save such as are placed by industries or plants embraced within preference list; and

Provided further, That each producer of pig iron and of steel-manufactured products shall, at the end of each week, ending with midnight Saturday thereof, prepare and forward to the director of steel supply of the War Industries Board a detailed statement of all shipments made during such week not covered by such priority certificates.

Be it further resolved, That should any producer of pig iron or of steel-manufactured products have any surplus war material or manufacturing capacity after filling (*a*) all orders covered by priority certificates and (*b*) all orders embraced within the schedule of purposes entitled to preference treatment or placed by industries or plants embraced within the revised preference list, after it shall have been promulgated and certified by the priorities board, then, in such event, such surplus materials or capacity may be disposed of by such producer or manufacturer to other customers, subject to the approval in writing of the director of steel supply first had and obtained.

Be it further resolved, That the director of steel supply and a committee, appointed by the American Iron and Steel Institute, shall jointly make a careful study of the present and prospective iron and steel requirements of each and every department and agency of the Government of the United States and of its Allies, and the capacity of the iron-producing and steel-manufacturing plants of the United States to meet such requirements and present to this board as early as practicable (1) a report of their findings, together with (2) recommendations of measures, if any, which should be taken to stimulate and increase the production of iron and steel products in order to meet the direct and indirect war requirements and the demands of industries of exceptional or national importance.

APPENDIX XVIII.

TENTATIVE UNITED STATES LANDED POOL PRICES FOR NITRATE OF SODA.

1918	Refined, per 100 pounds.	Ordinary, per 100 pounds.	1918	Refined, per 100 pounds.	Ordinary, per 100 pounds.
May	$4.10	$4.05	September	$4.50	$4.32½
June	4.10	4.05	October	4.52½	4.40
July	4.20	4.10	November	4.52½	4.40
August	4.45	4.32½	December	4.55	4.42½

APPENDIX XIX.

FINAL UNITED STATES LANDED POOL PRICES FOR NITRATE OF SODA.

1918	Refined, per net hundred-weight.	Ordinary, per net hundred-weight.	1918	Refined, per net hundred-weight.	Ordinary, per net hundred-weight.
January	$4.68582	....	June	$4.040585	$3.936585
February	4.3494512	$4.2900512	July	4.03641	3.91755
March	4.0564571	3.9970571	August	4.138794	4.019934
April	4.0569056	3.9727156	September	4.169396	4.050536
May	4.00846	3.93913			

STORY OF THE NITRATE PROBLEM.

The obtaining of the necessary supplies of nitrate was one of the most difficult of all the problems that faced the Board.   There were no substitutes in sufficient quantities to take the place of the product from Chile.

Upon the declaration of war by the United States, the demand for Chilean nitrate was tremendously increased and, even before the requirements of the Government had become known, prices in Chile advanced rapidly because it was recognized that the United States Government would have to be a large purchaser.   By April, 1917, there had been an advance from the prewar price of 2½ cents per pound to about 7½ cents.   It was at this time that the raw materials division of the Council recognized that some action was urgently necessary, and an order was issued to all ammunition manufacturers, or others bidding on Government work, that inquiries or options for nitrate would be unnecessary, and all proposals could be made to the Government on a basis of 4¼ cents a pound for the nitrate necessary to fulfill the contracts.   It was believed that this would prevent contractors from bidding against one another and thus prevent a run-away market.

As the actual consumption of nitrate had not yet been greatly increased, the raw materials division had a period of a few months in which to arrange a program for making good on the 4¼-cent nitrate.   Through the Naval Intelligence Division advice came of a discussion between the German Government and the Chilean Government regarding the national gold reserve of Chile which was on deposit in Berlin.   When the German Government finally made the definite decision that it would not permit the Chilean Government to withdraw this gold, overtures were made immediately by the United States to the Chilean Government offering to restore the Chilean gold reserve in Chile, on condition that the Chilean Government would seize the German-owned nitrate there and sell it to the United States, the price offered being about 60 per cent of the current market price.   There was an embargo on the shipment of gold at this time so that the cooperation of the Secretary of the Treasury was necessary to the transaction.   This deal was consummated in the summer of 1917 and all mention of it was kept secret.

Great numbers of speculators had entered the Chilean market in the spring and summer of 1917 and were bidding actively for shipments of nitrate that were to be delivered in October, November and December.   This had caused a rapid rise in prices.   To break the rise, arrangements were made with the Allies by which all Allied purchasing should be curtailed for the months of October, November and December, it being possible to supply the urgent needs from the German nitrate which the United States had bought.   In order to ship this nitrate from Chile, it was necessary to get Great Britain to waive the regulations against trading with the enemy and allow jute sacks to be shipped from Calcutta and allow British docks and ships to handle the German-owned nitrate.   Delivery of this nitrate was started in October and caused consternation in the Chilean market. The outside speculators who had purchased nitrate expecting that there would be a huge demand and that they could sell at any price found that there was no market for their goods. The American-owned German nitrate had taken its place. They had counted on this nitrate being tied up through inability of German subjects to sell or ship it. While this collapse of the nitrate speculators was being brought about and the Chilean market was being steadied, the Allies supported the demand market and covered all requirements at a price about 60 per cent below the current prices of the previous summer; and, as a result of all this, our Government was able to make good on the price of $4\frac{1}{4}$ cents a pound, fixed by the raw materials division in April, 1917, when the market was 7 to $7\frac{1}{2}$ cents. The fact is, when all accounts for the whole war period were in, it was seen that the nitrate cost our Government about $4\frac{1}{8}$ cents per pound.[1] This undertaking, originating in March, 1917, required for its fulfillment eight months of continuous effort under most trying conditions and involved most difficult negotiations with the Allies and with the Government of Chile.

The success of this operation, eliminating as it did the international speculators in Chilean nitrate, led to an urgent request on the part of the Allies that America join with them in the formation of machinery for centralizing the purchases of nitrate for all the Allies and America. This was accomplished through the formation of the International Nitrate Executive, which so successfully functioned throughout the balance of the war period, through the support and cooperation of the Honorable Winston Churchill, then Minister of Munitions of Great Britain.

It was apparent early in 1917 that the production of nitrate by Chile, which was the sole source of supply for the United States and the Allies, was insufficient to meet the war program which would be contemplated if the United States was to have an Expeditionary Force in Europe. Notwithstanding the fact that agriculture and industry in every nation had been curtailed to the utmost, the production of nitrate was barely sufficient to meet the requirements of the Allies themselves without counting the great increase in demand occasioned by America entering the war. By the early part of 1918, it was clear that some effort would have to be made to produce a substitute for Chilean nitrate.

Methods had been developed in Germany by which nitrates could be produced, by a fixation process, from the nitrogen of the air. The United States had but one small plant of this character; and the Allied nations, though they had made the effort, were still unable to produce any appreciable quantity. Urgent representations were made to the War Department, as the largest consumer of nitrates, to continue its activity in the construction of fixation plants to meet the situation. The plant at Muscle Shoals had been authorized in the fall of 1917 but progress on the work had been disappointing. A special commission was appointed by the Secretary of War to investigate the available processes and to advise in regard to locations for additional plants. Two additional plants

---

[1] See page 357.

were eventually authorized by the War Department and construction on them had made considerable progress before the Armistice. News in Chile of the extensive plans and the beginnings of construction in a large way of these fixation plants had an undoubted effect in keeping Chilean prices down.

When it is considered that every pound of powder and every pound of explosive must have nitrate as its principal ingredient, it must be seen that the importance of this material for the Nation's defense cannot be overestimated. The location of the original battle between the German and British fleets off the coast of Chile was not by chance; it was occasioned by the necessity on the part of the Allies of securing shipments of Chilean nitrate. The retreat from the Chilean coast by the German fleet after its victory over the British fleet was made necessary by the arrival of the Japanese fleet. The sinking of the German fleet later, left access to the Chilean nitrate fields more open to the Allies for the remainder of the war. In any war an adequate supply of nitrate is the first step necessary in material preparedness.

APPENDIX XXI.

RULING OF WAR TRADE BOARD ON DYEWOODS AND DYES, EFFECTIVE OCT. 10, 1918.

Hereafter no licenses for the importation of dyewoods or vegetable-dye extracts are to be issued for the remainder of the calendar year of 1918, except to cover the following:

1. Shipments from Mexico or Canada by other than ocean transportation.
2. Shipments from Europe or Mediterranean Africa when coming as a return cargo from convenient ports where loading can be done without delay.
3. Shipments of the following commodities, including extracts and compounds thereof: Annatoo, roucou, rocoa, orleans, cudbear, archil, litmus, madder, safflower, saffron, sumac, cochineal, and indigo, natural or synthetic.
4. Shipments of the following commodities in the amounts stated:
   a. Logwood, 22,500 tons.
   b. Fustic, 1,250 tons.
   c. Gambier, 400 tons.
   d. Cutch (used exclusively for dyeing, not to include mangrove bark extract), 1,250 tons.
   e. Nut galls, 750 tons.
   f. Mangrove-bark extract, from West Indian and South American countries only, not to exceed 375 tons.
   g. All other dyewoods in crude state, 500 tons.
   h. Extracts and decoctions for dyeing or tanning, not otherwise provided for, from Central and South America, 450 tons.

The amounts of the commodities permitted to come forward under section 4 above are to be allocated by the bureau of imports in accordance with the recommendations of the tanning material and natural dye section of the War Industries Board.

CLASSIFICATION OF INDUSTRIES USING ACETIC ACID.

[Subject to revision upon presentation of suitable evidence.]

Class A. Those concerns which are to receive their requirements for the month in full: Cellulose acetate, insecticides, Paris green, laboratory work, synthetic indigo dyes, salvarsan.

Class B. Those concerns which are to receive their requirements for the month in full as to specific Government orders and 50 per cent of their requirements for other purposes: Medicinal preparations, white lead, enamel ware.

Class C. Those concerns which are to receive their requirements for the month in full as to specific Government orders and 25 per cent of their requirements for other purposes: Dye manufacturers, photographic materials, dye pigments, tanners, sugar lead; resale (except to industries classified in Class D), mordants, textiles, for use in manufacture of blue for leather trade, for mixing with glue and paste for bindery purposes, cobalt acetate, paper mills for chrome yellow.

Class D. Those concerns which are to receive their requirements for the month in full as to specific Government orders and no part of their requirements for other purposes: Laundries, toilet articles, food products, soap manufacturers, miscellaneous, for rendering natural foliage and flowers permanent, for resale to small consumers in millinery trade.

Appendix XXIII.

QUESTIONNAIRE TO ELECTRODE CONSUMERS.

1. Number and size and type of furnace you operate.
2. What product do you produce by use of electrodes?
3. Total weight of electrodes in stock at end of the month.
4. Size, number, and weight of each of the electrodes on hand.
5. Whether graphite or carbon electrodes.
6. Number and weight of electrodes used during the month.
7. Number and weight of electrodes received or en route during month.
8. With what companies have you orders placed for electrodes?
9. Give list of unfilled Government orders placed with you for which electrodes are necessary.
10. Is any of your product being used by nonessential industries? If so, what percentage of your total production, and what are these nonessentials?
11. Can your product be made by any process that does not require the use of electrodes?
12. Estimate of your actual monthly requirements per month for the next three months.

MAXIMUM PRICES FOR COTTON GOODS.

[Fixed July 8, 1918.]

36 inches, 48 by 48, 3 yards per pound sheeting, 60 cents per pound.
36 inches, 56 by 60, 4 yards per pound sheeting, 70 cents per pound.
38½ inches, 64 by 60, 5.35 yards per pound print cloth, 83 cents per pound.
38½ inches, 80 by 80, 4 yards per pound print cloth, 84 cents per pound.
Standard wide and sail duck, 37½ per cent and 5 per cent from list.
Standard Army duck, 33 per cent from list.

GOVERNMENT REGULATIONS FOR HANDLING WOOL CLIP OF 1918.

The War Industries Board has fixed the prices of the 1918 clip of wool as established by valuation committees and approved by the Government as those established on July 30, 1917, at Atlantic seaboard markets. These values are figured on scoured basis. (See table on p. 7.)

Rights of the Government.—The Government shall have a prior right to acquire all of the 1918 wool clip, or any portion thereof which it may require, at the prices fixed by the War Industries Board. The remainder will be subject to allocation for civilian purposes under the direction of the War Industries Board.

A very large portion of the wool-manufacturing machinery working on Government contracts is located close to the Atlantic seaboard, and in order to avoid the possibility of railroad delay and congestion late in the season when the crops are moving, it is desirable and necessary that the wool clip shall be collected as soon as possible at points near the manufacturing centers. For these reasons it has been considered advisable to designate as distributing centers those centers which are close to points of consumption and which have the necessary facilities for handling wool.

Necessity for concentration.—The necessities of the Government at this time are such as to require the use of all existing agencies for concentrating the wool near the centers of consumption. Therefore all the wool of the 1918 clip must be distributed through approved dealers in approved centers of distribution.

"Approved dealers" defined.—"Approved dealers" shall be those dealers authorized by the War Industries Board to handle wool who are located in the distributing centers and who buy from growers direct, through agents, or from country merchants; and also those dealers authorized by the War Industries Board who are located in wool-growing districts, and who buy direct from growers and resell or consign to the dealers in distributing centers.

Approved distributing centers are the usual well-recognized points of distribution.

Classes of wool.—In a general way, the clip may be divided into fleece wool and territory wool.

Fleece wool shall be considered as that which is grown in the States east of the Mississippi River, and also the States of Minnesota, Iowa, Missouri, Arkansas, and Louisiana, and also those parts of Kansas, Nebraska, North Dakota, and South Dakota, and other localities where the same general conditions prevail. All wool not listed as fleece wool shall be considered territory wool.

In order that the collection of the clip may proceed in a rapid and orderly manner, the following regulations are promulgated by the wool division of the War Industries Board:

FLEECE WOOL REGULATIONS.

Compensation of grower and dealer.—Approved dealers shall be entitled to a gross profit in no case to exceed 1½ cents per pound on the total season's business, this profit to cover all expenses from grower to loading wool on board cars.

The grower shall receive fair prices for his wool based on the Atlantic seaboard price as established on July 30, 1917, less the profit to the dealer, as stated above, and less freight to seaboard, moisture shrinkage, and interest.

In no case shall this be construed to mean that there shall be more than 1½ cents gross profits made from time wool leaves growers' hands until it arrives at the distributing center.

On consignments forwarded to distributing centers the prices to be paid for the wool to the approved dealers therein shall be those established by the valuation committee on Atlantic seaboard values of July 30, 1917, to which shall be added a commission of 4 per cent to be paid by the Government, if bought by the Government, or by the manufacturer to whom the wool is allotted for other than Government purposes. This commission is to include grading and other expenses of handling. The consignor shall be charged with the freight on his shipment and interest on all advances made for his account to the date of the arrival of his wool at a distributing center, as shown by the railroad receipt.

On any lot remaining unsold in his possession for a longer period than six months the dealer shall be entitled to charge storage and insurance at the market rate, and this additional charge shall be added to the price of the wool.

Pooling by growers is advised.—Growers who desire to do so will be allowed to pool their clips in quantities of not less than minimum carloads of 16,000 pounds and consign the wools so pooled as one account to any approved dealer in any approved distributing center. Growers are urged to adopt this latter course through county agents or others, thus eliminating the profits of one middleman.

Government price.—Approved dealers in approved distributing centers will be required to open and grade all their purchases or consignments as rapidly as possible after the arrival of wool at point of distribution. Prices on all wools, as soon as graded, will be fixed by a Government valuation committee appointed for that purpose in the different distributing centers. Prices to be paid by the Government at distributing centers for such wool as it may require are to be those established as of July 30, 1917, at the Atlantic seaboard markets. In addition to said prices the Government is to pay a further sum equal to 4 per cent of the selling prices to cover compensation or commission to approved dealers for their services in collecting and distributing wool. On wool not taken by the Government for its own use and which may be allocated for other uses, prices will also be fixed in accordance with July 30, 1917, values at Atlantic seaboard markets, and on such wool approved dealers shall be entitled to a commission or compensation of a sum equal to 4 per cent of the selling price, and this commission or compensation shall be a charge against said wool and shall be collected from the manufacturer to whom said wool is allocated.

Profiteering prohibited.—As a guard against profiteering, the books of all approved dealers in distributing centers shall be at all times open to Government inspection, and if it be found that their gross profits, including the aforesaid commission of 4 per cent, are in excess of 5 per cent on the season's business then such gross profits shall be disposed of as the Government decides.

The books of the country dealers shall likewise be open to Government inspection. If it be found that their gross profit for the season's business is in excess of 1½ cents per pound, then such excess profits shall be disposed of as the Government may decide.

Distributing centers.—The approved distributing centers for fleece wools are: Boston, Mass.; New York, N. Y.; Philadelphia, Pa.; Chicago, Ill.; St. Louis, Mo.; Detroit, Mich.; Louisville, Ky.; Baltimore, Md.; and Wheeling, W. Va.

TERRITORY WOOL REGULATIONS.

Exceptions.—In the Willamette Valley, Oreg., and the Puget Sound district of the State of Washington, the regulations in regard to fleece wools shall apply.

Distributing centers.—For the reasons before stated, in order that the 1918 wool clip may be promptly concentrated near the manufacturing centers and to make use of every available agency for storing and grading, all territory wools must be consigned to one of the designated distributing centers which are as follows: Portland, Oreg.; Chicago, Ill.; New York, N. Y.; St. Louis, Mo.; Boston, Mass.; and Philadelphia, Pa.

The only exception is that clips of under 1,000 pounds may be sold by the owner. In buying these small clips, the buyer must recognize that he is entitled to only a small profit, which must not exceed 2 cents per pound. Growers, if they desire for any reason to consign their wool through their banker, country merchants, or others, may do so and said bank, country merchant, or others may receive a commission or compensation for handling said growers' wool (in no case to exceed one-half cent per pound); such commission or compensation to be paid by grower. Growers are, however, urged to consign their own wool and get the full price.

Shipping.—As soon as possible after wool reaches the railroad, the owner should load it and consign it to any approved dealer he may select in one of the designated distributing centers, who will there deliver the wool to the Government or to some manufacturer to whom the Government may allot the wool. These approved dealers will store, insure, handle, and deliver the wool under Government regulation. The grower should procure two copies of the shipping invoice and of the railroad bill of lading, and forward the original invoice and bill of lading to the dealer whom he has selected to handle his wool, retaining the duplicate in his own possession.

Advances, interest and freight.—The grower shall be entitled to receive an advance up to but not exceeding 75 per cent of the fair estimated market value of his wool. He shall pay interest on this advance at the rate of 6 per cent per annum from the date he receives such advance until his wool arrives at the distributing center as shown by the railroad receipt. It is not intended that the grower shall pay interest on advances after the date of arrival as shown by the railroad receipt, and he shall be entitled to receive interest on the selling value of his wool after freight has been deducted from date of arrival. The Government is fixing the price of the 1918 clip on a basis delivered at Atlantic seaboard points. It is therefore incumbent on the grower to deliver his wool at the designated distributing centers, and the expense of delivering the wool at such centers will be charged against the wool on a basis of the freight rate from point of origin to the Atlantic seaboard.

Valuing and grading.—As soon as possible after the arrival of the wool at a distributing center, if the wool is to be taken in the original bags, it shall be valued by the Government valuation committee. If the wool is to be graded it shall be valued in the piles by the Government valuation committee as soon as the piles are graded and ready for delivery. All grading will be conducted under Government supervision. The grades out of each clip will be weighed separately and the books of the dealer, as far as they pertain to any grower's wool, shall be open to him. Tags, bucks, black, and other recognized discount fleeces will be paid for at prices fixed by the Government. Bags will be paid for in the same manner.

Payments to growers.—Growers shall be entitled to payment on a basis of the date of the arrival of the wool as shown by the railroad receipt. However, as it would be impossible for obvious reasons to make settlement on each clip on the date of its arrival, in order that the grower may lose nothing by any delay in settlement he shall be entitled to draw interest on the selling price of his wool less freight from the date of the wool's arrival until the date of final settlement.

Final returns will be made as promptly as possible in all cases.

Commissions.—The grower does not pay the commission or compensation for handling wools in the designated distributing centers. This commission or compensation for handling will be added to selling price of the wool and paid by the buyer.

If sold in the original bags, the commission or compensation shall be 3 per cent of the selling price. If the wool is graded, the commission or compensation shall be 3½ per cent of the selling price. This commission or compensation includes drayage, storage, and insurance for a period not exceeding, on any lot, six months after arrival. On any lot remaining unsold in his possession for a longer period than six months the dealer shall be entitled to charge storage and insurance at the market rate, and this additional charge shall be added to the price of the wool.

Mills located in wool-growing districts.—In order that the Government may have full control of the wool situation with a view to conserving as far as may be necessary the wool supply for military purposes, it is considered necessary to prohibit manufacturers from buying wool except in the designated distributing centers, and then only with the permission and consent of the Government under such regulations as the Government may hereafter make.

However, mills located in wool-growing districts not near to the designated centers of distribution, and which are working on Government orders, will be given permits through the wool division of the War Industries Board to buy certain amounts of wool in their immediate neighborhood. In making applications for such permits, the manufacturer applying should state the number of his Government order, the amount of goods yet to be delivered against such order, the amount of his wool stock on hand, and the amount and class of wool required to complete said order. The manufacturer receiving such a permit will be required to report to the wool division of the War Industries Board all purchases made against permit issued to him.

Permits to dealers.—All dealers in approved centers desiring a permit to operate should apply to the wool division of the War Industries Board, stating their capacity for storing and grading.

All country dealers should apply for a permit to operate by writing to the wool division of the War Industries Board, giving name and address.

In order to expedite movement of wool, dealers in country districts and distributing centers may operate immediately in accordance with the above regulations, pending application for and granting of permit.

LEWIS PENWELL,
Chief of Wool Division, War Industries Board.

APPENDIX XXVI.

[P.C. Form 75.]

PRIORITIES CIRCULAR NO. 45.

EMBODYING RULES AND REGULATIONS GOVERNING THE DISTRIBUTION OF ELECTRIC ENERGY BY LIGHT AND POWER COMPANIES.

Under date of September 3, 1918, there was published by the Priorities Division of the War Industries Board Circular No. 20, known as Preference List No. 2, which furnishes a guide to all governmental agencies and all others interested in—

(1) The production and supply of fuel and electric energy;
(2) The supply of labor; and

(3) The supply of transportation service by rail, water, pipe lines, or otherwise, in so far as such service contributes to production of finished products.

Where the supply of electric energy is equal to the demand, there is obviously no occasion for use of the preference list.

But where the demand exceeds the available supply, due to lack of generating capacity or any other cause, then the producers and distributors of electric energy are directed to use the said preference list as a basis for distribution.

Whenever an individual plant has a preference classification differing from that of the industry to which it belongs, the individual plant classification shall govern.

Consumers having 100 horsepower connected load or less will, save in extreme cases, be treated as in Class I, irrespective of their preference list classification. It has been determined that, speaking generally, the saving of electric energy through a curtailment of these small consumers would not justify the loss, damage, inconvenience, and industrial disturbance that would follow. Where, however, it becomes absolutely necessary to do so in order to supply important Class I plants, even such small consumers should be curtailed.

Industries and plants grouped under Class I are only such as are of exceptional importance in connection with the prosecution of the war. Their requirements must be fully satisfied in preference to those of the three remaining classes.

The requirements of industries and plants grouped under Class II, Class III, and Class IV shall have precedence over those not appearing on the preference list.

If, however, after satisfying the requirements of Class I the requirements of the industries and plants grouped in the remaining three classes cannot be fully satisfied, then they shall be rationed, giving to each class a per cent of its requirements in the ratio of 5, 3, and 2, which represents the relative value or importance of each class as fixed and determined by the priorities board.

A simple illustration of the application of this "method of weighted needs" as applied to the distribution of electric energy may tend to clarify this rule, under which there should be applied as nearly as practicable the formula following:

(a) The aggregate kilowatt demands of each of the four classes of all industries and plants shall be approximately ascertained.

(b) The available supply of electric energy shall be ascertained.

(c) Should the available supply equal the requirements or demands, then the requirements of all industries and plants on the preference list shall be fully satisfied.

(d) But should the requirements or demands exceed the available supply of electric energy, then there shall be deducted from such supply the requirements of Class I, 100 per cent of which must be delivered, and the remainder shall be prorated between Classes II, III, and IV, giving to each a per cent of its requirements in the ratio of 5, 3, and 2.

Assume that the available supply of electric energy in a particular city or district is 100,000 kilowatts, while the requirements are as follows:

	Kilowatts
Class I. Requirements (including customers having 100-horsepower connected load or less)	20,000
Class II. Requirements	40,000
Class III. Requirements	50,000
Class IV. Requirements	60,000
Total requirements	170,000
Available supply	100,000
Supply Class I in full	20,000
Balance for distribution between Classes II, III, and IV	80,000

After having allotted Class I its full service, obtain the amounts of power to be served to the other classes as follows: Multiply the requirements of Classes II, III, and IV by their priority ratio of 5, 3, and 2, respectively, to obtain the "relative figures" as shown in the example following. The total available power for Classes II, III, and IV (80,000 kilowatts) is then divided by the total of their "relative figures" (470,000 kilowatts) giving in the example a decimal of 0.17021. If the "relative figure" for any class is multiplied by this decimal, the result will be the power allotted to that class.

Class	Require-ments	Multiplied by priority ratio—	Equals relative figure—	Multiplied by decimal—	Equals power allotted—	Proportion of requirements served	Ratio of service
	Kilowatt				*Kilowatt*	*Per cent*	
II	40,000	5	200,000	0.17021	34,042	85.10	5
III	50,000	3	150,000	.17021	25,532	51.06	3
IV	60,000	2	120,000	.17021	20,426	34.04	2
Total			470,000		80,000		

NOTE.—$\frac{80,000}{470,000} = 0.17021$.

Under this formula it will be seen that the power allotted to each of Classes II, III, and IV will always fill a proportion of the demands of the classes in the ratio of 5, 3, and 2.

It will, however, sometimes happen, when Class II or III, or both, have extremely small requirements in proportion to the total requirements of the district, that the formula will allot to one or both of these classes (II and III) an amount in excess of their respective requirements. In such a case, the overallotted class or classes should be given 100 per cent of their requirements and the balance of their allotment under the formula should be distributed either—

(a) Between the classes given incomplete service by the formula, in the ratio of their respective priority ratios (5, 3, or 2). This procedure is to apply where two classes are left incompletely served, or (*b*) If only one class is left incompletely served by the formula, the over-allotments of the other two classes are to be assigned to the incompletely served class.

The allotment of more than 100 per cent under the formula to a small class of high importance shows that the shortage in the district was primarily caused by the large amount of less important work in the district, and that the small class or classes of higher importance should not be penalized, since they are not responsible for the shortage.

It is not practicable, and it is not intended, that an attempt should be made to apply this formula with literal and mathematical accuracy, but it will afford a workable basis for rationing industries and plants embraced within Classes II, III, and IV, where the available supply, after satisfying Class I, is less than their aggregate requirements or demands.

In case any consumer shall be dissatisfied with the applications made and the electric energy furnished him under these rules and regulations, such consumer may present his complaint in writing to the priorities division of the War Industries Board, sending a copy of such complaint to the power company interested. Pending further directions from such priorities division the power company shall continue to distribute electric energy in accordance with these rules and regulations notwithstanding the lodging of a complaint by a dissatisfied consumer.

The War Industries Board fully appreciates, and is grateful for, the support and whole-hearted cooperation which it has received at the hands of both the producers and distributors of electric energy on the one part, and their consumers on the other, in connection with the handling of such cases of power shortages as have already arisen. These rules and regulations have been promulgated with the view of stimulating production to meet the requirements of the war program, and at the same time reduce to a minimum the inevitable disturbance to industry due to power shortages. With confidence we bespeak the continued cooperation of all interested parties in our efforts to reach sound and just solutions of these difficult and constantly recurring problems.

Yours very truly,

EDWIN B. PARKER,
Priorities Commissioner.

WASHINGTON, D. C., *October 7, 1918.*

BOOK TWO

Taking the Profit
Out of War

IN THREE PARTS

Editor's Preface to Parts I and II

THE TWENTIES were hardly fertile years for preparedness planning; certainly they were not plentiful ones.

In the illusory decade of Locarno and Geneva's rise, of the Washington Naval Conference and the Kellogg-Briand Pact, there were not many who raised their voices to warn against the day when "this, too, shall pass away."

To be sure, Congress in 1920, still mindful of the sad plight of the nation in 1917, did enlarge upon the National Defense Act of 1916, thereby authorizing the Assistant Secretary of War to institute and take active charge of M-Day planning (1) through a Planning Branch, to make studies and plans for wartime mobilization of industry, and (2) through the Army and Navy Joint Munitions Board, to study and co-ordinate the needs of the two services so as to prevent the disastrous competition in procuring supplies which had crippled both services in the last war.

Moreover, to supplement the planning work of the Army War College, there was also established the Army Industrial College—and before both of these bodies Mr. Baruch, Hugh S. Johnson, and many others frequently lectured on their World War experiences.

But despite all this, it was not until a decade had passed that an M-Day plan began to take definite shape—the first Industrial Mobilization Plan being submitted to the War Policies Commission in 1931.

The War Policies Commission was created by a joint resolution of Congress approved June 27, 1930, and the hearings, which opened on March 5, 1931, continued through the following May. Secretary of War Patrick J. Hurley was chairman. The other Cabinet representatives were: Secretary of the Navy Charles F. Adams; Secretary of Agriculture Arthur M. Hyde; Secretary of Commerce Robert P. Lamont; Secretary of Labor William N. Doak; and Attorney General William De W. Mitchell. Representing the Senate were David A. Reed of Pennsylvania, Vice Chairman of the Commission; Arthur H. Vandenberg of Michigan; Joseph T. Robinson of Arkansas; and Claude A. Swanson of Virginia. House members were Lindley H. Hadley of Washington, Secretary of the Commission; William P. Holaday of Illinois; Ross A. Collins of Mississippi; and John J. McSwain of South Carolina.

Colonel Hurley, before becoming Secretary of War in December, 1929, had served for the better part of a year as Assistant Secretary of War and had come into immediate contact with the problem of M-Day planning. Even before he was elevated to full Cabinet rank, he had begun agitation for the creation of a joint commission to review the work already done and set forth the essential needs of the country in any future war emergency.

Colonel Hurley frequently has told of the importance of Mr. Baruch's contribution to the work of the War Policies Commission—first, in exerting his influence in behalf of the joint resolution in Congress, and second, with his presentation to the Commission.

It remained for the phrase-makers of a later day to bring forth such words as *all-out* and *total war*—but the concept of the entire nation at war, the requirements for its prosecution, are clearly set forth, and completely so, in the presentation of Mr. Baruch, to which he has given the heading of *Taking the Profit Out of War*—a title that he used for an article in the *Atlantic Monthly* in January, 1926.

According to customary procedure, Mr. Baruch's presentation is two-fold: (1) his general statement at his first appearance before the Commission; and (2) a supplementary statement amplifying his views in the light of the statements of other witnesses.

R. H. H.

PART I

SUGGESTED POLICIES TO PROVIDE, WITHOUT CHANGE IN OUR CONSTITUTION, FOR INDUSTRIAL MOBILIZATION, ELIMINATION OF PROFITEERING, AND EQUALIZATION OF THE BURDENS OF WAR

A Memorandum submitted to the Joint Congressional and Cabinet Commission constituted pursuant to Public Resolution No. 98, 71st Congress.

Introduction

I TAKE IT that we are of the common belief that war ought to be avoided if possible, but that we must plan in such a way that, if war comes, we shall meet the enemy with our maximum effectiveness, with the least possible injury and violence to our people, and in a manner which shall avoid inflation and waste. Our plans should eliminate war profiteering and they ought to provide that each man, thing, and dollar shall bear its just proportion of the burden. They should be designed to avoid the prostrating economic and social aftermath of war and, finally, they should be laid with full recognition that modern war is a death grapple between peoples and economic systems rather than a conflict of armies alone, and to that end we should merit for industrial America something of what Field Marshal von Hindenburg in his retrospect of the World War had to say of its efforts in 1918:

Her brilliant, if pitiless, war industry had entered the service of patriotism and had not failed it. Under the compulsion of military necessity a ruthless autocracy was at work and rightly, even in this land at the portals of which the Statue of Liberty flashes its blinding light across the seas. *They understood war.*

I. Scope of Inquiry and Feasibility of Its Purpose

The principal requirements of your organic Joint Resolution are that you consider and report whether a Constitutional amendment is necessary:

(1) To authorize Congress to take private property for public use during war;
(2) To remove the profits of war;
(3) To equalize the burdens of war; and
(4) To consider and report policies to be pursued in war.

The Committee is not to consider conscription of labor.

For purposes of discussion I venture to paraphrase the subject of inquiry thus:

"A plan to mobilize effectively the resources of the nation for war which shall eliminate war profiteering, prevent wartime inflation, and equalize wartime burdens."

I assume that, if a Constitutional amendment is not necessary to this end, a recommendation of policies is nevertheless desired and also that such policies should provide for war profits at a lower rate than peace profits.

Since there was never a war without inflation, profiteering, and unequal burdens, the resolution seems a large order, but it is with no hesitation that I can say from our own experience in the World War and from methods that were actually in practice here at its close that the ends sought are possible of attainment and that means to those ends are simple. This is neither dream nor theory. I shall recommend no principle that was not in actual practice and accomplishment in 1918.

II.   *Requirements of Modern War*

Prior to 1870, nations hazarded their existence in reliance on small fractions of their strength. In the Franco-Prussian War, Germany showed some dim conception of what she called the "Nation in Arms," by which was meant that, in war, her entire resources of men, money, and things should suddenly become a compact instrument of destruction. The true intendment of this conception was fully grasped by none of the belligerents in 1914 and became clearly apparent only in the last months of the World War.

What it really means is that in the next major conflict the entire population must suddenly cease to be a congeries of individuals, each following a self-appointed course, and become a vast unitary mechanism composed, in our case, of some hundred and twenty-five million co-related moving parts all working to the end of directing practically all our material resources to the single purpose of victory. Modern war requires that the full power of the nation be exerted in the shortest possible time not only to the violent beating down of the enemy by any destructive material force we can invent or use, but also to every process of slow and often insidious economic strangulation and political isolation that we can devise and administer.

The battlefield effort (while now only a part of what we shall be called upon to do) has become of itself a monstrous thing. Twentieth century means of transportation, communication, and supply have made possible—and therefore necessary—the massing of men in numbers never before deemed possible. The accelerating progress of science has created destructive forces which require for their use or for defense against them the products of practically the whole of industry in quantities many times those required for the uses of peace. Thus war requires that, at the very moment when productive effort is deprived of millions of men for military service, the country's facilities for production must be speeded up to disgorge unprecedented volumes of supplies. Civilian morale becomes as important as military morale and it is necessary to make this cosmic change with the least practicable interference with the normal life of the nation. Furthermore, the increasing dependence of each principal nation on uninterrupted contacts with practically all other nations entails the necessity—for both offense and defense—of an economic strategy and an intense economic tactics which must include practically every other nation—hostile or neutral—in its far-flung application.

No such results as these are at all possible without a sanction, control, and leadership in industry sufficient to organize and deal with it as practically a single unitary system instead of a highly competitive community. Once this unity is attained, however, experience has shown beyond question that the mobilized industry of America is a weapon of offense or defense far more potent than anything the world has ever seen—more terrible, I think, than the mind of any man has ever imagined.

War on this vast modern scale has hitherto so violently disturbed the pattern of the normal economic structure of belligerent nations that, regardless of the side with which rests military victory, the aftermath of struggle prostrates both the conqueror and the conquered. With these most serious considerations you must deal. They depend on principles which we seem loath even to talk about—much less to provide for. These principles, while generally conceded in a vague uncomprehending way, are hardly understood at all. Yet they are of such sinister and overwhelming importance that the neglect of them is, in my opinion at least, one of the most threatening aspects of our governmental policy. From my experience I am convinced that it is quite possible to prepare, in peace, plans that will make the transition from Peace Industry to War Industry without serious disruption, to carry on the feverish industrial activity of war with the least possible harm to civilian morale, to accomplish all in the economic struggle that we shall ever need to accomplish and, even with all this, to lessen the destructive after-effects of major conflict. It is for these reasons that I regard the work of this Commission very seriously and that I am

much gratified to be able to lay before it the results of the experience
of the War Industries Board in the World War.

III. *Preventing War Inflation*

The following sequence has attended every major conflict in history:

(1) Shortages of services and things develop rapidly.

(2) Competitive bidding among the procurement agencies of Government and, in the last war at least, other procurement agencies, and
for the civil population sends all prices into a rapidly ascending spiral.

(3) Expenses of government multiply. The abnormal need for
money requires vast issues of certificates of governmental indebtedness. The inherent threat of destruction of Government impairs national credit. The combination of all these things rapidly debases
the exchange value of money, thereby still further increasing the prices
of things. The consequent destruction of buying power in the markets of the world begins almost immediately to impair the economic
strength of the nation in the conflict. This sapping of economic
strength will, in future wars, be the determining cause of defeat. As
Ludendorff has so bitterly complained, his military front remained im-
pregnable long after what he called "the home front" had crumbled.
Destruction of civil morale defeated Germany.

This process intensifies as time elapses with the following inevitable
results:

(1) Destruction of domestic morale through a just and bitter re-
sentment by soldiers, their families, and indeed by all persons of fixed
income, at the spectacle of grotesquely exaggerated profits and income
to those engaged in trade or in services for sale in competitive markets
and the constantly increasing burden of bare existence to all those
who are not so engaged. This is the greatest source of complaint of
"unequal burdens." The present demands for "equalizing burdens"
and "taking the profit out of war" both go back to this single phenomenon of war inflation. There is no more important problem to
solve—whether we consider it purely as a means to maintain the solidarity and morale of our people, or as the basis of our economic strength
for war purposes, or to avoid war's aftermath of economic prostration,
or on the broader grounds of humanity and even-handed justice.

(2) The inflationary process affords opportunity to individuals and
corporations to reap profits so large as to raise the suggestion of com-

placency if not of actual hospitality toward the idea of war. That
any human being could be persuaded, by prospect of personal gain,
however magnificent, to invoke the horrors of modern war is almost
unthinkable; nevertheless the certainty that war could never result in
the enrichment of any man would give us all security and comfort.

(3) Inflation enormously increases the cost of war and multiplies
burdens on the backs of generations yet to come. The war debt of
the nation is necessarily incurred in terms of debased dollar values.
In the inevitable post-war deflation, the debt of course remains at
the inflated figure. Thus the bonds that our Government sold in the
World War for fifty-cent dollars must be paid through the years by
taxes levied in one-hundred-cent dollars. For example, our total war
expenditure was $39,000,000,000 incurred in terms of 1917, 1918, 1919,
and 1920 dollars. In terms of the purchasing power of 1913 dollars
it would have been only $13,000,000,000, or in terms of 1930 dollars
probably not more than $15,000,000,000. Such a grotesque result would
be almost unbelievable were the figures not living facts. If anything
can be done to avoid this practical *doubling* of the economic burden of
war, certainly we should spare no effort to accomplish it.

When we entered the World War, the frantic demands and un-
co-ordinated counterbidding of our future associates in war had already distorted our own price structure out of any semblance of its
normal scheme. In other words there was a robust inflation here
before we ever entered the war. Furthermore, nearly twelve months
elapsed after our declaration before we had evolved controls and organization capable of co-ordinating our own and our associates' procurement activities and of controlling price. Notwithstanding this
delay and the dimness with which controlling principles were at first
perceived, we did, in 1918, arrive at a method which checked the process
of inflation in America and kept it in check until all controls were
released in November, 1918. It is to this experience that I refer when
I say that we have proved in practice a method to control inflation.
That proof convinces me that it would also prevent inflation if applied
at once upon the advent of war and before the inflationary process
begins.

To measure inflation of price and profit we must have some norm.
The obvious norm is the whole price structure as it existed on some
antecedent date near to the declaration of war on which the normal
operation of the natural law of supply and demand can be said to
have controlled price. That determined, we need a method of freezing the whole price structure at that level. The obvious way to do

this is simple: by proclamation to decree that every price in the whole national pattern as of that determined date shall be the maximum that may thenceforth be charged for anything—rents, wages, interest rates, commissions, fees—in short, the price for every item and service in commerce.

In these few words reside the basic principle of war control of national industry and of the present suggestion for elimination of war inflation in America. The superficial objection is, "You propose to repeal the law of supply and demand." We may as well take this bull by the horns. In modern war, administrative control *must* replace the law of supply and demand.

In the national pattern of peace, all economic forces are operating under the work-a-day influences of that natural law. Prices, production, and finance all are factors of competition—in other words, of that law. But in peace, the various parts of what will eventually be the economic engine for war are neither co-ordinated nor subject to any single guiding control. Indeed, to prevent such combination and control is the basic effort of peacetime administration. *"Competition is the life of trade."*

Suddenly war appears. The whole tempo, volume, and quality of the force of *demand* becomes distorted. Things that yesterday were of no great importance (e.g., toluol, picric acid, and sodium nitrate) suddenly become the aim of all endeavors. As to these as well as to all other fundamental commodities there is an almost instantaneous shortage. Now, in peacetime shortage, the highest bidder takes all. That *is* the law of supply and demand. In war—at least in major modern war—we cannot permit this. The Government must assume control of the whole supply and ration and apportion it—not to the longest purse but to the most necessitous use. Furthermore, the distinguishing characteristic of peacetime economic operation is *competition*, and basic prices are largely determined thereby. Also it is literally the object of one great competitor to secure as great a proportion of all business as possible. Under war conditions the entire process is reversed. There is more business than all the facilities of the country can handle. Competitors must become co-operators in order to meet the very minimum demand for shortage items. Control of this co-operation rests in government. Thus, both because governmental determination (*and not price*) controls demand, and because only complete co-operation (*and not competition*) can produce supply in sufficient quantity, the law of supply and demand adjourns itself.

These principles apply to shortage items. The crystallized price structure is a schedule of maxima. Items in ample supply are left free to fall below the fixed price level.

Furthermore, this provision, which places control of and responsibility for supply of shortage items in the hands of government, by no means solves the shortage problem. Under the law of supply and demand, rapidly increasing demand (and consequent rising price) is the force relied upon to provide increased supply. In war we cannot wait for this and we cannot stand the waste and confusion incident to it. We must use other means such as were very fully developed in 1918. By way of introduction let us name them:

(1) Elimination of waste, loss, and unnecessary accumulation through frantic competition by all procurement agencies, which elimination is achieved by a rigorous control and co-ordination of them and the funneling of all demand through one central control agency.

(2) Rationing and allocation of shortage items in order that more necessitous uses (such as equipment and supply of field armies) may have priority in time with careful provision against undue hardship to the civil population.

(3) Conservation, by which is meant: standardization of type and design; elimination of any but necessitous uses; prevention of hoarding and accumulation; postponement of all deferrable uses, thus increasing supply by sharply curtailing demand.

(4) Substitution—by which is meant substitution of items of greater availability for shortage items.

(5) Discovery of new sources of supply.

The resiliency of a great people like ours—their capacity to "do without" or adapt themselves to new conditions—makes the potentiality of the above expedients very great. No one who has not seen these expedients in operation would be likely to imagine the vast quantities of essential commodities, power, storage space, transportation, money, and labor which can be made available in this way. An explanatory word as to some of these expedients may be in order. Conservation is among the most effective of wartime expedients. Multiplicity of type and design in almost every commodity of commerce wastes a vast amount of component material. Had the war gone on another year, our whole civil population would have gradually emerged (as wardrobes and inventories became exhausted) in cheap but serviceable uniform. Types of shoes were to be reduced to two or three. The manufacture of pleasure automobiles was to cease. Flaps from pockets and unnecessary trim in clothing would have disappeared. Steel had already been taken out of women's corsets.

The conservation program was of course much broader than this. It affected practically the whole field of commodities. We had instituted a deferment of every type of building construction except that indispensable to the prosecution of the war. We had gasless, meatless, sugarless, fuelless days and, in ways and methods too numerous to mention, we were greatly increasing the supply for essential uses by cutting off supply for non-essentials.

Yet after all these things are done there will remain an unavoidable necessity for adjusting the crystallized price structure upward in individual cases. We always have low-cost producers and high-cost producers. War requires *all* producers. This presents the most difficult aspect of the problem:

"If we raise the price sufficiently high to pay a reasonable profit to the high-cost producer, we will thereby create inordinately high profits to the low-cost producer."

There are only two alternatives—create a system of bonuses to the latter class or limit, by an excess profit tax, the return on invested capital to the former class. After exhaustive study during the war, the former method was considered inpracticable and the latter was adopted. The most cogent objection to it is the great variety of accounting systems and the consequent confusion and opportunity to conceal profit. Owing to the income tax and the increasing ownership by the public of the securities of great corporations, accounting is now much simpler. Some of the difficulty still remains but it is a hindrance—not an insuperable obstacle.

Besides the necessity of revising some prices upward, there will also be a variety of occasions for revising others downward. A method must be devised to adjust the initial frozen price pattern to the changing situation.

We did this during the war by a Price Fixing Commission which reported directly to the President, who passed final judgment and announced the price. There was nothing in the experience of that Commission to suggest that a similar system would not be entirely effective in the future.

The frozen pattern of price will also have to be protected against the situation in export trade. If, as is almost certain, the inflationary process is in operation in the rest of the world, means will have to be applied to prevent extravagant foreign prices from upsetting our domestic schedule. Government, in its world economic strategy, must have almost plenary control over foreign trade. We shall see the agency for such control purchasing for export at the controlled domestic price, selling in export at world price, and using the profit to buy necessitous imports at inflated world prices and to sell to domestic needs at the controlled schedule.

Of course the basis of the present suggestion is price fixing. The student of the economic history of war will say, "There is nothing new about this. Every nation with a debased currency has tried to force acceptance of it at a fiat figure. None has ever succeeded."

One did succeed. It was the price-fixing policy of the World War. The distinction between that and previous attempts was that, for price fixing in 1918, the whole of industry was mobilized and under control of government in a sense never even imagined in any other country or in any other war. This I shall later demonstrate. Another distinction between all previous attempts with which I am familiar (including that of the World War) and the present suggestions is that what is here proposed is that we apply the organization and methods developed in 1918—not *after* rampant inflation has run away with our economic structure—but at the very outset.

As illustrative of these distinctions, New York, in the Revolution (1 Cook's New York Laws 1780, p. 210), enacted a law by which the profits of manufacturers, wages of mechanics and laborers, and the prices of a long list of commodities were fixed at a figure *"not to exceed twenty fold of the prices paid in 1774"*—the latter date was taken as reflecting the normal operation of the law of supply and demand and the "twenty fold" as measuring the debasement of the Continental currency. Here was an attempt to check inflation *after it had occurred*. The basic idea is the same as the one here suggested, except that we now propose to check inflation *before* it occurs.

Similarly, in the 1917 Food Control Act, profits in July, 1914, were set as the maxima for wartime profits of bakeries. The New York price fixing was a failure. The Food Control Act succeeded. Why? The former was a fiat with no adequate means of enforcing it. The latter was backed by the whole system of licensing, commandeering, and regulating powers slowly evolved by our War Administration.

A re-creation of that Administration at the very outset of another war would insure the success of the suggestions here advanced.

IV. The "Nation in Arms"

Your resolution requires you to recommend policies to be pursued in event of war. President Wilson once stated such a policy thus:

The power against which we are arrayed has sought to impose its will upon the world by force. To this end it has increased armament until it has changed the face of war. In the sense in which we have been wont to think of armies, there are no armies in this struggle. There are entire nations armed. Thus the men who remain to till the soil and man the factories are no less a part of the army that is France than the men beneath the battle flags. It must be so with us. It is not an army that we must shape and train for war; it is a nation.

In specific terms, what we seek is:

(1) The adequate supply to our fighting forces of every item in the vast congeries and astonishing volume of things required for modern armies, navies, and air fleets, *when they want it, where they want it, and in the quantity they want it.*

(2) Provision to meet this tremendous additional task of our industry without undue dislocation of its normal functions and without too rigorous deprivation of our civil population.

(3) Maintenance of superiority of economic strength *vis-à-vis* the whole world to the end that we may not fail in the economic struggle which in modern war has become almost if not quite as vital as military conflict.

(4) Avoidance of the economic and social aftermath of war.

We have already lightly touched some of these subjects. Some repetition is necessary. I shall endeavor to keep it at a minimum.

The first problem is how to mobilize our industry. Industrial mobilization requires the creation of a central control agency charged with the entire problem of industrial mobilization. It must:

(a) provide an immediate and effective organization of both supply and demand;

(b) insure proper functioning of the interior control of each such organization and constantly regulate them both;

(c) bring them together, compose their differences, and insure the uninterrupted flow of goods from one to the other.

V. Central Agency to Control Industrial Mobilization

It is impracticable to maintain in peace any such powerful agency as is necessary in war to administer the gigantic effort of national economic mobilization. We should prepare a complete plan for such an organization but even that must be in the broadest of terms. It is impossible to foresee the precise circumstance and requirements of any future war. Perhaps a skeleton organization might be provided for —merely to insure the development of a personnel. The Congress has attempted to do this by making the Assistant Secretary of War responsible for making plans for industrial mobilization. Devoted work has been done in the War Department but there is some danger in this method. It is absolutely impracticable for the War Department to control industrial mobilization because:

(a) It is an economic problem requiring the ablest leadership in industry and utterly unsuited to military administration.

(b) The central control agency must act as arbiter of conflicting demands—the greatest of which is that of the civilian population. No single competitor such as the War Department should be entrusted with such arbitration.

(c) The job of the War Department is our armed forces. That is a big job. To pile on top of it the task of economic mobilization would insure the failure of both.

There is an inevitable tendency in the War Department to forget these principles even in planning. Their function is to say what they want and when and where they want it. The job of industrial control is to see that they get it strictly on their specification. We must neither militarize industry nor industrialize the army. While I do not advocate change in the present law, the facts just stated should forever be borne in mind.

These and other considerations are of equal force against any thought of calling upon any peacetime agency to assume this task. Our industry must, at last analysis, mobilize itself. What is required is leadership of a type that will persuade co-operation in every branch. This leadership must be backed by sanctions of far greater force than can or ought to be used in peace. It is a spontaneous sort of function utterly inappropriate to any imaginable form of bureaucratic organization.

The War Industries Board was slowly developed by a method of trial and error during the war. Its organization was as follows:

(1) The Chairman. All the power of the War Industries Board and complete and undivided responsibility for the performance of its tasks were vested in the Chairman.

The Board was composed of the heads of its grand divisions plus a representative of the Army, the Navy, and Labor, a legal adviser, and, when necessary, the heads of other war administrations were called in—they were always in intimate contact through representatives of grand divisions of the Board or otherwise.

This organization was created on the principle "Committees for counsel—a single responsible head for action." The Board members had no vote. The object was to obtain their views, to discuss their problems in common council, and to co-ordinate their action. As a matter of practice there was never a lack of unanimity and the Chairman never was called upon to overrule a member. This organic principle was carried down through every committee and commission of the Board. The chairman of each was individually and solely responsible and he had undivided authority. As someone has facetiously said, this principle kept the Board from being long and wooden.

The very essence of the Board's positive control of industry lay in three of its functions:

(1) the determination of priorities;
(2) its exclusive control over commandeering;
(3) power to fix the price of basic commodities.

(2) Priorities. The Government, through the Railroad Administration, controlled transportation. Because of the power of government to commandeer supplies and facilities (in some small part definitely expressed by statute delegating some of it to the President and, in large and completely comprehensive part, generally known to reside in Congress) every producer in the country was aware that failure to co-operate with the war measures of government might, and very probably and promptly would, result in the appropriation by government of all that he had. These two sanctions enabled government to obtain complete compliance by industry with the orders and regulations of the Board.

Practical regulation was achieved as follows:

Principal shortages were in transportation, power, fuel, and basic raw materials. In general, the Board prescribed that nothing of these and the other shortage items should be furnished by a supplier to any manufacturer who did not have a so-called Priority certificate. To obtain such a certificate of any grade, every manufacturer had to make to the Priority Division of the Board a satisfactory showing that his proposed use of these materials was one determined by the Board to be essential to the winning of the war.

The flexibility of this system was very great. Priorities could be granted to whole classes of industry or they could be restricted to only a few producers. Priorities were graded from those of the most urgent necessity to those only slightly preferred to normal uses. One of the essential conditions of any priority order was that the recipient must agree to abide by all governmental regulation on pain of forfeiture of his priority.

The priority system proved effective beyond the hopes of its proponents. It affords a method of almost instantly marshalling the industries of the country and thereafter synchronizing and controlling their operation in a far more effective way than if the Government were in actual control and operation of any of them.

The criterion of the priorities administration was that of relative essentiality. Its power to support essential industry and to curtail or cut off less essential uses was very great. By such curtailment or suppression, it released vast quantities of supplies, labor, transportation, power, and money to necessitous uses. By the very complete conspectus of relative need and available facilities and supplies which necessarily developed under its hands, the Board was enabled to know very definitely the location, size, and emergency of most of its major problems. By the utter dependence of both supply and demand on priorities, regulation and co-ordination of both were greatly facilitated. It rendered relatively simple that which (at first sight) seemed complex beyond hope of effective administration.

Other methods of control were used by other war administrations— the most usual being the licensing system typical of Food Administration practice. In this case the statute required a license by the Food Administration to certain classes of manufacturers and distributors of food and it was unlawful for these classes to do business without such license. Like priority orders, these licenses were granted only on condition that the recipient would abide by governmental regulation and were revocable on failure to comply with such conditions.

This system accomplished the same ends as the priority system but I have always regarded the latter as the more flexible.

(3) Commandeering. The true basis of our control of industry was the latent (and in part expressed) power of Congress to commandeer. Portions of this power had been expressed in statutes and delegated either to the President or to other agencies. There was some initial confusion in the exercise of these delegated powers (or the threat of such exercise) by un-co-ordinated users of it. The President finally ordered that no commandeering order should issue without approval of the Chairman of the War Industries Board.

This provision is absolutely essential. The final essence of control of all industrial activity must be lodged in a single responsible pair of hands. If there be one single authority charged with (a) determination of priority, (b) commandeering, and (c) price fixing, then the details of the integration of various war administrations become of less importance and a great flexibility is permissible.

Thus in 1918 we had nine major war administrations. Each of them reported separately to the President. Each was set up independently of the others. The War Industries Board administered everything not controlled by others. For example, one of its functions was control of the iron and steel industry. It is difficult to see why that industry should have been treated in a manner different from that used for the fuel industry. In strict theory, I suppose it could be said that proper co-ordination and control would have dictated the grouping of all these administrations into a single central control agency for war administration.

As a matter of practice, no conflict ever arose. I attribute this to the fact that in the War Industries Board was centered the essence of all control—commandeering, priority, and price fixing. All the administrations were in the hands of very capable men. Methods did not differ greatly. The whole structure was synchronized and co-ordinated by the fact that essential control in the three functions just named was centered in one place.

The actual process of commandeering was simple. A Commandeering Committee was set up to determine the question of just compensation. It was provided that every commandeering order should be signed by the Chief of the Priority Division (representing the Chairman of the Board) and by the Army and Navy representatives on the Board.

In practice the power to commandeer was very rarely used. It remained in the background as the effective persuasive force which vitalized the whole program of regulation.

(4) Price Fixing Commission. The Price Fixing Commission included the Chairman of the War Industries Board, the Fuel Administrator, the Labor Member of the Board, a member of the Tariff Commission, representatives of the Army and the Navy, a representative of Agriculture, and a Chairman of the Commission.

In practice, prices were fixed by agreement. When a necessity arose to consider a price, the expert staff of the Federal Trade Commission was called in to investigate costs. The particular branch of industry affected was represented either by the appropriate War Service Committee, hereinafter described, or otherwise as it should elect. Organized demand was represented by the appropriate Commodity Committee of the Board and the procurement officials directly affected. The Commission itself sat in a quasi judicial capacity. While doubtless the resulting "agreement" as to particular price schedules was somewhat influenced by the latent control of the Board, there has never been, to my knowledge, any charge that prices so determined were either discriminating or unfair to industry on the one hand, or burdensome and extravagant to the public interest on the other. Prices were fixed for stated periods and subject to revision on hearings.

The President finally passed upon the agreed price and announced it to the public.

With the whole price schedule crystallized at the outset, as is here suggested, the function of the Commission would come into play only when necessity appeared for changes in the fixed maximum prices. Price control would be much simplified.

(5) Commodity Committees. Industrial production falls into two natural classifications—raw material and finished products. The Board had a division for each. The head of each division had under him a group of so-called Commodity Committees—one for each principal grouping of commodities. There were in all sixty of such committees. In the raw materials division, for instance, there was one committee for iron and steel; one each for copper, zinc, and brass, one for each of the ferro alloys, one for each principal metal and chemical, and so forth throughout the whole list of raw materials. Under the Commissioner of Finished Products there were similar committees for finished goods, as, for example, one for each: machine tools, cranes, chains, boots and shoes, cotton goods, and so forth throughout the whole list of products.

Each committee was composed of a chairman expert in the subject assigned to it but divorced from financial interest in any company within it. Representatives of each procurement agency were members and also such assistants as the Chairman or Chief might choose.

The method of functioning of these committees is more fully described under the heading "Organization of Demand." Briefly, to each of them was assigned responsibility for supervision of both organized supply and organized demand in the subject assigned to it. They studied requirements, investigated sources of supply, suggested conservation, priority, curtailment, and price schedules, worked out means to increase supply or render it more available, brought supply and demand into contact, allocated facilities, regulated prices in contracts, and were responsible for delays in production due to failure of transportation, power and fuel, raw material, or labor supply. Most problems were settled by conference between those affected but, where something more was needed, each committee was merely auxiliary to the grand divisions of the Board and, at the call of the Chairman of the Committee, the whole vast power of the Board was instantly available to him. The Commodity Committees were thus the working points of the grand divisions of the Board, just as those grand divisions constituted the support and sanction of the Commodity Committees.

Opposite to each Commodity Committee of the Board was a War Service Committee—more fully described under the heading "Organization of Supply." These committees were the "war overhead" of each branch of organized industry—which branches fell into the same classifications as the Commodity Committees of the Board. They were usually composed of the leaders in the branch of industry to which each pertained. While the War Service Committees were purely voluntary on the part of each industry, no industry could afford to neglect their formation, since they were the most efficient if not the sole method of organized representation at the seat of power and were thus quite as necessary to industry as to government.

Thus with organized *demand* classified and represented by membership on each Commodity Committee of the Board and organized *supply* classified and represented by a War Service Committee in daily contact with the Board, and with the powerful and searching power of the grand divisions of the Board behind each Commodity Committee—control of both supply and demand was systematized, sufficient, and complete.

(6) Conservation. The function and effects of conservation have been sufficiently described. The organization consisted in another Division of the Board which surveyed the whole field of possibilities and instituted the studies that were necessary to arrive at decisions. The projects thus instituted as policies were perfected and executed through the Commodity Committees, which were able to move systematically on a broad front through the whole of organized industry and bring matters to conclusions with a rapidity not possible in peacetime administration. Here, also, regulation once promulgated had the whole power of the Board behind it and was invariably effective.

(7) New Sources of Supply and Substitution of Uses. Enough has been said in description of the Commodity Committees and the grand divisions of the Board to make clear, with a word, its other principal functions.

Whenever shortages developed in any item, there was immediately instituted a searching study of substitution and new sources. These studies were carried out simultaneously through the whole fabric of industry by the Commodity Committees. When such study indicated new *foreign* sources, the power of the Board in the field of international economic strategy was immediately called into play. Some of the incidents of this administration were almost romantic. We withheld Swedish iron from the Central Powers by buying it ourselves, persuaded Chile to disgorge nitrates by the discovery that her gold reserve was sequestrated in a Berlin bank, cajoled from Spain the mules she had refused us by dangling before her a supply of ammonium phosphate for which she was starving, procured jute at a reasonable price by threatening to cease the withdrawal of silver dollars from our monetary circulation which we had done to stabilize Indian currency, etc., etc. It was a varied control and we were enabled to exercise it solely because of the perfection of economic organization which was erected on the principles here advocated.

(8) Industrial Control Outside the Board. There were nine War Administrations outside the War Industries Board. They will be discussed here only as their functions contribute to the principle of economic administration here considered.

a. *The control of money.* Money was controlled on exactly the theories here described for the control of other commodities.

A Capital Issues Committee was constituted and the sale of all securities in our money market without the approval of this Committee was practically prohibited. Such approval was given only when the purpose of the issue was for an effort or enterprise contributory to victory and consonant with the policies here outlined.

A War Finance Corporation was created to provide federal financial assistance to essential enterprises. A moment's reflection will reveal the universal principle of the present suggestions at work here. The short supply was being rationed and allocated to essential uses. Priority was being given such uses. Conservation was being practiced by interdicting the use of money for non-essential uses. When these other means were insufficient, additional supply was provided by the War Finance Corporation. The net effect was to:

(1) Increase the available supply of money.

(2) Prevent inflation by inhibition of competing, conflicting, and wasteful uses.

(3) Add strength and flexibility to our whole fiscal structure.

What is the use of vain talk of drafting dollars when dollars can be made to serve every purpose of government by the regulation of their use?

This fiscal administration was carried on in such close relation with the administration of the Board and in such complete accord with, and support of, its policies that it might as well be considered as having been a part of the Board organization.

b. *The control of man-power.* To the extent that the interdiction or curtailment of less essential enterprises and the whole priority and conservation programs of the Board affected the supply of labor, that supply was in control of the Board. But the great central administration of man-power was (under the Selective Service Law) in the hands of the Provost Marshal General.

The Selective Service Law classified most of the able-bodied men of the nation in the inverse order of their necessity to industry and agriculture and then made those in the advanced classes liable to selection for military service. It left key men in industry untouched but it made great inroads into the available supply of industrial labor.

In practice the Provost Marshal General kept in close touch with the Board. He placed in deferred classes those groups of men who were employed in important positions in industries determined by the Board to be essential. Before planning particular drafts he consulted with the Board to determine where to get them.

But there was in the Selective Service Law a provision profoundly affecting the labor supply which was not utilized until the spring of 1918 when it first saw the light of day as the famous "Work or Fight" order.

Even in the classes under the draft which were otherwise available for military service there were hundreds of thousands of able-bodied men who, by reason of their domestic relations or of late members in the list prescribing the order of call, were deferred temporarily or completely. The Work or Fight order merely said to these men:

"No matter what the grounds for your deferment may be, unless you are faithfully, continuously and usefully employed in a capacity and for an enterprise determined by the Government to be essential to the prosecution of the war, your deferment will be cancelled and you will immediately be called for service with the colors."

I note that the Joint Resolution prohibits any consideration of the conscription of labor. We have heard a good deal of a slogan: "Draft every dollar, every thing, and every man." The attempt to draft labor is as impossible and dangerous as the attempt to draft dollars. It has been attempted several times in a small way in the war history of the country and it has never succeeded. Fortunately no informed and responsible authority ever advocated any general draft of labor. The ill-considered argument that has been advanced is:

"If the nation goes to war as a unit—if the men who remain in industry are as much a part of the national war-team as the men who march with the colors—why should not the same principles apply at least to both of these cases? Why should men in industry, in whatever capacity, be rewarded by inflated war wages which they may accept or decline in their own discretion? Why should they not be drafted on exactly the same principle as soldiers?"

That labor should be inordinately rewarded is unnecessary, wrong, and—under the plan here suggested—easily avoidable, but *not* by drafting men to work for other men. A soldier serves the nation directly. There is but one master in the case and that master is America. He serves to profit no one but the country as a whole. There is no distinction between him and his comrades. He enters an immemorial status. His entry is not contractual. He is clothed, fed, housed, and attended.

As long as our present industrial organization maintains, industry is in the hands of millions of private employers. It is operated for profit to them. The employee therefore serves in private industry operating for gain. Enforced and involuntary service for a private master is and has been clearly and repeatedly defined by our Supreme Court as slavery inhibited by the Thirteenth Amendment to the Constitution of the United States.

If any such provision were made, it might be used to break a perfectly justifiable strike and so at one sweep destroy all the social advance of our labor system in the last century.

All this does not say, however, that men not under military discipline are free agents in war. The Government cannot say, "Work here. Work there," or "Work for Mr. A." But it can say—as it did say in 1918: "Work or Fight!" That principle was barely invoked, but it was and is capable of immense expansion. The Government can specify classes of employment for which, in emergency, women, men without the draft age limits, and men not fully capacitated for military service are sufficient. It can specify whole classes of employment which are not considered essential at all and, as we have seen, can say, "Every man not in military service—whatever may be his domestic or other circumstance warranting deferment or exemption—must be usefully and faithfully employed in an occupation essential to the military purposes of the nation." It can go much further. It can say that if a man be called and found unfit for military service but fit for other work in the essential lists, he must so employ himself or be cut off from rations, transportation, fuel, and supplies. Also, in the organization of the nation here considered, there is the force of public opinion more potent than any governmental compulsion. If our organization for the next war proceeds from the lessons learned in 1918, our man-power will be so classified and organized that no man can shirk and show his face among his fellows.

The draft of men for industrial employment is not only impossible.

It is wholly unnecessary. The Work or Fight method is a better way. It is compatible with our institutions and far more effective than any chain-gang or impressment that could be invented.

There is no doubt that in any future major emergency there must be just such a control of human effort as has here been suggested. The productive effort of war must be very much greater than the productive effort of peace and it must be made at a time when the very cream of the country's physical man-power is being withdrawn by millions from productive effort. Such vast demands can be met only if everybody goes to work.

Labor policy and industrial disputes were also under a separate "War Labor Policies Board," but a close integration through the Labor Member of the Board prevented any conflict in this respect.

c. *War Trade Board.* Complete control of exports and imports—indeed of all war trade—is an absolute necessity to the success of the plan developed in this memorandum. It has a profound effect on the worldwide economic strategy to which I have hitherto adverted. During the World War it was handled by a separate administration called the War Trade Board, but (as with the other such functions just described) it was all done in such close contact with the work of the Board that there was no conflict or lost motion whatever.

The only point to emphasize in respect of this and the other war administrations mentioned below is that each is a necessary part of the perfected whole of war organization which is so necessary to make this country the very powerful unit which I have tried to picture here. As I have said, centralization of the essence of war powers—i.e., commandeering, price fixing, and priority—in the hands of one agency will synchronize and co-ordinate the efforts of all others whether they be formally attached to it or not.

The other necessary war administrations were: Food, Fuel, Shipping, and Railroads. Enough has been said of the functions of each to make the entire picture clear without further repetition.

So much for the organization of the Central Control Agency—call it Industrial Strategy Board, War Industries Board, Administration of Resources, or what you will. Briefly, to recapitulate, it consists of:

I: *A Chairman* in whom is vested complete and final authority and responsibility, subject to appeal to the President.

II: The following Divisions:
   (a) Priority (to determine preference of all uses).
   (b) Commandeering (to enforce all regulations).

II: The following Divisions:—(*Continued*)

(c) Price Fixing (to make or adjust price schedules).

(d) Conservation (to regulate, prohibit, or substitute uses and to discover new sources of supply).

(e) Commodity Committees or Sections. (These are in two groups under a Raw Materials and a Finished Products division. Each is a miniature War Industries Board for each one of the separate branches into which Industry naturally divides itself. They are the working points of the Board and are supported by all the powers of the Board.)

III: Other War Administrations in close contact with the Board:

(a) Food.

(b) Fuel.

(c) Shipping.

(d) War Trade.

(e) Railroads.

(f) War Labor Policy.

(g) War Finance and Capital Issues.

(h) Provost Marshal General.

VI. Organization of Demand

Demand in time of war flows from the procurement agencies of (a) the Army, (b) the Navy, (c) the civilian population, (d) auxiliary agencies which arise in time of war. For example, in the late war these were the Allies, the Shipping Board and Emergency Fleet Corporation, the Red Cross, Salvation Army, and so forth.

At the beginning of the war these agencies, with procurement programs of such tremendous volume as had never been seen in the history of the world, rushed into our markets. They were absolutely unco-ordinated. The right hand knew not what the left hand did. They competed with each other on prices, for the use of facilities, and for delivery. The result was a tremendous increase in price, the congestion of certain areas and certain factories beyond any possibility of efficiency, and a general condition of chaos in industrial production which actually threatened the continuity of supply.

The War Department alone maintained at first five and toward the end of the war eight separate procuring agencies. The Navy had only one such agency and, generally speaking, all other procurement bodies had only one. The demands of the separate Allies were not well co-ordinated.

One of the first steps toward the elimination of waste, inflation, excess cost, and confusion will be to insure that no such situation shall ever again develop in a future war.

The War Department still clings to its plan of multiple purchasing agencies. They are prescribed by statute. While, in the opinion of most industrial observers, the method is unnecessary, archaic, and costly, there has as yet been no change and it is probable that change will be difficult. The War Department has attempted to co-ordinate these activities by providing that no two of the War Department's agencies shall be utilized for the purchase of the same thing. This same theory was applied during the latter part of the war, but never with complete success; and, while it is probable that important difficulties will be raised in another emergency by this system, I believe that they will be somewhat minimized by the steps the War Department has taken and the greater knowledge it now has of the trouble occasioned by its peculiar form of organization.

The first necessity for effective organization of demand is the assembly into one central control agency (or the direct control by one central authority) of the responsible head of each of the great procurement or supply agencies. To that central forum (which, as we have seen, and shall see in more detail, also controls organized supply) they must bring

First: A general statement of their procurement programs in finished goods and also broken down into initial estimates of their bulk requirements of such basic commodities as steel, wool, copper, etc.

This is difficult not only in the early days of a war, but also during war, because of the rapidly changing military situation. Nevertheless it is necessary to make the best possible estimates to the end that the central planning agency may make preparation to provide the necessary raw materials and fabricating facilities.

Second: They must bring to the same central agency currently during the entire period of the emergency the specific orders that they intend to place with industry.

This is necessary because, in order to prevent competition and congestion of facilities, to insure that the manufacturers with whom such orders are to be placed shall have prompt and adequate supply of raw material, labor, power, transportation, and sometimes capital, and to carry out other features of mobilization, the central agency must allocate these orders to particular facilities, fix the price to be paid, and insure the prompt provision of the necessary constituent materials.

In practice the tremendous volume and variety of the things and types required by such orders is impossible of clearance by any one control unit. Industry groups itself naturally into strata of commodities or cognate lines of endeavor. Thus there is a leather industry, an iron and steel industry, a chemical industry, a textile industry. Each procurement division has a separate buying department for each of these industrial groupings. As we have seen in the central control agency, there is a Commodity Committee for each of these groupings. Each Committee is composed of men of leader-calibre who are experts in the particular industrial stratum involved. In the War Industries Board the head of each governmental commodity procurement subsection actually sat on the particular Commodity Committee of the Board in which he was interested. For each of these groupings in industry there was a so-called War Service Committee corresponding to each Commodity Committee of the Board. Each War Service Committee was composed of interested leaders of its branch of industry who were usually the principal figures in the Trade Associations of that industry. These men were intimately familiar with their particular branch of industry. They presented its problems promptly and were able to advise the corresponding Commodity Committee of the Board on all perplexing questions that arose. By bringing the heads of each procurement sub-section into contact with the appropriate War Service Committee in the forum of the proper War Industries Board Commodity Committee, organized "demand," organized "supply," and the governmental control agency were placed in intimate contact and co-operation. The method proved itself.

In such contacts bulk requirements were determined and plans made to meet them. All particular commodity procurement programs of the government and associated agencies were then co-ordinated and synchronized to the avoidance of conflict and the insurance of supply. Details of the application of the general principles discussed in this memorandum were practically all determined in this manner.

It is not for a moment intended to say that this system functioned perfectly. Indeed it did not get into really effective practice until the summer of 1918, but it did progress far enough to enable every informed observer to conclude, "*This is the way to organize demand and supply in any future emergency and completely to avoid the folly, waste, and loss of frenzied competition.*"

It must be remembered that the bulk of wartime requirements will still be for the civil population. The latter demand is not subject to organization and representation on the above plan. Nevertheless one of the prime purposes of war administration is to see to it that the public does not suffer unnecessarily. It follows that in all allocations and priorities the Chairman of the Commodity Committee is the representative of the public. He constantly studies the public demand and every act of his is controlled by that necessity.

While only the heads of grand divisions or Commodity Committees of the Board had the sole power of decision on any matter within their jurisdiction, any of the procurement representatives had the right of appeal to the Chairman of the Board. As a matter of fact, there was only one appeal in the entire history of the Board and that controversy was merely referred back and settled by agreement and without further appeal.

The method here so sketchily outlined will be effective in any emergency for the organization of supply and demand and their complete control by whatever central agency it is decided to set up.

Further organization of demand is accomplished by the integration of higher departments or officials of the various procurement agencies with the Central Control Agency already discussed.

For example, as active members of the War Industries Board itself, there was an officer of high rank from each the Army and the Navy. These men were in daily contact with all the problems of the Board. They participated in all its deliberations and even in its organization. They were part of it.

Similarly each principal procurement agency had responsible representatives sitting in all the grand divisions of the Board, and usually these men were the officials of those departments of the procurement agencies most directly interested in the work of the grand division on the Board of which they were themselves members.

VII. *Organization of Supply*

Some of the details of supply organization have already been necessarily stated here and there in the foregoing paragraphs. To recapitulate, under the guidance of the Central Control Agency (and in the Great War this was done through co-operation of the U. S. Chamber of Commerce) the various trade associations voluntarily create War Service Committees composed of leaders in each industry. These Committees represent the industry in its contact with the central control. They provide for whatever further organization or closer contact of companies within their industry is necessary. The final result is that each of the different branches or strata in the whole of industry is organized within itself and is represented in Washington by an appropriate War Service Committee.

If this sort of organization seems loose and impracticable now, it is simply because the war is thirteen years away. We forget the great surge of enthusiasm and idealism which engulfed our country in 1918. People were not seeking to obstruct government—they were grateful for any leadership which could show them the way to aid government. The sacrifice and devotion of American businessmen in the emergency is an unwritten history. Through the organization of industry here suggested, competition was adjourned. Companies within each branch of industry pooled patents, trade secrets, facilities, and resources. Only a telegraphic request was ever necessary to bring immediately to Washington the busiest heads of the greatest industrial concerns in the country. Responses to any suggestion were instantaneous and the final result was a solidarity and a co-operation the effects of which remain in our industries to this day.

Neither should the force of public opinion be overlooked. There was no shirking in that war and there will be none in another war for the simple reason that nobody could lead this country into a war without aroused and enthusiastic public opinion behind him.

The thought is often expressed: "If we can solve our industrial problems in war by this method, why can't we use the same methods in peace?" The answer is: Incentives in peace are individual freedom and the hope of reward. Incentives in war are love of country, idealism, and defense against a common danger. President Wilson struck the keynote of the whole matter when he said:

The highest and best form of efficiency is the spontaneous co-operation of a free people.

However harsh may appear the principles of control here announced, it must be kept in mind that there was no harshness in their application. We regulated only where it was necessary to regulate in order to avoid confusion. Industry mobilized itself. The great bulk of accomplishment must be credited to spontaneous enthusiasm and self-abnegation and not to artificial control.

VIII. Statutory Requirements

As I have said, I do not favor an involved statute attempting to anticipate the requirements of another war.

I think plans should be made and revised yearly. I think some steps should be taken to keep selected industrial leaders informed of these plans so that when the principal actors in the 1918 mobilization pass from the scene there will be a nucleus of personnel to take their places. I do not believe that we can go further.

But for a very special reason I do believe that there should be one statute on the books, the very existence of which would be a constant warning to everybody that never again in America will any man make as much profit in war as he can make in peace. There need be nothing complex nor involved about it. Purely for purposes of discussion I have prepared a rough draft eliminating enacting clauses and formalities. It follows:

That, whenever Congress shall declare war or the existence of an emergency due to the imminence of war, then, from and after a date prior to such declaration which date the President is hereby authorized and directed to determine and announce, it shall be unlawful for any person to buy, sell or otherwise contract for any service, right, or thing at a higher rate, rent, price, wage, commission, or reward than was in effect at the date so determined.

Whenever in the sole discretion of the President he shall determine that any maximum price, wage, rent, rate, commission, or reward should be adjusted either upward or downward, he is hereby authorized to make and proclaim such adjustment and such adjustment shall have the full force and effect under this statute of such price, wage, rent, rate, cómmission, or reward before such adjustment.

During the period of any war or emergency declared by Congress hereunder, the President is authorized to determine, and by proclamation announce, what classes of public service, or of dealers or manufacturers of any article or commodity, shall be required to operate under licenses, to fix the conditions of such licenses, and to grant licenses under such conditions. After such determination by the President it shall be unlawful for any public service, dealer, or manufacturer in such determined classes to engage in business without such license.

During the period of any war or emergency declared by Congress hereunder, the President is authorized to determine the order of priority in which any manufacturer, dealer, or public service in the United States shall fill customer's or other orders and after such determination it shall be unlawful for any such manufacturer, dealer, or public service to fill such orders in any other order of priority.

There should also be enacted a general commandeering statute giving the President plenary authority in the usual terms to commandeer in time of war any manufacturing facility or any supplies deemed by him necessary to the successful conduct of war.

In addition to some such statutes as these, the essential principles of the Overman Act (approved May 28, 1918) should be re-enacted authorizing the President in time of war to make such redistribution of functions of executive departments as he may determine.

This is all the statutory authority that should be attempted in time of peace. Additional war legislation will of course be necessary, but the presence of these statutes would be notice to the world that we will enter the next world conflict effectually organized and that we shall conduct it without inflation and with no war profits to any man.

IX. Constitutional Amendment Unwise and Unnecessary

I am no authority on Constitutional Law and I have consulted none. But I am familiar with the wartime discussions of this subject and I also know the practical side of it.

The whole structure of wartime control of American industry was built on the right of Congress to commandeer property in war. This Government has always had this right, has frequently exercised it, and has never been denied it by the courts. It is plenary and subject to the sole conditions of due process and just compensation. Certainly at no time during the World War—nor so far as I have ever heard during any war—has this Government ever been hindered or embarrassed in wartime administration by any restriction on this Constitutional power. While our regulatory power, built upon this right, was frequently used, the requisitory power was seldom used. It served rather as a reservoir of persuasive force which proved amply sufficient to provide prompt and general acquiescence in all federal regulation of industry we ever found necessary to war administration.

This brings us to the question of Constitutional restrictions on the right to commandeer. The only ones I know are the "due process" clause and the Fifth Amendment: "Nor shall private property be taken for public use *without just compensation.*"

Your resolution does not specifically direct that you inquire whether this provision should be repealed, although there is a clear suggestion that you may have to consider that as the only way to eliminate war profits and equalize war burdens. For reasons I have fully discussed, I think no such amendment is necessary. For further reasons, I think that the mere suggestion of such an amendment is unwise.

I see only two possible purposes of a right in government to take private property without just compensation:

(1) To provide funds for the prosecution of war.

(2) To impress facilities for production or transportation on the

theory that material things can be had with more speed or at less price or in greater quantity by federal operation.

Confiscation as a means for financing war. The total of our expenditure for the World War was thirty-nine and one-half billion dollars. The nearest antecedent census estimate of total national wealth was one hundred and eighty-six billions in 1912, of which only 1.4 billions was in gold and silver bullion. Real estate, plant, and equipment (including railroads) was $141,000,000,000. Transportation systems (except railroads) was $10,000,000,000, and all other forms of wealth (agricultural, manufactured and mining products, clothing, furniture, carriages, etc.) was $34,000,000,000. It is interesting to inquire how the war could have been financed by confiscating any or all of these items. The billion and a half in hard money would not have been a drop in the bucket if all had been taken. As to the seizure of physical properties, their use for finance would require resale. But who, under the patent threat of reconfiscation, would buy such properties? And since such capital levies would of course first reach the more liquable forms of wealth, who would have anything to buy them with? There may be an idea that seizure would nevertheless finance war because we would simply take war material without paying for it. The error in this is that there is no considerable amount of material available for war under peace conditions. It has to be manufactured from raw resources. The bulk of all fabricated costs are labor costs. We cannot conscript labor; therefore we would have to pay labor and that requires finance. There being no available war material for seizure, no one would expend his money to produce war material merely to have it seized as fast as he made it and without reimbursement. The whole idea is absurd.

There has been a good deal of talk of drafting dollars. Even if there were ample Constitutional authority, there is a very cogent reason why that could not be done. Every man with fair warning that his dollars were about to be taken away from him and never given back would cause them to disappear with amazing rapidity on the first rumor of war. The experience of France and Germany in attempting to draw existing distributed supplies of gold into their treasuries for war purposes clears this point. The gold went into stockings, baking powder cans, and other convenient receptacles and these into the ground. Panic-stricken efforts in every direction to avoid such confiscations would disarrange the whole fiscal structure of the country and, adding to the general confusion and dislocation caused by invocation of the broad principles of confiscation, would paralyze the country's sinews of war at the outset. No project more destructive of adequate defense could be conceived.

It is also pertinent to ask on what theory of assessment could such confiscation of property for financing war proceed. If—as under the present theory of commandeering *with compensation*—the new idea would be simply that the Government should take the first property that came to hand arbitrarily and without equalization, we could have a complete subversion of the very purpose of all government. No such political system ever existed and there can be no question that such is not the purpose of the suggestion. If the thought be that government shall take equably from all those who own, it is simply a process of capital levy in the form of tax. Nothing in our war experience has ever indicated a necessity for this. No belligerent nation of the World War even at the limit of its extremity ever adopted the capital levy, and it seems unnecessary to believe that the resolution intended such a thought in this connection.

This Government has unlimited power of taxation in the fields allotted it by the Constitution—by income tax, by duties, imposts, excises and all forms of indirect taxation, and by capitation or direct tax in proportion to census determinations. The power to tax is the power ultimately to appropriate and in this nation it is sufficient to any current levy that ought (in prudent administration) ever to be assessed against any generation in any single year.

I think I was the very first advocate of the plan to take the profit out of war and to make every man, dollar, and thing bear an even proportion of the burdens of war. I hold no brief for especial protection of wealth in war, but my experience tells me that the draft of dollars is quite as absurd and impossible as the draft of labor. For reasons elsewhere considered, such wholesale impressment is both impossible and unnecessary, but in the considerations under this heading it is crazy. The fiscal strength of a nation lies not in what government owns *but in what its people own*. The sinews of war are not dollars—they are efforts. In order to produce things, money is necessary, but it is not necessary that government *own* the money by taking it away from the people who do. Monetary wealth is potential productive capacity just exactly as a factory is and, exactly as the factory capacity of the country must be administered, rationed, and controlled for war purposes in order that the vastly increased demands of war may be met and, at the same time, that the normal requirements of the civil population be not denied, so must wealth be similarly administered, rationed, and controlled. The method of doing this has been fully discussed. There is no more reason to confiscate wealth in order to make it work for government than there is reason to confiscate factories for the same purpose. Simply put it to work where it will best serve the public good.

Confiscation of facilities as a means for insuring production. The "Draft Everything" proponents seem to think that confiscation of productive facilities promises a more effective use of them in the interests of government and for the purposes of war. During the World War, government had power to commandeer factories and to operate them under bureaucratic direction. I do not recall a single important industrial enterprise that was thus taken over. This does not mean that the use of the power was never advocated. On the contrary, it was seriously urged in respect of a great industrial plant which was thought by some not to be giving full co-operation to its government. The proposal split on the rock of this argument:

"Who will run it? Do you know another manufacturer fit to take over its administration? Would you replace a proved expert manager by a problematical mediocrity? After you had taken it over and installed your government employee as manager, what greater control would you have then than now? *Now* you can choke it to death, deprive it of transportation, fuel, and power, divert its business, strengthen its rivals. Could any disciplinary means be more effective? If you take it over, you can only give orders to an employee backed by threat of dismissal and with far less effect than you can give them now. Let the management run the plant and you run the management."

Nobody with any familiarity with industry could seriously urge a wholesale assumption by any federal bureau of the responsibility for management of any or all of the vast congeries of manufacturing establishments upon which we must rely for extraordinary effort in event of war. Even if such bureau management could prove adequate to the task (which it could never do), the mere process of change would destroy efficiency at the outset.

The industrial pattern of the United States is a delicate mesh of inter-related strands. It has been evolved in response to the needs of the nation and under natural economic law but is dimly understood. It is a sensitive living organism, and the injection of arbitrary and artificial interference could be attempted only at the risk of starting a sequence of upheavals, the ends of which no man can foresee. To approach it, on the advent of war, bearing in one hand demands for a vast stepping-up of output and a heavy draft on its man-power and, in the other, a broadaxe of governmental confiscation with which to wreck its vitals—is no way to win a war.

There may remain some question as to whether wholesale price fixing might not itself be construed as a taking of private property without just compensation. Of course, just compensation is usually taken as "market value." I know of no better way of assessing market value than to refer to the actually existing schedule of prices as they stand under the influence of the law of supply and demand. That is exactly what the present suggestion contemplates as the standard. It would be difficult, I think, to spell confiscation out of that.

There should be no Constitutional amendment, not only because it would be unwise and destructive but because it is wholly unnecessary.

X. *Conclusion*

I am confidently of the belief that, on the policies here briefly outlined, this country would achieve the following benefits:

(1) It would pass from a peace to a war status with a minimum of confusion, waste, and loss.

(2) It would mobilize war supplies almost as quickly as it could mobilize men.

(3) It would reduce the cost of war by 50% and I believe by an even greater figure.

(4) It would eliminate war profits and inflation.

(5) It would preserve its credit and its economic prestige throughout the world.

(6) Its war effort would be conducted with less interference with normal economic processes and the lives of the civil population than has ever been the experience of any nation in the history of the world.

(7) It would conserve its resources and preserve the morale of its people to such an extent that it would be able to outlive any antagonist in a long-drawn struggle.

(8) It could pass from a war status back to a peace status with a minimum of the prostrating economic aftermath that has hitherto been the invariable experience of every ex-belligerent in a great war.

(9) The efficiency of the combined military and economic machine that could be derived from these policies would constitute this nation an instrument for war effective beyond the imagination of any military expert even of this advanced date—powerful beyond the possibilities of any antagonist and perhaps of any combination of antagonists.

(10) Considering the obvious fact that the military aspirations of this nation will never disturb the peace of the world, the mere acceptance of (and deliberate provision for) the kind of organization here suggested would go very far toward keeping the peace of the world.

And the last result, I take it, is the hope and aim of all of us.

SUPPLEMENTARY STATEMENT SUBMITTED TO THE WAR POLICIES COMMISSION IN SUPPORT OF THE MEMORANDUM SUBMITTED MARCH 6, 1931

I. General Statement

A MONG the many distinguished witnesses before this Commission
there is expressed a variety of opinion on the suggestion of war
policies submitted by me on March 6. While all do not concur fully,
none is in total disagreement. There is some opinion which springs
from a misapprehension of the policies proposed and some from a lack
of knowledge of what was done. For the convenience of the Commission, out of deference to the earnestness of the witnesses themselves,
and also because I believe most sincerely in the soundness of the plan
submitted, it has seemed to me appropriate to digest and attempt to
answer every instance of dissent.

As a result of a further study of the Constitutional aspects of the
suggestion and the bearing upon them of certain expressions in post-
war decisions of our federal courts, the skeletonized statute which was
submitted in my earlier testimony has been modified and amplified
and is appended.

On pages 28 to 50 [1] of the record, I epitomized the organization and
method of industrial mobilization for war as developed in 1917–1918.

In no testimony did I discern any dissent from this broad outline
which was generally concurred in by Commander Ralph T. O'Neil
representing the American Legion (p. 8), former Commander Paul V.
McNutt (p. 206), General Palmer E. Pierce (p. 145), Commander
John M. Hancock (p. 153), Colonel Leonard P. Ayres (p. 165), Daniel
Willard (pp. 170, 171), George N. Peek (p. 219), Eugene Meyer
(p. 238), Ex-Assistant Secretary of War Charles B. Robbins (p. 253),
General C. C. Williams (p. 283), Julius Barnes, Chairman of the
U. S. Chamber of Commerce (p. 287), Howard Coffin (p. 306), and
Homer Ferguson (p. 317). As I read the testimony of Ex-Secretary
of War Newton D. Baker (p. 124), he also concurred in this suggested
organization with a qualification, excepting what he called a "little
war." With that qualification, I am in complete agreement. I understand that what is proposed by Gen. Douglas MacArthur is in agreement as to broad organizational outline. I submit herewith an
organization chart showing the system as it existed in 1918.

---

[1] All page numbers refer to the printed record of the War Policies Commission
hearings, published in three volumes by the Government Printing Office.

Such disagreement as I observe in the testimony centers chiefly on the plan for general price stabilization. The comment on this subject was so varied as to require systematic and comprehensive treatment in this reply.

In the first place, it must be made clear that the proposed enabling statute (see Appendix) vesting power in the President to determine a day as of which the statute speaks to stabilize prices is discretionary and not mandatory. This is necessary for two reasons: (1) as Mr. Baker pointed out, it might not be required in a minor war; (2) no one can foresee the circumstance of future conflict. A situation is conceivable in which none of the policies of 1917–1918 would be appropriate.

Also, while I thought I had exhausted ingenuity to make clear my suggestion as to price stabilization, things that some witnesses have said to me in conversation and much that is contained in the record convinces me that I was not altogether successful. At the risk of prolixity, I want at the outset to try to restate more clearly just what I do propose.

I do *not* suggest the fixation of any price. The effect of the proposed statute is simply to say, "Unless later adjusted by the President upward, no price *shall rise above* the figure at which it stood at a certain named day." In a word, we clamp a ceiling down on the existing price structure. All prices are free to fluctuate below that maximum.

Next, what is proposed is not the artificial determination of price by fiat or otherwise. There was not a single witness who did not propose *price fixing*. Those who opposed me want to fix prices individually. Now that means studying the costs of a few producers selected by design or at random and (based upon such study) taking somebody's *judgment* as to what a particular price should be. My proposal suggests initially nothing of the kind. It addresses the whole interrelated pattern of prices as it exists under natural economic law and says of it, "Since arbitrary governmental rationing will henceforth govern supply and governmental determination of priority— and not price—will control demand, we propose to keep intact this last natural price schedule which we are likely to see for many a day."

It is a preservation of a natural determination rather than substitution of a collection of artificial determinations, and I think I can show later that it is the only fundamentally sound way in which the problem can be handled under the usual circumstances of the coming of war.

Some witnesses seemed to think that, once this existing maximum is established, there are to be no changes. I tried to make it clear that there is at once to be set up a competent tribunal to adjust any maximum prices, either upward or downward, whether to cure incidental injustice or hardship or to increase production. That, of course, will inject artificiality, but artificiality will be the exception and not the rule, as would be the case with plans which propose fixing the prices of basic commodities separately. On the other hand, some witnesses say, "He proposes to freeze prices and then immediately to unfreeze them." I propose to unfreeze nothing. I propose to adjust the few exceptions. Those who suggest partial price fixing propose to create what amounts to an entire artificial price structure and (as I shall later show), because they leave the generality of prices free, they will be obliged to adjust fixed prices so frequently— and always upward—that, at least in the usual circumstances of war, they would perhaps better leave the whole schedule free.

With so much said by way of explanation, what I propose is to have a statute which shall say in effect, "From and after a day to be determined by the President, it shall be unlawful to charge a *higher price* for anything than was in effect on that day, except that the President may and will (to relieve hardship or meet an exigency of war) adjust any particular price either upward or downward."

One misunderstanding I have discovered and am particularly happy to clear up is this: Some witnesses construed my language to mean that the President is not to select M-Day or approximately M-Day— the beginning of the war—but that he is to reach far back (let us say 90 days as a fixed period), in search of "normal" relationships notwithstanding substantial changes that may have occurred in the interim. Of course, if in such meantime, there has been a marked inflation, to go back to a period of lower prices would constitute confiscation in many cases. Such was not the intent. The reason for not naming M-Day in the statute is that, in the usual circumstances of the advent of war, the first thing that happens is a marked and sometimes panicky price depression. Since the frozen schedule is one of maxima—a kind of ceiling clamped down on the whole price structure—one purpose of providing for a slight leeway was to prevent an abnormal *depression* from governing future price.

As I shall later show, it does not make a great deal of difference what day the President selects. His task is to select one reflecting the instant conditions and the fewest number of distortions. Since his very next step is to set up a Commission to adjust distortions and injustices, another purpose of giving some little leeway in naming the day is to minimize the work of that Commission and to determine a day, the circumstance of which seems fairest and wisest—all things considered.

I now understand from Gen. George Van H. Moseley that the opposition of the War Department to general stabilization was largely based on this misunderstanding, and now that this has been cleared up there is no substantial disagreement between the War Department and myself on this subject.

II. The excess profits tax is not a substitute for price stabilization.

Senator Swanson has brought out by questions to nearly every witness an opinion by some that, by letting prices rise to magnificent heights, we can induce extraordinary effort by holding out hope of extravagant profits and then later frustrate that hope by an excess profits tax which shall recapture 80 per cent of such profits. Other witnesses seemed to think that all the equalization of war burdens that would ever be necessary or practicable could be accomplished by the excess profits tax. For example, on page 135 of the record appears the following colloquy:

Senator Swanson: . . . During the war prices were fixed so as to stimulate production and people produced night and day, thinking they were making money. Afterward we took 80 per cent of the profits in taxes and they realized they were not making so much as they thought they were making. . . .

Mr. Baker: . . . Now the price of coal had to be fixed so that the people who had the high-cost producing mines could still live, and, when you did that, the surface mines . . . got very much more than a good profit for them. That was recovered by an excess profits tax.

Senator Swanson: You think you can equalize that better by exercising the power of taxation than by trying to fix the price?

Mr. Baker: That would be my judgment.

Senator Swanson: You think if Congress will exercise its power to tax it can equalize in substantial degree—not entirely exactly but in substantial degree—the inequality of the profits by the power of taxation?

Mr. Baker: Yes, sir. I think Congress did try to do that and tried very earnestly and conscientiously to do it and I think they succeeded probably in accomplishing as nearly a perfect job as could have been done by *the other process* with less disturbance while the war was going on.

By "other process" I understand Mr. Baker to mean price stabilization.

I hope I shall not be understood as being opposed to the excess profits tax. The war policy advocated here by me could not be effectuated without it, It was intrinsic in my recommendation. But I must emphasize, in all earnestness, that (except for human slaughter and maiming and all that goes with them) *inflation* is the most destructive of the consequences of war. As I have maintained before and shall more clearly demonstrate later, it is inflation that doubles the cost of war, imposes the severest hardship on our people and, through inevitable deflation, burdens the future with a constantly increasing debt and a long period of painful and bitter readjustment such as we see today.

Excess profits taxes—standing alone—have no effect whatever to check inflation. Their only effect is to increase it. Thus 20 per cent of $500,000 profit is $100,000 and 20 per cent of $1,000,000 profit is $200,000. One way to increase $500,000 profit to $1,000,000 profit without increased risk or effort is to double price. For this reason there is more incentive to increase prices—and therefore profits— under an 80 per cent excess profits tax than there is without it. Indeed, the main result of such a system is to induce rapid price increase to absorb the tax. Precisely because it accelerates and in no wise checks inflation, the excess profits tax—without more—offers no cure at all for war evils. On the contrary, it aggravates them.

In the colloquy quoted above it seems to be assumed that the sole purpose of the excess profits tax is to equalize between low- and high-cost producers. That is one purpose but it is far from being the only purpose.

Consider for example the simple case of a company capitalized for $1,000,000, selling $1,000,000 worth of goods annually, making 20 per cent gross profit or $200,000 on its turnover, and having $100,000 of expenses of administration and selling, leaving a net profit of $100,-000 or 10 per cent on both its normal turnover and its capital. Suppose, also, that 10 per cent of its costs of manufacture or $800,000 are fixed overhead charges—depreciation, maintenance, supervision, taxes, etc. Then its costs for material and direct labor are $720,000 for every million dollars' worth of goods it sells. Now suppose that war comes and we need the full capacity of that plant. We give it orders for $4,000,000 worth of goods to be delivered in a single year. It has no increased selling and general administrative expense because the demand is so great that no such effort is required. Neither do the fixed overhead elements of its manufacturing costs increase greatly—say only to $90,000. What happens to the profits of that plant? Its material and direct labor costs on its $4,000,000 sales are $2,880,000. To this it must add $90,000 for fixed overhead charges in its factory and $100,000 for general and administrative expense, making a total cost for goods sold of $3,070,000. Its net profit is therefore $930,000 *or* 930 per cent *of its normal profits in peace.* It is making nearly 100 per cent on its investment and its net profit on turnover has increased from 10 per cent to 23 per cent. Even if we assess a tax of 80 per cent on the $830,000 of excess over peace profit, that plant will still be making $260,000 or 260 per cent of its normal profits.

I want you particularly to note that this example considers *no increase in price whatever.* I have stated the case in this way to show that neither the object nor the theory of the excess profits tax is confined to equalizing benefits or burdens due to increased price, and further to show that—standing alone—an excess profit tax such as we had in the World War will not wholly eliminate huge war profits. I understand that your Executive Secretary is to submit an improved plan for such a tax and, from what I know of it and him, I believe it to be the best that can be devised, but he will not contend, I think, that it offers any check on war inflation.

I recall vividly that, during the war, even after we had, by price fixing, compelled a reduction of 35 per cent from the peak index figure of iron and steel, and even after the 80 per cent excess profits tax was in effect, some high-minded and public-spirited steel men came to me expressing apprehension over the enormous profits they were making under our restrictive system operating at its best. The reason they were making such profits in spite of all we could do is made clear by the example I have given you. If to the enormous increase in profits shown by that example we add the profits due to a runaway market, the figures of profit become even more astonishing.

The suggestion in the colloquy I have quoted—that we can entice extraordinary effort by a bait of huge profits, later to be magicked away—is hardly appropriate now because the whole of industry is on notice that we shall have an excess profits tax in any war—it is a recognized incident of war operations everywhere.

Finally, I concur fully in Mr. Baker's answer to that suggestion (p. 135): "I do not think prices were ever fixed high as a means of increasing production. I think it was not necessary to stimulate anybody to produce in America."

There are reasons supporting Mr. Baker's view which stand entirely apart from the stimulation of patriotism—which, in itself, is sufficient: Our modern production plant is highly mechanized. Mechanical mass production brings low costs, but only when the machines are operating close to capacity. The system has grievous faults from which we are suffering severely today. Those machines represent enormous aggregations of capital on which fixed charges are very great.

When they are idle there is nothing to absorb these charges. Losses mount rapidly and there is nothing that can be done to lessen them. Conversely—as in the example given above—when they are speeded, the results in reduced cost per unit of production are sometimes almost fabulous. It is this economic circumstance which insures us against any faltering of production, and the expedient of increasing prices (with the excess profits tax to offset profiteering) is wholly unnecessary to increase production. The circumstance of modern industrial organization just recited will take care of that.

While the excess profits tax is an indispensable concomitant to proper industrial mobilization, the points I have tried to demonstrate and now emphasize by repetition are:

(a) Even with a fixed price structure and a high excess profits tax there will be huge war profits.

(b) It is both futile and unnecessary to try to stimulate production by high prices—relying on an excess profits tax to recapture these profits.

(c) The excess profits tax—standing alone—as a means for equalizing the burdens of war and eliminating the profits of war is fatally defective because it aggravates inflation and therefore fails to protect us against the most destructive phenomenon of modern war.

III. Improved control of governmental purchasing will alleviate but can never prevent inflation.

General MacArthur says that all economists agree that one major factor of inflation is purely psychological. The witness then outlines several suggested improvements in Army purchase control which he thinks will go far toward preventing inflation. These improvements are good. I cannot speak too highly of the work of the War Department in this regard in the recent past. Their new methods will reduce waste, confusion, and competitive governmental bidding. This will alleviate the tendency to high price, but the principal cause of inflation is beyond the reach of even this improvement.

In the six listed causes of wartime price disturbance on page 18 of General MacArthur's statement, I do not see the major effective cause—withdrawal of millions of able-bodied men from production, diversion of vast quantities of essential commodities and productive facilities from production for civilian uses, and their appropriation to destructive and wholly unproductive uses, with consequent universal *shortage of things.* It is the immutable law of supply and demand that in the face of scant supply prices will rise. This is inflation, and the only effective prevention is price control.

General MacArthur also says:

. . . It is conceivable that a war might be conducted with such great regard for individual justice and administrative efficiency as to make impossible those evils whose existence in past wars inspired the drafting of Public Resolution No. 98—71st Congress. It is also conceivable that the outcome of such a war would be defeat. With defeat would come burdens beside which those we are considering would be relatively insignificant. In all we do and in all we say with reference to preparedness, and to policies to be pursued in event of war, we must never overlook for one moment the fact that while efficiency in war-making is desirable, effectiveness is mandatory.

No one can quarrel with most of this statement. It was the guiding principle of all our war administration, but I find it difficult to distinguish between efficiency and effectiveness. What we must not overlook is that, in modern war, there are economic weapons other than those used by soldiers. International credit is one; economic strength is another; and civilian morale is another. Finally, if experience in the World War goes for anything, a war is possible in which the victor is left in a state of economic prostration approaching that of the vanquished. In the next war we must plan for military victory without economic defeat.

IV. The fixation of a few individual prices is a wrong war policy; first, because, in the usual circumstances of the advent of war, it would be confiscatory and wholly impracticable; second, because, in any case it has only a fragmentary effect on inflation; third, because, in theory, it is basically unsound; fourth, because it is much more difficult than general stabilization.

There was no witness who considered the subject at all who did not affirmatively declare that some measure of price fixing would be necessary, in major war, but several very distinguished witnesses contended that it would be a sufficient protection to confine this activity to prices of a few particular commodities.

On page 125 of the record, Mr. Baker, after discussing the War

Industries Board method of arriving at prices through industrial conferences, thus fixing certain prices separately, said:

. . . it would be far better to secure the results which Mr. Baruch is aiming at by following his processes rather than by attempting in any arbitrary way to install his procedures at the outset as an arbitrary and fixed thing.

Also, on page 127, after expressing apprehension lest general stabilization result in a wrong price for some industries, and after Senator Robinson had suggested that this might be true of individual price fixing after war had begun, he said:

I think that would not be true, Senator, if you would call in the industries one by one . . . and reach a conclusion as to each industry as to where its price ought to be frozen, etc., etc.

Commander Hancock (p. 156) (after stating that he had had no opportunity to examine the suggestion of general price fixing) also inclined to Mr. Baker's opinion favoring fixing of prices one by one, and so also did Colonel Ayres (p. 156) and Ex-Assistant Secretary of War Robbins (p. 255). Daniel Willard (p. 171) declined to express a preference as between general and particular price fixing without further study. There is some indication that General Williams (p. 284) misapprehended the plan. He seemed to think that it was proposed now to fix the price of copper ten years from now. Of none of these witnesses, except Commander Hancock, can it be said that they have had direct personal experience with the problem of wartime price fixing.

(1) **In the usual circumstances of the advent of war, individual price fixing is confiscatory and wholly impracticable.**

I think a good deal of this divergence of view may result from a failure to distinguish between the usual circumstances of the advent of war—a rather rapid transition from a state of peace to that of war in which the normal peacetime schedule of prices is suddenly shattered by the abnormal demands of war—and the really unusual case (such as ours in 1917) where we encounter a distorted price pattern due to the influence of several years of a war of worldwide percussion elsewhere but in which we have not been belligerents.

The former was the case with England in the Napoleonic wars, with us in every war of the nineteenth century, with the Russo-Japanese and Sino-Japanese wars, with the belligerents in all European

wars of the nineteenth and twentieth centuries, except for us and perhaps for Italy in the World War.

We should consider, first, then, and prepare for, the usual circumstance of the advent of war and not the exceptional circumstance.

In the normal peacetime price pattern, every price is a resultant
of the combination of all other prices. Thus the price of steel is a
direct resultant of the price of ore-lands, mining, transportation,
conversion, and distribution. Resolving each of these direct elements
into its components, we shall see each of them at last analysis as a
direct function of the cost of labor, which is dependent on the cost
of living, which in turn is a composite of the cost of almost every
element in commerce. Irving Fisher has well shown that, in making a
general price index, it makes little difference in the result whether
we select the weighted average of the prices of fifty commodities or
of five hundred commodities. There is such inter-relation of component costs that the general effect is the same in either case.

Returning to our example—the price of steel. If we fix the price
of that alone and leave other prices to the mercy of *laissez faire*, all
war experience goes to show that the components of the cost of steel
will rise like so many skyrockets. To put it another way, when we
impose upon a general price schedule in a fairly normal state an influence for rapid general inflation, and, at the same time, apply a
repression to a single commodity, we automatically and almost instantly destroy the exchange value of that commodity. There is as
little doubt about the unconstitutionality of that procedure as there
is about its impracticability. Under the Constitution it would be confiscation, and from a practical standpoint it would paralyze production. In other words, such a project, on the most superficial examination, proves futile and impossible. To try to make this clearer
in a practical way, suppose war were to break out tomorrow. Knowing, from invariable experience, that general prices will soon go skyward, we try the individual price-fixing formula and call in the makers
of iron and steel and say to them:

"Gentlemen, we are embarked in a great war. We know the market
price of steel is where it is today by force of the law of supply and
demand. We also know from the history of every great war that
all prices in our markets are about to begin a dizzy upward spiral.
But, as to your prices, we ask you as patriotic citizens to keep them
where they are."

The instant answer would of course be:

"Why, in that case our selling price will almost immediately be
below our costs. You can't ask us to finance the war alone. You
are simply proposing confiscation of our product."

There of course would be the end of the attempt.   It is impossible.
Even if our request should be:

"Well, we are going to fix a price somewhat higher than your
present price in order to prevent profiteering and inflation."

The answer would be:

"What price?   All other prices control our costs.   The only way
you can do that is on 'cost-plus basis.'   That we must insist upon
because, if you leave other prices free to rise as they will, we can
have no way of knowing at what price we shall be safe."

If I were conducting such a negotiation, with all the experience of
the World War at my command, I would not know how to answer
these supposed arguments of industry.   If other witnesses who so
strongly advocated this procedure here can answer them, I think this
Commission should call upon them to do so.   The issue they raise is
one of pretty nearly first magnitude.

How can any seller accept a price which he knows will be exceeded
by his costs?   How can anyone contract at a fixed price in a runaway
war market when all he knows about his costs are that they are on an
upward spiral and may run to any figure?   It was this reasoning that
afflicted us with the vicious cost-plus contracts of 1917–1918.

It seems to me so apparent, from the examples I have given, that
individual price stabilization in the usual circumstances of a great war
is wholly impracticable that no further argument or exposition is
necessary.   In briefest terms, under those circumstances (i.e., where
we start with a relatively normal price structure), we must either
stabilize every price or stabilize no price.

(2) In any circumstances of the advent of war, individual price fixing cannot eliminate inflation.

It is only when we start from a distorted schedule of prices that we
can stabilize prices piecemeal, and then only in respect of such prices
as we find to be so grotesquely out of line with their component
costs that there is no confiscation in fixing them until component
costs rise to relative parity with the prices fixed.

There are only three conditions in which such general disorganization is likely.   One is that which we encountered in 1917—domestic
disorganization due to foreign war; another is some temporary disturbance not due to war; and the last is, if, apprehensive about general stabilization on the outbreak of war, we sit still while all prices
whirl upward and then (after some have gotten unreasonably out of
line) attack the peaks.   In any circumstance, of course, we could then
call in such an industry as that of iron and steel and say (as we did
in 1917):

"Gentlemen, your prices are away out of line with the costs of labor, materials, money, and things in general. We are going to ask you to lower prices to a figure which still leaves you safely above your normal level relative to other prices even though it represents a 30 per cent reduction from what you are getting."

Nobody could justly complain of that—which is an entirely different thing from trying to do this at the outset of war when prices are not disorganized.

If, in the next great war, we are to be as unfortunate and unskillful as we were in 1917, or so fatuous as to refuse general stabilization and let the normal schedule run away, it is *possible* to stabilize such prices as have outdistanced the general advance. But that will not stop inflation. The following table of ratios of wholesale price indexes for April, 1917, and November, 1918, to indexes for July, 1914, is very interesting:

	Column I July, 1914 Index	Column II April, 1917 Ratio	Column III Nov., 1918 Ratio
All commodities	67.3	170%	202%
Grains	69.6	243%	227%
Iron and Steel	59.5	285%	253%
Non-ferrous Metals ..	75.1	244%	200%
Chemicals	86.1	210%	210%
Bituminous Coal	34.8	271%	235%

The table shows in Column I what we may call the normal supply-and-demand relationship, at the outbreak of war in Europe, between the price of the named commodities and the general price index. In Column II we see the distortion due to Allied buying in our markets. We observe that the general price index was up 70 per cent but grains were up 143 per cent of the July, 1914, index; iron and steel 185 per cent, non-ferrous metals 144 per cent, chemicals 110 per cent, and bituminous coal nearly 171 per cent. Obviously in this distortion there was no confiscation in downward price revision designed entirely to bring these particular exaggerated prices back toward their normal relationship to the all-commodity index. But glancing at Column III will make two things clear. First, our partial price fixing did *not* stop inflation. The all-commodity index rose another 32 per cent by November, 1918; second, only in the case of non-ferrous metals did we succeed in reducing any of the principal commodities to their normal place in the general pattern of prices. While, in the period of our participation in the war, we did succeed in *reducing* the degree of distortion in the prices of grains, iron and steel, and bituminous coal, we never cured it. All we did in respect of these controlled prices was to reduce the spread between the abnormal relation we found in 1917 and the normal relationship of 1914—in the case of grains a spread of 73 points was reduced to a spread of 25 points; iron and steel was reduced from a spread of 115 points to 51 points; non-ferrous metals from 74 points to —2 points; chemicals from 40 points to 8 points; coal from 101 points to 33 points. Thus, in the unusual conditions of 1917 there was ample room to attack the exaggerated prices singly without any such injustice as would have happened if, for example, we had held the 1914 price of iron and steel at an index figure of 59.5, letting the other prices rise to the figures shown in Column II.

These figures show, I think, that individual price fixing did not stop inflation. We made an exhaustive study of this after the war which is published in a joint book by the War Industries Board Price Section and the War Trade Board. (W. I. B. Price Bulletin No. 3.) The net result of that study is sufficiently shown in the tables I have given. We checked the *rate* of inflation but the process still went on. Of course it *must* go on when we fix only a few prices, leaving the rest free to rise—as rise they must if only because of inflation of the currency, which is an inevitable concomitant of any war. Individual price fixing can never stop inflation.

(3) In any circumstance of the advent of war, the theory of individual price fixing is fundamentally unsound.

I have shown—and, I submit, incontrovertibly—that individual price fixing of a few commodities in the usual circumstance of the advent of war is necessarily confiscatory and wholly impracticable. Also, that, even if we start with a distorted schedule or wait for the initial schedule to become distorted, the individual method does not reach the chief evil you are convened to consider, namely, *inflation.* I wish to go further and say that in the unusual (as in the usual) case of the coming of war the piecemeal system is equally unsound in principle and for the same reasons in each case.

Since the uncontrolled component costs of the fixed price are constantly rising, the fixed price is moribund at the moment it is uttered and may be dead before it can be placed in practice. We had something of this experience with our fixed prices in 1918. It became rapidly apparent that the rising tendency of the elements of the cost of living—retail prices—would soon obsolete our whole schedule and that we would be faced with the alternative either of adjusting our fixed prices upward or of entering the complex field of retail price fixing in a disorganized price structure. We chose the latter method and were proceeding vigorously with it when the armistice came. We had started, just as these witnesses start, with the idea of fixing a few basic prices and letting other prices go free. The uneven upward trend of free prices was threatening the structure. To maintain it we were driven to consider an enormous extension of the price-fixing field. Out of that experience my present suggestion was born. It was simple and obvious that—at last analysis—what we were really groping toward was the creation (under a rapidly but irregularly rising trend) of a stabilized homogeneous and balanced general price schedule, the very condition that normally exists at the beginning of nineteen out of twenty wars. Two conclusions were obvious. First: *"If what you have naturally at the beginning is the very thing you are striving to recreate artifically at the end, why not preserve the initial relationship?"* Second, *"This thing you are trying to recapture, in an irregularly rising market, by arbitrary piecemeal stabilization—no matter how comprehensive—is, by its very terms, arithmetically impossible."* It is like a dog trying to catch himself by running rapidly around a tree. Or (because the free components of the fixed price continue to increase) it is like a command to a moving regiment— "Regiment, halt! But all the soldiers shall keep on marching!"

When we reflect that the price of anything is simply the resultant of the price of everything, it must be clear that, in war, we cannot justly or practicably halt the rise in the price of anything unless we halt the rise in the price of everything, and this is true—in different degree—whether we start with a balanced schedule or a distorted schedule.

For this reason even in a repetition of 1917, I can see no logical argument against general stabilization first to stop the rising trend everywhere—followed by an immediate attack on each exaggerated price.

(4) General stabilization requires less machinery and is simpler and easier than stabilization piecemeal.

One of the most astonishing aspects of the testimony before the Commission was an opinion by several witnesses that general stabilization would require a more complex machinery or would be a more difficult administrative procedure, or would create more confusion than piecemeal price fixing. General Williams (p. 284), Commander Hancock (p. 155), Mr. Baker (p. 128), Colonel Ayres (p. 162).

Commander Hancock, Mr. Baker, and Mr. Willard all expressed themselves as feeling that it would be too difficult a matter for the President to determine a day to use as a standard. It was a trifle unfortunate, I think, that some of the questions referred them to a day 90 days or some specific number of days prior to a declaration of war. As I have shown earlier, such was not the intent but only that the day should be one that reflected practically the current condition at the outbreak of war and that the only reason for allowing some leeway was to permit selection of a day on or about the day of declaration when there should be the fewest downward distortions. Colonel Ayres (p. 165) thought that all that was necessary would be to freeze twenty commodities at the outbreak of war—a proposition already shown to be wholly impracticable. Mr. Baker thought there would be less confusion if prices were fixed piecemeal (p. 127).

In order to examine this criticism we must consider two cases: first the usual case where we start with a more or less homogeneous and normal price structure; second, the unusual circumstance of 1917 where many prices were far above their normal relationship with general prices.

(a) *Price stabilization in the usual case of the advent of war.* As I have shown, if (in the usual circumstances of the outbreak of war) we adopt the individual-fixation plan of these witnesses, we cannot fix prices at all at the outset. We must wait, while the whole structure advances, until distortions appear, and then move against them.

Under my suggestion we would at once freeze the whole price structure in its normal relationship and thereby stop advances. This does not mean that we would decree any price. The frozen structure is a schedule of maximum prices. Economic influences making for price *declines* would operate freely. We are simply clapping on a ceiling against advances and we immediately set up a Commission to rectify any incidental injustices. In my opinion the mere fact that such a power and plan exists would have a very great stabilizing effect on any tendency of prices to rise.

The President would have no difficulty in naming a day. On any day he names, some prices are sure to be somewhat above and others somewhat below their usual relationship. We would have to consider them separately and at once. The President's only problem at the start is one of convenience—to name a day when these exceptions are fewest, and of course he must guard against selection of a day reflecting material changes of prices as compared with the situation existent on the day stabilization is to become effective.   There is no machinery complexity or difficulty whatever in this.

Let us assume that the day is named and the schedule of maxima effective.   It now becomes necessary to consider the exceptions which we may have caught in our net.   These are of two kinds: first, prices for some reason temporarily depressed which if left free would, under war stimulus, rise to parity with other prices or far above them; second, prices which for some reason are temporarily *above* their just relationship.

The most obvious instance of probable depressed price is that of some farm products mentioned here by George Peek.   These are now and long have been much submerged below their pre-war relationship to general prices.   In every war in history farm prices have been among the most volatile.   If left free they would rise exorbitantly. Mr. Peek stated the solution with the problem.   If the problem occurred today, we would probably raise the frozen maxima to a figure which bears the pre-war relationship to the general price index.   No machinery, no study, and no administration is required for this kind of case.   It is a simple arithmetical problem in ratios.

It must be constantly emphasized that the maximum price so adjusted would not be a fiat nor even a minimum guarantee such as we made for wheat in 1917.   It would simply be a price above which farm products or any other unduly depressed commodity must not rise.   If economic forces did not raise them to that maximum, they would never reach it.

The second class of cases is that of the unduly exaggerated price requiring downward revision.   First we must note that, in the usual case we are considering, there would be very few of these and none of the exaggerated distortion we found in 1917.   In peacetime, individual prices rarely if ever get very far out of line with their normal relationship.

It is a much more difficult thing to revise maximum prices downward than to revise them upward.   It requires exhaustive cost studies and long and difficult negotiations.   All that involves machinery and trouble, but it requires not nearly so much of either when we start from a stabilized base, with only a few minor exceptions to deal with, as it would to sit still while all prices spiral dizzily upward and then finally to move against a confused mass of exaggerated exceptions and attempt to haul them back into line while the whole schedule is still scurrying skyward—and to what end?   Simply to try to restore a balance that we had at the beginning and could have maintained without effort and on a much lower level.

One method *stops a runaway* and keeps the whole team in line. The other submits to the runaway and then tries to keep some of the horses from running faster than the rest.

Between these two alternatives I can see no room for hesitation. Why should we submit the nation to the disorganizing and destructive process of general inflation? Why lose the time and suffer the loss? Why multiply work and difficulty? Why abandon the natural structure of price relationships and then later seek to create a wholly artificial pattern of relationships by a conjectural method under well-nigh impossible circumstances?

In this case surely the proponents of piecemeal (as opposed to general) stabilization had not clearly understood what is being proposed.

(b) *Price stabilization in a distorted price structure.* This brings us to consider the relative merits of general price stabilization as against piecemeal price fixing in such a case as we encountered in 1917. The witnesses whose testimony we are considering say that the former would be more difficult and require more machinery. But why would it? The sole difference between the two plans is that under my suggestion we would clap a ceiling on the whole schedule—at first— to stop the upward trend and then proceed to bring down the peaks by attacking them one at a time. As these witnesses would have it, we would do exactly the same thing as to the peaks but leave the generality of component prices to run wild. I have already tried to show that this is fundamentally unsound in economics. But we are here considering *relative difficulty of administration* and not economic theory. Why is it more difficult to reduce an exaggerated price when its component costs have been stabilized than when those costs are fluctuating wildly? I think the question answers itself. The number of prices to be considered, the machinery and method for determining the maxima, the administration and negotiation are exactly the same in either case. Anyone who had actual experience with the process must know at a glance that the task would be far more simple when performed from a stabilized base than when performed from a fluctuating base. I think that point requires no argument.

V. Miscellaneous Criticisms

(1) General price stabilization would not disproportionately burden any economic group.

It should be obvious without argument that general stabilization of a natural price structure is inherently a rule of equality especially when compared with individual price fixing and yet the project has

been attacked here on the argument that, if we had stabilized prices
in April, 1917, the savings to our people would have come largely
out of two specific economic groups.

On page 162 Colonel Ayres says that price changes in different
groups during our participation in the war were:

Food	+ 6%
Textiles	+39%
Chemicals	+ 4%
Leather	—10%
Iron and steel	—11%
Other metal products	—20%

From these figures he concludes that, if there had been general
stabilization in April, 1917, "it would have had its impacts largely in
those two general fields of the farmers and the textile workers," since
most of whatever saving had been made would have come from
farmers "who would have received far less from food products . . . and
from the textile workers."

This is so remarkable a statement that it is difficult to believe that
it was not an inadvertence. In the first place the "food" group of
prices is not a true reflection of the farmer's situation. Even if it
were, it is manifestly unfair to compute the farmer's relative condition
by comparing even his own prices with those of such random groups
as leather or metals. The obvious way to find out how the farmer
fares is to compare the index of his prices with the all-commodity
index or with the non-agricultural price index. The April, 1917, ratio
of farm prices to the U. S. Department of Labor all-commodity index
was 109.6 per cent and to the same department's non-agricultural price
index was 113.8 per cent. The corresponding November, 1918, ratios
were 110. per cent and 114.7 per cent—all of which means that the
farmer, at the armistice, would have been in almost the identical
economic situation if all prices had been frozen in April, 1917, as he
was in the circumstances that really existed at the armistice. The
difference is negligible.

As to textiles, it is true that piecemeal control of prices was attempted far too late and was ineffectual. Consequently textile prices
ran further away from their proper relationship to other prices than
did any other group, and therefore Colonel Ayres is right in saying
that if we had stabilized all prices in April, 1917 (when textile prices
were in an eminently fair relationship with other prices), they would
never have risen to such exorbitant heights as they reached in 1918.
Precisely to prevent such distortion is equally the whole aim and endeavor either of general stabilization or partial stabilization such as

Colonel Ayres advocates. Colonel Ayres shows that steel and iron prices declined 20 per cent between April, 1917, and November, 1918. He does not add that they fell under compulsion of price revision downward. On the contrary, he compares that forced fall with the uncontrolled rise of textiles and concludes—as though it would have been a grievance—that if control of textile prices had been equally effective with control of steel prices, the savings to our people would have come out of the textile workers.

Of course the fact is that no commodity group has a vested right in exorbitant war prices and that reduction of textile prices to an equable basis would have come out of swollen profits of textile companies and not out of textile workers.

Since the effect of general stabilization on farmers' relative prices would have been negligible, on textile workers nil, and on the textile companies only that justice for which all such plans are devised, one wonders why "farmers" and "textile workers" were emphasized. Both the Fuels group and the Building Materials group also got badly out of line in 1918 in spite of individual price fixing. They were not mentioned in the conspectus of this witness. In the same statement in which this witness used the example of textiles as an argument against initial price stabilization, in advocating individual price freezing, he said:

Price freezing . . . should be undertaken . . . at the beginning of the war in those commodities which clearly are going to be purchased . . . in such large amounts that the new and added demand threatens to lift the quotations unusually high . . . those products include, clearly, iron and steel . . . *they probably include several different types of textiles* . . . perhaps there might be, let us say, twenty commodities.

As I have already shown, such a plan would be confiscatory and impracticable in the usual circumstances of the advent of war.

> (2) **General price stabilization does not insure profiteering by producers whose prices are in a declining trend because it does not fix fiat prices—it only clamps a ceiling on the price structure existing at the advent of war.**

This witness' next assertion (p. 162) is even more remarkable. It is that, if prices were frozen, nobody would try to get a frozen price adjusted *downward* and so "where the trend was downward the freezing would constitute a governmental sanction for an ever increasing profit."

This would be true only if the frozen price was a fiat price. He apparently does not understand what was explicitly brought out in my statement (p. 35): "The crystallized price structure is a schedule of maxima. Items in ample supply are left free to fall below the fixed price schedule."

Obviously if any trend is downward it is because supply exceeds demand and it will be wholly unnecessary for anybody to "make application for reductions." The law of supply and demand will attend to that as it traditionally does—not occasionally, or now and then, or part of the time, or here and there—but at every place and all of the time.

Furthermore there was no basic commodity in the whole list during the war where the price *trend* was downward in the sense in which the words are used here. The only conspicuous and sustained downward progress (relative to the general price index) that was not the result of artificial price control of one kind or another in this country was in leather (and that has been shown [W. I. B. Price Bulletin No. 3] to have been the result of price control in England in 1916) and in manufactured fuel and lighting gas, which was the result of vastly increased production due to the demand for coke and by-product derivatives such as toluol. The very fact that the gas price went *down* bears out my statement that the law of excess supply and reduced demand forces prices downward and refutes this witness' criticism that by-products in general not necessary for war uses under a frozen price system would "yield greater and greater profits" under governmental protection.

Therefore the statement that the cases where "the trend was downward would constitute a governmental sanction for an ever increasing profit which in the case of a large part of our expenditure in that (the World) war would have been of considerable proportions" is almost meaningless (1) because, except as just noted, there were no downward trends that did not result from the downward fixation of price, and (2), more importantly, because we are not dealing with a fiat price but only with a stabilized maximum price.

> **(3) General price stabilization will freeze some maximum prices at figures too low to bring out necessary production. The easy and obvious remedy is to raise such prices.**

On page 162 Colonel Ayres also mentions as an objection the circumstance that freezing might find a particular commodity necessary for war abnormally below its normal relative place in the general price structure. Of course this is certain to happen. It will happen as to particular commodities and it will also happen as to particular localities. This was thoroughly developed in my statement on page 36, where, after showing the reason why we must provide a price incentive to increase production in particular cases, I said:

"A method must be devised to adjust the initial frozen price pattern to the changing situation."

I then referred to the method of the 1917–1918 price-fixing commission and said, "There was nothing in the experience of that Commission to suggest that a similar system would not be entirely effective in the future."

As I have already shown in my initial statement and in this statement, there is neither difficulty nor complexity nor administration in revising a price upward. This criticism is almost trivial.

I will go a step further and say that, as upward adjustments become necessary to govern particular cases, their effect on other costs may require small flat percentage increases in the whole pattern. Both processes are provided for in the suggested statute and both are simple.

(4) General price stabilization can easily be protected against the price situation in other countries.

On pages 162 and 163 Colonel Ayres and, on page 126, Mr. Baker bring up the obvious situation in the rubber and tire industry in which the price of tires may be frozen in the domestic market and the price of rubber is free and probably grossly inflated abroad, and say, "It would be quite impossible to keep on producing tires at present prices."

This situation was fully considered in my prepared statement (p. 36):

The frozen pattern of price will also have to be protected against the situation in export trade. If, as is almost certain, the inflationary process is in operation in the rest of the world, means will have to be applied to prevent extravagant foreign prices from upsetting our domestic schedule. Government, in its world economic strategy, must have almost plenary control over foreign trade just as it did in 1917–1918. We shall see the agency for such control purchasing for export at the controlled domestic price, selling in export at world price, and using the profit to buy necessitous imports at inflated world prices and sell to domestic needs at the controlled schedule.

It is only fair to conclude that these witnesses had not read my testimony. It was particularly unfortunate for their argument to have used rubber as an example. They have apparently forgotten what happened during the war under War Trade and War Industries Board control of rubber prices through agreements with rubber-producing countries. Notwithstanding tremendous demand and acute shipping shortage, the price of rubber went down during 1917 from an index figure of 178 to one of about 128, where it remained until the armistice.

I never hear this branch of the subject discussed that I do not recall the case of Chilean nitrates. The price of nitrates—an absolutely critical and indispensable war commodity—was being deliberately controlled against us and, by reason of apparently ideal circumstances for speculation, threatened to rise to any height. By a relatively simple use of plenary governmental war control of foreign trade we handled the nitrate price situation quite as effectively as we controlled the domestic price of any commodity. I could cite similar cases of regulation of import price through government control of foreign trade. There is no danger to the proposed plan inherent in the superficial objection we are now considering.

(5) Governmental price fixing is not possible in peace, but it is in war.

General MacArthur's suggestion that governmental price regulation is a failure does not apply to price control during the World War, as your record plainly shows. I do not read this statement as importing anything more than my own observation on this subject, that price regulation in peace is impracticable, because, shortly after making it, he proposed an immediate control of prices of raw materials which "might finally cover the whole range of commodities." This general assertion about price regulation which we are all prone to use overlooks the fact that one very large section of American industry is, and for many years has been, operating under fixed prices—the whole railroad and public utility field—the combined total of which accounts for a very substantial proportion of all business done in the United States.

Also, while we all know that peacetime price fixing is a visionary dream because economic law and not governmental determination control both supply and demand, if the World War proved anything it proved that, in major war, government must, for all practical purposes, exercise a rigorous control over principal sources of supply as well as over principal channels of demand. As a matter of fact neither General MacArthur nor any other witness has failed to urge that price fixing is necessary. The only real point of disagreement disclosed in the record is as to whether it shall be an artificial and arbitrary fixation of individual prices or preservation from the outset of the natural pattern of price relationships.

One curious aspect of this and all other arguments that have been advanced against general war stabilization is that it applies with precisely equal if not greater force to partial stabilization.

(6) General price stabilization in war has not been adjudged unconstitutional.

General MacArthur said: "Since the Supreme Court has definitely determined that no price-fixing agency of government may set a price on a citizen's property and compel him to give that property to the Government at that price, any fixed price is effective only when it is enforced by public opinion."

I fully agree that no drastic war policies opposed by public opinion can succeed, but I am assured that no such pronouncement ever dropped from the Supreme Court as applying to wartime price stabilization. If this statement, in the broad language quoted, were the law, we would have no procedure in eminent domain, no railroad and other public utility rate regulation, and no usury laws. We would have had no history of war control of prices with which this record is redundant. I understand that your legal section has arrived at no such conclusion as to the law on price fixing.

(7) There is nothing conjectural or impractical in general price stabilization.

General MacArthur also said: "So many factors are involved (in general price stabilization) that injustice must follow. Evasion and court appeals are inevitable. Attempts at enforcement would likely create antagonism and government would lose good will. Without complete and unstinting popular support no nation can hope to fight to victory. The citizens' road to judicial appeal should not be made long or difficult."

As I have observed earlier, these remarks are applicable with at least equal force to partial price fixing as to general price fixing and some of them, I think, apply with more force to partial price fixing.

What witnesses overlook is that we are not proposing here a fiat—an artificial determination of price. We are proposing to clamp a ceiling down on a whole pattern of existing prices created by the operation of economic law. The justice which we insure is the justice of the laws of trade as they are working at the time the ceiling is clamped down.

An individual fixed price is a pure artificiality—an invention, if you please. The very reason for using it is that we are dissatisfied with the product of the law of supply and demand under war stress and wish to substitute a designed price in its place. For reasons fully developed in this statement, I see no escape whatever from the conclusion that this method is an economic impracticability if applied early in any major war under the usual circumstances of the coming of war and it is impracticable precisely because it insures injustice. In other words, some incidental cases of injustice (immediately to be relieved) might conceivably arise from general stabilization but, as I have tried to show, partial stabilization, in the usual case of the advent of war, has invariable and unavoidable injustice as its inherent essence.

Some evasion and some court appeals are inevitable. They would be inevitable under any form of price control. A glance at the appended statute will show that they have been provided for and that the citizens' road to judicial appeal is made short and easy.

One curious aspect of the difference of opinion on this subject is that everybody (including myself) stresses the importance of civilian morale and then proceeds to use it as an argument for the thing he proposes. That of course presents to the Commission the choice between the effect on civilian morale of a stabilized price structure or that of a time of wild inflation. To my mind there is small room for hesitation.

As to the morale of the generality of civilians, we all know how it was affected—especially among soldiers' families and people of fixed income—by the upward spiralling of the cost of living and the lavishness of reward to those who were in a position to profit by it as compared with the hardship imposed on those who were compelled to suffer from it.

As to the morale of industry at large in the World War, the uncertainty of the daily fluctuation of price and the inevitable rising trend on all sides was matter for common commiseration. I am aware of no able and experienced business administrator who does not prefer operation under stable conditions to operation under a price schedule in an unforeseeable state of flux.

We have also to consider here the apparent thought of some witnesses that morale would be better conserved if the Government moved against individual prices to control distorted peaks than if it stabilized an initial normal supply-and-demand relationship.

I am completely unable to get this point of view. When government approaches a distorted price schedule to control individual prices, it moves every time for the purpose of *reducing a price*. It goes in to break up an enjoyable situation and to impose a severe restriction. It is simply not in human nature to welcome this. I never experienced in such a situation much of the cordiality referred to by some witnesses.

What is here proposed is a very different thing. At the outset in the usual case, we are not going to reduce anything. People are simply put on notice that prices are not going to be allowed to rise. They know from the experience of the World War that the power of the longest purse is going to be considerably curtailed because essential things, at least, are going to be pretty much rationed anyway. Every producer and every merchant knows that, while his price may not rise, it is unlikely to fall and, as to his profits, that regardless of price, his turnover will increase because, by reason of scarcity, he is in a sellers' market and he can plan with confidence because his price is constant.

I feel confident that, assuming the effect to be as I have stated it, ninety-nine out of one hundred businessmen would infinitely prefer such a situation to the one that is absolutely certain to supervene under any plan for individual price stabilization. In other words, to the extent that morale, content, satisfaction, and calm are involved, my suggestion encourages them while the contrary suggestions are designed to impair them.

VI. Price control through "leadership" alone is not feasible.

On page 124 et seq., Mr. Baker said:

What Mr. Baruch did with his organization in the last war was to make it the leader of American business rather than the boss of American business. When he wanted, for instance, to fix prices in an industry or to divert the capacity of an industry from one occupation to another, the way he did it was to send for the leaders of that industry, seat them around the table with him, tell them the national need, lay out the economics of the situation to them with experts in their own field at his elbow, and, at the end of the conference they were not only informed of what was to be done but they knew why it was to be done, and they were enthusiastic for doing it. . . . My recollection is that there was no single instance in which an industry was invited to a conference of that sort in which it did not enthusiastically conform to the desire of the War Industries Board as soon as it was all explained and worked out.

. . . For that reason I am inclined to believe it would be far better to secure results in the next war, to secure the results which Mr. Baruch is aiming at, by following his processes rather than by attempting in any arbitrary way to install his procedures at the outset as an arbitrary and fixed thing. I am not economist enough to comment on Mr. Baruch's suggestion that there ought to be an instantaneous freezing of prices, but I am willing to be foolhardy about it and venture a disagreement. . . .

Take the steel industry, for example. There was in the office of the Secretary of War a meeting of some 25 or 30 men who controlled the steel industry, or controlled its management in this country, and the problem of what ought to be the price of steel in the United States after we went into the war was proposed for discussion and an agreement reached under the advisory direction of the Secretary of the Navy and the Secretary of War which reduced the price of iron and steel products, which are the most necessary things in a war, so that the net effect of that kind of price control, through the leadership which we exercised, was that the general price level of iron and steel products went down after America went into the war.

General MacArthur also said:

Prices promulgated as fair and reasonable should be determined by agreement between government and the representatives of industry . . . (p. 19). Price control efforts . . . will be directed gradually. . . . Good will and cordial acquiescence will assure their success. Injustice and hastiness will be avoided because in the determination of prices industry will have a voice. The spontaneous co-operation born of patriotism and enthusiasm will not degenerate into an enforced and begrudging compliance. . . . Citizens will feel that the restrictions to which they submit are restrictions they themselves have imposed in the interests of the common welfare.

What these witnesses are really referring to when they talk about spontaneity and co-operation in general public acceptance of price fixing and all other war tasks is not that there was not compulsion behind the duty imposed on citizens. They are referring to the universal confidence that was placed by government in the people themselves to enforce the more or less arbitrary and distinctly sacrificial requirements of government. As if by common consent, every war administration adopted the policy of decentralization reliance on unofficial civilian co-operation, public education as to necessity, and—to put it frankly—universal and highly organized propaganda.

Thus the draft—instead of being enforced by soldiers carrying bayonets as in the Civil War—was turned over to small boards of local civilians who were given almost unlimited and final authority. Largely they served without compensation and at great sacrifice. Much was made of the service of these men and conscription took on the aspect of a great spontaneous *levée en masse*. But there was a provision in the Selective Service Act under which, if any member of these draft boards had refused that duty, he could have been sent to jail. Many men who failed to register did go to jail.

Thus the Food Administration actually absorbed into its organization not only bakers, millers, dealers, and elevator companies—but also thousands and thousands of housewives. But in the act under which this was done there were many penal and criminal provisions and there was the standing threat to every one of the hundreds of thousands of licensees under that act of being put out of business on a moment's notice by the arbitrary act of the administration and of being sent to jail if he did not stay out of business.

Thus, also, as I have repeatedly explained, industries were called into consultation whenever the War Industries Board fixed a price and, while we had no penal statute, we had plenty of threat to enforce what we thought was just.

In other words it was an enlightened policy of *administration* of those laws—not an absence of teeth in their jaws—which obtained an unusual degree of popular co-operation for them. I see no reason to suppose that the suggestion now made would be administered in any less sensible manner. No industry is going to complain of our effort to protect it from a panic market. If any industry is hurt, the way to adjustment is wide open and adjustment would proceed on exactly the round-table "conference" method invented by the various War Administrations in the World War. It goes without saying that the agency responsible for production and industrial efficiency is not being set up to oppress industry.

I would be the last person in the United States to depreciate the spontaneity of wholehearted co-operation and self-sacrifice exhibited by American business during the war. That and that alone made my work possible. I agree with Mr. Baker's excellent statement: "The mobilization of America for participation in the World War is the most outstanding industrial achievement that has been accomplished in the history of mankind. . . . May I add to that by saying so spontaneously, so cheerfully, and so enthusiastically."

Yet I venture to think that there is not one of those industrial leaders who would not heartily agree with me in saying: first, that it would be impossible to prevent general inflation by any nationwide convention as to price; second, that no one—no matter how generous —could agree to restrict his own price unless all other prices affecting him were restricted, or unless his price was already so high that his profits were exorbitant; and finally, that substantial price reductions by agreement (even from highly profitable peaks) could not be secured unless those willing to agree through high-mindedness knew that the

Government body with whom they were dealing had *some* sanctions—some control with actual teeth or some disciplinary power to apply to recalcitrant or unwilling subscribers in the event of default.

I wish the record and my memories permitted me to agree with the picture presented by these witnesses of each commodity group gathering around to hear our price determinations and then going away "enthusiastic for doing it." I wish I could also agree that, after a meeting of steel leaders with the Secretaries of War and Navy before the war, "the effect of that kind of price control through leadership . . . was that the general price level of iron and steel prices went down after America went into the war." My recollection is of a long and tedious period of bickering attended at first by such public statements by the President as, *"Those who do not respond in the spirit of those who have given their lives for us on bloody fields far away may safely be left to be dealt with by opinion and by the law, for the law must, of course, command these things."* I recall a bitter controversy between the Chairman of the Shipping Board and the industry in June, 1917, leading to the Pomerene bill which proposed to authorize the President to fix iron and steel prices and to commandeer the plant of any producer who failed to comply. I remember also what I am free now to relate since Judge Geary himself has said—in effect—that he kept the steel industry from being nationalized. He was quite correct. Owing to the inability of the Government to reach agreement with the steel industry I was compelled to—and *did*—secure authority from the President to commandeer certain companies in that industry if it should become necessary. While all this was going on, the index figures of the U. S. Department of Labor show the following as to the prices of iron and steel:

1915	64.7
1917:	
April	170
May	182.7
June	204
July	230.2
August	227.6
September (price fixed)	214.3
November	143.7

As Commander Hancock expressed it in his testimony (p. 154) relating to price control through leadership and agreement:

. . . the President said to Mr. Brookings (Chairman of the Price-Fixing Commission), "Let the manufacturer see the club behind your door."

Now, as I have explained before, the club was of synthetic origin, in that, in all these conferences, our sole authority was the latent threat of commandeering and withdrawal of priority ratings. The strength of that synthesis has been seriously diluted by expressions of the Federal judiciary, which has said, as I shall presently explain, that the War Industries Board had no statutory authority to fix prices or to commandeer, that such "agreements" were induced by duress and were not binding, and that such a method was invalid. It is unwise and unfair to any future war administration to require effective results from a more or less truncated flush after the hand has been so publicly exposed. Price control through such "leadership" alone will never again be possible. We must have statutory authority in the broadest conceivable language.

So much has been said here about price fixing by agreement, or spontaneous co-operation, that I think it is necessary to say at this point that there was no such thing, generally speaking, as price fixing by agreement in any such sense as witnesses seem to have derived from reading and talks with others on this subject. Agreement there was in the sense of acceptance of a Federal price determination by a few leaders in each industry, and in many of our conferences the Government had the enthusiastic support of some producers and in some conferences the unanimous support of all, but, as a practical matter, there was no alternative to such acceptance and there was a distinct threat of effective reprisal in case of refusal.

Reference has also been made to Food Administration methods with perhaps a suggestion that greater reliance was there placed on spontaneous co-operation. Everyone knows the skill with which that administration molded public opinion, but the Lever Act, under which it was set up, fairly bristled with penal provisions. The President was authorized to prescribe reasonable charges and the President's determination of such charges was made *prima facie* evidence in any prosecution. It was also a crime for any food company doing more than $100,000 worth of business even to continue in business without a license, and the Food Administration conditioned these licenses on such considerations as it saw fit.

As a matter of fact, the wheat price established under that act was a *minimum* guarantee. The licensing system was used to establish a maximum price, and an angry agricultural community has not yet ceased to complain about that "agreed price."

It is far from my purpose to criticize the Food Administration. It did what it had to do and the record speaks for itself—it was one of the outstanding jobs of the war, or of any war or any administration

—but the Commission would be misinformed if it were to gather from any testimony here that there was price fixing by spontaneous co-operation in that department any more than in any other war administration. As a matter of fact, in the strict sense, there was no price fixing at all except as to wheat and its products. The Food Administration policy was to regulate profits rather than price. The Commission will be equally misinformed if it concludes that there was or can be price control without proper legal sanctions and determined administration.

I bore the heat and burden of nearly every one of the principal price determinations except food, and I am speaking from intense experience when I say that in most cases those prices, while eventually accepted wholeheartedly, were not unconstrained free-will offerings of all by any manner of means. We used a good many euphemisms during the war for the sake of national morale, and this one of "price fixing by agreement" is a good deal like calling conscription "Selective Service" and referring to registrants for the draft as "mass volunteers." Let us make no mistake about it: we fixed prices with the aid of potential Federal compulsion and we could not have obtained unanimous compliance otherwise.

VII. A statute authorizing general stabilization should not be deferred until war appears, on the argument that we can then improvise a more appropriate act.

On pp. 122 and 123 Mr. Baker said:

Modern war is essentially a process of improvisation. . . . As war progresses under modern conditions the inventive faculty . . . is stimulated. . . . I think this is also true about the economic situation. . . . There is only a limited amount of preparatory economic legislation that can be done. . . . . . . We of the War Department found ourselves perhaps more embarrassed by laws that had been passed than by the absence of law. . . . We were happiest when the laws that provided us power were more elastic and least in detail.

I concur fully with Mr. Baker that any law now to be passed must confer power in the very broadest language conceivable for the reasons he has given. But he seems to proceed on the theory that such powers as are here sought to be conferred are already in the President. I shall address this subject later. For the present let us assume that this theory is not correct. On this assumption we will have to have a statute conferring power and we must give it at least such definition in its provision of mechanics and methods as will make it conform to the Constitutional limitations heretofore laid down by the Federal Courts.

We improvised in 1917 because we had to. I know of no benefit that came from our total lack of prevision and consequent necessity for improvisation of fundamental war measures. And I know of no burdens that came from broad statutes which were enacted in advance of war for the purposes of better administration in war. Had it not been for the National Defense Act of 1916, I shudder to think what might have happened. That act really interested industrial leaders in War Department problems for the first time in our history. The Council of National Defense provided by that Act literally produced, one after the other, the great wartime industrial-mobilization agencies much as a hen lays eggs. I think it not too much to say that but for that little rift of statutory provision we could never have made our contribution in time to avert Allied defeat in 1918. The statutes that proved burdensome were not those enacted after careful consideration to provide broadly for war; nor were any statutes that conferred power burdensome. The clogging statutes were peace statutes which restricted power, imposed formalities, and neglected completely to provide for the overwhelming necessities of the emergency of modern war—such statutes as were virtually repealed by the Overman Act.

Improvisation is almost an obsession with us. Many of our manufacturers say that our refusal to adopt contemporary types of machine-guns, seventy-five millimeter projectiles and guns, airplanes, airplane engines, and even our own standard types of motor trucks, in order that we might improvise improvements on what the experienced Allies had already effectively used was largely responsible for General Pershing's recently published complaints about deliveries of technical equipment.

We improvised a Selective Service Act and the circumstance of its novelty required six weeks of study and debate before enactment. Except for unauthorized administrative action during those six weeks, every principal datum point in the history of our participation would have been set back exactly six weeks, with what result on the Western Front in March, July, and November, 1918, I hesitate to conjecture.

We are considering here a far-reaching step in war economics. It is based on specific experience. The results to be achieved are being demanded from the nation by such soldier organizations as the American Legion and have been promised by both political parties because there is a general feeling that our present system of distributing war burdens is grossly unfair. In other words, maintenance of military and civilian morale requires these results from the Government.

Under modern conditions, if we do not provide for them, our military effectiveness for defense will be impaired. Yet the solution is not easy. If there is any one thing that has been brought out clearly here by the very diversity of opinion on this subject, it is the lack of understanding of the principles here involved by men who were in positions of the highest responsibility in our war effort but who, by reason of the intense centering of that responsibility in their particular departments and the furious effort to which they were driven, had neither time nor opportunity to know or understand what was going on in the next compartment of governmental war effort. How much less informed and more bewildered would a hastily assembled war organization or a new War Congress be when presented with this problem in the panic of a world upheaval?

I submit that here is no situation for consideration and decision in the white heat and confusion of a war emergency. It is a situation for the most deliberate study and unhurried decision. The suggested statute is mandatory in nothing. It is permissive merely. It simply creates powers in the President to be used when necessary and appropriate to the kind of emergency we may encounter. It leaves the way for necessary improvisation wide open but it does not remit the country to improvisation of a basic and fundamental economic policy in the excitement and confusion of a lethal attack.

VIII.   *The Constitution implies no war powers in the President which would enable him, without statutory authority, to regulate prices and control industry or even to commandeer property for the support or maintenance of the Army or Navy—much less to do these things for the civilian population. Consequently a broad statutory donation of such powers would not limit supposed plenary implied war powers of the President.*

The Capper-Johnson bill (p. 112) authorizes the President, in case of the existence or imminence of war:

(a) To determine and proclaim the material resources, industrial organizations, and services over which Government control is necessary to the successful termination of such emergency, and such control shall be exercised by him through agencies then existing or which he may create for such purposes.

(b) To take such steps as may be necessary to stabilize prices of services and of all commodities declared to be essential, whether such services and commodities are required by the Government or by the civilian population.

Speaking of this bill, Mr. Baker said (p. 123):

It is really an express donation to the President of what has always been tacitly regarded as the war power of the President . . . confers by statutory enactment what has always been assumed to be the war power of the President.

And on pages 141 and 142:

Secretary Hurley: Now, on the question of a Constitutional amendment or the enactment of a law by Congress to give the President the power suggested for the freezing of prices, minimizing of profits, stabilizing the economic situation during an emergency, I understood you to say that under the present Constitutional powers, under the laws heretofore enacted on that subject, and under the implied power which the courts have held to be in the Chief Executive in time of emergency, all of these things can be done without further enactment?

Mr. Baker: I think they can, Mr. Secretary. Of course I have not examined any of these laws since 1921 and do not know what has been repealed since then; but I think that can all be done under the combination of the flexibility which was introduced by the Overman Act and the normal constitutional power of the Executive. If the Overman Act has been repealed (and I suppose it has been), then so much of the Capper-Johnson Act as restores that power, removing the objection pointed out by Mr. McSwain, which had not occurred to me when I read the act, would seem to me to be a very proper act to have on the statute books at all times as an element of flexibility in the executive power.

And on page 142:

Secretary Hurley: Invasion by statutory enactment of a field that is now left to implied powers. The purpose of my question is to bring out whether or not a statutory enactment usually limits implied powers or enlarges them.

Mr. Baker: It usually limits the implied powers. . . .

Secretary Hurley: In other words, you found, where you relied upon implied power, you could always go ahead; but where you had to rely upon a statutory enactment, you found your way obstructed usually by the enactment?

Mr. Baker: Yes, sir.

and finally, on page 143:

Mr. Collins: You spoke about the war powers of the President. Where do you find anything like that? I have heard that expression.

Mr. Baker: Well, the place to look for it, sir, is first to read the description of the President of the United States, as Commander-in-Chief of the Army and Navy, and then in the decisions of the Supreme Court. There is no definition of it; there is no donation of it, but the Supreme Court has found it in abundance.

The Overman Act simply authorized the President to

. . . make such redistribution of functions among executive agencies as he may deem necessary including any functions, duties, and powers hitherto by law conferred upon any executive department, commission, bureau, agency, office, or officer.

. . . utilize, co-ordinate, or consolidate any executive or administrative commissions, bureaus, agencies, offices, or officers now existing by law, to transfer any duties or powers from one existing department, commission, bureau, agency, office, or officer to another, to transfer the personnel thereof or any part of it either by detail or assignment, together with the whole or any part of the records or public property belonging thereto.

. . . establish an executive agency which may exercise such jurisdiction and control over the production of airplanes, etc.

and provided that:

. . . moneys heretofore and hereafter appropriated for the use of any executive department, commission, bureau, agency, office, or officer shall be expended only for the purposes for which it was appropriated under the direction of such other agency as may be directed by the President hereunder to perform and execute said function.

. . . should the President, in redistributing the functions among the executive agencies as provided in this Act, conclude that any bureau should be abolished and it or their duties and functions conferred upon some other department or bureau or eliminated entirely, he shall report his conclusions to Congress with such recommendations as he may deem proper.

The Overman Act thus granted no new powers whatever to the Executive Branch as a whole and specifically withheld power even to abolish a bureau. It has expired by its own limitations.

I think it is fair to conclude that Mr. Baker's opinion is that the President derives by Constitutional implication all the power that is necessary to stabilize prices and control resources or to carry into effect the recommendations I have made, and that the only statutory enactment necessary is a revival of the Overman Act. As I said in my original statement, I think the Overman Act should be revived in a future war.

To a similar result as to the effect of specific enactment to limit implication and the so-called war powers of the President was the testimony of Commander McNutt (p. 212).

It may appear somewhat inconsistent to those who were in or near wartime administration for me now to express an opinion against this point of view. I think I was one of the original protagonists of "no definition." Every other wartime administration had some specific statutory authority but the War Industries Board had none. When it was offered, we were afraid of it for the very reason Mr. Baker states. As I have repeatedly explained, we built up our whole system of control on the threat of commandeering, price fixing, and the priority system. But I cannot agree with Mr. Baker that we thought we were acting under a war power in the President that was wide enough to include every power sought to be donated by the Capper-Johnson Act (price regulation, control of industry and resources, draft of men for military service).

We had no power to commandeer. The War and Navy Departments had that. But they did not get it from the President. They got it from Congress by specific statute. Everybody acknowledged that Congress had that power and the threat to invoke it was sufficient whether we were to get it by utilizing the War and Navy Departments' specific authority or to ask Congress to give it to us for new necessities. Similarly, there was specific authority in the President (by statute, not by implication) to prescribe priority in car service. Also, under the National Defense Act and in several other acts, manufacturers of war supplies were under the President's orders to give priority to war orders. We built our whole complex system of priorities on these two statutes, at last analysis, by threatening to refuse priority on car service if other priority ratings made without such specific statutory authority were not acquiesced in. There was such close co-ordination between our Board and the War, Navy, Treasury, Food, Fuel, War Trade, Shipping and Emergency Fleet Departments, that although we had no statutory commandeering powers or priority powers our orders were backed by their specific statutory authorities and the authority of the President under the Overman Act to reallocate and redistribute functions and organizations.

In none of the legal advice taken as we set up these extraordinary functions do I recall any to the effect that such powers rested in the President by implication. Had that been the case there would have been no problem in controlling industry during the World War—there were plenty of problems.

We are here discussing a purely legal question. I am no lawyer. However, I am advised that this view is entirely correct. Briefly, as I understand it, the reasoning is as follows:

The power of the President as Commander-in-Chief of the Army and Navy relates to the administration and use of those forces as what they are—the military arm of the nation. The office of Commander-in-Chief does not of itself, even in time of war, extend powers of the President *vis-à-vis* the co-ordinate great branches—Legislative and Judicial—of our Constitutional Government.

Certain acts of President Lincoln—as, for example, the emancipation proclamation—are often adverted to, but there is no question that the Commander-in-Chief in respect of conquered territory or even perhaps of territory under martial law has authority in its nature legislative and to some extent judicial. Lincoln was acting under express statutory authority from Congress to suppress rebellion, and his acts were done under recognized principles of the law of war as applied to occupied enemy territory. The emancipation proclamation was justified as a military measure *against a common enemy.*

We are here considering implied powers of the President affecting not an enemy but the domestic civilian population—in other words, we are considering powers relating to the President not as Commander-in-Chief of military forces but as Chief Executive of the nation. I am advised that the Constitution implies no war powers in anybody in derogation of its specific provisions, among which is a clean-cut definition as between the functions of the legislative, the executive, and the judiciary. In this view the President could not draft soldiers on any implied powers. He could not commandeer plants and facilities even for military supplies without statutory authority, because the Constitution specifically provides that *Congress* shall "raise and support armies" and "provide and maintain" a navy. I understand that the Supreme Court, in the case of *Mitchell vs. Harmony,* passed very directly on this point. Similarly the President, relying solely on implied powers, could not, to the complete exclusion of the courts, fix prices, because the Constitution provides specifically for "just compensation," and it has been invariably held by our Supreme Court that at least final determination of what constitutes just compensation is a judicial and not an executive function.

I am further advised that the Supreme Court, instead of finding such war powers as we are here discussing in the President "in abundance," as Mr. Baker suggests, has invariably denied the existence of such powers in every single instance in which a case which relied on that theory has come before it.

True it has found almost unlimited war powers in *the Government,* but it has traced those powers to the same great branches of government to which the Constitution allocates them in peace, and the matters we are discussing all fall within the domain of legislative and not executive war powers.

As a layman I hesitate even to express a conjecture in the face of the opinion of so distinguished a Constitutional lawyer as Mr. Baker, and of course the Commission will take its own legal advice. On the other hand, I sincerely believe in the suggestions I am making. I earnestly hope for their adoption. I could not sit silently and see them impaired by such an opinion if it is possibly in error, and I have been shown language of the Supreme Court which inclines me to think very strongly that it *is* in error.

In the case of *United States vs. Smith* (39 Federal 851) a Circuit Court of Appeals specifically addressed our method of fixing prices and regulating industries by a sort of synthetic authority (such as I have described) based on the commandeering and priority powers of other departments of administration. The court in its opinion described the process much as I have described it here and then declared it wholly invalid in its application to the circumstances of the case before it— regulation of the wool industry and fixation of wool prices. The gist of the decision was that a body without any statutory powers whatever could not use powers created for other purposes to accomplish a purpose not contemplated by any statute. When I recall that we were then operating under the Overman Act and that the President had funneled all commandeering power through us, I get little comfort from Mr. Baker's view that the Overman Act coupled with the President's war powers is sufficient.

Entirely apart from technical legal precedent and reasoning, it certainly is a novel conception to think that the President, without any statutory authority, can raise an army by selective draft, take over any property he deems necessary, regulate prices, and control any resources of the country. It is simply to say that, in war, whenever the President decides that a dictator is necessary, he actually becomes (by the force of his own decision alone) a dictator.

I think we must have this statute and, considering the breadth of its terms, I can see no restriction on implied powers even if they exist. If they do not exist, of course no amount of definition or specific donation could limit them.

IX.   *General stabilization would very substantially reduce the cost of war and conversely would prevent enormous post-war increases in the real burden of war debts.*

In my prepared statement I concluded, among other things, in respect of the effect of general stabilization (p. 54): "It would reduce the cost of war by 50 per cent and I believe by an even greater figure." On page 33 I said:

Inflation enormously increases the cost of war and multiplies burdens on the backs of generations yet to come. The war debt of the nation is necessarily incurred in terms of debased dollar values. In the inevitable post-war deflation the debt, of course, remains at the inflated figure. Thus the bonds that our Government sold in the World War for 50-cent dollars must be paid through the years by taxes levied in 100-cent dollars.

On the same page I placed our total war expenditures at $39,000,-000,000.

On page 126 of the Record appears the following:

Senator Robinson: If I understand you, Mr. Baker, your opinion is that a statute authorizing the freezing of prices as of a given date is not only not necessary but is undesirable.

Mr. Baker: In my judgment it is, Senator. We had no such statute in the World War and, in my judgment, after we got going and realized the character and extent of the emergency, we were able successfully to cope with the price situation with the law as it was then.

Senator Robinson: What would be the natural effect on prices if no limitation were imposed at the beginning of the war?

Mr. Baker: Well, Senator, I hesitate to try to answer that question comprehensively. I cannot. But I think you will find, and I think that Colonel Ayres can prove it to you, that the thing that happened in this country was that prices went up enormously before we went into the war. . . .

Colonel Ayres' testimony begins at page 151 of the Record. After saying, "We spent roughly $22,000,000,000 from the time we entered the war," he remarks, "if one takes those various allocations of expenditure and the shifting prices of commodities during the whole period, he may then address himself to answering the questions of what would have happened in the matter of war costs if prices had been frozen as of the first day of the war. The result seems to indicate that for our entire effort . . . there might have been effected a total saving of approximately 10 per cent of the cost."

On page 168 the following appears:

Mr. Collins: I take it that you feel that a general price freezing would not be of as much benefit to the country as has generally been assumed?

Col. Ayres: No sir. I think on the contrary that it would on the one hand bring very great administrative difficulties and, on the other, that it would insure a good deal of profiteering.

(These suggestions of profiteering and difficulty have been answered on pages 25 and 30 of this statement.)

Before proceeding to discuss the issues raised by the divergencies just quoted, it is pertinent, I think, to notice the fact that within a few days after his testimony here, Colonel Ayres was widely quoted in the metropolitan press of April 16 as showing that, by reason of the decline in purchasing power of money since the settlement of the British war debt to us, and notwithstanding payment by the British of one third of their debt to us, the actual burden of that debt on the British people had been doubled. On this reasoning he seems to conclude that the only way to restore prosperity is for us now to step in and, by debt adjustment, to take on our own backs this more-than-doubled burden. So much of this as pertains to the effect of deflation to double debt is, of course, merely repeating in different words what I said when I estimated that the effect of inflation during war and inevitable post-war deflation was to double the burden of war debts on our people.

Since Mr. Baker seemed to predicate at least a part of his opinion on what Colonel Ayres later said and since the latter's statistical conclusions are so different from those I have seen and used, I must consider his testimony in detail. He said (p. 161) as a basis for his deduction that we might have saved 10 per cent by general price stabilization:

"We spent for the war roughly $22,000,000,000 from the time we entered the war."

Pausing here only long enough to observe that 10 per cent of twenty-two billion dollars is two billion two hundred million dollars, which happens to be about double the total gross public debt of the United States in 1916, I trust that we would not exactly smile such a saving away in these discussions. I am, of course, wholly unwilling to accept Colonel Ayres' estimate as the limit of possible savings.

In the first place Colonel Ayres' method of computing savings, "if prices had been frozen on the first day of the war" is entirely inappropriate to my statement before this Commission.

I said (p. 33), "There was a robust inflation here before we ever entered the war. Furthermore, nearly twelve months elapsed after our declaration before we had evolved controls and organization capable of conducting our own and our associates' procurement activities and of controlling price."

In concluding that my suggestion would reduce the cost of war 50 per cent, I made it quite clear that I referred to savings possible in any future war where price freezing would be applied before inflation had started (p. 36): "Another distinction between all previous attempts" (at price control) "with which I am familiar (including that of the World War) and the present suggestion is that what is here proposed is that we apply the organization and method developed in 1918—not after rampant inflation has run away with our economic structure—but at the very outset."

For these reasons Colonel Ayres' statement that this suggestion would have saved only $2,200,000,000 if applied in April, 1917, is not responsive to my statement here and not really germane to the issue. Also the effect of his method of computing a possibility of 10 per cent saving in the World War and then using that computation to base a conclusion that initial price freezing would "not be of much benefit" in a future war is, of course, very misleading. I think I can show ample justification for the accuracy of my statement that general price stabilization will save 50 per cent of the cost of any future war.

Even with this qualification, however, I must still take issue with Colonel Ayres' advice to the Commission that price freezing in April, 1917, would have saved only $2,200,000,000.

According to the report of the Secretary of the Treasury, 1927, pp. 646–647, our war expenditures by fiscal years for the technical period of the war were roundly:

1917	$1,233,000,000
1918	12,339,000,000
1919	17,459,000,000
1920	5,172,000,000
1921	3,817,000,000
Total	$40,020,000,000

The purchasing power of the dollar according to the Department of Labor index was as follows:

1913	143.3
1917	85.5
1918	76.4
1919	72.3
1920	65.4
1921	102.9
March, 1931	134.2

I do not want to get into an argument on figures with a distinguished economist, but it does seem to me that, in order to establish the conclusion that general stabilization at the outset of a future war would not be of as much benefit to our people as has generally been assumed, Colonel Ayres took an initial figure of outlay, 45 per cent too small, used the wrong base for estimating savings in a future war (April, 1917, instead of July, 1914) and arrived at a percentage of savings (even on his own inappropriate assumptions) about 29 per cent too small.

There is a wide variety of figures extant on costs of the war. Variation is due to variety of assumption. What we are here considering is the effect of inflation to increase war cost and of inevitable deflation to double war debt. From this point of view I think we should take *total outlay* as the figure from which to compare effects. That is the figure which we have to finance by taxation or borrowing. That is the figure which determines our debt and the future burden on the backs of our people. That is the inflated figure whose inevitable deflation invariably inflicts the world with seasons such as we are suffering now.

The annual report of the Secretary of the Treasury for 1928 (p. 564) shows our total war outlay, including continuing costs to June 30, 1928, as over $49,197,000,000, including some nine billion six hundred thousands of loans to the Allies in respect of which the Secretary of the Treasury, in his report for 1927, estimated there had been a reduction of 40 per cent from "present values" by reason of the debt settlement.

To reduce this forty-nine billion odd dollars to a workable figure of total outlay involves a maze of bookkeeping and a variety of assumption. In an exhaustive analysis published by the Bankers Trust Company and referred to as authority by the Secretary of the Treasury in a letter to me dated August 7, 1930, Harvey Fisk (p. 325, *Inter-Ally Debts*) computes for each nation what he calls "total expenditure" in the war to include the technical end of the war—June 30, 1921. His figure of "total expenditure" for the United States is $39,447,000,000. It was to this figure that I had reference in saying that our total outlay was $39,000,000,000. The report of the Secretary of the Treasury for 1927 (p. 647) computes this item at over $40,000,000,000. Mr. Fisk also computes what he calls *"net"* cost for each nation and ours is $36,186,000,000. This is very close to what the Treasury computes as net cost—$36,360,000,000. The lowest figure used by the Treasury after deducting over six billions paid by us as interest on the debt, one billion of military and naval compensation, over one third of a billion in property turned over by the War Department to other departments without cost, *and the entire portfolio of Allied obligation to us,* is $27,189,000,000. Mr. Fisk also computes what he calls "direct cost" for each nation for the fiscal years 1917–1920 inclusive and that for the United States is $26,593,000,000. In all this confusion of final figures, I have been unable to find Colonel Ayres' figure of $22,000,000,000.

I am not particularly interested in finding it because, for reasons already stated, it seems clear to me that whatever amount we might have been able to reduce from total outlay would have been net saving of public treasure. No matter what figure we take, the effect of 100 per cent inflation on that figure will be to double the cost or—conversely —the result of an inevitable 50 per cent post-war deflation will be to double the debt.

An interesting confirmation of my estimated 50 per cent or more saving by price stabilization, and also of the beneficial effect of our partial price fixing, will be found at page 328 of *Inter-Ally Debts* referred to above, where Mr. Fisk computes the direct cost to Allies (including ourselves) and enemies for the "second part" of the war (fiscal years 1917–1920 inclusive) and then recomputes this cost in "1913" dollars. Results are as follows:

	I Direct Cost in currency dollars 000,000 omitted	II Direct Cost in "1913" dollars 000,000 omitted	Ratio Column I to Column II
United States	26,593	12,212	217%
Associated powers except U. S.	78,528	21,259	369%
Central Powers	41,774	12,428	336%
Total for all belligerents	146,895	45,899	312%

On these figures I based my conclusion on page 54 of the record with reference to general price stabilization at the outset of war:

"It would reduce the cost of war by 50 per cent and I believe by an even greater figure."

It might interest the Commission to know that wholesale prices in England showed a rise of 88 per cent during the Napoleonic wars, followed by a decline of 14 years to the pre-war norm. During the four years of our Civil War, wholesale prices in the United States practically doubled and reached the pre-war norm after fifteen years of deflation. Wholesale prices in the United States reached a peak of 226 per cent of the pre-war figure in 1920, stood at 120 per cent at the end of 1930, and are now—eleven years after the peak—about 104 per cent of the pre-war level. (Computations, except of present status, are to be found in *Economic Outlook for Agriculture* by G. F. Warren, Professor of Agricultural Economics, Cornell University.)

In the face of such facts as these, it is a little difficult to follow this witness' statement that general stabilization "would not be of as much benefit to the country as generally has been assumed."

Another aspect of Colonel Ayres' testimony which seems critical of the suggestion of general stabilization but which is cast in such form as to make it difficult to bring it to a clear-cut issue is that, in computing what he calls a saving of 10 per cent possible, if we had general price freezing, his method omits to consider that we *did* have partial price freezing and that it did save a great deal more than $2,200,000,000.

For example, he considers what the price of iron and steel was at April, 1917, then says it declined 11 per cent during the war, and obviously omits to include the effect of that decline in concluding that general stabilization would not be of as much value as has generally been assumed. The fact is that the Government's index for iron and steel prices for 1914 was 61.4. In April, 1917, it was 154.2. In July, 1917, it was 227.6. We fixed prices in September, 1917, by a flat downward revision, and in October, 1917, *by reason of such fixing* it was 143.7. The effect of this on the general price index was very great. Considering the magnitude of the textile industry and the effects of rents on the cost of living, it is interesting to speculate on what would have been the savings if those two price groups had also been stabilized.

I will not weary the Commission with similar figures for other controlled commodities. There is, I think, in your record an exhaustive study showing all these controlled movements (Bulletin No. 3, War Industries Board Price Section). It will show you in a series of amazing graphs beginning at page 507 similar results, varying of course in degree and time, for sugar, wheat, iron and steel, coal, coke, and petroleum—and by great groups (pp. 26 and 27) the effect of control on prices of food, clothing, rubber and paper, metals, fuels, building materials, and chemicals. I shall not attempt to try to estimate what these savings were, but I venture to say that no one who examines these data will be greatly impressed by Colonel Ayres' computation that price freezing at April 1917 would have saved this government only $2,200,000,000.

One way to get some idea of the saving is to observe the table on page 57 of this statement which shows that against an inflation for us—over 1913 prices—of 117 per cent, our associates suffered an inflation of 269 per cent and our enemies 236 per cent. Price control abroad was not as effective as it was here.

X. *Statutory Provisions*

I have had drafted and append hereto a form of statute. I want to make it very clear that this draft is not submitted as a suggested bill. It is lacking in many details. I had it prepared solely for the purpose of raising in form appropriate for discussion by your legal advisers some of the incidental matters raised by my principal suggestion. This was necessary because, without some such vehicle of exposition, a legal precisionist might possibly conclude that this or that resultant application of the principal suggestion would raise Constitutional barriers and so dismiss the whole suggestion.

I shall not weary the Commission by reading the draft and certainly I shall not attempt to discuss the legal questions involved. General Johnson, who was instrumental in drawing up the Selective Service legislation, as it was submitted to Congress during the war, and who wrote the Selective Service Regulations, assisted in preparing this draft. He has been called by you and can discuss any legal questions you may have.

In brief synopsis:

Section 1 limits the extraordinary powers donated to the President to the period of the war.

Section 2 authorizes the President to proclaim a day on or about the day of declaration of any war as of which he thinks abnormal disturbances in the general price structure are at a minimum.

Section 3 provides that ten days after such proclamation and thereafter during the war prices in effect on that day shall be deemed fair market prices.

Section 4 authorizes the President to adjust any such fair market price either upward or downward.

Section 5 makes it unlawful for anyone to buy or sell at a higher price than the fair market price or that price as adjusted, and obliterates legal rights to recover any excess charged or contracted for, and contains a penal provision for violations.

Section 6 is a safety provision against the contention that the frozen price might catch somebody with goods on hand bought at a higher price than fair market price on the proclaimed day and that the proclaimed price therefor constitutes confiscation. It permits such an individual to sell at a selling price in excess of the fair market selling price but not in greater excess than that of his cost over fair market cost price.

As a matter of practice it is doubtful whether such a seller could find a buyer at the higher prices in a case when the market would have been stabilized at a lower price by the proclamation, but this circumstance has been held by the Supreme Court not to constitute confiscation.

Section 7 authorizes the President to fix prices piecemeal if he decides against general stabilization, and contains a safety provision similar to Section 6.

Section 8 legalizes the power of the President to create such a priority system as was synthesized in 1917 by the War Industries Board.

Section 9 donates to the President general commandeering power with a provision for just compensation.

Section 10 provides that if a person accepts fair market price as determined by the statute, he shall be deemed to have accepted it as just compensation and makes it clear that the statute itself compels nobody to sell at the fixed price.

Section 11 is another safety provision. It gives any person a right to complain to executive agency that the fair market price deprives him of just compensation. That agency may then commandeer, in which case the question of just compensation is first determined administratively with a right of appeal to the Courts. If that agency does not commandeer, the complainant is given the right to have the United States Attorney proceed against his property by libel in condemnation and judicial sale, analogous to proceedings in admiralty, but at a price no higher than whatever the Court deems just compensation. This section applies only to things and not to services or estates in real property, in which latter cases it would be inappropriate.

Section 12 entitles a person who complains of a rate of service or rental, determined by the statute, to apply to enjoin the rate as to his particular case alone on the ground that the established rate is not just compensation. If successful, the rate is enjoined as to him, but the injunction is to be of no effect if the particular rate is adjusted upward by at least 10 per cent under the authority of the President, except that the complainant may again apply for an injunction with similar effect.

The obvious purposes of Sections 11 and 12 are to leave open an appeal to the courts in any case. Except for a few particular instances of unforeseeable hardship, which *ought* to be relieved, it is not believed that these provisions would result either in much administration or in material effect on the general purpose. If under Section 11 the property is a shortage item in great demand, the Government will commandeer. If it is not, then nobody will pay more than the stabilized maximum because, that being the market price, everybody knows that the material is available at that price.

There are three possible conditions as to general prices: (a) a fairly normal situation such as, let us say, that of 1928; (b) an unusual depression such as 1921; (c) an unusual distortion such as 1917. In any one of the three cases we simply clamp down a ceiling on the whole structure and then move to correct inequities. In cases (b) and (c) there would be much for the price-fixing commission to do. In case (a) there would be very little to do.

We must try to reconstruct for ourselves, in considering all these matters, the whole plan of control here advocated and the psychological aspects of a great war. I am prepared to agree with anybody that without the whole system of integrated industrial control recommended here no price stabilization can be effective. I am also prepared to agree that without a great surge of popular and patriotic inspiration neither the Selective Draft nor price fixing nor any other sacrificial statute can be enforced. I have no apprehensions as to the effectiveness of these proposals.

My view is that a price ceiling would establish a recognized market. I believe that, with vigorous education on the principles here proposed, that market would have an almost fanatical support by the public, in whose interest the whole scheme is devised—just such a situation as Mr. Baker described here in telling how our people voluntarily accepted and made their own heatless, meatless, gasless, breadless, etc., days, and woe to him who violated them! I believe that this spirit would be even more intense to support prices against inflation because that adds acute self-interest to enthusiasm.

For these reasons I feel sure that resistance even by appeals to courts would be very unpopular, that under the safety provisions, whether by judicial sale or permission to sell at a higher than market price, no complainant would get a higher price, that the courts would not be generous in dealing with such cases, and that after a few early educational attempts to use the safety provisions we would hear no more about them.

As I have said, framing of the statute is work for other hands than mine. There may be—and doubtless are—other and better mechanical and legal methods. The one before you is merely a vehicle for discussion.

XI. Conclusion

I regret that this reply had to be so long and so much in detail. I felt that, having made a suggestion here in respect of which some contrary opinion was expressed, it was incumbent upon me to show that the suggestion was not imposed upon you lightly and after immature deliberation.   On the contrary, because the experience of nearly every witness was confined to his particular valley of effort and because my own place happened to be at the confluence of all valleys, it seemed to be my duty to this Commission to examine for it every detail of criticism from each of these particularized points of view, in the light of the broader and more intense experience of prime responsibility.

In my own mind, at least, these criticisms have been very welcome because they have enabled me to test my original conclusions from a variety of angles—an experience which has strengthened and confirmed me in my opinion that the suggested plan is right and of overwhelming necessity to this nation.   The War Department criticism was particularly helpful.   It enabled me to clear up a misunderstanding, with the elimination of which, I am informed by General Moseley, we are in complete accord on the subject of general price stabilization.   If there is any doubt about this, Secretary Hurley can clear it up or, if the Commission sees fit, it can call General Moseley.

Finally, in closing, I think I should disclaim any desire to appear here as either a dictator or a doctrinaire.   Having been accorded unusual responsibility and honors in the war, I feel a duty to record with meticulous care my experience and recommendation.   It seems to have brought me into slight differences of opinion with some men of great distinction in career and attainment, nearly all of whom are my personal friends, the objects of my affection and regard.   I trust that, in the warmth of advocacy, I have given offense to none and that all these men will credit me with the same motives which I know actuated them—a sincere and earnest desire to preserve in the record opinions based on experience which may prove of value to our common country.

Expository Draft of Statute

AN ACT to provide for the national defense by equalizing the burdens of war; preventing inflation and excessive profits during war; reducing the cost of war; maintaining the credit of the United States and procuring supplies for, and preserving the morale of, the military and naval forces and the civil population during war.

Be it enacted by the Senate and House of Representatives of the United States of America in Congress assembled:

Section 1. That those provisions of this Act which create extraordinary powers in the President shall be in effect only during the period of any war declared by Congress.

Section 2. That at any time during the period of any war declared by Congress, the President may determine and, by proclamation, announce a day on or about the day of such declaration as of which, in the opinion of the President, abnormal disturbances in the general structure of market prices in the United States are at a minimum.

Section 3. That whenever the President shall determine and by proclamation announce a day, as provided in Section 2 hereof, then, ten days after such proclamation and thereafter during the period of the war, the highest market price, as of such proclaimed day, at any place within the United States, for any services, right, or thing, except for the fee estate in real property, shall be deemed, and is hereinafter called, the fair market price for the same or a similar service, right, or thing at the same place and in similar circumstances.

Section 4. That, whenever the President shall determine and by proclamation announce a day, as provided in Section 2 hereof, he may at any time thereafter adjust, either upward or downward, and by proclamation announce, any fair market price as determined by Section 3 hereof and ten days after such proclamation and thereafter, during the period of the war, such adjusted price shall have the same effect under this Act as such price before such adjustment.

Section 5. Whenever the President shall, by proclamation, announce a day, as provided in Section 2 hereof, or, by proclamation, adjust a price, as provided in Section 4 hereof, then, ten days after such proclamation and thereafter during the period of the war, it shall be unlawful for any person to buy, sell, or otherwise contract for any service, right, or thing at a price higher than the fair market price in effect as of such day or than such fair market price as adjusted and proclaimed by the President; and no purchase, sale, or other contract at a price in excess thereof shall carry any obligation between the parties thereto in respect of such excess; and whoever shall buy, sell, or otherwise contract for any service, right, or thing at a price in excess thereof shall, upon conviction thereof, be punished by a fine of not more than $2,000 or by imprisonment for not more than two years. Each transaction shall be a separate offense.

Section 6. Whenever, in any criminal proceeding charging a violation of Section 5 hereof, or in any civil suit for the excess of any price over fair market price as by this Act determined, the person alleging it can show that the seller (or person bound by contract to render, transfer, or deliver any service, right, or thing) purchased or contracted for the same prior to the date of the President's proclamation and at a cost price higher than the fair market cost price as by such proclamation determined, and that the excess of selling price charged or contracted for over the fair market selling price as by such proclamation determined did not exceed the amount by which his cost price exceeded the fair market cost price as by such proclamation determined, then such transaction shall not be deemed unlawful, the obligation as between the parties of such purchase, sale, or other contract shall not be deemed by Section 5 of this Act to be impaired, and such showing shall be a sufficient defense to any prosecution hereunder.

Section 7. That after any declaration of war by Congress and before the proclamation by the President of a day, as provided in Section 2 hereof, the President is hereby authorized and empowered, wherever and whenever in his judgment necessary for any of the purposes recited in the title of this Act, to fix and by proclamation announce the price of any service, right, or thing, except the fee estate in real property, and thereafter to adjust, either upward or downward, any price so fixed and by proclamation to announce such adjustment. Ten days after any such proclamation of a price or adjustment thereof and thereafter during the period of the war, it shall be unlawful for any person to buy, sell, or otherwise contract for any service, right, or thing in respect of which such price has been so fixed or adjusted, at a price higher than such fixed price or such price as adjusted; and no purchase, sale, or other contract at a price in excess thereof shall carry any obligation between the parties thereto in respect of such excess; and whoever shall buy, sell, or otherwise contract at a price in excess thereof shall, upon conviction thereof, be punished by a fine of not more than $2,000 or by imprisonment for not more than two years. Each transaction shall be a separate offense: Provided, however, that, whenever, in any criminal suit charging a violation of Section 7 hereof, or in any civil suit for the excess of any price over such fixed or adjusted price, the person alleging it can show that the seller (or person bound to render, transfer, or deliver any service, right, or thing) purchased or contracted for the same prior to the President's proclamation—at a cost price higher than that fixed or as adjusted thereby, and that the excess of selling price charged or contracted for over the fixed selling price, or such fixed selling price as adjusted, did not exceed the amount by which his cost price exceeded the fixed cost price or such fixed cost price as adjusted, then such transaction shall not be deemed unlawful, the obligation, as between the parties, of such purchase, sale, or other contract shall not be deemed by this Section to be impaired, and such showing shall be a sufficient defense to any prosecution under this Section.

Section 8. That the President is hereby authorized during the period of any war declared by Congress to determine the order of priority in which any manufacturer, dealer, public service, or any other person or classes of persons shall fill customers' or other orders and, after any such determination and thereafter during the period of the war, it shall be unlawful for any such manufacturer, dealer, public service, or other person or classes of persons to fill any such order in any other order of priority, and whoever shall fill any such order in any other order of priority shall, upon conviction, be punished by a fine of not more than $2,000 or by imprisonment for not more than two years. Each transaction shall be a separate offense.

Section 9. That whenever, during the period of any war declared by Congress, the President shall determine that all or any part of any property, real, personal, or mixed, or any estate, right, interest, use, or tenure in all or any part of any such property should be seized for the furtherance of any purpose recited in the title of this Act, he shall first determine and tender just compensation therefor and thereafter he is hereby authorized to requisition or commandeer the same. Whenever any person having been tendered just compensation as just provided shall not be satisfied with the same, he shall be paid seventy-five percentum of the amount tendered and shall thereafter be entitled to sue the United States in the manner provided by Section 24, paragraph 20 and Section 145 of the Judicial Code for an amount which when added to such seventy-five percentum of the amount so tendered shall be just compensation.

Section 10. Whenever, during the period of any war declared by Congress, any person sells or contracts to sell any service, right, or thing, he shall be deemed to have accepted the price in such purchase, sale, or other contract as just compensation, whether the same be in violation of, or in accordance with, this Act, and he shall have no further rights under this Act in respect thereof, but this Act shall not be construed as compelling any person to buy, sell, or otherwise contract for any service, right, or thing at any price as hereby determined.

Section 11. When any person shall refuse to accept any price as determined hereby for any right or thing, except such price for estates in real property or for services, whether personal or not personal, on the ground that the same does not afford just compensation, he may, within thirty days after the date of the President's proclamation by which such price is determined, notify such agency as the President shall designate in such proclamation. Such notice shall be in writing and shall set forth the circumstances, shall describe the property, and shall be accompanied by a demand upon him to sell such property at such price in writing, including a tender of such price, and signed by any Federal officer, or a similar demand and tender signed by a citizen of such state, territory, or district resident in the city, county, or township in which such property is held and certified as to the facts recited therein by a justice of the peace of such county or any magistrate of similar or of higher jurisdiction. If, within thirty days after the mailing of a notice as provided for in Section 11 hereof, such property has not been requisitioned or commandeered by the President as provided in Section 9 hereof, such person may, in a writing setting forth the circumstances and attaching a certified copy of such notice with all enclosures thereto, notify the United States Attorney for the proper district. It shall thereupon become the duty of such United States Attorney to proceed against such property in any district court of the United States within the district where the same is found by a process of libel for condemnation as in this section authorized. Jurisdiction is hereby conferred upon the district courts of the United States to hear and determine such suits in libel for condemnation and, if it shall be finally adjudged that such price so refused does not afford just compensation, such property shall be sold in such manner as the court may direct, but not at a price in excess of the minimum which the court shall in each case determine to afford just compensation, and the proceeds of such sale, less the legal costs and charges thereof, shall be paid to the party entitled thereto. The proceedings in such libel cases shall conform as near as may be to the proceedings in admiralty, except that either party may demand trial by jury of any issue of fact joined in any such case and all such proceedings shall be at the suit of and in the name of the United States.

Section 12. If any person shall complain, in respect of any price for services, personal or not personal, including rates of rental for real estate, as by this act determined—whether it be a rate or rent for any real estate or any service not personal or a wage, fee, commission, or reward for any personal service—that, in the case of a service not personal, it does not admit of a fair return on his investment, or in the case of a personal service, that it does not afford just compensation, he shall be entitled to file a written complaint under regulations made by the President or under his authority to an agency to be designated by the President and to a prompt hearing before such agency, and if, within sixty days after the filing of such complaint, such price shall not have been adjusted, or if it shall have been adjusted but such person shall still complain that, as adjusted, it does not admit of a fair return on his investment or afford just compensation, he shall have a right to file a bill, in the proper District Court, for an injunction against all officers and agencies of the United States to prevent their enforcing such price as to the petitioner under any of the provisions of this Act. District Courts are hereby given jurisdiction to hear such complaints and, if it be adjudged in a particular case that such price does not admit a fair return on investment or afford just compensation, to issue such injunction to apply only to the circumstances of that particular case; provided, however, that if, at any time thereafter, such price shall be adjusted upward by not less than ten percentum by the President or under his authority, such injunction shall thereby and thereafter be of no effect, but nothing in this section shall be construed as preventing such complainant from again complaining in the manner and with the effect herein provided.

Editor's Preface to Part III

THE INDUSTRIAL MOBILIZATION PLAN that was approved by the War Policies Commission in 1931 underwent many drastic changes in the revisions of 1933 and 1936 and 1939. For example, the proposed program for strict control over propaganda and censorship was knocked out of the 1936 revision because of the vigorous opposition of the Nye Committee.

Completely eliminated from the 1939 revision was the proposal for strict control over the labor supply—reflecting the influence and pressure of those who, like Mr. Baruch, feel that the Army has never demonstrated an understanding of labor's problems, nor an ability to think and plan with a fairness toward labor.

However, the basic pattern of centralized authority developed by Mr. Baruch and his associates in the War Industries Board remained throughout all the revisions. This pattern included, furthermore, the separation of the price control authority from the central administration of wartime industry.

But the program for control of prices, and profits, has remained only a proposal, without any statutory basis. Because there was insufficient agreement on every proposal, the War Policies Commission passed by the question of a statute. Legislation has been introduced in Congress from time to time, but nothing has ever been done about it.

Before the Nye Committee in 1935, Mr. Baruch pursued again his quest for legislation outlined in Parts I and II—but the Nye inquiry got off on so many tangents that it became impossible to find a program mutually acceptable to the Nye group and the President's committee, of which Mr. Baruch was chairman.

As a result, the country entered upon the present emergency still without any direct price- and profit-control legislation upon the statute books. Which, to a large extent, accounts for the further presentation of Mr. Baruch's views on price control and priorities that follows in Part III.

While this article was written directly for the *Harvard Business Review*, Mr. Baruch had before him the belief that it should be used as a concluding word in this re-publication of his views.

R. H. H.

PRIORITIES—THE SYNCHRONIZING FORCE*

THE DEMANDS of total warfare upon a nation's economy have become overwhelming. Even in the United States, with its present excess capacity and its unemployed reserves of labor, the requirements of an all-out rearmament effort are large enough to tax some industries beyond their limit, and the unfolding of the full-fledged program appears now to be rapidly extending this condition to the whole industrial structure. In World War I, which the country entered without the advantage of past experience and of the present reserves of industrial capacity and labor, the demands of the war machine were terrible in their sudden hugeness, and would have buried and asphyxiated the entire economic system if some means had not been found to channel the flood of orders and to govern the facilities for filling these orders. Unimportant goods were being made before essentials, commodities were being produced that could not find transportation facilities to take them to their destinations, while other articles were carried to embarkation points by the railroads only to find no ships available to take them to France. Freight accumulated so overwhelmingly at some ports that the railroads could no longer approach the docks but had to unload freight in empty fields ten or twenty miles back.

At the same time the un-co-ordinated Army and Navy supply bureaus competed against each other, with the other Government procurement agencies, with the Allies, and with civilian buyers. Manufacturers found themselves swamped with conflicting orders far beyond their capacity to produce and yet continued to try to grab as many more orders as they could, at the same time being harassed by demands from the Government agencies for preferential treatment and threats of commandeering.

To deal with such a situation, the system of industrial mobilization headed by the War Industries Board was developed during the World War, and was later elaborated in the planning carried on by the Army Industrial College and the office of the Assistant Secretary of War after 1920. Briefly, according to this plan all Government purchasing is routed through one agency, the War Industries Board, which is divided into numerous committee or "commodity sections," one for each important industrial product. Representatives of each interested Government department sit on these committees, so that

* Reprinted by permission from the *Harvard Business Review.*

465

the demand is fully represented. On the other side of the picture, supply is represented by a number of corresponding War Service Committees, formed with the co-operation of the various trade associations, to represent each industry and to aid the Government in determining resources and other questions affecting the industry. Each commodity section can thus deal directly with the corresponding War Service Committee representing organized demand.

At the heart of this simple but battle-tested plan is the Priorities Division, another subcommittee of the War Industries Board, whose duty it is to administer the priorities system. The functions of the priorities system are to determine whenever necessary the precedence of production and delivery of the above-mentioned products, and the proportions of any of them and of all other necessities which are to be made accessible to the various and varying demands for them. Such necessities may involve, besides plant facilities, (a) the supply of raw materials and finished products, (b) fuel supply or electric energy or both, (c) transportation by road, rail, water, pipeline, or otherwise, (d) labor, and (e) access to the capital markets.

RAW MATERIALS AND FINISHED PRODUCTS

The problem facing the Priorities Division in allocating the supplies of raw materials and finished products is to determine what amount of these commodities is to be made available to the many competing demands for them. Should locomotives go to the front to help the transportation of troops and supplies, or should they be held in this country to facilitate the production and shipment of these supplies? Should steel go to fighting ships whose mission is to destroy submarines, or to merchant ships which have been thinned down to the breaking point of the whole supply system? Should nitrates go to munitions without which guns would be useless, or to fertilizer without which the men who fire these guns would be foodless? And so forth, down to the smallest and seemingly most insignificant articles of production.

The concrete problem in allocating these scarce supplies is to provide some system whereby each producer can determine easily in what sequence his many competing orders should be filled. If he is faced with a large backlog, he should not be left to deal with it on the basis of his previous business relations with the purchasers as he would in peacetime, nor should he be allowed to fill the orders according to his own private estimate of their importance. Rather his contracts should be filled in the order of their urgency in relation to the war effort as a whole as determined by the Priorities Division, working on the basis of carefully planned time schedules of the whole nation's production. During World War I this was accomplished by a system of priorities certificates administered by the Priorities Division. All orders were divided into the following classifications:

Class AA—Emergency war work of an exceptional nature.

Class A —All other war work.

Class B —Orders and work which, while not *primarily* designed for the prosecution of the war, are of public interest and essential to the national welfare, such as textile machinery, railroad and farm equipment, machine tools, refinery supplies, etc.

Class C —Orders and work not covered by the above classifications, which nevertheless are to be utilized in furtherance of one or more of the purposes outlined in the lists of "industries demanding preferential treatment."

Class D —All work not embraced in the above classes.

All Government agencies or private purchasers, before placing orders for scarce commodities or facilities, had to submit applications to the Priorities Division, giving the name of the concern with whom the order was to be placed, the quantity and description of the material, the delivery date desired, and the amount of war work that the purchaser was doing. The Priorities Division took this application, referred it in some cases to the other branches of the Government or of the War Industries Board in charge of the industry in question, and then issued a priorities certificate, ranking the order according to the classes outlined above. The purchaser could then attach this certificate to his order and place it with the factory. The factory itself, in case it was short of anything necessary to this order, could get priority ratings and so on throughout the whole sequence of production.

Guided by these certificates, factory operators were thus able to arrange their production schedules so that all their contracts would be filled in the proper order. Class AA had to be given immediate preference, Class A had to be attended to before Class B, Class B before Class C, and Class C before Class D. This rule did not mean, however, that all operations had to be suspended on Class B work until the orders under Class A were finished. Production on lower-class work could be continued as long as it was possible to complete the orders in higher classes in time to meet their delivery dates.

Later these larger classifications were split down into subdivisions of descending importance, such as A1, A2, A3, B1, B2, B3, and so forth. The whole schedule, moreover, remained subject to revision as the war effort expanded and new shortages appeared.

During the World War this system proved to be smooth-working beyond all expectation in routing the supplies of necessary materials away from less essential industries into uses more essential for the armament program. However, the Priorities Division did not attempt to draw too sharp a line between essential and non-essential industries. Some were recognized to be more and some less important to the defense effort; but the whole economy was viewed more as a series of activities of gradually decreasing urgency in relation to the entire structure of mobilized industry. Cutting off some portions of the demand by denying materials to less essential industries was most helpful, but it was never done completely, and only when absolutely necessary. Even those among the least vital, such as the jewelry industry, were not marked out for complete elimination but were subject only to the strict curtailment incident to being placed in the last priorities classification. In such cases it is possible to skeletonize an industry if necessary, but it is extremely unwise ever to destroy one completely. An Industrial Adjustment Committee appointed by President Wilson to investigate this problem during the World War decided that to do away with these trades entirely would have caused hardships unwarranted by the small amount of materials, labor, and transportation saved.

After July 1, 1918, the system of classifying orders was made automatic and was left to the responsibility of the purchaser in all classifications below A3. Instead of applying for priorities certificates, the purchaser had only to attach an affidavit to his order stating the facts essential to its automatic rating and naming the uses for which the materials were needed. The Priorities Division remained merely as a sort of watch dog to catch any violators who might take advantage of this privilege.

In administering the priorities system, the Priorities Board must pay careful attention to the timing problem. Priorities should be applied as soon as the action of the Government in carrying out the armaments program has made impending shortages apparent in any of the above components of production. Then there is a more delicate timing problem after the system has been launched, which must be dealt with carefully to attain the maximum possible synchronization of all elements of the nation's industry.

This problem may be made clearer by a specific example. An airplane ready for fighting is made up of a number of component parts: wings, body, motor, gasoline tanks, radio equipment, guns, ammunition, bombs or torpedoes, armor plate, and so forth. It is useless to accelerate the production of these parts unless all are expedited in the same fashion so that all are ready for assembly at one time. If the wings, fuselage, and gasoline tanks are rushed through the factories only to have to wait until engines can be attached, the whole system in this case has been useless in speeding up the completion of the finished instrument of war. The Priorities Administration, therefore, must make special efforts to attain synchronization of the manufacture of all the parts of each essential armament.

Not only that, but all the industrial processes behind the manufacture of these parts, from the extraction of the raw materials down to the fabrication of the finished goods, should be kept under cognizance. The production of machine tools to manufacture the engine, the building of factories for assembling the fuselages, and the construction of aluminum plants to produce raw materials for the coverings—all have to be co-ordinated with the central effort in order to get maximum speed and to attain the utmost possible use from the scarce commodities involved. A well-administered Priorities Division will act in such cases before bottlenecks can occur, allocating the supplies of scarce goods and services among the more essential demands and shutting off supplies from the less essential. By the proper timing of allocation and production, bottlenecks can be very nearly eliminated.

Such close synchronization can be approximated by means of the priorities certificate system, and particularly by insuring that all producers obtain the goods they need on the delivery date specified on their priorities applications. This delivery date is the most important single factor in attaining proper synchronization. Producers must be urged to exercise all possible care in determining the date when the necessary raw materials and finished products will actually be required. They should not ask, through fear of future unexpected shortages in the market, to have delivery made before they are prepared to use the article. To do so would not only throw the whole time schedule off, but would also distort the supply-demand picture by enlarging the apparent demand above actual needs.

Priorities in the field of consumers' goods present a different problem. Commodities of which shortages exist in wartime cannot be distributed only to those able to pay the highest prices, as under the normal laws of supply and demand. The need for preserving civilian morale forbids that necessities should be given only to those with the longest pocketbook. For this reason food, clothing, and all other vital elements that go to make up the cost of living, if they become scarce, must be rationed equitably among all consumers. The most satisfactory method is a system of ration cards together with the licensing of wholesale and retail distributors. It should be said that, with our large capacity to produce the staple foods and clothing in this country, the situation never became so critical in the last war that such a drastic system as the ration-card method became necessary, nor does it seem likely in any emergency of the near future; but, by the time of the armistice in 1918, plans were being formed to reduce all shoes and clothing to a few simple styles, which, if necessary, would have been rationed, and to extend the rationing system more thoroughly in the case of goods. Licensing of food distributors was used by the Food Administration to attain some control of distribution and the price structure, while a similar plan to license shoe stores, to go into effect in July, 1919, had been drawn up by the War Industries Board by the end of the war.

TRANSPORTATION AND LABOR

Transportation likewise must be governed by a priorities system if shortages start to appear, to insure that facilities will not become over-congested in certain parts of the country and that they will be used for purposes most essential to national defense. The supply of man-power also is a component of production that must be controlled by a thorough priorities system if the demands of the fighting forces and of industry start to exceed the total number of employables. The pools of skilled labor, of managerial ability, and of men trained to be fighters should be parcelled out according to a central plan based on the most vital needs of the war machine. If the shortage of man-power becomes acute, some general rule such as the "Work or Fight" regulation of General Crowder and the Provost Marshal's office in the World War must be invoked to provide that very man either enters the Army or the Navy or takes part in some essential war work. Close co-operation is necessary here between (1) the war industrial administration, (2) the organization handling labor relations, disputes, and so forth, which under the best plan would be an integral part of the industrial administration machinery, and (3) the personnel departments of the Army and the Navy. Through this liaison, the recruiting policies of the Army and the Navy can be correlated as closely as possible with the labor needs of the essential industries so that the latter are not deprived of their skilled labor or their minimum requirements of unskilled workers. At the same time the industrial administration can see to it that the remaining supply of labor, after the levies are taken into the Army and the Navy, is allocated throughout industry in a way that will most wisely promote the production of war materials. This does not mean "conscription" of labor or any compulsion on any man to work for some particular employer not of his own choosing. Lastly, the co-operation of the labor relations branch will see that the labor priorities system and all the regulations preventing undue shifting of jobs and competition for the labor supply do not work undue hardships on the laborers themselves. Strikes are sure to occur, and justifiably, if any effort is made to take advantage of the situation to reverse labor's hard-won advances. The labor relations branch will serve an invaluable purpose in preventing such strikes either by opposing unjust encroachments on labor's rights or by winning the backing of labor for any sacrifices that are found absolutely necessary.

As I pointed out in my testimony before the War Policies Commission in 1931—at which time I laid down a complete program for the economic and civilian mobilization of America:

. . . that labor should be inordinately rewarded is unnecessary, wrong and easily avoidable, but *not* by drafting men to work for other men. A soldier serves the nation directly. There is but one master in the case and that master is America. He serves to profit no one but the country as a whole. There is no distinction between him and his comrades. He enters an immemorial status. His entry is not contractual. He is clothed, fed, housed, and attended.

As long as our present industrial organization maintains, industry is in the hands of millions of private employers. It is operated for profit to them. The employee therefore serves in private industry operating for gain. Enforced and involuntary service for a private master is and has been clearly and repeatedly defined by our Supreme Court as slavery inhibited by the Thirteenth Amendment to the Constitution of the United States.

If any such provision were made, it might be used to break a perfectly justifiable strike and so at one sweep destroy all the social advance of our labor system in the last century.

Access to sources of capital must come under the cognizance of the Priorities Administration. Some authority such as the War Finance Corporation in the World War, under the direction of the Treasury Department but in close co-operation with the Priorities Division, should co-ordinate all loans for plant expansion and other war purposes and must license private capital issues, limiting those that are not for purposes vital to the war effort.

Finally the priorities system must be extended to the control of exports and imports. If a shortage of shipping arises, some supervision should be exercised to see that the scarce cargo space is used only for the most vital purposes. During the World War this problem was assigned to the Shipping Board, although because of the international nature of the question, most of the functions devolved upon the Allied Shipping Control in London. The Export-Import

Bank or some body similar to the War Trade Board in World War I must also be formed to license all transactions in foreign trade, preventing the export of essential materials which should be kept for the domestic war industries or the import of nonessentials at the expense of more vital commodities.

To serve as a guide to other war agencies during the World War in allocating the above components of production, the Priorities Division issued a "General Classification of Purposes Demanding Preferential Treatment" which listed all manufacturers of ships, munitions, Army and Navy supplies, fuel, food and collateral industries, clothing, railroads and public utilities.

The Division itself governed the allocation of finished products and raw materials by means of its priorities certificates system but used the above classification to help guide the other Government boards. Fuel was administered by the Fuel Board and transportation facilities by the Railroad Administration. Labor relations were under the jurisdiction of the War Labor Board and the War Labor Policies Board, while the problem of supplying man-power for the essential industries was handled by the United States Employment Service. Priorities questions in labor were administered by the Employment Service and also the industrial advisers of each of the local draft boards, who based their policies on the decisions of a Labor Priorities Section set up under the Priorities Division in Washington. All these authorities worked in close co-operation with the policies of the War Industries Board, but undoubtedly in the future smoother operation could be obtained if all their priority functions were centralized under one organization.

PRICE CONTROL

The priorities system cannot work alone. It is the heart of industrial mobilization, but it needs the other organs. Above all, it must have the assistance of price control, conservation, the search for substitutes, and commandeering.

Price control is necessary because the priorities system is actually a means of short-circuiting the laws of supply and demand. Scarce commodities, instead of being distributed to those who can pay the highest price as under a free economy, are allocated to those needs that are most important to the armament effort as a whole. Such a violation of natural law makes it absolutely necessary to supplement the priorities system with some control of prices. If the prices of rationed goods were left free to fluctuate, price competition would immediately occur and, under the pressure of competitive bidding for the scarce items, the whole system of distribution by priorities would break down. Sellers would be given an irresistible incentive to distribute their commodities to those willing to pay the highest prices rather than to those indicated by the Priorities Administration. Bootlegging and other forms of evasion would inevitably appear.

There is no system of price control that does not have its shortcomings, but no method has yet been found that has so few as does that of placing a ceiling over all prices above which they cannot rise but below which they are free to fall. When industry has reached full capacity and price fixing is admittedly necessary, this ceiling should be clamped down, and all prices, wages, rents, and other forms of remuneration limited to the highest levels obtaining on a certain specific day. Thus the whole structure of that day will be preserved, with two important exceptions: all rates will be free to fall below the fixed level, and certain prices may be adjusted upwards by a Price Adjustment Committee organized to correct inequities. All rates should stay in effect for some set period such as three months, after which they may be subject to change upon presentation of data by the industry in question.

There is no need for such a thoroughgoing plan until a general rise in the price level is threatening. If industry is working below capacity and the price level is resting fairly stable, it will be sufficient to attack the prices of individual commodities where scarcity is causing the price to be bid up above all equitable cost relationships. If a general inflation is evident, however, there are numerous reasons why the attempt to fix individual prices would be unwise and why the method of clamping the ceiling down on the whole structure would be both easier and more equitable.

In the first place, fixing individual prices after the whole structure has started to move upwards would mean studying the costs of the producers involved and then taking somebody's judgment, on the basis of these studies, as to what the particular price should be. The price-ceiling plan initially proposes no such application of human judgment. It addresses the whole interrelated pattern of prices as it exists under present natural economic law and says of it, "Since arbitrary governmental rationing will henceforth govern supply, and governmental priority—and not price—will control demand, we propose to keep intact this, the last normal price schedule which we are likely to see for many a day." It is a preservation of a natural existing determination rather than a substitution of a collection of artificial determinations.

Secondly, the fixing of individual prices at a time when the whole of the rest of the structure is moving upwards would be both unjust and confiscatory. In a normal peacetime pattern every price is a resultant of the combination of all other prices. The price of steel, for instance, is a direct function of all the costs of ore lands, mining, conversion, and distribution. Resolving each of these into its components, we shall see each of them in the last analysis as a direct result of the cost of labor, which is dependent on the cost of living, which in turn is a composite of the cost of almost every element in commerce. It is evident, therefore, that we should either stabilize every price or stabilize no price. A steelmaker cannot be expected to submit to price fixing when he sees the costs of his own materials and labor free and spiralling upwards.

In the third place, individual price fixing is not effective to stop inflation. During World War I, the actions of the Price Fixing Committee held certain prices in line, and the effect of that was to reduce the general price index but not nearly to such good effect as general price control. Many individual prices continued to rise. The price ceiling, therefore, as a check to inflation, has its own justification in addition to its use as an adjunct to the priorities system. By preventing inflation, price control will hold down the price of goods the Government will have to buy, thus reducing the national debt. It has been estimated that a curb on the 1914–1918 inflation would have cut national expenditures on the war in half, and a similar situation in the present emergency is foreshadowed by a recent announcement that because of rising prices the national defense program during the first year may cost two and one half billion dollars more than the original estimates. Likewise control of inflation will prevent the usual unfortunate consequences of war, the phenomenon of the government piling up a national debt in inflated dollars which has to be serviced and repaid in more valuable deflated currency after the inevitable post-war deflation. The evils of inflation in lifting the cost of living, dislocating the wage-price relationship, and thus causing labor unrest and strikes is another justification for the price ceiling as a method of expediting industrial mobilization. Labor cannot be blamed for demanding higher wages if it finds itself being squeezed by the rising costs of the necessities of life and at the same time sees industry receiving inflated profits, of which it does not feel it is getting a fair share.

Lastly, the theory of fixing individual prices in a period of general inflation is unsound, because at the moment you fix a price under such conditions, all its components are at the same time rising, and that price becomes immediately out of date. If you fix individual prices, you later, as inflation occurs, are faced with the choice of either (a) adjusting them upwards to meet their costs or (b) of entering a disorganized retail market and fixing its prices. The Price Fixing Committee of the War Industries Board was faced with this problem towards the end of 1918 and chose the latter alternative. They discovered, however, that what they were actually striving for was a stabilized, homogeneous price schedule, the very thing that exists at the beginning of most wars. Why, therefore, in any future emergency should we not attempt to capture this while it still exists, at the beginning of the war? To capture it piecemeal later is actually arithmetically impossible.

The administration of a price ceiling should not present insuperable difficulties. It has already been successfully introduced in Germany and a partial attempt has been made in Great Britain. Price fixing has been applied so widely in the latter case that there would not be much more difficulty in extending it to an overall ceiling. In fact, most of the difficulties experienced so far have arisen largely because the initial attempt was not more thorough rather than because of any flaw in the program itself.

Whether or not it becomes necessary to clamp down a price ceiling in order to check inflation, and whether it will be sufficient to attack a few individual commodities in cases where scarcity has caused their prices to be bid up above the levels of normal profits, in any event, the important consideration is that priority and price controls are completely interdependent. It is impossible to ration scarce commodities without some method of controlling their prices.

A necessary adjunct to these systems of price fixing and priority is a strict control of the money supply. One reason for rising prices in wartime is that under conditions of full employment consumers are being given purchasing power greater than the value of consumers' goods and services being produced by the economy. If production is at an annual rate of 85 billion dollars, 10 billion dollars of this may represent munitions. The public, therefore, is left only 75 billion dollars of consumers' goods to buy with its 85 billion of purchasing power. The result is inevitably rising prices unless some restraints are exercised. Much pressure can be taken off the price ceiling by attempting to bring down this purchasing power of 85 billion dollars somewhere nearer the 75 billion mark of consumers' goods. This may be done by persuading the consumers to save, as for instance through Liberty Bond campaigns or, with much more certainty, by heavier taxation. The latter method has a double advantage: it decreases purchasing power and minimizes inflation at the same time that it increases the ability of the Government to "pay as it goes."

The policy of the Government in financing the defense program likewise should be conducted with an eye to preventing an inflation of the money supply, which might put pressure on the price structure and make the task of administering prices and priorities more difficult. All effort should be made to raise the necessary funds first through taxation, then by borrowing out of savings whether through bonds sold to the public or from savings banks and insurance companies, and only as a last resort by inflationary borrowing from commercial banks.

CONSERVATION AND THE SEARCH FOR SUBSTITUTES

Priorities are a method for allocating inadequate supplies among a number of competing demands, but the institution of a priorities system should not make the industrial administration neglect the necessity for raising these supplies up as close as possible to existing demand. Capacity should be increased as much as is feasible, peacetime industries should be converted to war use wherever possible, and finally a thorough conservation program should be started, together with a scientific search for substitutes.

A Conservation Division should be concerned with eliminating waste throughout the economy, releasing more materials and man-hours of labor for the war program. One of the most important efforts in this direction during World War I was the reduction of styles and designs to a few basic varieties, reducing greatly the costs in materials, labor, handling, and cataloguing. At the same time, a wide effort was made to cut down the use of strategic materials in less essential products and to find satisfactory substitutes. The elimination of tin from tin plate in canning, for instance, would have released annually around 4,680 tons of pig tin, while the reduction of bicycle designs saved 2,265 tons of high-quality steel. It is remarkable how many of our accustomed wants and needs can be eliminated under the pressure of a rigid war economy and how many of them, under the stern light of war, prove to be unnecessary luxuries. If World War I is a trustworthy precedent, the public usually accepts these limitations willingly, even enthusiastically, if the reasons for the restrictions are made clear to them.

Under the free price system, when demand exceeds supply, rising prices offer an automatic incentive to entrepreneurs to develop new means of manufacturing. In wartime, however, in most cases this mechanism is too slow. The Government cannot wait for rising prices to attract new capital and management into an enterprise, and also, in many cases, when the industry has reached capacity and shortages of labor and capital have appeared, rising prices are powerless to bring forth any more production. The Industrial Administration, therefore, must choose carefully whether it wants to allow prices to rise in certain instances where it knows that this will bring out more production, or whether it should fix these prices and attempt to expand production more rapidly by its own measures. In any case, when the priorities system and a price ceiling have been applied, the industrial administration must set up a special division to carry out vigorous efforts to develop new methods, encourage inventions, and find substitutes to fill the need of scarce items, activities which under a normal economy would be attended to automatically by the action of higher prices.

The Priorities Administration, to be effective, must also have some voice in the determination of commandeering policy. The power to take over plants that are essential to national defense has been given the President in the Selective Military Service Act, while the right to commandeer stocks of commodities would also probably be granted him under the war powers, but neither of these measures should be used except as a last resort when other means have failed.

Thus we see that any industrial mobilization must have as a center of everything a Priorities Division which synchronizes the whole war effort, at the same time providing for the maximum possible satisfaction of civilian needs. To be efficient, the Priorities Administration must also envisage price and money control, conservation, inventions, commandeering, and the use of substitutes. Lastly but no less important, priorities and price control will insure that the nation not only win the war but *survives* it economically, with a low price structure and an industrial system dislocated to a minimum degree, well prepared for post-war conditions in the international markets.

Indexes

Index for Book One

Conservation (*cont.*):
industries affected by, 70
knit goods, 67
lessons from work in, 71
plan and purpose, 62–63, 65
pledges, 66
publicity, 63
regulations, 65–66
return of goods, 63
sanctions for, 66
sentiment of industry, 66, 71
spools, 68
styles and types, 60–65
tin in silk, 69
war service commissions, 64
wool, 249–251
Conservation Division of Army, 95
"Conspectus of progress," 45
Construction:
emergency, 233
nonwar, 230, 234
Control, method of, 16
Conversion section, 40, 41
Conversions, 38, 39, 41, 42
Conveying apparatus, 304
Cooperation in industry:
benefits of, 105
dangers of, 106
effect of war on, 104, 105
Government's attitude, 104, 106–107
Cooperative delivery, 63
Copper, 136–143
conferences on price fixing, 139
control of distribution, 142
European demand, 139
labor problem, 137–138, 140
maximum production, 136
price:
advance, 141
comparisons, 136–137
control, 136
fixed, 140
producers' pledge, 141
purchases for allies, 138
regulations, 141–142
sales on memorandum, 137
spirit of industry, 143
study of costs, 139–140
technique, 136
voluntary price to Government, 136–137
wages, 137
Copper and brass, 136–148
Cordage (*see* Jute, hemp, and cordage)
Cork, 262
Cornell, Irwin H., 159

Cost of production, 79, 80
Cotton:
goods, 243–247, 362
linters, 181–184
raw, 245–247
prices, 245–247
special committee on, 247
Council of National Defense:
law creating, 17
relation to War Industries Board, 19
staff of, 18
Cover, T., 264
Crane, Mr., 157
Cranes, 284–285
Creosote, 196–197
Cromwell, Lincoln, 252
Cross-hauls, 127
Crowder, Gen. Enoch, 95
Curtailment, 67, 114

D

Darling, Ira C., 197
Darlington, Fred, 298
Davis, Mr., 157
Declaration of war, 50, 77
Delivery methods, 63
Dental instruments, 217
Devastated regions, 100
Dillon, Clarence, 26
Donnelley, T. E., 236
Downman, R. H., 232
Draper, F. W., 162
Drugs:
prices, 219–220
production, 216
Du Bois, Henry C., 210
Dunn, H. T., 272
Dyes (*see* Artificial dyes *and* Tanning materials, etc.)
Dyewoods, regulations, 360

E

Economizers, 304
Edgar, Chas., 233
Editorial section, 45
Electrical apparatus and supplies, 300–301
Electrical power and equipment, 300–304
boilers, condensers, etc., 303
steam turbines, 301
Electrodes, 210–211, 361
Electrodes and abrasives, 210–212
Emergency Construction Committee, 233

Labor, competition for, 88
Labor conference, February 28, 1917, 87
Labor Conference Board, 89, 344
Labor disputes, 90, 91
Labor division, 95, 96
Labor policy, 87, 88, 344
Labor priorities bulletin 1, 94, 345, 358
Labor priorities section, 58, 94
Labor problems, 86–96
Labor program, 87–90
Labor turnover, 88, 92, 93
Lanoline, 199
Lauck, W. Jett, 90
Lead, 157–159
Leather (see Hides, leather, and leather goods)
Leather and rubber, 263–275
Leather clothing, 271
Legal basis of price fixing, 76–78
Legal basis of priorities, 49–51
Legal status of board, 23, 24, 27, 28
Legge, Alex, 26, 35, 56
Leith, C. K., 214
"Lessons," 102
Lewis, H. J., 264
"Liberty shoe," 270
Linoleum, 262
Linters (see Cotton linters)
Lithographic felt, 257
Llewelyn, Sir Leonard, 154
Locomotives, 43, 293–294
Logwood, 197
Loree, L. F., 89
Lovett, Robert S., 20, 33, 48
Lumber, 224–233
 airplane, 228, 229
 black walnut, 226
 committee, 224
 conservation, 230
 construction, nonwar, 230
 costs of production, 225, 227–228
 domestic production, 227
 Emergency Construction Committee, 233
 fir, 227
 Government purchases, 226
 mahogany, 229
 price agreements, 225–229
 price fixing, 227–228
 prices, 225–229
 priority administration, 229–232
 priority Circular No. 54, 232
 production, 226
 regional administrators, 229
 requirements, 224

Lumber (cont.):
 ship lumber, 228
 softwood, 229
Lumber and labor, 94–95
Lumber emergency bureaus, 225

M

MacDowell, Charles H., 165, 167, 178, 184
Machinery and tools, 276–288
Machine tools, 276–279
Mackall, Paul, 98
Magnesia (see Asbestos and magnesia)
Magnesium, metallic, 204–205
Manganese, 149–151
"Market value," 79
Martin, Dr. Franklin H., 18
May, George, 59
McCormick, Vance C., 59
McCutcheon, Prof. T. P., 205
McLennan, D. R., 58
Mediation and Conciliation, United States Board of, 87
Mediation Commission, 87, 341
"Mediation service," 87
Medical industry section, 216
Medical supplies, 216–220
Medicinals, 219–220
Mellon Institute, 205
Merrill, W. H., 297
Merryweather, G. E., 276
Metals, miscellaneous, 149–164
Methods of control, 16
Mexican sisal, 260, 261
Meyer, Eugene, jr., 137, 143
Mica, 213–215
Michael, C. Edwin, 89
Middlemen, 123
Military optical glass, 286–288
Miscellaneous chemicals, 203–205
 bromine, 204, 205
 camphor, 204
 celluloid, 204
 metallic magnesium, 204–205
 white arsenic, 204
Mitchell, Prof. W. C., 44
Montgomery, Lieut. Col. Robert H., 82
Moody, Prof. H. R., 205
Morehead, J. M., 194
Morey, Dr., 287
Morss, Everett, 147
Motor trucks, 292
Munitions (see Forgings, ordnance, etc.)
Munitions, chemicals for, 165–190

Index for Book Two

Industrial mobilization:
  control through central agency, 386–397
  methods of control, 389–397
  plans for, 386–387
  system of, 465
Industrial Mobilization Plan, 373, 463
Industrial Strategy Board, 396
Industries, essential and non-essential, 468
Industry:
  morale in World War, 434
  positive control of, 388
  self-mobilization of, 401
  war control of national, 382
Inflation:
  aggravation of, 417
  alleviation of, 417–418
  control of, 381
  elimination of, 398, 421
  general, 427
  preventing war, 380–385
  prevention by price control, 418
  results of war, 380–381, 416, 448
Inter-Ally Debts, 451
International credit, 418
Iron and steel:
  price, 1917, 453
  price index figures, 438
Iron and steel industry, control of, 390
Italy, 420

J

Johnson, Hugh S., 373, 454
Joint Resolution:
  prohibition of labor conscription, 394
  requirements of, 377
"Just compensation," 446

L

Labor:
  conscription of, 377
  draft of, 394
  representative on War Industries Board, 387
  under priorities system, 470–472
Labor, Department of:
  all-commodity index of, 1917, 428
  purchasing power of dollar according to index of, 450
Laissez faire, 420
Lamont, Robert P., 373

Leadership, price control through, 435–440
Lever Act, 439
Liberty Bond campaigns, 475
Lincoln, Abraham, 446
Licensing of distributors, 469–470
Locarno, 373
Ludendorff, 380

M

MacArthur, Douglas, 411, 417, 418, 432–433, 436
McNutt, Paul V., 411, 444
McSwain, John J., 374
Man-power, control of, 393–396
Market value, assessing, 407
Marshal, Provost, 470
M–Day, 413
M–Day planning, 373, 374
Meyer, Eugene, 411
Mitchell, William De W., 373
Mitchell vs. Harmony, 446
Mobilization, industrial:
  central agency for, 386–397
  methods of control, 389–397
  plans for, 386–387
  requirements, 386
  system of, 465
Mobilized industry, as weapon, 379
Modern war, requirements of, 378–380
Money, control of, 393, 475
Morale, civilian, 469
Moseley, George Van H., 414, 457

N

Napoleonic wars, 419, 452
National defense, act to provide for, 458–462
National Defense Act of 1916, 373, 441, 445
"Nation in Arms," 378, 385–386
Navy, representative on War Industries Board, 387
New York price fixing laws, 1780, 385
Nitrates, 393
Nye Committee, 463

O

O'Neil, Ralph T., 411
Orders, classification of producers', 466–467

Warren, G. F., 452
Waste, elimination of, 476–477
Wealth, confiscation of, 405–406
Wholesale prices, rise of, 452
Willard, Daniel, 411, 419, 425
Williams, C. C., 411, 419, 425

Wilson, Woodrow, 385, 468
Wool prices, fixation of, 447
"Work or Fight" order, 394, 395, 396, 470
World War I, expenditures by United States in, 404, 451